THEY DIDN'T WANT TO DIE VIRGINS

They Didn't Want to Die Virgins

Sex and Morale in the British Army on the Western Front 1914-1918

Wolverhampton Military Studies No.15

Bruce Cherry

Helion & Company Limited
26 Willow Road
Solihull
West Midlands
B91 1UE
England
Tel. 0121 705 3393
Fax 0121 711 4075
Email: info@helion.co.uk
Website: www.helion.co.uk
Twitter: @helionbooks
Visit our blog http://blog.helion.co.uk/

Published by Helion & Company 2016
Designed and typeset by Bookcraft Ltd, Stroud, Gloucestershire
Cover designed by Paul Hewitt, Battlefield Design (www.battlefield-design.co.uk)
Printed by Gutenberg Press Limited, Tarxien, Malta

Text © Bruce Cherry 2015
Images © as individually credited

Every reasonable effort has been made to trace copyright holders and to obtain their permission for the use of copyright material. The editor and publisher apologize for any errors or omissions in this work, and would be grateful if notified of any corrections that should be incorporated in future reprints or editions of this book.

Front cover: 'Changing Billets', William Orpen, official war artist. Rear cover: The brothel house number '606' was a coded message with the number referring to 'compound 606', a drug called salvarsan, developed in the early 1900s to treat syphilis. The number identified a 'safe' house. In reality, the girls were forbidden to show themselves at the windows. (Postcard courtesy: Stephen Likosky collection)

ISBN 978-1-910777-70-1

British Library Cataloguing-in-Publication Data.
A catalogue record for this book is available from the British Library.

All rights reserved. No part of this publication may be reproduced, stored in a retrieval system, or transmitted, in any form, or by any means, electronic, mechanical, photocopying, recording or otherwise, without the express written consent of Helion & Company Limited.

For details of other military history titles published by Helion & Company Limited contact the above address, or visit our website: http://www.helion.co.uk.

We always welcome receiving book proposals from prospective authors.

Contents

List of Illustrations — vi
Series Editor's Preface — x
Acknowledgments — xii
List of Abbreviations — xv

1 'Un peu d'amour?': Introduction — 17
2 'Avoiding an unsavoury and malodorous discussion': The British Army's attitude towards sex — 39
3 'Every man had his Story': Quantifying and qualifying the extent of sexual activity — 65
4 'It's Not Something a Gentleman Talks About': The soldier and his moral code — 81
5 The Road to Hell: From morals to morale — 99
6 'Volez vous couches avec moi?': Fraternisation with the local population — 124
7 A Moral 'No Man's land': The billet — 162
8 A Red lamp to Guide Mars to Venus: Regulated prostitution — 177
9 Following the Drum: Unregulated prostitution — 207
10 Je Ne Regrette Rien: Prostitution and the impact on morale — 225
11 'Satisfies 'is lust, I s'pose': The obscene, pornography and masturbation — 231
12 Not Guilty! Sex crimes: Assault, rape and sodomy — 259
13 'Inkey Pinkey, Parlez-vous': Conclusion — 286

Appendix: Imperial War Museum oral records cited — 295
Bibliography — 299
Index — 319

List of Illustrations

No order was needed to turn a soldier's head. Controlling and channeling their natural desires became one of the army's key challenges. (Author's collection)   20

Serving Officer and cartoonist, Bruce Bairnsfather, captured the soldier's preoccupation with the pursuit of local women and hints at their general availability. (Courtesy Mark Warby. ©2015 Estate of Barbara Bruce Littlejohn)   22

The Army faced the challenge of reconciling the sexual needs of the citizen in uniform with the demands of military efficiency. (Author's collection)   48

French and British troops alike were subjected to the embarrassing and much disliked 'short arm inspection'. It was not always considered a joke.   71

Predatory women might lead to many problems, including venereal disease. (Courtesy Mark Warby. ©2015 Estate of Barbara Bruce Littlejohn)   76

The regular soldier's reputation was well established. (Author's collection)   83

La Vie Parisienne's illustrations made astute and accurate observations of life outside the war zone. Their caption reads; 'The Little lady, with frantic admiration and recognition, "Then it's true, my little Tommy, that your miserable little army has three million fellows like you…"'. And over the four years of 'occupation' many little Tommies would be stealing away from a French boudoir. (Author's collection)   98

Peronne was certainly not Eden, nor the offer of sex the first moral collapse, but this scene could very well have illustrated the young and innocent T.S. Hope's Peronne experience (see chapter six). Official war artist, William Orpen's allegorical painting, 'Adam and Eve at Peronne'.   105

Out of the line, and especially in the back areas, soldiers had few problems in meeting women. In fact, it was often the case of 'fighting them off'. (Courtesy Mark Warby. ©2015 Estate of Barbara Bruce Littlejohn)   118

The brothel house number '606' was a coded message with the number referring to 'compound 606', a drug called salvarsan, developed in the early 1900s to treat syphilis. The number identified a 'safe' house. In reality, the girls were forbidden to show themselves at the windows. (Postcard courtesy: Stephen Likosky collection)   119

List of Illustrations   vii

Tommy's continental amours were the subject of comic speculation as these postcards illustrate. These were probably produced post-war for purchase by day-trippers to Ostend and depict the 'plight' of interned British soldiers (from the Naval Brigade sent to Antwerp in 1914). Note the play on 'It's a long way to Tipperary'! (Courtesy: Anthony Gracier collection)   125

The shared attraction between soldier and locals is satirised in this *La Vie Parisienne* cover illustration entitled 'L'Entente Cordiale', and equally celebrated in a widely-sold postcard. (Author's collection)   129

'I want to devote my life to you to make you happy, dear'. Seductive words that could be attributable to either or both parties. (Author's collection)   130

Entitled 'La Peche', *La Vie Parisienne* once again brilliantly captures the flirting game played out by the hunters and the hunted. (Author's collection)   134

Speaking the local language delivered more prosaic benefits than 'owning two languages is to have two souls' as *La Vie Parisienne* poetically observed in the title of this print. Interestingly, the advert on the wall behind guarantees 'success', implicitly for the local in attracting the ANZAC officer. (Author's collection)   157

Billets provided potential for sex and romance for all combatants as this German postcard illustrates. (Author's collection)   167

The situations parodied in Bairnsfather's cartoons would have been instantly recognisable to the troops on the Western Front. (Courtesy Mark Warby. ©2015 Estate of Barbara Bruce Littlejohn)   175

Despite Bairnsfather's intimation of a gap between the dream and the reality, there was an allure and the girls of the billets often provided romance and sex. (Courtesy Mark Warby. ©2015 Estate of Barbara Bruce Littlejohn)   176

French postcard entitled 'The Lust' captures the spirit of the maison de tolerance. Note the black prostitute, popular in some areas and mentioned as being found in one Calais brothel by a Tommy. (Courtesy: Stephen Likosky)   180

Even though this French postcard is meant as a humorous comment on aggressive prostitutes and naïve soldiers, it is easy to see why young British soldiers might find the atmosphere intimidating. (Courtesy: Stephen Likosky)   180

Wartime French humour magazine, *La Rire*, captures a crowd of Poilu's being turned away from a shared brothel as two smug-faced Tommies leave. There is an implicit joke over the British having precedence, referring back to the 1745 Battle of Fontenoy. On a wall behind the madam can be seen a sign, 'The Establishment is closed at 8 clock for British troops'; a kilted soldier is seen slipping in. (Courtesy: Anthony Langley)   182

These rare photographs taken by Lieutenant William Morgan, illustrates how the officer 'Blue Lamps' were usually more club-like in their atmosphere. Note, too, the ubiquitous Kirchner pin-ups on the walls. (Courtesy: Jonathan & Fran Gluck, descendants of William Morgan)   190

These photographs, taken by Lieutenant William Morgan, are very probably of the girls who worked in the 'Blue Lamp' he visited. Such women would have been of a better class than those working at the Red Lamps frequented by the other ranks. (Courtesy: Jonathan & Fran Gluck, descendants of William Morgan)   191

Photographs taken of 'Tableaux Vivants' often offered in high class brothels would be turned into erotic postcards and sold to the soldiers. 'Satisfies 'is lust, I s'pose'. (Courtesy: Stephen Likosky)   194

This postcard captures the spirit of the notorious 'Breda' district of Paris but similar streets existed in Amiens, Calais, St Omer, Le Havre, Poperinghe, Boulogne and many other base camp areas. (Courtesy: Stephen Likosky)   196

The notorious 'Le Cayeux' pass issued to soldiers enjoying Harve town leave in 1917. The number of banned cafes and localities gives some idea of the huge number of brothels (presumably both regulated and unregulated) operating in this one town. (TNA WO/150/8)   198

Legally, women were forbidden to appear at the windows but such soliciting was prevalent. The house number '69' suggests exotic 'French practices'. (Courtesy: Stephen Likosky)   203

The threat of the Provest Marshal was actually not a great discouragement to finding available women, and officers were only really at risk of censure if bringing disrespect to the uniform. (Courtesy Mark Warby. ©2015 Estate of Barbara Bruce Littlejohn)   208

Soldiers reporting with, or discovered on examination to have VD contracted from an unregistered prostitute, were made to complete a questionnaire by one diligent APM so that the source of infection could be identified and the woman removed to a lock hospital. (TNA WO 154/8)   218

Australian soldiers enjoyed a perhaps surprising freedom to seek out female company. The map shows the distribution of army sanctioned 'red lamps', known non-regulated brothels, and – through analysis of mid-1918, 3rd Division APM returns, where VD had been reported as contracted - locations where soldiers had found sex in back area villages. (Source: TNA WO/154/77)   224

Whether sex was dreamed of or a reality, whether it was paid for or freely given, the thought of a local women brightened up the soldier's life. (Author's collection)   229

Prints taken from magazines were pinned to dug-out and billet walls as glamour pin-ups now adorn a thousand garages and workshops. Many included a military motif. (Author's collection)   243

'I only dream of Kirchner's naughtiest chromo'. (*La Vie Parisienne* prints from author's collection) 245

Idealised representations of women, drawn by the soldiers themselves, found their way onto many different objects such as shell cases. (Courtesy: Mesen Museum) 254

Hand-drawn Christmas Menu from an unidentified Officers' Mess, Landrecies, 1918. (Courtesy: Private collection, Richard Marshal) 254

Representations of women found themselves onto all manner of souvenirs that could be bought by the soldiers from shops in back areas. Sometimes it was trench art made by the men themselves. (From collection 'In Flanders Fields', Ieper) 254

The fantasy of the girl in the estaminet helped a soldier dream of better times, even if he had eventually to wake to harsh reality. (Courtesy Mark Warby. ©2015 Estate of Barbara Bruce Littlejohn) 290

Leave; the ultimate morale booster but it was not always taken at home, and not always with what might have been a recognised 'girlfriend'. (Courtesy Mark Warby. ©2015 Estate of Barbara Bruce Littlejohn) 294

The Wolverhampton Military Studies Series
Series Editor's Preface

As series editor, it is my great pleasure to introduce the *Wolverhampton Military Studies Series* to you. Our intention is that in this series of books you will find military history that is new and innovative, and academically rigorous with a strong basis in fact and in analytical research, but also is the kind of military history that is for all readers, whatever their particular interests, or their level of interest in the subject. To paraphrase an old aphorism: a military history book is not less important just because it is popular, and it is not more scholarly just because it is dull. With every one of our publications we want to bring you the kind of military history that you will want to read simply because it is a good and well-written book, as well as bringing new light, new perspectives, and new factual evidence to its subject.

In devising the *Wolverhampton Military Studies Series*, we gave much thought to the series title: this is a *military* series. We take the view that history is everything except the things that have not happened yet, and even then a good book about the military aspects of the future would find its way into this series. We are not bound to any particular time period or cut-off date. Writing military history often divides quite sharply into eras, from the modern through the early modern to the mediaeval and ancient; and into regions or continents, with a division between western military history and the military history of other countries and cultures being particularly marked. Inevitably, we have had to start somewhere, and the first books of the series deal with British military topics and events of the twentieth century and later nineteenth century. But this series is open to any book that challenges received and accepted ideas about any aspect of military history, and does so in a way that encourages its readers to enjoy the discovery.

In the same way, this series is not limited to being about wars, or about grand strategy, or wider defence matters, or the sociology of armed forces as institutions, or civilian society and culture at war. None of these are specifically excluded, and in some cases they play an important part in the books that comprise our series. But there are already many books in existence, some of them of the highest scholarly standards, which cater to these particular approaches. The main theme of the *Wolverhampton Military Studies Series* is the military aspects of wars, the preparation for wars or their prevention, and their aftermath. This includes some books whose main theme is the technical details of how armed forces have worked, some books on wars and battles, and some books that re-examine the evidence about the existing stories, to show in a different light what everyone thought they already knew and understood.

As series editor, together with my fellow editorial board members, and our publisher Duncan Rogers of Helion, I have found that we have known immediately and almost by instinct the kind of books that fit within this series. They are very much the kind of well-written and challenging books that my students at the University of Wolverhampton would want to read. They are books which enhance knowledge, and offer new perspectives. Also, they are books for anyone with an interest in military history and events, from expert scholars to occasional readers. One of the great benefits of the study of military history is that it includes a large and often committed section of the wider population, who want to read the best military history that they can find; our aim for this series is to provide it.

Stephen Badsey
University of Wolverhampton

Acknowledgements

The following poignant and sad letters were written home by 23-year old Lance Corporal Ben Hyde to his parents while serving as an NCO in the Military Police in Iraq, 2003, and reported in the *Guardian* of 2 December 2006. He was one of the many British servicemen who did not come home, dying in the 'war against terror'. With five other 'Red Caps' (Military Police), he was murdered by a mob besieging a police post in the Southern Iraqi town of Majar-al Kabir.

> 15 May 2003
> Mum and Dad, I thought I'd write again and tell you about the list of things I want to do when I get home. Here goes …
> 1. Have sex
> 2. Get drunk
> 3. Eat steak
> 4. Have a bath
> 5. Sleep in a bath
> 6. Sleep at all
> 7. Get up when I feel like it
> 8. Have a shit in peace
> 9. Have a shit on a toilet
> 10. Use a proper toilet paper
> 11. Have sex again
> 12. Get drunk again
> 13. Persuade Mom to buy clothes me and the boss ordered from the catalogue …
> 14. Get a car
> 15. Drive it
> 16. More sex
> 17. Look at pictures of my naked girlfriend for hours after sex
> 18. Go to a supermarket
> 19. See white people
> 20. See people who don't smell
> 21. I don't want to smell any more
> 22. Put some hair gel on

23. Put clean clothes on
24. Not start sweating again ten seconds after having a wash
25. Watch telly for a week.

Lance Corporal Hyde's list, with the exception of those particularly twentieth-century inventions of 'cars' and 'telly', could well have been written by his great-grandfather had he served in the trenches on the Western Front. Nearly twenty per cent of his wish-list concerns sex: perfectly normal for a young man in his early twenties, as it would have been for his great-grandfather's generation.

The next letter his parents received was post-dated.

June 2003
Mum and Dad,
If you are reading this, then you will know that I'm not coming home. I'm up in the stars now looking down on you making sure that you are safe. I'm sorry for all the times I've been a pain, but I know the good times outweigh the bad tenfold … You have both got long lives ahead of you so make sure you make use of every second you have because sitting here, writing now, I know just how precious time is …
Look after yourselves,
All my love,
Ben xxxx

At least Ben's body came home, unlike those who died in the same region during the Great War.

This book is dedicated to all those Tommies of the Great War, and in the wars succeeding the 'war to end all wars', including the current conflicts, who used sex in thought and deed to get them through the trials and tribulations they faced. It is especially dedicated to all those who died virgins, never enjoying perhaps the main rite of passage from boy to man.

The delicate and sensitive nature of the subject of this research inevitably meant that material was hard to find. I am greatly indebted to all those who assisted in suggesting sources or who pointed me specifically to relevant information. The staff at both the Imperial War Museum and The National Archives were tireless in their efforts, as were the staff of Reading University Library. I should particularly like to thank Julian Putkowski, who not only provided access to his extensive library, which included microfilm of the CEF courts martial records unavailable elsewhere, but also gave me invaluable early feedback on my approach to the material. This book owes much to the support so generously given during trying times of Professor Richard Hoyle, then of Reading University. Dr Matthew Worley, Dr Frank Tallet and Dr Michael Snape have my gratitude for their invaluable input during the long process of research and writing up of the PhD thesis that formed the core of this book. Equally, much is owed to those whose belief that this study could, and should not be undertaken, spurred me on to prove them wrong. Very special thanks are due to Nora De Bievre for her moral support, and who assisted me in finding and translating materials in the original Flemish, to Malcolm Brown, and to Nigel Jess who provided some final 'spit and polish'. Equally, I would like to thank all those parties including Mark Warby, Dr Richard Marshall, Anthony Langley, Stephen Likosky and the Metropolitan Postcard Club Blog, who have very kindly given their permission to use original cartoons and illustrations in their possession. Thanks are also due to the Ypres 'In Flanders Fields' and Messines Museums, and last but certainly not least, to Jonathan & Fran Gluck, descendants of William Morgan, who kindly allowed the reproduction of their Grandfather's unique photographs. Many others, who I have not specifically been able contact, deserve my thanks for use of their information. Thanks are also due to Duncan Rogers and his team at Helion & Company for their interest and professional assistance in publishing and marketing this title. Apart from recognising these academic and publishing debts, my wife, Thelma, is owed great thanks for putting up with her husband's long obsession with the Great War, to the exclusion of our taking 'normal' holidays and sacrificing weekends to research.

List of Abbreviations

AIF	Australian Imperial Force
ANZAC	Australian and New Zealand Army Corps
APM	Assistant Provost Marshal
ASC	Army Service Corps
AWOL	Absent Without Leave
BEF	British Expeditionary Force
Bn	Battalion
CD Acts	Contagious Diseases Acts
CEF	Canadian Expeditionary Force
CO	Commanding Officer
COC	Chief Officer Commanding
Coy	Company
DORA	Defence of the Realm Act
EEF	Egyptian Expeditionary Force
FANY	First Aid Nursing Yeomanry
FOO	Forward Observation Officer
GHQ	General Headquarters
HQ	Headquarters
IWM	Imperial War Museum
Lt	Lieutenant
MO	Medical Officer
MP	Military Police
NCO	Non-Commissioned Officer
NVA	National Vigilance Association
NZEF	New Zealand Expeditionary Force
OP	Observation Post
OTC	Officer Training Corps
PBI	'Poor Bloody Infantry'
RFC	Royal Flying Corps
RAMC	Royal Army Medical Corps
TNA	The National Archives

VADS	Voluntary Aid Detachment
VC	Victoria Cross
VD	Venereal Disease
WAACs	Women's Army Auxiliary Corps
YMCA	Young Men's Christian Association

1

'Un peu d'amour?': Introduction

> Jack and Bill
> Went up the Hill
> To see a Frenchman's daughter:
> The censor's here
> And so I fear, I can't tell you what they taught her.[1]

Sex is not a subject that either a professional military historian or an interested amateur would immediately associate with the story of the Western Front. Rats, lice, the carnage of the trenches, shootings at dawn and mud, mud, mud; these images readily come to mind – but sex?

The subject of sex is often limited in more formal academic accounts of the war to a passing reference of venereal disease in the troops, if mentioned at all. A trawl through files at the National Archive will turn up a 1917 Imperial conference on the problems associated with the prevalence of the disease and the disquiet of Dominion governments over the lack of any strategy to curb predatory women. Further investigation in the relatively few extant APM reports adds some interesting 'colour' detailing the problems encountered along the Western Front with local prostitutes. Other than this sparse official acknowledgment, there is little to suggest that sex in any form existed for the average soldier.

Yet, conversely, you don't have to read too deeply into the history of the war as told by the men themselves before the subject of sex is mentioned, though often obliquely. In the soldier's own memoir, and occasionally in letters home – from British, Dominion, French, German, even Indian soldiers – there is often a coy reference to a liaison with a local girl, or a discreet mention of a 'red lamp', the army's official brothels. In some memoirs the reference is not so shy; some are even full of frank reminiscences. Two of the most well-known British accounts of the war, those of Royal Welch Fusiliers,

---

[1] Cambridge University Library: *The Minden Magazine,* August 1916. This wartime trench newspaper was the creation of the Lancashire Fusiliers.

Robert Graves and Frank Richards, openly recount stories of the soldier's sex life. Indeed, it is Graves who provides the title of this book; 'They Didn't Want to Die Virgins'. Many other implied references are there for those who look; in 'true to life' novels written by returning soldiers, in song lyrics, in trench 'newspapers', in jokes and marching songs, in 'naughty' postcards of the period, and occasionally it is even given substance in erotic trench art.

Even allowing for the legendary and oft caricatured British reticence to admit that sex exists, should we be surprised that it is an integral part of the story of the Great War, and particularly the Western Front?

Historically sex has been regularly employed on a strategic level as a weapon of war. Violation or seizure of an enemy's women has been used explicitly as a weapon of demoralisation, denigration and control. History is littered with examples of mass sexual slavery, forced marriage and impregnation. The Roman 'rape of the Sabine women'; the Christian Serbians' treatment of Muslim women in the Balkans civil wars of the late 20th century; the more recent horrors of schoolgirl abductions by Boko Haram in Nigeria; and wholesale enslavement of Yazidi women by ISIS/Daesh have all had subjugation of an enemy as their core objective.

Furthermore, at the level of the individual soldier, sexual gratification and 'conquest' has traditionally been an accepted as one of the spoils of war; the reward of the victor usually, though not uniquely, taken forcibly. Sometimes this has been openly condoned, more regularly excused by the expedient of turning a blind eye. The Red Army excesses during the fall of Berlin in 1945 had its precedent on the Eastern Front of the Great War and, to a lesser degree, rape was one of the main atrocity accusations levied against the German Army during their initial advance into Belgium. Even the British Army cannot claim historical innocence when it comes to rape as accounts of its behaviour in the Peninsular Wars and suspicion of cover-ups in colonial outposts attest.

Throughout modern times the importance of catering for the soldiers' sexual needs, while keeping them both physiologically and psychologically healthy has been recognised, if not always explicitly, as fundamental in conflicts spanning the American Civil War to Vietnam. When the full histories are written it will probably be uncovered as part of story of the Gulf Wars and in Afghanistan. Sometimes it has involved using slave or forced labour for camp brothels, as the Japanese notoriously did for their troops in World War Two. At other times – in the French and German sanctioned soldier brothels of the Great War, for example – the service providers were arguably volunteer. As we'll see, the British took advantage of these existing French arrangements but the years of Empire building had already given them wide experience in running their own establishments.

Aside, however, from what are now rightly recognised as war crimes, sexual activity in war often occurs at another level; at a level where the sex can be defined as consensual (though where there is an economic imperative the woman's freedom of choice might still be argued to be limited). It would be a strange army that did not have its camp followers and the allure of a uniform has been an immemorial one. There has been fraternisation between members of the military and local population in virtually every war that has involved an extended occupation of civilian regions. It is a quite natural phenomenon that where males and females are placed in close proximity, and over an extended time, social intercourse will lead to that of a sexual nature. British soldiers have always returned from wars or foreign occupations with brides, and across the globe the blue-eyed or fair-headed amidst a majority dark-skinned population bear witness to historic interracial contacts. The war on the Western Front, being essentially a near four-year siege with 'foreign' soldiers living side-by-side with the indigenous population, provided an environment conducive for the former to quite literally embed with the latter. The fact that the men of the local tribe were themselves away at war simply hastened the inevitable.

In times of war moral constraints are noticeably loosened. The German sexologist, Hirschfeld, argued in the 1930s that a 'war fever' took hold across Europe during the Great War years, leading women as well as men to abandon the social norms of peacetime. Others have postulated that in times of conflict, with men facing an uncertain future, the normal pursuit of sex becomes heightened by a primordial need to recreate before premature death. Arthur Osburn, a regular medical officer, wisely observed that 'plants and animals, when stress or privation threatens the extinction of their species, will hastily, even prematurely "cast their seed"'.[2]

Deeper still run the waters of sadomasochism, torture, bestiality and other variants of human sexuality that rise to the surface with the breakdown of social constraints.

Pursuit of sex in war or peacetime is part of soldiering. Armies are largely comprised of testosterone-fuelled young men (the average age of the Western Front combatant was under 30); it would be a surprise to find that natural, genetically programmed instincts were not followed. For some the urgency grew in direct proportion to the danger, and one soldier's lasting memory of going up the line in the Second Battle of Ypres (1915) was of a young Highlander, kilt pulled up, making passionate and very public love to a shop girl in a doorway.[3]

Furthermore, 'birds, bombs, booze and bullets' have been a great motivator of recruitment through the ages. BEF regular, Bob Mariner VC asked for nothing more than 'booze, a woman now and again, a bit of excitement, and a chance of making a bit of "tin" on the side'.[4] Frank Richards, another 'old soldier' reservist recalled on the outbreak of war, sums up the regular soldier's priorities: 'On arrival at a new station, we pre-war soldiers always made enquiries as to what sort of place it was for booze and fillies. If both were in abundance it was a glorious place from our point of view'.[5]

---

2   Osburn, A. C. *Unwilling Passenger* (London: Faber & Faber, 1936), p. 355; similarly Cloete, Stuart, *A Victorian Son: An Autobiography* (London: Collins, 1972), p. 258.
3   Holmes, Richard, *Tommy* (London: Harper Collins, 2004), p. 596.
4   Eyre, Giles, *Somme Harvest* (London: Jarrolds, 1938), p. 21.
5   Richards, Frank, *Old Soldiers Never Die* (London: Berkley Publishing Corporation, 1966), p. 12.

No order was needed to turn a soldier's head. Controlling and channeling their natural desires became one of the army's key challenges. (Author's collection)

Indeed, the implicit promise of sexual adventure, preferably in a foreign clime, has often has been a more effective inducement than the promise of the King's shilling and a square meal. Colonial postings for the British soldier, both officers and men, further offered the opportunity of indulging in practices frowned upon at home.

On the Western Front, sex, in its widest incarnation, played a much larger role in the soldier's existence than has been acknowledged. Whatever the underlying motives, the hunt for sexual gratification was virtually universal and an integral part of many a soldier's wartime experience. In this book the focus will be almost exclusively on the soldiers who comprised the British and Dominion armies but no matter the colour of the uniform, *khaki, feldgrau,* or *bleu horizon,* underneath was a man with similar sexual needs and desires.

Thomas Dinesen, a Danish volunteer and VC-winner serving with a Canadian division, explained how, out of the line and away from life-threatening fire, it did not take long for human nature to reassert itself and carnal concerns to come to the fore:

> When living in the trenches and amongst the ruined houses there, we take no interest in women and love beyond the usual jokes and funny stories – such is my impression at any rate. We do not think or talk much about love-making. Life is so hard, and so full of exertion and intense excitement that all such thoughts and desires are quite imperceptibly put aside. But ... in ... peaceful surroundings with so much spare time on your hands, the old Adam of the flesh again comes to life.[6]

6 Dinesen VC, T., *Merry Hell! A Dane with the Canadians* (London: Jarrolds, 1930), p. 185.

Dixon, a young subaltern whose recollections form part of the Imperial War Museum's collection of unpublished manuscripts, expressed much the same sentiments: 'We were not monks but fighting soldiers and extraordinarily fit – fitter than we had been in our young lives, and fairly tough – certainly with an abundance of physical energy … full of beans or bull juice'.[7] When he was not concentrating on basic survival, sex was never far away from the soldier's mind. Manning, in a novel not only widely recognised as a memoir but as one that best captures the spirit of the time, lists the priorities of the front line soldier out of battle and places women on a par with food as a basic appetite: 'all the insubordinate passions released by battle … find no adequate object, unless in the physical ecstasy of love'.[8]

Whether that 'physical ecstasy' was engaged in with a compliant local population, paid for from myriad local, officially-regulated or unregulated 'wayside' prostitutes – at home or abroad – or simply obtainable only as pornography, sex was almost as ubiquitous as the rats and lice. For many the search for sex dominated periods of leave or the quieter times spent behind the front line; and it was also quite possibly *the* subject that dominated trench talk.

Neither was it restricted to those 'old soldiers' of the professional army as might be expected, but to be found throughout the new volunteer citizen soldiers irrespective of age, class, culture or even race. The younger raw recruits of these new volunteer armies saw the pursuit of alcohol and women as a rite of passage or, as one soldier put it, 'I knew that to grow up one must get drunk and sleep with women'.[9] Older recruits, used to the pleasures of the marriage bed, were not going to forgo such pleasures if opportunity arose. Erotic adventures were enjoyed by farm lads from Frodsham, mill lads from Manchester and miners from Merthyr. Public schoolboys and even the Royalty lost their virginities to French femmes. Diggers, Kiwis and Canucks took war-brides home while the turbaned troops of the Indian Army enjoyed the delights of the normally forbidden and 'untouchable' white memsahibs.

Even doctors reportedly had their 'kept' women; nursing assistant, Ellen La Motte writing in 'Backwash of War' tells of male doctors having women who they went to once a week, or at night, including one who had 'a pretty 14-year old'. And they resorted to prostitutes, sometimes paying the price of catching VD, as Alfred West, NCO, Monmouthshire Regt recalled: 'Even the doctors [caught it] … the old doctor who had been giving the lectures came in to flush himself out'. And perhaps less credibly, soldiers like L. Stagg, an NCO with the RAMC claimed when working in a base hospital that 'I even had a chaplain in there with VD' though their numbers were not

---

7   IWM 92/36/1, Dixon, R., 'Wheels of Darkness' (unpubl. memoir).
8   Manning, Frederick, *Her Privates We: the Middle Parts of Fortune* (London: Penguin, 2005), p. 55.
9   Cloete, S., *Victorian Son*, p. 206.

22 They Didn't Want to Die Virgins

Nil Admirari
"Now, then, never mind about those demi-mondaines; look straight to your front!"

Serving Officer and cartoonist, Bruce Bairnsfather, captured the soldier's preoccupation with the pursuit of local women and hints at their general availability. (Courtesy Mark Warby. ©2015 Estate of Barbara Bruce Littlejohn)

'Un peu d'amour?': Introduction   23

large as Robert Graves warned that, 'The troops took a lewd delight in exaggerating the proportion of army chaplains to combatant officers treated here'.[10]

Naturally, the opportunities for sexual adventure changed over the four years of war and according to circumstance. Sex was understandably more readily available to those who had the time and the money. Officers, as a class, had both. Dominion troops, being paid more, had more money. Women were more easily accessible in the back lines than in the front where men spent considerable time, but as F.P. Crozier admitted, it was not only 'base-wallahs [who] had all the luck'.[11] Talbot Kelly, a gunner, wrote that 'infantrymen lived a restricted life, week in, week out, with discomfort and danger whereas I as a gunner was able to move about on the battlefield at large, seeing far more, and, although frequently in danger, finding something by the way to ease the burden of war.' Kelly, remembers the 'good things in life rather than the bad' and one of those was sex.[12]

The real surprise is not that there was sexual activity along the Western Front, but that it has not been explored in more detail. Respected historians of the period have denied or underplayed the amount of sexual activity. Most soldiers we are also advised, 'seldom had the opportunity' being too busy fighting a war. Until comparatively recently military historians have been more interested in studying the 'bombs and bullets' than the 'booze and birds'. This is surprising since the social aspects of soldiering have had, as they will no doubt continue to have, an impact on recruitment, morale and, if sexual health is considered, even fighting efficiency.

This relative silence is not only confined to British writers. Historians charting ANZAC involvement on the Western Front are equally obtuse; Bean and Gammage, two of the most consulted authorities either leave the subject unmentioned, or deny sex activity existed. David Kent found 'only one candid mention of a sexual encounter with a prostitute' in his extensive study. At least Watson was unafraid to lift the lid on ANZAC antics in pre-Gallipoli Egypt and anyone researching the redoubtable Kiwi condom campaigner and feminist, Ettie Rout, will find material on Venus and the lonely Kiwi.[13] It is particularly interesting that until Craig Gibson started exploring the general, behind the line relationships with the French, in his ground-breaking

---

10   La Motte, Ellen, *Backwash of War* (London: Putnam 1916); IWM Sound Archive, No. 12236, West, Alfred, Monmouth Regiment, reel 6, on padres with VD. See also Wheatley, Dennis, *Officer and Temporary Gentleman* (London: Hutchinson, 1978), p. 152; and IWM Sound Archive, No. 8764, reel 4, Stagg, L. NCO, Royal Army Medical Corps. Graves, Robert, *Goodbye to All That* (London: Penguin,1960), p. 195.
11   Crozier, F. P., *A Brass Hat in No Man's Land* (London: Jonathan Cape, 1930, Gliddon Books repr., 1989), pp. 106-7. Taylor, F. A. J. *The Bottom of the Barrel* (London: Regency, 1978), p. 112.
12   Talbot Kelly, R B, *A Subaltern's Odyssey; a memoire of the Great War*, (London: William Kimber 1980), p. 166.
13   Bean, Charles, *The Official History of Australia in the War of 1914-1918* (Australian War Memorial) is a twelve-volume series covering Australian involvement in the First World War. Gammage, Bill, *The Broken Years: Australian Soldiers in the Great War* (Canberra:

and informative study, Canadian authors had also confined themselves to the VD controversy.[14]

Where sex is mentioned by those retelling the histories of Imperial or Dominion troops, a lack of evidence is often employed to discount its role as insignificant or, implicitly, to raise a barrier to further research:

> The violence that took place during the Great War gave rise to very specific taboos. One of them concerns sexuality: it can be reasonably assumed that the moral norms that were common in peacetime were weakened among soldiers cut off from the home front and exposed to front line dangers. And yet, aside from some very rare allusions in the combatants' accounts of their wartime experiences, masturbation, prostitution and homosexuality are shrouded in the deepest silence.[15]

The issue is not that there is absence of material from either Imperial or Dominion troops; far from it. The 'colonials', including the Indian troops, were as willing to mention the 'unmentionable' as their Imperial counterparts both in letters home and even in their illegally-kept dairies, yet in the work of those now exploring these sources, there is a common and somewhat inexplicable assertion that sexual activities were rare. Joanna Bourke typically contends in her insightful work on the impact of the war on concepts of masculinity: '[I]t is probably correct to argue that the majority of British servicemen never had casual sex with any woman during their active military service'.[16]

Baynes writes that, despite the rank-and-file soldier 'being ready to have sexual intercourse with almost any women wherever they could', in France it was not often possible:

> Even where there were brothels available, few private soldiers could spare the money to use them ... and within the area his life was lived, women were rare. The few attractive ones by all accounts became expert in rebuffing the amorous advances of the hordes of soldiers who passed through the villages they lived in.[17]

ANUP, 1974). Kent, David, *From Trench to Troopship. The Experiences of the AIF 1914-1919* (Sydney: Hale and Iremonger, 1999), p. 127.
14 Gibson, K. C., 'Relations between the British Army and the Civilian Population on the Western Front 1914-1918' (unpubl. Leeds University PhD Thesis, 1999). Cassel, Jay, *The Secret Plague: Venereal Disease in Canada, 1838-1939* (Toronto: University of Toronto, 1987).
15 Audoin-Rouzeau, Stephane and Becker, Annette, *1914-1918, Understanding the Great War* (London: Profile Books, 2002), p. 43.
16 Bourke, Joanna, *Dismembering the Male. Men's Bodies, Britain and the Great War* (Chicago: University of Chicago, 1996; London: Reaktion Books edn, 1999), p. 157.
17 Baynes, *Morale: A Study of Men and Courage 2nd Scottish Rifles at Neuve Chapelle* (London: Cassell, 1967). Baynes was, however, writing about one battalion over a short period of time.

This situation may have applied to the single battalion of Baynes' study but it was certainly not universal. The fact that there was a relative paucity of woman did not necessarily imply a shortage of sex. Not only were brothels organised to process men numbered in hundreds, as we shall see, but even a single compliant woman was capable of entertaining a considerable number of individuals. A young T.S. Hope met a farm girl, patently one of a type who would come to be called 'clandestine' prostitutes, who illustrated just how many men just one woman might entertain (and infect):

> … ma'm'selle at our farm, is any soldier's meat … Rather a pretty girl; she was pointed out to us as being willing to teach any soldier the art of love making for a matter of a paltry five francs … a few men in our battalion are already praising her as being a proper artist in her profession, but … three of them, including the colonel's groom, have been sent down to a base hospital.[18]

Other writers, implicitly dismissing the existence of sexual activity, have claimed, using a Freudian concept, that men sublimated their desires, especially in battle: 'It may be that fight-flight conduct, as psychologists would term battlefield behaviour, inhibits sexual desire'.[19] This argument not only dismisses the activity itself but misses the importance of other sexually related activities, such as the use of pornography.

Even the most cursory investigation questions the validity of these positions; if sexual activity was so unusual why are venereal disease infections so high? Why do so many memoirs demonstrate working knowledge of the army brothels? Why indeed did the army sanction use of the brothels? Why did soldiers include tales of romance in their memoirs? Are the adventures recounted in interviews with old soldiers undertaken for oral history projects re-imagined? Are sexual storylines contained in novels written by ex-soldiers truly fictional, a story sexed-up to encourage commercial sales or are they, more truthfully, an outlet for truths not able to be told in 'polite' society? Why is it that there has been an apparent refusal to read between the lines, to follow the logic of unarguable facts to reach a conclusion or to suggest areas worthy of further research? Why is the subject of sex seemingly taboo?

It must be acknowledged that a large number of Great War participants claimed, probably honestly, not to have had any sexual experiences. Morals and a host of other influences held them back. We cannot doubt that, in an army in which approaching six million British men served over a four-year period, there would have been men of every moral hue and shade. It is unsurprising, therefore, that there were soldiers who boasted a moral outlook and the strength to forswear any perceived immorality. Clifford Lane, an NCO in the Bedfords, noted of his battalion: 'it was only a small proportion who went to the red lamps areas … might have come to 10 per cent perhaps

---

18 Hope, T. S., *The Winding Road Unfolds* (London: Tandem Books, 1965), p.68.
19 Winter, Denis, *Death's Men* (London: Allen Lane, 1978; Harmondsworth: Penguin edn, 1979), p. 151.

… most people had a higher standard of morals'.[20] Though it should be noted that even ten per cent, however, implies between eighty and ninety men. It is also unsurprising that some men claimed not to have seen immorality, though they had heard reports of it. It would certainly have been possible for a man serving a relatively short time, to have done so almost exclusively in the front line and, perhaps, to be invalided out before getting to a rest area, where sexual activities were most commonly found. Also, as the war wore on, with fewer civilians inhabiting the battle zone and running estaminets or billets, fraternisation would have become less likely. It is, however, unlikely that there were many soldiers like Pte F. Lewis (Royal Warwickshire Regt) who claimed he 'never saw any women all my four years in the trenches – and I was in the trenches the whole while. I never seen any woman in the services near the Front line'. Even Lewis's disclaimer has to be taken with a pinch of salt given no battalion of his regiment actually served on the Western Front over the complete four years.[21]

This lacunae in the social history of the soldier on the Western Front has many probable causes. First and foremost, there is perhaps a subconscious desire not to denigrate the memory of those involved. The Great War soldier has been sanctified as much by the writings of over-sensitive poets, the post-war disillusioned school of historians and 'Oh, What a Lovely War' satirists and writers, as by the fact that when we talk of the Tommy we are talking of our own kith and kin. This 'parfait knight', was driven in tens of thousands by callous generals to lay down his life for our freedoms in the most horrendous circumstances; he cannot be guilty of perceived sin. The looting of homes, the killing of prisoners, the robbing of dead comrades, the gambling, the alcoholism, the fornication, the descent of the man into beast; none of this can be readily admitted. Every man 'shot at dawn' is guilty only of having shellshock; none robbed, murdered or truly deserted. These were our fathers, brothers, uncles, husbands, grandfathers; gentlemen all, none were capable of crime, none of immorality.

Their reputation was protected from the beginning: how else can we explain what Tiplady, the Wesleyan chaplain of the 56th Division, wrote in 1917:

> Here, on the actual Front, I have come across no proved [sic] case of immorality. There is no possibility of immorality in the trenches, and in the villages where the men rest when out of the trenches I have neither seen nor heard of any misconduct. Our soldiers are friendly and respectful to the French women and girls, but there is no 'walking out' with them, and no unseemly familiarity.[22]

---

20 Imperial War Museum: IWM Sound Archive, No. 7257, Lane, Clifford James, NCO, 7th Bn Bedfords.
21 Lewis, F., *The Colonel's Runner. The Account of 1713 Pte F. Lewis (Royal Warwickshire Regt)*, ed. T. Oates, at http://www.hellfire-corner.demon.co.uk/runner.htm (accessed 19 June 2010).
22 Tiplady, Thomas, *The Cross at the Front: Fragments from the Trenches* (1917), an online version of which is available at http://www.lib.byu.edu/~rdh/wwi/memoir/cross/crossTC.

This can only have been for 'public consumption' on the home front unless Tiplady chose not to see the obvious. Had he gone through a few of the soldier's pockets, or listened a little more carefully to his flock's conversations, he might have found his evidence. Writing in the 1930s, Williamson was also aware of this tendency to paint a saintly picture:

> A characteristically English reaction has begun against the truthfulness of good war books, which are said to malign our armies. An effort is being made to maintain that our soldiers, in addition to being heroes, were archangels. For myself I prefer them to have been what they were: men.[23]

Sexologist Magnus Herschfeld's ground-breaking 1930 investigation of the German soldier's sexual life received little attention in a Britain as much alienated by his advocacy of tolerance for homosexuality as by his claim that the findings applied equally to allied armies and populations. A British copycat and admittedly inferior work by Fischer and Dubois, focusing solely on the British army experience, would only get a limited-run, privately printed publication. De Groot noted, in the negative reaction seventy-years later to the otherwise popular TV drama series, *The Monocled Mutineer* (1986), how ingrained the saintly reputation of the Tommy had become, and how important it still was to protect; 'the idea of a Tommy who cheated, lied, fornicated and mutinied was abhorrent'.[24]

The story that has until relatively recently dominated the literature of the Great War is of the 'flower of a generation' wasted futilely in the mud of Flanders: thrown away by the military incompetence, political duplicity and jingoism of armchair generals. The 'soldier's story' essentially ennobles the individual: they all become 'knights'. Central to this school of writing is that sexual activity is – consciously or sub-consciously – ignored, exorcised or denied. A reputation has thus been developed that no one either thinks, or wants, to question: 'we had become knights in shining armour' remembered one soldier.[25] Thus historians are guilty, though probably more by simple omission than conspiracy, from acknowledging what some might find as uncomfortable facts.

Tommy's sexual adventures have also been smothered by an over-emphasis on studies of the front line. Perhaps unsurprisingly, given the fascination we have with the truly alien environment of 'the trench', there has been a morbid obsession with this aspect of the war. Everything is seen through the limited prism of the 8-foot

---

htm (accessed July 2012).
23 Williamson. H., *The Patriot's Progress* ((London: Geoffrey Bles, 1930, Sphere reprint), preface.
24 De Groot, *Blighty: British Society in the Era of the Great War* (London: Longman, 1996), p. 161. See The National Archives (TNA): WO 154/77, APM report illustrative of troop behaviour.
25 See Simkins, Peter, 'Soldiers and Civilians: Billeting in Britain and France', in Beckett and Simpson (eds.), *A Nation in Arms* (Manchester: MUP, 1985), pp. 168-71.

ditch. This is evident in the plethora of books on the subject, the ubiquity of trench photographs in popular media articles and the dominance of trench scenes in plays and films from *'Journey's End'* to *'Blackadder'*. The fact that the army had a long tail and that the vast majority of men never saw a front line trench, other than in comparatively rare instances of delivering supplies to it, is ignored or worse, lost. The doings of the Highland Light Infantry, Liverpool Pals and 9th Hussars become the dominant story; the Royal Army Medical Corps get a look in but the Army Service Corps – largest of all regiments – might as well not have been involved for the popular recognition it gets. Even the Artillery play second fiddle to the 'PBI'.

This myopia further often conceals how relatively little time a man actually spent in the trenches, and how much time he had out of the line – often seeking diversions that would take him physically as well as mentally away from the battle lines. The 7th battalion Royal Sussex Regiment, for example, formed part of the BEF from 1915 to 1918 and spent 42% of this time in the front line or support, 38% in the billeting areas, and 20% in the rest areas. The Canadian 16th Battalion were 34%, 35% and 31% respectively and other battalions show similar proportions. There was plenty of time away from fighting when men needed to be entertained; in just these two random examples, more than half their time. Thus a figurative veil is drawn over life behind the lines, when in reserve, at training or camps, in recuperation hospitals or at popular leave destinations.

There are further, more practical reasons why the subject of sex was originally sidelined. Though early and fairly conclusive evidence of the general promiscuity abounding in Flanders and Picardy (and, incidentally, also in towns and cities on the home front) was to be deduced from admissions to specialist hospitals for venereal disease, this was not a statistic either the government or army were keen to publicise. Patently, it was not in the general interest to expose what the boys were up to overseas when not at Hun throats defending the poor Belgians. It would have adversely affected recruitment if mothers had thought their boys were coming home with less than honourable wounds. Socially, 'thou shalt not fornicate' often presented a stronger moral imperative than 'thou shall not kill'.

It was certainly not in the personal interest of individual sufferers, especially those with 'decent' family back home, to admit to the probable source of their 'venereal', if indeed they admitted to the infection. Initially, the relatively high incidence of venereal disease in the general population on the Home Front helped conceal the source of infection. Discussion of the issue was perhaps understandably muted though by 1917 this high incidence did became a better known and highly contentious statistic, especially in Canada and New Zealand. Where to point the finger of blame for this 'epidemic' was nevertheless still highly contested by those centrally involved in the issue. Such discussion as there was, both during and immediately following the war, avoided any of the obvious moral conclusions to be drawn from the statistical information available. Discussion instead concentrated on how to curb the activities of the infected with the objective of limiting pass-on rates, and in finding an acceptable cure for the individual – whether it was introducing preventatives to prevent infection or new chemical treatments to treat it. The causal link between the initial promiscuity and the unlucky outcome was conveniently ignored.

Another common excuse given for neglecting sexual history has been that of a paucity of evidence available. This is only partially true; quantitative evidence can be extrapolated from various official sources such as the VD statistics, war diaries and APM reports, as will be demonstrated, and there is much to be gleaned from memoirs. The latter simply have to be well-read with the understanding that much is written 'between the lines'.

In the moral climate of the day sexual reminiscences were not conventional and as a result often the subject was raised only obliquely. R. Hilton, a middle-ranking officer in the Royal Garrison Artillery in 1916, was a man typical of his age who described the Edwardian era from which he sprang as one that 'marked a golden age of good manners, good taste, and "good form"'. He excused his omission of more colourful tales by reference to his upbringing, while nevertheless obliquely admitting to have experienced 'romantic' interludes in Béthune: 'I was not married then, nor even engaged. Though I know it is unfashionable, I still hold the prehistoric view that a man's amorous adventures are not a fit subject for public reminiscence'.[26]

There were, during the war itself, those British soldiers with less gentlemanly attitudes but even Irish-Cockney, Edward Casey, aka 'The Misfit Soldier', whose colourful sexual adventures will be recounted later, chose initially to use the pseudonym 'Rowarth' when telling his story; we must assume out of general embarrassment. Others may, however, have held back from writing about their adventures to friends because they knew that their words were not private and a degree of self-censorship was probably driven by fear of whom, other than the intended respondent, might read a letter once it was delivered rather than any moral reticence. Memoirs simply have to be carefully digested and, while conscious of not reading too much into reported situations, being alive to inference and subtle 'codes'. A young subaltern of the Dorsets, J.H. Butlin wrote of a sexual adventure while in Rouen initially wishing he could be more informative:

> However the fact that this letter has to pass through a number of hands prevents me from saying any more except that I am supremely happy. Of course you must never mention all that I have told you to a living soul'.[27]

Obviously having received suitable reassurances, he later wrote considerably more graphic accounts of his adventures. New Zealander, Deward Barnes, was equally circumspect, writing in one letter home that '[t]here is an immoral life in the army

---

26 Hilton, R., *Nine Lives* (London: Hollis & Crater, 1955), pp. 46-7.
27 IWM 67/52/1, J. H. Butlin [6th Dorset Regt, France], 'Letters collection', 29 Jan. 1917.

that I can't write about'.[28] It must have been a significant 'secret' life; Kiwi soldiers exhibited one of the highest VD infection rates of any of the allied contingents.

We have to recognise, too, that many memoirs were not written with a view to publication; they were intended simply for family history. It is possible that family members reading the memoirs later put a blue pencil though any of the more colourful memories that had escaped initial self-censorship.

While more openly honest memories might have been expected in the flood of war books that characterised the publishing world of the late 1920s and early 1930s, post-war censorship also limited what might be written, despite the writers themselves becoming less coy about recording their experiences. Many books fell foul of the Lord Chancellor's office and were either banned or their content bowdlerised for perceived obscenity. As a strategic alternative, authors simply left out or circumvented what they knew the censor would ban. Most authors, and certainly publishers, would have been aware of the constraints imposed by the Obscene Publications Act of 1857 thanks to a number of high profile court cases. Content in the inter-war period was further constrained by the activities of social purity movements, who dictated what was published both directly, through the censor, and indirectly by influencing distribution, effectively further forcing authors into self-censorship.[29]

An interesting example of the impact of the moral-police can be seen in the differences between Sassoon's wartime diaries and his subsequent literary 'Sherston' trilogy; the former records men on leave 'eating and drinking and being bored, and looking for lust', while in the later version, with the fictional character, Sherston, they were merely 'eating and drinking and being bored'. Sassoon is particularly careful with any suggestion of homoeroticism, perhaps realising that emotions and actions close to base nature would not easily fit with the image of the heroic soldier that was being cultivated.

Public and critical reaction in the inter-war years to any implied denigration of the soldier would certainly have acted as a restraint to men wanting to write the whole truth of their war time experiences. Lamont found that the adjectives 'nasty, disgusting, pornographic and revolting were hurled at me for not remembering that England is the last refuge of sexual cant, prudery and hypocrisy', following publication of his sexually-explicit memoir, *War, Wine and Women*.[30] Equally, in truth, there were also a number of more sensationalist authors who attracted justified criticism for 'sexing-up' their work with an eye on sales; these, however, were rather more obviously 'novels' rather than old soldier accounts but it is possible that factual material was omitted by the true memorialist for fear of being branded as one of the 'bandwagon'

---

28   Boyack, N., *Behind the Lines: The lives of the New Zealand Soldiers in the First World War* (Wellington, NZ: Allen & Unwin/Port Nicholson, 1989), p. 283, letter home.
29   Bristow, Edward, *Vice and Vigilance* (Dublin: Gill & MacMillan, 1977), pp. 224-6.
30   Harvey, R., *Muse of Fire* (London: Hambledon, 1998), p. 151. Lamont wrote under the pseudonym of Wilfred Saint-Mandé, *War, Wine and Women* (London: Cassell, 1931, repr., 2003). See also Williamson, *The Patriot's Progress*.

brigade. It may be that some authors aspiring to sales took note of reviews such as that appearing in the *Times Literary Supplement* of June 1930 concerning the title '*The Garlands Wither*': 'what good does realism do? ... are brothel visits in Amiens and Béthune anymore edifying than visits to brothels in London or Chicago?'.[31] Perceived 'course' references might well have been omitted in favour of positive reviews.

Where their accounts passed the censor, however, their truthfulness cannot be in doubt. Such references were likely to have been made openly and honestly by men who assumed their books would be read by contemporaries, who would be quick to point out exaggeration or downright lies. A. M. Burrage, as an example, writing in 1930, was typically conscious of possible criticisms and caustic of those he felt had played fast and loose with the facts or sensationalised their story and his disclaimer justifies his inclusions of sexually-related material: 'I have not grubbed in the dirt for obscenity and horror in the hope of selling a few extra copies, but I have shirked nothing, and I think have contrived to be frank ...'.[32]

Later in the century, public attitudes had changed, old soldiers became less concerned with how others might view them and the invidious censorship of pre-Elizabethan days had disappeared. Charles Carrington wrote: 'When writing for readers in the nineteen-sixties there is one topic I dare not shirk, though for 1914 readers it would have been a topic I dare not face – the sexual conduct of the young soldier'.[33] Interestingly, by the 'Swinging Sixties' other memoirs go further, also mentioning the once taboo areas of homosexuality, pornography and even masturbation.

The honesty and reliability of all memoirs of course reflect, to an extent, the period in which they were written – rather than the period they recall – and depend on the objectives of the writer. Some memorialists undoubtedly 'sexed up' their memoirs with an eye to sales, some were concerned to discount this possibility, while still others buried their sexual adventures. Although a tradition of telling the unvarnished truth – however unpleasant or discreditable to a memorialist – developed from the late 1920s, it has to be recognised that any author might have problems with recording objective and ascertainable fact. In an environment where the senses were quite literally bombarded, a man could forget, confuse facts, or imagine events, not so much making them up as confusing trench gossip or remembering someone else's story as his own experience.

What we cannot discount, whatever the challenges of the sources, is that the Tommy had an active sexual life. Despite the chastity of some, there is no denying that sexual activity was taking place; it is the scale and frequency, and with whom it occurred, that requires illumination, as does the impact that sex, or lack of it, had on the men. Gunner McCormack made the telling point: 'Everyone had their history,

---

31 *The Times Literary Supplement*, June 1930.
32 Burrage, A.M., *War is War* (London: Victor Golanz, 1930), p. 7.
33 Carrington, C., *Soldier from the Wars Returning* (London: Hutchinson, 1965, Arrow Books repr., 1970*)*, p. 183.

everyone in the war had some tale to tell … [women] were few and far between but they were still there'.[34] This fact was acknowledged by both professional soldiers such as Charles Carrington and Frank Crozier[35], and also by the ordinary rank and file like infantryman, Percy Clare:

> I speak of the subject because I am writing faithfully of my life in France and as wherever you find an army you will find the thing; it is better to know the truth than to get the erroneous idea that it is a libel on either the women or the men. [36]

If even a very small percentage of men committed their experiences to paper, or who orally recounted them later for posterity, the percentage that does mention or allude to sex – especially given the contemporary tendency towards self-censorship – gives a broad indication of its extent throughout the army.

The question might justifiably be asked, especially given the somewhat sensitive and occasionally distasteful nature of the material, why uncovering this aspect of the soldiers' life matters. In peering into the boudoir, so to speak, is there a danger of being a 'Peeping Tom', or of seeking cheap titillation? Is there a danger, too, of denigrating the men, of moving the focus somehow from their sacrifice?

Perhaps there is titillation there for the puerile or who wish to see it as such, as there will be material for those who wish to exercise narrow, subjective moral judgement. The rational, emotionally mature and objective reader, however, will appreciate that by ignoring the social side of the combatant's experience, being content with the muddy details of the front line, we get a hugely distorted picture of the individual's war experience. This is especially so if focus is always on the infantryman; even then understanding his performance in battle is enhanced by understanding the full and uncensored realities of his life both in and out of the line.

One fundamental question for all who have an interest in the Western Front is how men endured the horrors and privations of this 'war to end wars' without more individual lads experiencing a personal breakdown or collectively resorting to mass indiscipline.

On the Western Front the average soldier's battles were fought on two fronts. In spirit-sapping trench warfare he periodically fought bloody and horrific engagements against the forces ranged against him on the other side of no man's land. When not engaged on that front, he had the daily fight against the boredom and tedium that constituted army life. For the majority there was another subsidiary battle; the battle of the 'amateur' civilian-soldier, many volunteers in only 'for the duration', to maintain

---

34 IWM Sound Archive, 24539, reel 2, W. Hill, Private 8th Bn Rifle Bde; IWM Sound Archive, No. 22739, reel 2, McCormack, Leo, gunner Royal Artillery.
35 Carrington, *Soldier from the Wars Returning* (London: Hutchinson, 1965, Arrow Books repr., 1970), p. 184.
36 IWM 06/48/1. Clare, Percy, 'Reminiscences 1914-18', unpaginated.

their individual civilian identity in the face of army bureaucracy, rigidity, uniformity and often apparent stupidity.

The maintenance of good morale was the key to success on both fronts. Though unique in many ways, in this aspect the Great War was no different from others, with morale the singularly most important constituent of the soldiers' armoury. In both pitched battle and the attrition of trench warfare morale underpinned a combat effectiveness, essential for both maximising individual survival chances and for beating the opposition army. Out of the fight, morale gave men the fortitude to endure what seemed the endless and mind-numbing routine of army life in a war with seemingly no end. In the face of an alien environment that often appeared to want to dehumanise the individual, morale, in the sense of 'never letting the bastards grind you down', was essential for civilian-soldiers in the preservation of their individual humanity, and probably sanity. The study of morale has thus become central to understanding why men continued to fight and endure this unprecedented war when mutiny, desertion, surrender, or even personal physical or psychological breakdown appeared easier alternatives.[37]

---

37 For those wishing to explore aspects of morale see, Marshall, S. L. A., *Men Against Fire. The Problem of Battle Command* (Norman OK: University of Oklahoma Press, 2000); Watson, Alexander, *Enduring the Great War. Combat, Morale and Collapse in the Germany and British Armies, 1914-1918* (Cambridge: Cambridge University Press: 2008); Baynes, *Morale* (1967); Fuller, J., *Morale and Popular Culture in the British and Dominion Armies, 1914-1918* (Oxford: Clarendon Press, 1990). Englander, David, 'Discipline and Morale in the British Army, 1917-1918' in Horne J. (ed.), *State, Society and Mobilisation in Europe during the First World War* (Cambridge: Cambridge University Press, 1997); Sheffield, G. D., *Leadership in the Trenches: Officer-Man Relations, Morale and Discipline in the British Army in the Era of the Great War* (Basingstoke: Macmillan, 2000); MacKenzie, S. P., 'Morale and the Cause: The Campaign to Shape the Outlook of Soldiers in the British Expeditionary Force, 1914–1918', *Canadian Journal of History*, 25 (1990); MacKenzie, S.P., *Politics and Military Morale. Current Affairs and Citizenship Education in the British Army, 1914-1950* (Oxford: Clarendon Press, 1992); Snape, M., *God and the British Soldier. Religion and the British Army in the First and Second World Wars* (London: Taylor & Francis, 2005); French, David, *Military Identities. The Regimental System, the British Army, and the British people, 1870-2000* (Oxford: OUP, 2005); Bowman, Timothy, *Irish Regiments in the Great War, Discipline and Morale* ((Manchester: MUP 2003); Strachan, Hew, 'Training, Morale, and Modern War', *Journal of Contemporary History*, 41 (2006), pp. 211-27. Bourne, J., 'The British Working Man in Arms' in Cecil, Hugh and Liddle, Peter (eds.), *Facing Armageddon. The First World War Experienced* (London: Leo Cooper, 1996), pp. 336-52; Watson, Alexander and Porter, Patrick, 'Bereaved and Aggrieved: Combat Motivation and the Ideology of Sacrifice in the First World War', *Historical Research*, 83 (2010), pp. 146-64; for the importance of humour see Robertshaw, Andrew, '"Irrepressible Chirpy Cockney Chappies"? Humour as an Aid to Survival', *Journal of European Studies*, 31 (2001), pp. 277-87, and Winter, J., *The Experience of World War One* (Oxford: OUP, 1988); Simkins, P., 'Everyman at War. Recent Interpretations of the Front Line Experience', in Bond, B.(ed.), *The First World War and British Military History* (Oxford: Clarendon Press, 1991). McCartney, Helen, *Citizen Soldiers: The Liverpool Territorials in the First World War* (Cambridge: CUP, 2005).

The study of morale in any period of warfare falls into four overlapping areas; the recognition of its importance and relationship to other military variables; agreeing an operational definition of the concept; identifying and exploring what impacts on an individual's morale; and examining how morale has been sustained or lost.

Xenophon, the Greek historian, soldier, mercenary and philosopher was probably the first to acknowledge that 'in action, the sustaining of morale was an imperative'. Centuries later, Napoleon give this more substance advising that morale outweighs the material by three to one (much to the detriment of French soldiers in Autumn 1914 whose leaders, emphasising *'cran'* over a pre-attack artillery barrage, followed his dictum perhaps too literally). Clausewitz wrote 'That the moral(e) cannot be omitted being amongst the most important subjects in war is evident in itself, for the *condition of the mind* [emphasis added] has always been the most decisive influence on the forces employed in war'. Historical judgement aside, the importance of sustaining high morale continues to be a key issue in contemporary conflicts.

It is one thing recognising that positive morale fundamentally contributes to a desired military objective but defining it presents greater problems. While theorists continue to struggle with the concept, one thing agreed, however, is that Clausewitz's *'condition of the mind'* translates as the will to win, and this is often the decisive factor in obtaining victory. 'Morale' is synonymous with this will to win, or to endure whatever hardships war brings. This was cogently summarised in the Great War by Field Marshal Foch as 'Victory = Will'.

Clausewitz somewhat side-stepped advancing a deeper explanation, content to note that the subject 'will escape from all book-analysis' being 'neither bought into numbers nor into classes, and require[d] to be both seen and felt'. He wrote that he preferred 'to remain rhapsodical, content to have drawn attention to the importance of the subject in a general way'.[38] This might be seen as a bit of a 'copout' though, Fennel, a more recent historian of the British Army's WW2 North African campaign, echoed this difficulty; 'it is obviously not amenable to quantification'.[39]

This difficulty notwithstanding, scholars and theorists following Clausewitz have, however, attempted to deliver an operational definition. Baynes, in one of the first studies of the subject pertaining to the Great War, defined morale as the 'quality of mind and spirit which combines courage, self-discipline and endurance … having as its hall-marks cheerfulness and unselfishness'.[40] The outcome of this 'quality of mind' was observable both in peace and in war. In peace it was immediately identifiable from the way a battalion conducted itself; from the smartness of salute to the warmth of welcome for its guests. In war it was manifest in perseverance and in having a belief in ultimate victory. Kipling perhaps summarised it best in his poem *'If'*:

---

38 Clausewitz, *On War* (Ware: Wordsworth Editions, 1997). Book Three, Ch. 3, pp. 150-52.
39 Fennell, Jonathan, *Combat and Morale in the North Africa Campaign; The Eighth Army and the Path to El Alamein* (Cambridge: Cambridge University Press, 2011).
40 Baynes, *Morale*, p.108.

> If you can force your heart and nerve and sinew
> To serve your turn long after they are gone,
> And so hold on when there is nothing in you
> Except the Will which says to them: 'Hold on!'

To a soldier of the Great War, high morale prosaically meant being 'in the pink' when writing home from a water-soaked trench; joining in with a marching song when faint with physical exhaustion; putting up with either interminable boredom or endless fatigues; going 'over the top' while knowing the odds of survival were low; and basically being prepared to 'see it through' – whatever that meant.

Identifying the outcomes of this positive frame of mind is, however, easier than identifying the constituent elements that underpin morale and subsequently managing those variables to bring about the desired positive 'will'. Lord Moran's 1945 definition in his explorations of 'Courage' was open-ended; a soldier's morale was, he noted, 'governed by the thoughts however elementary that pass through his head.' Sixty-years later, Michael Snape, while making a pitch for religious belief as an under-pinning element, opined morale was, 'that mysterious quality without which an army is like a machine without fuel'[41], but was not an easy concept to evaluate. What is agreed, however, is that it has many constituents though inevitably historians cannot always agree on these, or on their relative importance. Perhaps the most inclusive definition has been provided by a veteran turned scholar, S. L. A Marshall:

> Morale is the thinking of the army. It is the whole complex body of an army's thought: The way it feels about the soil and about the people from which it springs. The way it feels about the cause and their politics. The way it feels about its friends and allies, as well as its enemies. About its commanders and goldbricks. About food and shelter. Duty and leisure. Payday and sex. Militarism and civilization. Freedom and slavery. Work and want. Weapons and comradeship. Bunk fatigue and drill. Discipline and disorder. Life and death. God and the devil.[42]

In those periodic but violent and destructive battles of the Great War, where actual combat performance was of primary importance, less nebulous and somewhat easier to define military factors were of greater importance. Men, it is argued, did not break; courage held because of factors like belief in their cause, regimental tradition and pride, realistic training, leadership and allegiance to their primary group. Specific battlefield explanations are also advanced by some seeking to explain the phenomenon. There may, in addition, have been other deeper psychological factors at play,

---

41 Snape, *God and the British Soldier*, p. 91.
42 Marshall, *Men Against Fire*, p. 158, cited by Watson, *Enduring the Great War*, p. 140. Another veteran to mention the link is Fuller, *Morale*.

such as faith in the protection provided by unseen powers, or even for some it has to be admitted, the pure enjoyment of killing.

Outside of the violent eruptions of warfare, however, and in the daily battle to keep up an individual's spirits, to somehow mentally accommodate the horrors seen or anticipated, and to cling on to civilised peace-time mores, a different balance of factors came into play. Some of these overlapped with those required to ensure physical survival, others were at odds with those the military felt important. While life in peace-time had in various ways prepared the new soldier for the acute discomfort and deprivation that war entailed, and continuing connections to and support from home could be of importance, men needed to develop their own individual coping strategies, bolstering the natural capacity humans have to remain resilient in the face of adversity. John Baynes, in *Morale*, added to Marshall's list some prosaic factors underpinning resilience and endurance; food, rest, mail, proper medical attention and good welfare services for the men at home, in addition to pride in appearance and strong personal and imposed discipline.

Despite this growing list of variables, it is only comparatively recently that the role of sex, other than its use as a weapon in war, has been considered from the stance of what one historian has described as 'desire and delight, of consensual pleasures made possible by the anonymity of war and the disruptions of traditional constraints and communal and familial monitoring mechanisms'.[43] Or as Frank Richards would perhaps more prosaically describe it, 'the fun of getting up to some hanky-panky without someone looking over my shoulder'.

With a few exceptions sex has simply not been recognised as a constituent of morale by most theorists. Even Barnes, while not discounting sex like others, questions its prevalence and availability. Yet sex, encompassing anticipation, activity and consequence, while only of peripheral importance in underpinning actual combat effectiveness, was of vital importance in the soldiers' battles against the tedium of army life and in preserving his civilian identity and soul. Without considering and accepting this, we miss a huge aspect of the soldier's experience of war. But to understand the extent to which it contributed to morale there has to be a full appreciation of the extent of activities, and of the physical context in which they took place. One cannot debate whether morale was helped or hindered by a visit to an official brothel unless the very physical nature of that visit is envisioned. One cannot debate whether sexual interplay with women outside of the purely commercial experience helped a man cling to his civilian self unless the context of that relationship is understood. One cannot debate the impact on morale of the obscene and of pornography unless its availability, type and usage are fully appreciated. One cannot understand what role sex, consummated, imagined, or simply as a conversation staple, played in morale without a descriptive

---

43 Herzog, Dagmar (ed.), *Brutality and Desire, War and Sexuality in Europe's Twentieth Century* (Basingstoke: Palgrave 2009), p. 5.

audit. The facts, however potentially distasteful, are important and illuminating and enumerating them is the primary objective of this book.

Sex, in its multiple guises, whether successfully enjoined or merely anticipated, was undoubtedly a morale-builder, a distraction from the horror of war. Aubrey Smith, writing as 'A Rifleman' confirmed that when denied it was a morale-dampener: 'No civilians about – a fact that appeared to upset riflemen … who always had an eye for a pretty wench and an estaminet bar', he wrote.[44] I.L. Read's 'dream' of the future included 'unlimited scope for romance'.[45] For Frank Richards 'booze and fillies' equated with 'a glorious place'.

Sex beckoned from doorway and window throughout the war and in every theatre. The prospect of leave invariably meant women; in fact, the two were often inseparable. Further, new opportunities for sexual adventure were presented as battalions moved between fronts. Men resting in Marseilles or posted to Italy found their experience of life broadened, if only through observation, and carried their experiences, their pornography and, sometimes, their diseases back to France. This was especially true of men posted to Cairo, an epicentre of potential carnal adventure, where for many a visit to the Wazir brothel district was often the first taste of sex. Immediately after the Armistice men found themselves enjoying the favours bestowed on liberators in Belgian towns and villages, and visiting the brothels of Brussels. Then, when occupying parts of Germany itself, the British soldier was welcomed by local girls, literally with open arms, and not always purely for commercial gain.[46] And morale was all the better for these multiple opportunities.

There is too, another reason for investigating this sex life; 'it takes two to tango'. The soldier's story of necessity leads us to the woman's story. The debate is incomplete unless there is some demographic knowledge of the women who served their needs, either venally or otherwise, and their motivations. The interest in Tommy's Great War experience rarely touches on the life facing a civilian population, dominantly female, effectively captive in their own occupied land. We fail to appreciate the enormity of the battle inherent in struggling for physical and emotional survival in an economically-disrupted, socially-dislocated environment where men have left their woman folk behind to cope; where displaced populations, both refugee and a multi-national military, caused massive social upheaval; and where social tradition and morals in

---

44 A. Rifleman (Aubrey Smith pseud.), *Four Years on the Western Front: Being the Experiences of a Ranker in the London Rifle Brigade* (London: Oldhams, 1922, Naval & Military repr., undated), p. 278 and Richards, *Old Soldiers Never Die*, p. 12,
45 Read, *Of Those We Loved* (Bishop Auckland: Pentland Press, 1994) p. 213. See also Hope, *Winding Road*, p. 83; Stephen Graham, *A Private in the Guards* (London: Macmillan, 1919, Heinemann edn, 1928), p. 167.
46 Crozier, *Brass Hat*, p. 255; Gibbs, Philip, *Realities of War* (London: W. Heinemann, 2 vols, 1920, repr., 1938), p. 416; Hiscock, Eric, *The Bells of Hell Go Ting-a-ling-a-ling: An Autobiographical Fragment Without Maps* (London: Arlington Books, 1976), p. 90.

traditionally conservative and religious regions were challenged daily. The story of the soldier's sexual life is arguably also the story of a woman's survival strategy.

Prior to following these various stories, our next two chapters look at the army's attitudes to soldier sex and attempt to establish the extent of sexual activity but one final caveat must be added. While the material discovered for this study uncovers a new dimension to the soldiers' experience, and helps to paint a picture of the British soldier's sexual attitudes and activities, this author can only share in the frustrations of Ronald Hyam, one of the pioneers of sexual history:

> [T]he evidence uncovered in this investigation is patchy. It is necessarily impressionistic. The effect at times is rather like peering only into the relatively clear surface layer of waters of a particularly deep and opaque pool, since most sexual activity is simply not observable, still less recorded.[47]

---

47 Hyam, Ronald, *Empire and Sexuality: The British Experience*. (Manchester: MUP, 1990), p. 19.

2

'Avoiding an unsavoury and malodorous discussion': The British Army's attitude towards sex

If there had been a medal clasp for 'sex' to affix to any general service medal then most old soldier's ribbons from Wellington's time onward would have sported it. Sex had been seen as a recognised and important factor in the army's reward structure and most, if not all men had fought in the metaphorical battle for sex. Given the public's low peace-time regard for Tommy Atkins and knowledge, as Kipling wrote, that 'single men in barricks don't grow into plaster saints', few questioned how and where this particular and largely unpublicised battle was fought and certainly not the army itself – unless the casualty rate from VD became too high. Until, that was, the arrival of Josephine Butler and her allies fighting against the anti-Contagious Disease Acts.

In seemingly identifying women as the enemy in the fight to keep men healthy, the army, while employing tactics made possible by these acts, created for itself a redoubtable enemy. However, even under determined and sustained attack from any quarter, including Butler's brigades, they found ways around both the political and social objections to ensure that the soldier's continuing sexual needs would be catered for. This battle, starting in the mid-1880s, was to continue up to and through the Great War and even beyond, and although the army suffered occasional tactical defeats, in strategic terms it was the long-term victor. The order of battle was the same throughout; the Western Front, especially from 1915 to 1919, simply presented a different order of logistic problems in trying to manage the needs of both a much expanded army – in both size and demographics – and one whose sexual demands were largely unanticipated.

The agenda of the 1918 Inter-Allied Conference on Venereal Disease, a meeting called at the behest of the Dominion governments to discuss the problem of venereal disease in their troops, is the closest one gets to a single document presenting the army's 'official' line on sex during the war years.[1] This document generally reflected practical considerations but, as we will read below, while avoiding moral judgments

---

1 TNA: WO 32/11404.

in its defence of the tolerated brothel, the agenda represented a coherent summary of the army's attitude towards sex, and the problem of venereal disease. Unfortunately for the historian, the committee did not stick to its agenda and the file in the National Archives is incomplete, with some material lost and the minutes failing to record certain items listed for discussion.

Beyond this much-consulted file, it is hard to find other direct statements of policy. The previous decades had seen the army embroiled in a number of controversies over the provision of sex, often as a result of its own indiscretion;[2] there had been an 1886 controversy, for example, caused by the leakage of a circular memorandum tacitly admitting to the army's support and management of 'red lamps' in India. It had learned that holding its tongue was the best way of avoiding 'unsavoury and malodorous' discussion, as Lord Sydenham, Chairman of the Royal Committee on Venereal Disease, reminded them in a note of 15 March 1918, to the War Cabinet about the use of a regulated brothel at Cayeux.[3]

Elements of the army might ideally have wanted to uphold Victorian morals, but the impossibility of doing so in practice was generally recognised. In effect, the army created and sustained a culture that acknowledged a soldier's lust, its importance to the maintenance of his morale, and his right to satiate it. There was one proviso: that he kept himself fit for service. This involved turning an official blind eye to the use of prostitutes, unless it had an impact on military efficiency.[4] Pragmatism driven by military need became the determining factor. On various occasions over a 50-year period from 1865, the army or its civilian allies implicitly or obliquely stated or defended its position in letters, memoranda, and evidence presented to committees. Taken together they provide some confirmation of the army's attitude. If, after the repeal of the Contagious Diseases Acts, this position was challenged or the army was requested to amplify its policy, then the response was to deny that prostitution was officially sanctioned. Seldom did it lead to formal or sustained physical crackdowns on their use.

The army had traditionally been very good at establishing a position of which everyone was cognisant but about which there had been virtually no formal discussion. Probably reflecting the feelings of most observers, the soldier and scholar Charles Carrington wrote:

> I have never discovered the official attitude of GHQ to licensed prostitution, which had been the subject of much heated controversy in late Victorian England.

---

2 K. Ballhatchet, *Race, Sex and Class under the Raj* (London: Weidenfeld & Nicolson, 1980), pp. 56-61; Gill, Anton, *Ruling Passions: Sex, Race and Empire* (London: BBC Books, 1995), p. 131.
3 TNA: WO 32/5597 and CAB 23/5/WC366.
4 Douglas Peers, 'Privates off Parade: Regimenting Sexuality in the nineteenth-century Indian Empire', *International History Review* 20 (1998), p. 834.

The impression I formed was that it was accepted as inevitable in the first years of the war but driven underground in the later grimmer days.[5]

Everything was based on impressions and received wisdom, without the subject ever forming part of a manual or a training course. Despite this, the army did actually hold well-defined attitudes, or as they might be described today, 'a set of shared corporate values', known throughout the army itself and in the wider establishment. On various occasions over a fifty-year period from 1865, when the physical manifestation of those values were challenged by external forces, a sentence, or paragraph or two was generated in a letter, memorandum or in evidence presented to a committee, in which the Army, or its civilian allies, implicitly stated, or defended, its position. In short, this was to recognise the problem but turn an official blind eye to the solution unless it had an impact on military efficiency, then deny it was officially sanctioned.

Traditionally, providing a practical solution to the problem of sex was delegated to officers at regimental level. Even then, however, they would be disowned and abandoned if their actions caused any difficulties. Individual commanders often learned this the hard way finding themselves 'left hanging out to dry' by both their senior officers and civilian politicians in rushing to denial of any knowledge.[6] An unconvincing defence, and subsequent fall-out from a leaked circular memorandum from the CO of the Cheshire Regiment asking for 'sufficiently attractive' women for the Indian Lal Bazar in 1886, probably did more than anything to teach the army that silence was golden. 'Any despatch or statement which we may hereafter send home in defence of any policy which run counter the prejudices of … 'hysterical' interests' wrote Lord Dufferin, Governor-General, 'will be disbelieved and denounced as misleading and untrustworthy'. The silence is golden rule was still the preferred option 30-years later when an embarrassed APM Dieppe received a written rebuke from General Headquarters British Armies in France 20 Jan. 1918, noting him formally that 'he should not have issued any orders on such a delicate matter as brothels [there was] no excuse for any such stupidity'. In this case the offending memo was concerning the Chinese Labour Corps going into brothels. While this could have had a contentious race dimension it was going into print that was the crime, not excusing the brothel.

The individual soldier, for his part, was led to believe tacitly, with a wink and a nod, though sometimes overtly such as when Gibbons and comrades were literally forced marched to a brothel by a junior officer on the Somme in 1916,[7] that – if he could not control his carnal desires (self-control generally being society's preferred solution), or find a legitimate outlet for them – he could use the services of prostitutes, but would be punished if he contracted any disease that removed him from service.

---

5   Carrington, *Soldier*, pp. 180–82. See also TNA: WO 154/114: APM, HQ IGC, report 20 Dec. 1914 where the existence and usage of non-regulated brothels is explicitly recognised.
6   Balhatchet, *Race,* p. 62.
7   Gibbons, John, *Roll on Next War* (London: Frederick Muller, 1935) p. 55.

The range of information and advice provided during the war by MOs on preventing disease further illustrates the *ad hoc* nature of the policy: it was never uniform and ranged from total absence through their own innocence of the subject, to railing against fornication on moral grounds, to enthusiastic recommendations for having safe sex.

In truth, the army's ambivalent attitude gave it an irreconcilable problem. In Stephen Graham's Guards Battalion, he found that:

> Padres ... could not inveigh against lust because the medical officer was of the opinion Nature's needs must be satisfied ... all we had to do was use the safeguards and preventatives which were at our disposal to save us from disease. The padre could not go and reason with the men who upon occasion were to be seen in the queues outside the houses with the red blinds. Hundred of thousands of men who had led comparatively pure lives until they saw France learned and were even encouraged to go with impure women.[8]

Due to such inherent dichotomies the army often tied itself in knots trying to follow this position, especially when fettered by outside interests. The basic dichotomy is illustrated by the 1918 Conference agenda.

I. The Maison Tolerée as found in France
    A. As a safeguard against disease or otherwise
    B. Its psychological effect as a factor promoting sexual indulgence
    C. As a factor in preventing crimes of sexual violence or perversion
    D. The problems of policing the maison tolerée when placed out of bounds
       • In large cities
       • In smaller communities
    E. Local cooperation with restrictive measures
II The amateur prostitute and the army
III The drink question in relation to sexual indulgence
IV Prophylaxis or early treatment before or after exposure
V Disciplinary measures for officers and men found with VD
VI Measures against the publication and distribution of indecent literature and pictures
VII Constructive measures of meeting sexual problems in the army with special reference to overseas troops
    • Literature

---

8 Graham, *Privates*, p. 225.

- Lectures
- Recreative measures
- Leave

VIII Position of men infected with VD.

Sandwiched between the two primary goals of safeguarding against disease and avoiding sexual perversion is the nagging doubt that they might also be promoting moral incontinence. Another dichotomy was apparent in the Conference's justification of regulated prostitution, and its discussion of disciplinary measures to be taken against men who probably availed themselves of the non-regulated variety. Later, discipline gave way to prevention and cure, which might have attracted accusations of promoting immorality. The final item on the agenda introduces methods by which the sexual appetite might be suppressed, despite earlier tacit admittance of the need to tolerate prostitution given the strength of the sex drive in the soldier.

This historic belief in the rank-and-file soldier's need for sex was fundamental. Access to sex was seen as an essential contributor to morale. Towers believes that the British class leadership was convinced that army morale was contingent on sexual activity with Beardsley adding, 'Army leaders … regarded prostitution … as a necessary evil and a vital auxiliary service.'[9] This was an attitude carried forward from the pre-war professional army to the new army of the Great War: as Brigadier Frank Crozier famously held, 'A man – or a boy … could not fight well unless he could love well'.[10] Traditionally, the lower classes were thought by the military 'top brass' to lack the intellectual and moral resources required for continence. Although the army introduced several initiatives from the late Victorian period to try to improve the chances of the men remaining celibate, including shortening the enlistment time, any expectation of celibacy was seen as unrealistic given the working-class background of the soldiery and their attitude to premarital sex; 'While celibacy remained the ideal, pragmatism on the part of the military authorities won the day' as Trustram concluded.[11] Military effectiveness was deemed to be dependent on the interconnected foundations of discipline, morale and physical fitness; sex was part of the equation. In addition, at a subsidiary level, there was always an anxiety to avoid any problems, either in the barrack room, or with native populations, that frustration might have caused.

---

9   Towers, Bridget A., 'Health Education Policy, 1916-1926: Venereal disease and the prophylaxis dilemma', *Medical History* 24 (1980). Beardsley, Edward H., 'Allied Against Sin: American and British Responses to Venereal Disease in World War I', *Medical History* 20 (1976), p. 190.
10 Crozier, *Brass Hat*, quoted in Fischer H. C. and Dubois, Dr E. X., *Sexual Life During the World War* (London: F. Aldor, 1937, private printing edition), p. 78. Hyam, *Empire*, pp. 2-3.
11 Trustram, M., *Women of the Regiment. Marriage and the Victorian Army* (Cambridge: CUP, 1984), p. 27.

The general view of the military hierarchy was evident in the communication between the Acting District Magistrate of Ahmadabad and the Bombay Government in 1894, expressing the general view among officials and army officers:

> Private Soldiers are young men taken from the classes least habituated to exercise self-control – classes whom in their natural state marry very early in life. You take such men, you do not allow them to marry, you feed them well – better in most cases than they have been accustomed to be fed, and you give them sufficient amount of physical exercise to put them into good condition and no more. It is asking too much to expect that a large majority of such men will exhibit the continence of the cloister.[12]

A few years earlier, Dr W. J. Moore, the Surgeon-General of the Indian Army in Bombay, had summed up this philosophy from a semi-official standpoint: 'Physiological instincts must be satisfied in some way or other; or they must be repressed by force of will aided by severe physical exertion, abstemious habits, and the high moral capacity arising from culture'.[13] The army did not have much faith in the soldier's ability to reach the alternative goals, or considered the task of taking responsibility for them too costly. As such, the satisfaction of sexual desire became the overriding policy. In the more graphic and colourful language of the press, the *Almora Akhbar*, a Hindi weekly, wrote that 'not to provide women for European soldiers who are drunk and mad with lust would be like letting loose beasts of prey'.[14]

The views were prescient: it was similarly noted, though in slightly less colourful language in a letter from Le Commissaire de Police de Graville to La Maire de la Ville de Graville in June 1918, how the closure of a controlled local brothel led to problems in troop behaviour within his local French community: 'les soldats anaglais debauchent le jeunes filles et aussi les femmes de nos poilus'.[15]

It is no surprise that statements such as this came out of India rather than Britain, as officials at home wisely kept their heads down in response to the constant sniping of the forces of social purity. The last thing anyone wanted was to be accused of promoting licentiousness or immorality (as the Agenda on the Inter-Allied Conference item Ib, later implies). In 1897 however, the *Lancet*, implicitly on behalf of the wider establishment, stuck its head above the parapet to comment on regulated prostitution: 'We … must look the facts in the face. Nature has implanted in every man, in common with

---

12 Balhatchet, *Race*, p. 83.
13 Ibid., p. 10.
14 Ibid., p. 66.
15 TNA: WO 32/5597: 24 June 1918 to le Ministre de la Guerre. See also correspondence in the same file that recounts further French official concerns over the sexual activities of allied soldiers in the town.

the lower animals, an appetite so strong that it is hopeless to suppose we can successfully war against it'.[16]

Admitting defeat in this unequal contest against nature, the army turned to prostitution to satisfy that appetite. By the advent of the Great War the troops, Guardsman Stephen Graham included, often had little doubt over the army's attitude: 'Sexual intercourse was regarded as a physical necessity for the men. Besides being the medical point of view, it became the official Army point of view as well, and we were often told in lectures that it was natural'.[17] Or, as infantryman Harry Wells succinctly put it, prostitution was tolerated 'to keep the men quiet, I suppose that was the idea … otherwise they'd have had problems, I'd think'.[18]

A New Zealand Rifleman, Moloney, showed a mature and perhaps surprising understanding give his relatively lowly rank:

> 'Whatever our private views were on the subject of morality the Army being a soul-less machine, looked at morals from a purely practical aspect, that of the danger of needless waste of man-power. We were in the war to engage the enemy. To do this with the greatest efficiency it was necessary that each man be fit and therefore he should take every precaution to guard against infection by using the facilities provided by the blue lamp people and to use prophylactics which would be supplied.'[19]

The necessity of accommodating the sexual impulse was the foundation on which the army's attitude was built. However, it was beyond question that sex had to be with a woman. Second only to the realisation that natural heterosexual instincts would have to be assuaged was the determination that homosexual ones should not be. The army was well aware of the dangers inherent in their policy of maintaining a male-only society. Thus, running parallel with its concern to accommodate heterosexual desire, was its deep-rooted fear of sodomy. Not only was this seen as unnatural, but it also posed a threat to traditional hierarchy and military order and by implication, morale.[20] Furthermore, it was an offence under the Army Act.

Its importance in army thinking is represented by its position as Agenda item 1c at the Inter-Allied Conference, considering controlled sex as 'a factor in preventing

16   Balhatchet, *Race,* p. 83.
17   Graham, *Private,* p. 225; see also Boyack, *Behind the Lines,* p. 144, for a New Zealander's view.
18   IWM Sound Archive, No. 22740, Wells, Harry, Pte, 17th and 23rd Bn Royal Fusiliers, 1918. Boyack, *Behind the Lines*, p. 143. There is also the view of the much-quoted Crozier, *Brass Hat*, p. 143.
19   Boyack, *Behind the Lines*, p 14.
20   Davenport-Hines, Richard, *Sex, Death and Punishment* (London: Fontana, 1991), p. 147. See also Peers, 'Privates off Parade: Regimenting Sexuality in the Nineteenth-Century Indian Empire', *International History Review,* 20:4, (1998) p. 857.

crimes of sexual violence or perversion'. It is possible, however, given the pressure both the War Office and Home Office were under to 'do something' about the problems of VD in colonial troops, that this was introduced as an Aunt Sally, or a useful scare. The relatively low incidence of military prosecutions for indecency does beg the question of why such a fuss was being made of the offence unless the army authorities were aware of more (unrecorded) cases of homosexual activity.

While there is more evidence for homosexuality than the relatively small number of courts-martial might suggest, the fear of it was probably unwarranted. It certainly did not have the debilitating impact that venereal disease had. Even so a fear of homosexuality had historically fuelled the need to allow unfettered access to sex. The demoralisation and threat to discipline which homosexuality was thought to present were behind both the debates on allowing more marriages within the army, and also tolerating prostitution. As Balhatchet writes when examining the issue of sex in the Indian Army: 'referred to only in oblique terms, was homosexuality; it was despised as unmanly, and it was dreaded as a threat to military discipline'.[21]

This fear had a long history with buggery, mentioned in the articles of war since the seventeenth century, treated as seriously as desertion, mutiny or murder. In 1811 Ensign John Hepburn and Drummer Thomas White had been launched into eternity for their 'unnatural' activities, and in 1816, four members of the crew of the Aquitaine were hanged for buggery after a major naval scandal. Although execution was no longer the punishment, from the 1890s the armed services became increasingly anxious over any signs of homosexuality, an anxiety which probably arose from the general climate fostered by social purity concerns and the scandal of the Oscar Wilde trials.

By the 1890s, Indian Army commanders could protest that if 'disorderly houses' were suppressed, 'even more deplorable evils' than venereal disease would occur. As Viceroy Elgin put it, in 1894, 'there is already an increase in unnatural crimes'.[22] The matter was patently not far away from the minds of Home Office officials in Britain a decade or so later. An unsigned, hand-written note appended to the submission of the London Borough of Lambeth, commenting on the proposed reclassification of brothels in the Criminal Law Amendment Bill 1917, advises: 'I do not think the prosecution of single prostitutes should be encouraged. If prostitution in a reasonable manner is rendered impossible we are likely to see a large increase in worse forms of vice'. Commenting on what was hardly an epidemic the writer felt that, 'I expect the large number of cases of young officers convicted of indecency with males since the outbreak of war may be attributed to some extent to the closure of places which were "houses" of prostitutes'.[23] Similarly, during the 1918 controversy over the use of the Cayeux brothel, Sir Ernley Blackwell, assistant under-secretary in the Home Office

21 Balhatchet, *Race*, p. 10. Davenport-Hines, *Sex, Death and Punishment*, p. 146.
22 Hyam, *Empire and Sexuality*, p. 122.
23 TNA: HO 45/10724/251861/29A.

pointed out that 'if prostitution in a reasonable manner is rendered impossible we are likely to see an increase in [such] worse forms of vice [as a] number of young officers [committing acts of] indecency with young males'.[24]

Interestingly, the threat of indecency was not employed directly by any army spokesman when, in 1918 with their backs metaphorically to the wall – though this time fighting potential brothel closures rather than a Kaiser offensive – one might have assumed every justification would have been wheeled out. Haig's plea to maintain the status was based solely on the containment of venereal disease and the horrifying logistics of losing a further 350-400 men to policing and picket duties to keep the troops out of any brothels put out-of-bounds. That men might be forced into an 'unnatural' substitute is never mentioned.

In providing an outlet for lust whilst containing homosexual urges, the army had three main strategic options. It could control or corral passion; it could allow the presence of women, either as spouses or camp followers; or it could allow access to prostitutes or 'sex mercenaries'. Had the army had a totally free choice in the matter, the easiest option would simply have been to allow total access to the regulated prostitute. Its attempts to implement this policy in the post-Crimea environment, through such initiatives as the Contagious Diseases Acts, were quickly abandoned because of public antipathy and, by the later Victorian era, the army had decided, or was forced, to employ a combination of strategies, even if the accent was still firmly, if discreetly, on regulated prostitution.

Another obvious way for the army to provide for sexual needs would have been to allow greater freedom to marry and to allow men to have their partners (both legal wives and camp followers) with them. As part of the overall reaction to the varied weaknesses of the army highlighted during the Crimean campaign, there had been moves during the latter half of the nineteenth century towards changes in the rules governing marriage. They were tentative at best; at the turn of the century, still fighting shy of allowing too many married men to enlist, marriage in the army below rank of major was the exception though by 1876 a third of officers were married and less than 2% of those under the age of 24 were. Not unusually only twelve percent of the regiment overall was allowed to marry and only six to ten percent of privates could have their wives in barracks.[25] Even fewer were permitted to take wives and families to postings at overseas garrisons. Those favouring this argued that women would not only provide sex but an element of socialisation, perhaps even making soldiery more respectable and part of society rather than a caste aside from it. It could also provide an encouragement to recruitment and retention, both of which were perennial problems for the British Army. Finally, the women could be employed within their husbands' regiments as a source of cheap labour.

24 TNA: HO 45/10837/331148/38.
25 Trustram, *Women*, pp. 30-31.

The Army faced the challenge of reconciling the sexual needs of the citizen in uniform with the demands of military efficiency. (Author's collection)

While there were clear advantages, detractors saw greater problems. Salutary reminders of disasters and logistical nightmares that had involved camp followers on active campaigns littered the past from the Peninsular Wars to the Crimea and India. Not all men wanted a wife with them (many having anyway joined for the freedom to be 'o'er the hills'). To add to the mix, there were logistical problems over where they might live, and what to do with children accompanying the wives. The promiscuous behaviour of some of the relatively few women already on the strength had raised occasional questions about morality.

For the War Office, the pre-war question was one of balancing the positives with the cost that family welfare entailed, and assuaging a worry that domestic concerns might blunt the soldier's fighting prowess or commitment to the regiment.

The British military establishment found itself having to revisit these debates in late 1914 and early 1915. To compound matters, this war had several unprecedented aspects. Unlike earlier wars that largely saw soldiers passing relatively quickly through towns and regions according to the ebb and flow of battle, once stalemate had set in by December of the first year, the war became a quasi-medieval siege war, and stayed that way for over three years. The army of 1914-18, recruited to sustain this siege, saw an above ten-fold increase in numbers compared with the old regular army, and profound changes in its social composition and attitudes. It also comprised a high percentage of married men who, unless able to return regularly to the marital bed, would need other outlets for their awakened desires.

A further factor was that the soldier also had money, although sporadically paid and never a fortune, he had little to spend it on other than supplementing his army diet, buying the occasional souvenir, or the easily obtainable alcohol and vice. The occupied lands of Belgium and France were flooded with predatory women, some bored – with husbands and boyfriends away – but with many more needing to finance their survival, they provided an outlet for that money.

One obvious and seemingly easy way of overcoming the problems posed by married men was to mitigate the effects of absence by allowing home leave. In theory, this should have been easier to organise than in any other previous war, not only because of the relative proximity of the battlefront, but also as a result of the transport revolution in the second half of Victoria's reign. Steam power had replaced sail, railways lines criss-crossed both northern France and Britain, and motorised transport was replacing the horse-drawn. The battlefield was close enough to receive the London papers and next day postal delivery so in reverse, home was relatively easy for many soldiers to visit. Nevertheless, for a number of reasons, mostly concerning manpower shortages and logistic concerns, leave was to be a commodity in short supply, especially for the rank and file. Whatever the reason, preparations or implementation of a major offensive, or of the Germans expected of preparing one, or when shipping was needed for other tasks, or simply lack of military concern, it was not uncommon for a man to serve for up to eighteen months before getting leave; 'a poor woman wrote to me tonight begging me to send her husband home on leave; she hadn't seen him for fourteen months,' remembered Lieutenant Greenwell, 'I had to write to tell her that there are many who haven't been home for sixteen to eighteen months!'[26] Actually, it was not uncommon for a man to serve for up to eighteen months before getting leave.[27] In June-July 1917, more than 107,000 British soldiers had taken no leave for eighteen months, and 403,000 had had no leave for a year.[28]

Officers were treated somewhat better, receiving home leave more frequently than the men. Carrington noted that, on average, officers went home twice as often as other ranks.[29] They were also allowed to visit Paris, as were ANZAC troops. Things did improve as the war entered its fourth year, however. The French mutinies of 1917, partially attributable to dissatisfaction in French ranks over leave entitlement gave the High Command enough of a scare to see most men getting home leave after six months in France, and officers having the opportunity of home service after serving two years abroad.[30]

Periods of leave, when they finally came, posed special problems for dominion troops and for those British living in the far corners of the country, who patently could not go home to see loved ones. If they did not have relatives to visit, then London (or in some cases, Paris), with its sexually dangerous attractions, was the main alternative. At the Imperial War Conference on the temptations of overseas troops, W. F. Massey, the New Zealand Prime Minister, talked of seeing 'shoals of prostitutes in the Strand', and his compatriot, Joseph Ward, Minister of Finance, worried about:

> Some of these men who are out in France seven or eight months … coming over here seeing many women half-naked in the streets … I am talking about the effect of that, having regard to sex attractiveness, on men who have been away a long time and then they come across here and have this sort of thing placed before their noses practically all of the time.[31]

This temptation applied equally to British soldiers who were unable or unwilling to go to family homes on periods of leave, especially if they had sufficient money in their pockets. It was not only professional prostitutes that tempted the men. Young women, given the nickname 'flappers' in reference to the new hairstyle of ponytails, often practically assaulted men in public. These often very young women were notably free with their sexual favours, not exclusively for direct reward but in repayment for being taken out and given presents. More than any other figure, the amateur was deemed to be the greatest threat, especially to the Dominion troops whose healthy good looks and disposable income unsurprisingly proved magnetic. Sir Thomas McKenzie, reporting

26 Greenwell, G.H. *An Infant In Arms*, (London: Lovet Dickson and Thompson, 1935), p.41.
27 ibid, p. 41.
28 Fuller, *Troop Morale* p. 72.
29 Carrington, *Soldier,* p. 168. See also Fuller, *Troop Morale*, p. 72.
30 Ibid., p. 74.
31 TNA: WO 32/11404. See also Porter and Hall, *Facts of Life,* (London: Yale University Press, 1995), pp. 233-34.

at the Imperial Conference, recounted seeing 'two Tommies surrounded by 'four gaudily dressed girls', but it was the Australians they evidently wanted, drawn by 'the money, no doubt.'[32] Dominion representatives were concerned that the high incidence of venereal disease in their contingents emanated as much from home-based prostitutes and flappers as from the red lamps. This contributed to the passing of Defence of the Realm Act 40D, which made it illegal for a woman infected with VD to have intercourse with a serviceman. Whether this had much impact on sexual activities in practice is open to debate, as is the degree to which it was actually enforced.[33]

The army's view of the whole issue was, as ever, to look the other way. Policing morals on the home front was no concern of theirs unless there was an impact on manpower. The complaint of General Rawlinson, in response to the soliciting of men at Victoria Station 'in a most barefaced and persistent manner', as they arrived back from France, is instructive: his concern was not one of moral protection, but that the problem be dealt with because 'venereal disease removes men from the firing line'.[34]

Another strategic alternative to controlling the soldiers' desires, despite the inherent class-based cynicism of the 'old school' as to the likelihood of success, was by targeting behaviour through education and leisure. The Surgeon-General of the Indian Army, Dr. Moore, thought that whether working-class soldiers' sexual 'instincts [could] be repressed without ulterior serious consequences [was] a moot point on which it is not desirable to enter'[35] but the army, influenced more by the civilian social reformers than its whiskery traditionalists, tried in the post-Crimea period to wean the soldier away from immoral or licentious behaviour with the 'moralisation' of the army. The moralisation of the soldier, as the influential American educator and reformer, Abraham Flexner, observed in his 1913 study on prostitution in Europe, was a general goal throughout the European armies. With some prescience he noted that it was part of preparing soldiers for war: 'The nation that first manages to reduce [VD] will gain a considerable superiority over its enemies'.[36] 'Moralisation' was seen as an alternative to the provision of sanctioned prostitution.

Several of the major causes of immoral behaviour, notably boredom and alcohol, had been targeted by the introduction of libraries, sporting facilities, workshops, and other amenities intended to soak up the hours of enforced idleness that were traditionally a regular soldier's existence. Temperance was also preached to break the bonds of

32   TNA: WO 32/11404, Minutes of proceedings, p. 26.
33   De Groot, G., *Blighty. British Society in the Era of the Great War* (Harlow: Longman, 1996), p. 236. Buckley, B., 'The failure to resolve VD amongst Troops in Britain during World War I', in Bond and Roy (eds), *War and Society: a Year Book of Military History*, 2 (1977).
34   TNA: WO 32/11404. Minutes of proceedings.
35   Balhatchet, *Race*, p. 10.
36   Flexner, Abraham, *Prostitution in Europe: The regulation of prostitution in Europe* (New York: American Social Hygiene Association, 1915), p. 19.

alcohol and vice, and lectures and leaflets were provided to educate the young soldier against vice.[37]

Irrespective of who might have had the greater understanding – cynic or progressive – of the average soldier and his willingness to be 'moralised', this was another pre-war army policy that was sorely tested by the increase in recruitment numbers. The problems for the army of 1914-18 were how to 'moralise', or at least uphold existing morals amongst the vastly increased numbers of men involved, and to handle the logistical challenge of occupying the free time of over two million bored young men both in the trenches and when out of the action.

An initial response was the often risible attempt at education through training camp lectures. Inculcating fear of venereal disease rather than rational behaviour, however, had the greater impact on the troops, though for many this fear had been instilled long before signing up.

In absorbing any time not devoted to training or fatigues (the standard army response to the 'problem' of free time), some leisure activities were outsourced to volunteer organisations such as the YMCA, and others provided by the army itself. The army's efforts in this area have perhaps been under-valued, and they did much to fill the long periods men had out of the line with activities such as horse shows; inter-battalion sports such as boxing, rugby, and the ubiquitous football; travelling cinemas; concert parties and even excursions to the seaside. Despite their frequency and popularity, such activities were not, however, sufficient either to absorb all free time or to supress sexual desires.

Concluding that if morale was to be sustained then catering to the carnal appetites of the soldiery was an imperative, yet faced with the intractable problems of applying any of its pre-war solutions successfully given the sheer logistics and the suddenness of the war, the army was forced into adopting the simplest tactical solution: it fought sexual need in this war in the way it had fought it in others, by recognising the need for regulated and controlled brothels and allowing troops to use them. This was based on the French model of registration and inspection that had already proven, in their view, so successful when implemented in garrisons throughout the Empire.[38]

Influencing, if not totally controlling, the supply of prostitutes for the joint purposes of maintaining morale and protecting against venereal diseases and the other problems that unfettered access to vice might bring had a long precedent in the British Army. The East India Company had had prostitutes shipped out to the South African Cape as far back as 1806, and there is some evidence that during the Boer War the army knowingly acquiesced to the movement of women from Europe, Latin America and Egypt to South Africa to administer to Tommy Atkin's needs there. In India, the army had publicly recruited locally for the lal (literally meaning 'red') bazaars,

---

37 Fuller, *Troop Morale*, pp. 81-93.
38 See Hyams, *Empire and Sexuality*, p. 133; Balhatchet, *Race*, pp. 10-39, for a discussion of the operation of lal bazaars in India and Burma.

brothels established solely for the soldiers' use and designed to keep them away from the more public women.[39]

Despite such precedents, in 1914–15 it was not an easy matter to formally recognise brothels as 'British Army-owned', even if they were controlled by the French authorities. Regulation of prostitution had been a deeply controversial issue throughout the fifty years before the outbreak of war. The army was itself divided over the issue, with many believing that strong morals were the backbone of a strong and disciplined army. A well-meaning and obvious believer in Christian muscularity, Major H. Waite published his *Soldiers' Guide to Health in War and Peace* (1915), which advised that desire could be conquered by 'avoiding impure conversation and thought' and 'by regular employment of muscular and mental exercise'. Many retired senior army officers were sympathetic to the aims of the purity movements at home and not all, especially medical officers, were convinced of the efficacy of the provisions introduced by the Contagious Diseases Acts. As noted, the army largely avoided the issue when it could and was careful not to court controversy by sanctioning sexual activity in any official or overt way. Lord Derby's memorandum, discussed later, was the classic illustration of this approach. Only when its policies – on prophylactics or brothels, for example – were attacked did it defend its overall policy, such as it was.

This ambivalence caused confusion over the status of the regulated brothel both at the time and since. Evidence of the depth of the confusion lies in the social purity movement's conviction that the brothels were indeed owned by the British Army itself, or opened at its specific request. It alleged that they had been informed by the French branch of their Federation that, according to a letter received by General Dubois, 'it was at the request of the English authorities that this brothel was opened'. The British Government had to deny this vigorously. British policy also perplexed the local Granville mayor as his letter to le Ministre de la Guerre of 24 June 1918 illustrates; 'Je fus surprise d'apprendre que le Goverement Anglais avait consigne l'entrée de ces maisons a ses troupes, au moment meme ou les instructions prescrivaient l'overture des dites maisons'.[40]

Most soldiers appeared to believe the official red lamps were owned by the French authorities, even if policed by the British Army. Carrington thought it common knowledge that brothels such as the 'White Star' in Amiens was a French Government controlled brothel despite its Anglicised name. And both he and the less-educated rank and file, like Private Alban, Royal Ordnance Corps, believed 'these girls were inspected every day … by French doctors … that were (sic) their job'.[41] But in towns

---

39 Balhatchet, *Race*, p. 135. Also NAM 8210-13. Warrant Officer I.W.H Davies, 'Memoirs', cited French, *Military Identities*, p. 113, on the sanctioning of prostitution in Agra in the late 1890's.
40 'British Troops in France; provision of Tolerated Brothels', *Journal of the Association of Moral and Social Hygiene [The Shield]* (3rd ser., Jan. 1917), p. 397. TNA WO 32/5597: Cayeux file.
41 Carrington, *Soldier*, pp. 181-2. IWM Sound Archive, No. 6678, reel 2, Alban.

closer to the front control was thought to lie with British Town Majors. This was a common assumption and perhaps understandable given that the unregulated brothels and houses were most definitely and observably policed by the army's own police force.

Confusion over their status led some soldiers even to think the brothel formally 'off-limits': 'The thing was forbidden by Regulation, but that Regulation, like nearly all others in the Army, got occasionally defeated', remembered Harry Taylor, a NCO in the South Staffordshire regiment.[42] Interestingly, however, an APM report early in the war (12 Dec. 1914) mentions 'apprehending a considerable number of men in brothels after hours'. It was being there 'after hours' that was apparently the crime, not being there *per se*.[43] Soldiers, conscious of their desires, were even wont to believe that the army somehow controlled them. Some troops maintained that their tea was laced with all sorts of concoctions such as bromide, to keep sex under control. One Kiwi humorously remembered, 'Our old boys had a reunion in Auckland a few back. Two of them were going down the street and one said, 'You remember the dope they used to put in our tea to keep us in at nights? We'll, it's just starting to take effect on me now…'[44]

Needless to say, given the army's general record on committing anything to do with the subject to paper, there are no consolidated army records showing the number, location or size of the brothels. The nearest one can get to an official recording of their existence is when troops were banned from visiting them, usually because they had been identified as a source of infection. In this case, references can be found in the few APM diaries that still exist, and surviving soldiers' town passes listing banned or proscribed places.

The main objection to the regulated brothels was the reaction they provoked on the home front, a reaction that raised its head meekly, in 1914, but reared up again vociferously in 1916-17. The War Office and army hierarchy would have been all too painfully aware of the controversies and campaigns that had met attempts to control prostitution on the home front nearly 50 years earlier. Worried by rampant and seemingly out-of-control venereal disease amongst the troops in English garrison towns (with an incredible one in three hospitalisations being for venereal disease), the government had introduced the Contagious Diseases Act of 1864. The objective of the act was not actually to set up controlled brothels, but to subject those women suspected of suffering from venereal disease to a regime of medical inspection, and to remove those who were diseased to 'lock hospitals' until they could be safely returned to the streets. The act gave the police arbitrary powers of arrest and forced inspection of anybody suspected of prostitution and carrying disease.

---

42   IWM Sound Archive, No. 6617.
43   Gibbons, *Roll On*, p. 55. TNA: WO 154/114.s
44   Letter (L.H. Field), quoted in Coppard, G., *Machine Gun to Cambrai* (London: HMSO, 1969, IWM rev. edn, 1999), Appendix.

Initially, these arrangements were limited to eleven, named garrison towns but amendments were suggested in the late 1860s to extend the regulation northwards and, even more controversially, to include the general public in its provisions. Understandably, this provoked an immediate and vociferous response from those who disagreed and who saw the act as being directed against women in general and liable to impact on the totally innocent and respectable. An alliance of pressure groups, the most notable being Josephine Butler's Ladies' Association Against the Contagious Diseases Act, campaigned for the repeal of the act, finally achieving their aims in 1886.

Having achieved victory in its campaign on the home front, attention had turned to the overseas garrisons, and in 1888 the Indian cantonment arrangements were officially suspended. The incidence of VD among the troops shot up, reaching an official rate of 522.3 per thousand. Realising the likely political problems in Britain if the cantonment system were formally reintroduced, the practice of semi-regulated prostitution was brought back. As Hyam has put it, 'Essentially, the army outwitted the civilian objectors and purity-mongers'.[45]

Despite the controversy, to the military mind of 1914/18 the policy of recognising (if only semi-formally) the existing French regulated infrastructure was arguably their only realistic course of action. They were blind to the inherent dichotomies and firm in the belief that regulation worked; if VD was being spread, it was argued, it was being done so on the home front, not in France. Having taken the decision to use the convenient French system, the methods then employed to limit soldier usage were delivered in a rather half-hearted way. Educational lectures, keeping the men employed with training and – for those who contracted VD – pay stoppages and leave postponement, were no more than a smoke screen to assuage those who had reservations over the use of the tolerated brothel. The only 'active' policy for discouraging immorality was in the British High Command's reluctance to issue prophylactics in case it was seen as encouraging immorality (a debate that had been raging at home for some years), though no such reticence existed in Dominion army commands and even then this was in response to the problems generated by sex with unregulated women as much in London as overseas.[46]

Hirschfeld contributes one further rationale for opening the controlled brothels: they did it because they *could*:

> Trench warfare ... changed the conditions under which prostitution could be controlled in the army ... the sojourning of large military units at the front or at various intermediate stations, required a correspondingly sedentary or fixed form of prostitution. This form could only be found in brothelised prostitution. This

---

45 Hyam, *Empire*, p. 127. See also Balhatchet, *Race*, pp. 93-5.
46 Harrison, Mark, 'The British Army and the problems of Venereal Disease in France and Egypt during the First World War', *Medical History* 39 (1995), pp. 146-49.

had the added advantage of promising some protection against venereal disease and the possible interference with fighting power induced by the latter.[47]

Certainly the French military had no doubts about building brothels throughout the war, despite also having attempted the 'moralisation' of their soldiers throughout the late nineteenth century. The necessities of war reversed the decline in the number of *maisons de tolérance* that had been a feature of the 20 or so previous years. With education, appeals to moral fortitude and punitive action as ineffective for the French military as they were for the British, *maisons* were seen equally as convenient and necessary, both to preserve the purity of innocent local women and to control the spread of disease.

The Gallic allies could not understand the controversy over what was for them a sensible and proven approach to keeping the soldiers both healthy and happy. To question it could almost be taken as a cultural affront, as the openly hostile attitude the Americans encountered when banning use of *maisons* for the arriving AEF troops attested. The British were slightly more attune to their neighbour's sensitivity. In a memorandum to the War Council on the subject of the closure of the Harve and Cayeux brothels in June 1918, the Adjutant General perceptively wrote that such an 'action of the British military authorities would offend the susceptibilities of our ally'.[48] It was a happy coincidence for the British military that the political need to maintain good relationships at all levels, in addition to maintaining troop health, meant that the army was in a large measure 'forced' to accept the tolerated brothel.[49]

Dubois and Fischer make the pertinent point, somewhat caustically, that 'brothels grew up as though by magic in the military zones of France ... It is hardly necessary to point out that when the British Army took over a section of the line on the Western Front, these brothels were not immediately razed to the ground and their inmates banished from the vicinity'.[50] Furthermore, when there were changes in the line, and the British overran German lines, they inherited and used places that had been established by the Germans.[51]

In addition to the Inter-Allied Conference agenda, two other documents help pin down the army's attitude during the war years, with both further illustrating how the political consideration of not upsetting the French provided a convenient argument. Both emanate from the controversy over the Harve brothel closure. The first represents the wider, strategic view of the War Office and is perhaps the only truly official confirmation that the government of the day, as well as the army, not only accepted the concept of the tolerated house, but also implicitly sanctioned its use by the soldier.

47 Hirschfeld, *Sexual History of the World War*, p. 141.
48 TNA: WO 32/5597: Memorandum dated 21 June 1918.
49 See Levenstein, Harvey, *Seductive Journey. American tourists in France from Jefferson to the Jazz Age* (Chicago: CUP, 2000), p. 219.
50 Fischer and Dubois, *Sexual Life*, p. 332.
51 Crozier, *Brass Hat*, p. 254.

A War Cabinet memo written by the Secretary of State for War (Lord Derby) on 15 March 1918, is worth quoting in full:

> The undersecretary maintained what has been the accepted view of the Military Authorities since the beginning of the war. This view was also definitely asserted by the present Prime Minister when he was Secretary of State for War, in a letter of 8 August 1916. It was addressed to the Rt Hon T. R. Ferens MP … In this letter it said 'It must be remembered that the system of licensed houses is officially recognised by the French government and whatever our views on the matter, it is not possible or indeed prudent to overlook this fact'. Were all licensed houses to be put out-of-bounds, it is clear that the chances of contamination would be greatly increased.

While the case is made for keeping the brothels open for the purpose of soldier hygiene, French ownership and sensitivity is stressed. In case there should be any doubt over the former, Derby reinforces the point several more times during the memorandum:

> There is however no question of official sanction or control by the military of a system of queues. The licensed houses are mainly at base camps where the temptations are the most obvious and the risks greatest. Much can be done by example and precept, but human nature being what it is, it is incumbent on us to protect from themselves those who would not respond to such an appeal. The problem is with us here, and on the whole, I think it would be unwise to take so drastic a step as you suggest [close the licensed houses].
>
> These licensed houses are established by the French Government and are in no way under our control. They are part and parcel of the life of the country, and we can do nothing to disestablish them or close them.
>
> The Military Authorities have always regarded it as wise and prudent not to interfere with these institutions and so offend the susceptibilities of our Allies.[52]

In other words, and with all the political back-covering possible, the situation was beyond the government's control. While it could not be seen to be involved in actually running them, 'human nature being what it is', meant that the soldiers were going, *de facto*, to have access to brothels.

If Derby stated the initial strategic concerns, the second document, Haig's own memorandum defending the status quo, outlined the tactical considerations. If the red lamps were banned, he wrote:

> In the first place, I am of the opinion that it would be necessary for my force of military policemen to be increased by a number of from 350 to 400 men, if

---

52 TNA: CAB 24/45/g.t.3932, 121/France 1488.

maisons tolerées are to be so picketed as to ensure the observance of the order, and the nature of the work which would be required of them would render it necessary for them to be men of good physique who would have to be drawn from the ranks of those fit for active duty.

Interestingly, Haig goes on to explicitly recognise that both demand and supply would not so easily be managed;

In the second place, I do not think that enforcement of the order will have the consequences presumably expected. ... it seems reasonable to suppose that it was induced by pressure from certain sections of public opinion, whose main interest in the Army consists in the reduction of fornication on the part of its members ...

However, it will only lead to women leaving camps and becoming 'women carte' on the streets, probably with more success than before.

Haig's observation that 'women *carte*' (literally women holding registration cards but working the streets as opposed to working in the regulated brothels) would have more success suggests that he felt that the regulated brothel was as much channelling demand as protecting the soldier. More women on the street would mean greater temptation and opportunity. However, it is obvious from his conclusion that his main concern was not moral but logistic: 'Thirdly, the incidence of Venereal Disease will go up and England's combat strength would fall'.[53]

For Haig, it was simply a matter of manpower. Though certainly no libertarian, if there was any real moral concern it was lost amid his disparaging remarks on the source of the opposition. 'Certain sections of public opinion' – mainly the social purity lobby – patently concerned themselves with the wrong issues.

Despite all this, however, in the early part of 1918, the *maisons* were technically placed out-of-bounds. Lord Derby hinted at the reason for this: it was based on neither moral nor health grounds, but on political reasoning. Haig's *bête noire*, 'certain sections' had to be placated, and satisfying them was perceived as more important than the possibility of offending an ally. 'Quite recently', concluded Lord Derby in his memorandum:

There has been a great outburst of public indignation on this matter ... My opinion is that unless we take some steps, the outburst of indignation will continue to increase and might have far reaching affect [sic] upon the goodwill of a most respectable part of the community towards Government and the National cause.[54]

---

53 TNA: WO 32/5597: Sir Douglas Haig to Secretary of State for War, 4 June 1918.
54 TNA: CAB 23/5/WC366.

To summarise the army's attitude; it was in favour of regulated prostitution, favouring its consolidation into recognised brothels, which it saw as the best means of supplying safe sex, thus minimising manpower losses to disease and contributing to the upkeep of morale. It successfully followed this policy, albeit by the back door method of utilising existing and historic arrangements to be found in France, until the scale of Tommy's sexual activities, and the increase in VD especially amongst Dominion armies, shone an unwelcome spotlight into this hitherto dark corner of the Western Front. It had won its argument against the forces of social purity in India and, despite the temporary setback inherent in the Harve case, it had effectively won it again on the Western Front. Even with the supposedly general ban on access to brothels imposed after the 1918 Harve scandals, this was a ban in name only and soldiers still apparently continued to get authorised passes to visit the most notorious red lamp districts.[55] Had the essence of the conflict stayed as a siege, rather than changing to the wars of movement that characterised 1918, perhaps the army would have found itself under a more sustained attack on its moral flanks; but it did not and Tommy's sex life continued unabated.

So much for France; but how was the soldier's sex drive channelled in Flanders? It was not only in France that a *de facto* acceptance of prostitution was accepted and a system of regulation imposed. In the absence of army sanctioned brothels similar to those over the border, moves to tighten the regulation of general prostitution were introduced in Flanders early on in the conflict, though not always successfully. While the trail of primary source material now available demonstrates that the provisions were introduced through Belgian agencies such as the Health Department of the Ministry of Interior and Belgian military, and were as much directed at keeping Belgian soldiers healthy, one can see the hand of both the British and French army commands behind the move.[56]

Historically, Belgium had, like its southern neighbour, regulated brothels. In the Municipal Law of 1836 a stipulation was included in article 96 which gave local councils the power, if required, of supervising both people and places used 'for fornication', with the aim of protecting the safety, morality and public peace by introducing 'sanitation' and controlling the spread of venereal diseases. In the course of the nineteenth century several municipalities, though not universally, thought it necessary to invoke those powers. As with other countries attempting to administer such regulation, opposition came from an international movement, stimulated by the controversy over the British Contagious Diseases Acts. Regulation subsequently withered, though the ability of local councils to introduce measures remained on the statute book thus later

---

55 See Appendix III, 'Copy of the Harve Pass', showing open access to this district.
56 Provinciaal Archief West-Flanderen, Brugge: Correspondence can be found in the scattered and unpaginated sub-files of the main *Eerste Wereldoorlog* file. Also, Musée Royal. Centre de Documentation: see unsorted correspondence in between Belgium and French army liaison officers, in boxes 5616 and 2789.

allowing a re-introduction of renewed, if not exactly the same, regulatory procedures at will.

An increase in the incidence of venereal disease, which appeared to coincide with the massive influx of refugees in that small section of Flanders not under German occupation, saw regulation and policing gradually reintroduced from early 1915 and by mid-1916 a full and theoretically comprehensive regulatory regime had been imposed, though, as we will see, its efficacy was sometimes questioned by frustrated British APMs.

An analysis of the stages in the introduction of regulation and registration offers further confirmation of British army thinking and policy. The first mention of any regulation appears in a report dated 12 February 1915, from Trembloy, Commander of the Belgian Territorial National Guard in the zone occupied by the allied armies, to the Belgian army GHQ, and copied to the head of the 'English' army:

> The deputy police commissioner has introduced me to the measures prescribed by the special regulation concerning the matter … the following actions have been put in place once an infected woman is identified:
> 1. The denounced woman is subject to a judicial order.
> 2. She is subsequently removed, treated and kept at (illegible) until complete recovery.
> 3. The landlord of the music hall, house etc is himself prosecuted.[57]

These measures resulted from the visit of Trembloy to a prostitutes' place of work in a still partially inhabited Ypres, 'having learned that English soldiers have been affected with venereal diseases, contracted in Ypres'.[58]

From his declared interest in investigating the predicament of *English* soldiers (author's italics) who had contracted the disease, one can only assume that the visit was therefore at the instigation of concerned British army officials. His visit led to the subsequent suggestion that soldiers finding themselves infected immediately denounce the woman with whom they have had relations. This would allow the police commissioner to enforce a medical inspection of the denounced woman by the doctor of the vice squad who would prescribe the removal of the infected woman to a special VD hospital where she could be treated and kept until pronounced cured and allowed to return home.[59] These measures were identical to those imposed on clandestine prostitutes under the provisions of the Contagious Diseases Acts in Britain, and that were introduced and adhered to throughout the war in France's zones of occupation.

---

57 Provinciaal Archief West-Flanderen: Report of the Colonel, Commander of the Belgian Territorial National Guard in the zone occupied by the allied armies, to the (assistant) General of the General Headquarters of the Belgian army. No 1359.
58 Ibid.
59 Ibid. As claimed in letter dated 17 Feb.

Although Trembloy's suggestions were initially made for the single city of Ypres it was not long before the provisions were extended to the other administrative areas of West Flanders. A meeting of local mayors was held in Poperinghe on the 17 February, for example, where it was decided that a 'free health centre for women to visit or receive care could be established at the "House of the Incurables", Elverdinghe Road'. This was probably the asylum, Maison des Aliénés, which still exists as an asylum along the Poperinghe Road (which indeed is the prolongation of the Elverdinghe road). It all makes sense as the Ypres Hospital moved from the Market Square to the asylum when the bombardments became too troublesome (and after the psychiatric patients had been evacuated). A register of those treated (or who died) in the temporary hospital is kept at the Ypres town archive though VD cases are not mentioned. The mayors undertook 'to make appear before a medical panel all women denounced by the French or English soldiers who were being afflicted with venereal disease'. Weekly inspections were suggested for known prostitutes and, in the absence of the town having its own civilian 'vice squad' doctor, the appointment of a military doctor to fill the function of inspection was proposed and accordingly sent to the 'commander of the English army'. Unfortunately, the file contains no response though the centre was commissioned and began functioning. If indeed a British army doctor, as suggested, was then involved it would partially explain why British soldiers believed certain brothels outside of basecamps to be British army owned.

According to a February 1916 report of the Colonel, Commander of the Belgian Territorial National Guard in the zone occupied by the allied armies, to the Belgian GHQ and received by French and British authorities, the Poperinghe hospital was merely to be the first of many clinics to be established with immediate effect in each re-occupied part of the province.[60]

The system introduced patently did not satisfy the local British command as in February 1916 a more wide-ranging and comprehensive regulatory procedure was handed down by the Ministry to local administrations within the allied occupied zone after some discussion between interested parties. Once again, critically, the British army command was kept informed and it can be inferred from various comments that they contributed to the debate.

The resulting regulations featured all of the elements found in France and obviously favoured by the British military. Women identified as 'public women' or 'fornication daughters' were to be listed, issued with passbooks, submit themselves to regular twice-weekly inspections, and could be removed from the area (presumably to a hospital) if found to be infected. The local police were to administer the regulation. These provisions were published, generally though the medium of public posters, and came into immediate effect. Prostitution was regulated, if not, as we shall see, regulated effectively.

60 Ibid.

Although the regulations in theory proscribed the general soliciting activities of the women there is no outright ban on prostitution. In fact, there is no evidence to show that this particular part of the regulations was ever enforced and indeed for British soldiers, 'Pop' remained a place where he could quite easily turn desire and fantasy into fact. While this 'live and let live' approach may not strictly have complied with the letter of Belgian law, it is a further illustration of the 'double-standards' of the British army; prostitution was accepted *de facto*, just a long as it was sanitary.

Interestingly, however, not all British Army representatives agreed either that a VD problem existed or that regulated prostitution was a solution. A Guards officer, Captain Howells, wrote to the HQ of the Guards Division that he considered the proposed introduction of regulation in Poperinghe 'constituted a grave danger to troops billeted in, and in the environs, of the town'. His contention that 'It is well recognised that the institution of "Licensed Prostitution" had had no effect in reducing the incidence of venereal disease amongst the nations that have established the same' was, however, not the army view and the comment perhaps points more towards the Captain's wider politics and illustrates that there was a 'minority' view.[61]

The Flanders actions illustrate the 'majority' view and how the army attempted, throughout the Zones of Occupation, to control any 'clandestine' prostitution. They show that its underlying attitude was essentially akin to that held towards the brothels: it was inevitable that soldiers would use prostitutes. Although the army moralists might prefer an alternative course of action, the pragmatists won the argument. Once again, the army attitude could be described as 'turning a blind eye'. Women found to be infecting the ranks, and thereby having an impact on available firepower, were simply removed from their area of operation, and the APMs worked with local police (though not always harmoniously) to control the activities of identified clandestine prostitutes.[62]

The Flanders proclamations, banning women from idling on street corners, soliciting from doorways or the windows of their abodes, attending concerts or places of entertainment with the intention of soliciting, and even from engaging soldiers on the street in conversation, provide a vivid description of what sections of a back area town might look like if uncontrolled. Without some sanctions, 'public women' would patently have become just a bit too public and this, especially with so many civilians coming to the Western Front, from national politicians and volunteer workers to representatives of the moral pressure groups, was something the army needed to avoid.

How effective these and similar provisions were in effecting real control of the situation is not clear. Contact could, of course, not be completely stopped the women found ways of circumventing them.

---

61 Musée Royal. Centre de Documentation: Memo, Howells to HQ Guards Division, Box 2789.
62 For examples, see TNA: WO 154/8, WO 154/78 and WO 154/112: APM reports.

Outside of the soldiers' interface with the professional women, those working in either the recognised or unregulated sectors, they also met and socialised with a wide range of local females in 'innocent' contexts. The army's attitude to genuine fraternisation, where relationships were not based on any financial transaction, was based on the concern that relations between army and civilians should be as harmonious as possible. Kitchener's famed injunction to the troops was that they should 'avoid any intimacy' was the only official injunction and it was generally delegated to officers at the operational level to ensure that army and civilian 'got on'.[63] In reality, outside of the matters relating to matters such as property rights, it was hard to enforce any hard and fast rules for personal relationships, especially when ranks as high as – or even higher than – brigadiers were fraternising very publicly: only advice could be given.

As far as officers were concerned, however, discretion was expected; they were after all, 'gentlemen'. The only official concern on record was that officers should not 'disgrace the uniform' and be seen with prostitutes though even this was openly and knowingly flouted especially when on leave in cities like Amiens and Paris.[64]

Wherever and however the soldier, officer or other rank, sought it, the military knew the importance of allowing for his sexual release. History showed that, home or overseas, a soldier's morale was in part contingent on his access to women. It also showed it was a *sine qua non* that he would find it and very possibly, with an ever expanding population of women forced to finding their own survival strategies, it might earn him his first 'wound' stripe. Within weeks of the fighting settling down to a stalemate on what came to be called the Western Front the soldier was seeking out the companionship of women. As the size of the army grew, and the stalemate became more established, so the issues around sex became more obvious and more pressing.

Banning sexual contacts was a non-starter; it would be impossible to police especially given the growing size of the army. The logistical issues inherent in tackling both the health and morale issues by employing some of the more recent progressive policies that the army had been experimenting with, like health training lectures and establishment of wide-ranging leisure activities, was also immediately out of the question. The army was caught unawares and ill-prepared for handing the sex question. It is hardly surprising that, faced with so very many other more pressing challenges, the most effective policy was to turn a blind eye at operational level unless the liaison might end in venereal disease, be the subject of a complaint by a member of the civilian population, or involve personnel being AWOL. Given such, and with the regulated army brothel already having been established by the French allies in many of the base camps and back areas in which the BEF was to find itself, the easiest action was to accept both the status quo and the conditions as they found them.

---

63   See George, Sir Arthur, *Life of Lord Kitchener* (New York: Cosimo, 2000, reprint of 1920 ed., 3 vols), Vol. III, p. 27 for full transcript.
64   See TNA: WO 154/114 of C/APM: Appendix 1, 5 Mar. 1915.

What the authorities perhaps subliminally relied on was that the dramatic increase in the army numbers would largely be made up of men who would know and practise the self-restraint of civilian life. The question is whether this was an acceptable assumption; what sort of men had they now coming under their command and how far they would they be expected to avail themselves of the opportunities the environment was to provide?

3

'Every man had his Story':
Quantifying and qualifying the extent of sexual activity

The question is not one of whether Tommy had a sex life; that is *sine qua non*. It is establishing just how active he and his comrades were that is important. Quantification does, however, provide a challenge.

Five million or so men served on the Western Front; only a tiny proportion wrote of their experience. Of these, an equally small proportion committed their sexual reminisces to paper, let alone print. In arguing for the importance of sex as a general morale builder, one might be accused of selecting only the memories of those that supported the argument and ignoring the majority that contain no evidence. 'One swallow does not a Summer make'; a few reported sexual encounters cannot be taken as evidence of a general permissiveness.

There is, too, the obvious danger of taking too much from those limited first-hand accounts available. Given the small sample size, and with no way of knowing how representative that sample is of the men who served, we cannot extrapolate from their recollections to build any statistical picture of the extent and nature of sexual activity.

There is also the problem that many memoirs deliver impressions rather than hard facts; 'Our men are no sooner in a place than you see them with girls,' wrote Private Peter McGregor to his wife.[1] Private Lovegrove of the Royal Field Artillery recalled that 'they [the soldiers] used to line up outside No. 7 [an army sanctioned brothel] in St Omer',[2] Private Hill of the Rifle Brigade admitted he 'visited [the red lamps] myself, once or twice', and spoke for colleagues too: 'we all did!'.[3] Even though an individual talks of experiences in terms of 'our', 'they' and 'we', there is a vagueness to the numbers.

We can also get conflicting reports. One soldier noted from the cap badges of his fellow visitors to a red lamp that it was a popular pastime throughout the army;

---

1   IWM. McGregor, P. '*Letters*' (unpubl. memoir), 14 Sept. and 21 Sept. 1915.
2   IWM Sound Archive, No. 8231, Lovegrove, J., Royal Field Artillery.
3   IWM Sound Archive, No. 24539, Hill, P., 8th Bn Rifle Brigade.

'Gunners, Royal West Kents, Leicesters, Buffs, Welsh Fusiliers, Northumberlands, Durham Light Infantry. Cap badges from half the regiments in the BEF'.[4] Yet H. L. Silberbauer, an officer with C Company, 6th Battalion, Leicestershire Regiment, one of those regiments whose caps had been figuratively hanging over the bedstead, wrote that his men 'were a good lot and were devoted to their families – very seldom were they led astray by the French ladies'.[5] And for Gibbons, anxious to protect reputations, there were 'next to no gay ladies' in his service, although long.[6] Interestingly, despite the 'Leicesters' being 'a good lot', Silberbauer does nevertheless admit to 'seldom' rather than 'never' being led astray. And Gibbons concedes 'next to no' rather than none at all.

Equally, on the supply side, the purveyors of sex did not keep sales records, nor did officials keep data identifying the number and size of brothels that existed. The total number of clandestine or amateur prostitutes who plied their trade from the cellars of front line to the back rooms of billets can never be known. Other records that might help, such as police registers of regulated prostitutes or hospital admissions for diseased women have been lost or destroyed, sometime purposefully. There is no way of quantifying the non-pecuniary contacts between soldiers and local civilians; few would have been more than fleeting and even the more meaningful are unlikely to have been recorded in diary form, even if the relationship were socially acceptable. And unsurprisingly, the pornographers did not keep customer databases.

Ferris's observations in his study of 'Sex and the British' are equally relevant to the study of soldier sex:

> Before the 1980s, no one in radio or television was bold enough to coax frank sexual reminiscence from old codgers, and by then it was almost too late to catch living memories from the early years of the century … written records can be found here and there, the memories usually negative … mostly it is reports of mistakes that survive, not of the demand for pleasure that gave rise to them. The history of sex is written from the point of view of what went wrong, not of how much people enjoyed it.[7]

Thankfully, in the context of the Great War, it is exactly from a study of 'things that went wrong' that at least some quantitative evidence of Tommy's sex life can be gleaned.

---

4   Cloete, S., *How Young They Died* (London: Collins, 1969, The Book Society edition, 1969), pp. 55-7.
5   Silberbauer H. L., 'Reminiscences of the First World War', *South African Military History Journal*, 10 (1997).
6   Gibbons, *Roll on* (1935), p. 3.
7   Ferris, *Sex and the British: A Twentieth-Century History* (London: Michael Joseph: 1993), p. 2.

Of the many aspects of sex that could go 'wrong', catching a stigmatic, debilitating and sometimes untreatable disease was one, and it was reportable. Catching the disease meant the soldier was identified as sexually active. Although flawed, the medical record for venereal disease has provided a starting point for quantifying sexual activity during the Great War[8] even though, ironically, it has in the past been used as part of the argument to discount the activity.[9]

The key to using these statistics as a measure of activity lies not in reading them as they are baldly presented but in extending the analysis to understand how, and why, they were collected, the weaknesses inherent in the collection methodology and subsequently exploring what can be deduced from that broader understanding.

'Disraelian caution' is required in the use of any Great War statistics; the dictum that there are lies, damned lies and statistics is nowhere more evident. Data gathering did not always use scientific methodology, and the reasons for collection and subsequent interpretation were often politically driven. Inevitably, this has an impact on their validity. Further, alternative sources, when available, do not always correspond, making cross-checking the validity of any statistic difficult. There was, and still is for example, considerable debate even to the amount of venereal diseases in the population during this period. Official figures are extremely unreliable, a point acknowledged by the Royal Commission of 1916 in its conclusion that the rate of infection in the British military was approximately 30 per cent.[10]

In contrast, Bourke, in support of her contention that few men had casual sex, quotes that 'in 1911 the annual rate of admission to venereal hospitals was 61 in every 1000 soldiers, while in 1916 it was under 37'.[11] Patently, very much lower than the Royal Commission's 30% estimate. In addition, if one looks at 1916 in isolation and accepts Bourke's statistic, a figure of 37 in every thousand may well be lower than that of 1911 but the fundamental difference is that the army was at least ten times larger in the later year, and the absolute numbers with VD were thus considerably larger. Equally, one gets a different view looking at data for 1917, or 1918, or the war as a whole.[12]

---

8   TNA: HO 45/10724/251861/89: 1915, Canadians 287 per 1000; TNA: HO 45/10724/251861/89: Jan. to Aug. 1915, of 1,500,000 troops in England, 54,000 infections, report by Dr Arthur Newsholme of Local Government Board, 1917; TNA: HO 45/10802/307990/30: Anzacs infected in Britain, 144 Australian, 134 New Zealand; TNA: WO 32/5115: in 1917 between 101 and 198 per 100,000 (24,000 cases), Annual report of Infectious Diseases in France.
9   Bourke, J., *Dismembering the Male*, p. 156, quoting Hall, Lesley *Hidden Anxieties: Male Sexuality 1900-1950* (London: Polity, 1991), p. 37.
10 Towers, B., Health Education Policy, 1916-1926: Venereal Disease and the Prophylaxis Dilemma', *Medical History* 24 (1980), pp. 70-87.
11 Bourke, *Dismembering*, p. 156, quoting Hall, *Hidden Anxieties*, p. 37.
12 'In 1918 an average of 32 out of every 1000 men on the ration strength', Simkins, 'Soldiers and Civilians: billeting in Britain and France', in Beckett I. F. W, and Simpson K. (eds),

The figures cited for venereal disease within the New Zealand Expeditionary Force further indicate the problems. Various figures are presented in reports and surveys conducted throughout the period.[13] For the NZEF, the Director General of Health concluded in 1921 that '12,270 NZ soldiers had had venereal disease during the war, a rate of approximately one in nine', but a secret document to the government in 1919 had stated: 'The incidence of V.D. among NZEF has been extremely high. It is estimated that there was always a battalion out of the line suffering from V.D. There have been approximately 4,000 cases of syphilis and 12,000 of gonorrhoea'.[14] According to the British Colonial Secretary, in a secret official document to the New Zealand Government, the rate of venereal disease for NZ soldiers in 1917 was 134 per 1000 (or about one in 7.5). Boyack even holds that the figures were manipulated for the political reason of smoothing relations with the dominions. The official figure is too low, he claims: the real numbers infected may have been as high as 33 per cent of the New Zealand contingent.[15]

The figures for the British imperial troops are just as confusing. The *Daily Mail* on 25 April 1917, with reference to the report of the military authorities to the House of Commons, stated that there had been some 200,000 cases of venereal disease in the British Army in France alone. This did not include men in England or on the other fronts.[16] Sexologists Fischer and Dubois claimed that the VD rate of 17.5 per cent for the army of Great Britain far outweighed that of other combatant countries.[17]

Figure 1 shows the official picture for the BEF, citing a total of 153,531 British and dominion troops admitted to hospital with gonorrhoea, syphilis or other venereal diseases in France and Flanders. Yet Winter, using a second official source, can suggest that 416,891 men had been treated for VD by the end of the war.[18] Holmes accepts the same sources, quoting rates in ANZAC troops 'as high as 128 and 130 per 1000 of strength … compared with 24 per 1000 amongst British troops'. Another figure given for the Canadians is that a phenomenal 28.7 per cent of the men in the CEF were infected at the high water mark in 1915, whereas Jay Cassel 'concluded that 15.8 per cent of the Canadians suffered from VD'. Further, such statistics can be confusing in that they do not always make clear whether they are inclusive of British and dominion troops; or if they are figures for VD in troops just serving on

---

A Nation in Arms: A Social Study of the British Army in the First World War (Manchester: MUP, 1985), p. 186.
13 See n. 2.
14 Boyack, *Behind the Lines*, p. 146.
15 Ibid., p. 140.
16 Eddy, Sherwood, *With Our Soldiers in France* (New York: Association Press, 1917), Chapter VI.
17 Fischer and Dubois, *Sexual Life*, p. 373.
18 Winter, *Death's Men*, pp. 150-52. Holmes, *Tommy*, p. 483; see also MacPherson Sir W. G. (ed.), *Medical Services: Diseases of the War* (1923), II, pp. 118-22.

the Western Front.[19] Boyack, for example, concludes that the British had 'cleverly hidden the true rate by including dominion soldiers in their calculation'. Equally, we do not know, for example, how many of those treated were repeat treatments. In other words, there is a possibility of double-counting. Nor is there agreement over where the disease was contracted; how many cases were caught on leave (particularly in London) and how many in France?[20]

Figure 1: Admissions to hospital as a result of venereal disease in the BEF in France and Flanders, 1914-18

Year	Admissions	Per '000 troops
1914	3,291	17.3
1915	17,525	29.7
1916	24,108	18.2
1917	48,508	25.6
1918	60,099	32.4

Source: Michell T. J. and Smith, G. M., *History of the Great War Based on Official Documents. Medical Services: Casualties and Medical Statistics of War* (1931), pp. 73, 77, 131, 144-5, 156, 164. 174. See also MacPherson *et al.*, *Medical Services: Diseases of the War* (1923), II, pp. 123-5.

No wonder there is no agreement over the number! In truth, no one could confidently provide an accurate figure at the time, and no one can today even with the twin benefits of hindsight and research. At the time, even within the army differing views prevailed, with different statistics employed to support a number of political positions both over the extent of the disease and where the responsibility for its spread lay. One the one hand, Childs at the War Office claimed, during discussions with dominion representatives during the 1917 Inter-Allied Conference on Venereal Disease, that most disease was caught from casual and 'clandestine' prostitutes in France.[21] This was supported by evidence from Sir Edward Henry, Metropolitan Police Commander, who cited a figure of London-caught 200,000 cases versus 97,000 France-caught cases (most of which being from 'amateurs'). How and where this statistic might have been arrived at is left tantalisingly unanswered but it suited the London position; 'VD? Not our fault!' Conversely, the APM of the Canadian 2nd Division, wanting to protect his own back, could confidently argue the opposite:

19 Boyack, *Behind the Lines*, p. 140.
20 *The Official History*, quoted in Winter, *Death's Men*, pp.150-52. See also Cassel, *The Secret Plague*. p. 123, on the statistical challenge.
21 TNA: WO 32/11404.

> Mostly all the cases of Venereal Disease that come under my notice are contracted in England by men on leave and any woman found contaminated here can trace the contractors [sic] to their source … The licensed houses are only permitted in the large towns well behind the line. The inmates undergo medical inspection every two days and cases of Venereal Disease are almost unknown. Soliciting in the street is strictly forbidden and attracts a very severe penalty.[22]

On the basis of the firm evidence available in the APM report for the Australian 3rd Division, 60 per cent of the cases between July and August 1917 reported in the divisional area had been caught in France.[23] In incomplete records for the six months from early March to September, 44 percent of infections were ascribed to a French connection, and 56 per cent caught at varying points throughout the UK. Wherever the UK infections were caught, there is no way of knowing how many men were infected by their partners at home, rather than through casual sexual contacts. What is accepted, if not the reliability of the figures, is that a higher percentage of the dominion troops were infected, many through sexual contacts while in London.[24]

As all the above somewhat confusingly suggests, figures can only be used only as a jumping-off point for further analysis. The fundamental issue is, however, that whichever figure is used they are indisputably incorrect and understate the true level of infection. There are three basic issues: misdiagnosis, basic under-reporting, and distortion due to soldiers concealing they had the disease or dying before it could be diagnosed.

In the first instance there would have been a considerable level of misdiagnosis, through lack of time, experience or resources. One educated soldier and officer admitted there were inevitably men who were unwitting carriers of the infection, undetected by the medical authorities as Clothe observed, 'We had one penis inspection, 'short arm inspection' the men called it. An embarrassing performance for all concerned, but it was a divisional order … and the officers were supposed to check them for venereal disease which none of us, unless it was in its last stages, could have recognised'.[25] Even the French authorities, worried over the increasing incidence of syphilis in both civilian and military populations, were aware that misdiagnosis was a considerable problem. So much so that it undermined their confidence even in the cleanliness of tolerated brothels: many doctors were not able to diagnose the difference between syphilis and common herpes.

Given the incubation period of anything between eight days and six month depending on the disease contracted and its spread, it is difficult to know how many men contracted the disease during an all-too-brief period out of the line. With the

22 TNA: WO 154/122: entry for 16 Nov. 1916.
23 TNA: WO 154/77.
24 Cassel, *Secret Plague*, p. 123.
25 Cloete, *Victorian Son*, p. 215 (May 1916).

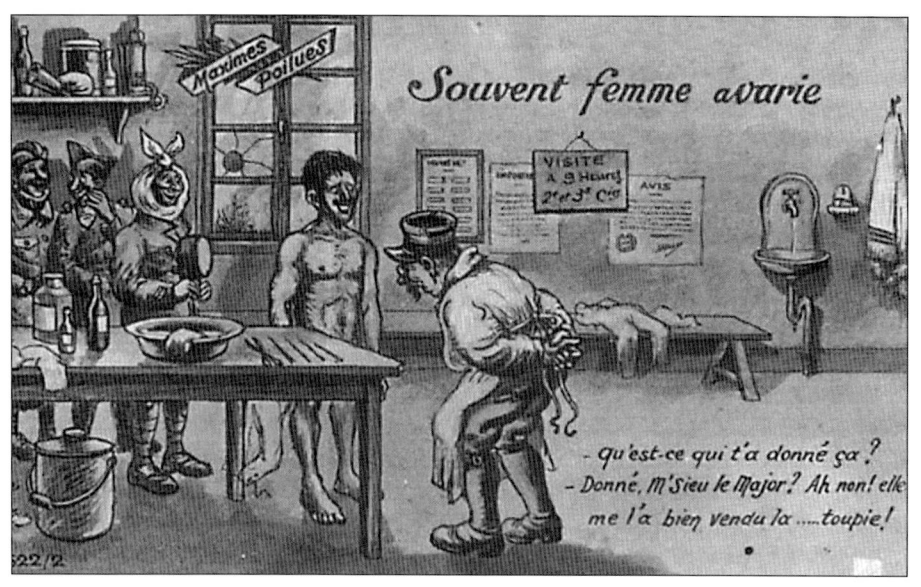

Quantifying and qualifying the extent of sexual activity

French and British troops alike were subjected to the embarrassing and much disliked 'short arm inspection'. It was not always considered a joke.

average life of an infantryman at the front being six months, and the face of an infantry battalion constantly changing, many certainly came off leave and went straight into either battle or active trench duties. There was, therefore, whether men contrived at concealment or were simply unaware of their affliction, every chance that infected men died before diagnosis.

There is no doubt that some men actively concealed their infection when they could, with attendant effects on the individual's morale. Holmes quotes an instance of a sapper concealing syphilis for six weeks by simply not reporting sick and there being no general 'short arm inspection' during the period. Concealment was not always possible, however, as there were diligent MOs, or the disease simply became too advanced to hide as this horrific description attests;

> 'We used to have a week's leave in Paris and some of the boys would return full of pox. On the train back, they used to have braziers to keep you warm, and one particular boy who'd been to Paris a few times said he'd sat too near a brazier with his legs open, that he had gone to sleep, and when he woke he found his trousers nearly alight and his private privates burned. That's what he said had gone wrong, but it wasn't that. He'd come back with pox, and his penis was nearly falling away it was so rotten ...'[26].

26 Ashurst, George, 2nd Btn Lancashire Fusiliers, IWM Sound Archive No. 9875.

The stigma associated with having the "shameful" disease often forced them into hiding their misery. Indeed, as George Coppard remembered, 'the stigma was such that very few front-line Tommies, in spite of the misery and danger they had to endure, would have swapped places with a VD man at a base hospital'.[27] Lieutenant Butlin gives a good indication of the climate of the times in a letter home from the Craiglockart Hospital for the 'shell-shocked', in May 1917:

> The inhabitants have two theories about us … Their first theory is that we are lunatics under careful surveillance … The second that we are victims of venereal disease and confined here as a punishment. From the looks of the population I gather that the second theory is most strongly held.[28]

The stigma was felt in several ways. There was the general social stigma, compounded in the early war years by notifying a man's family of his ailment, and there was the military stigma, with the men 'guilty until proven otherwise' of contracting a dishonourable, self-inflicted wound to avoid service. There was also a sound economic reason for keeping quiet, as contracting VD could mean that the man's pay was stopped and his wife's allowance cut, which had the added disadvantage of telling the wife exactly why she had no money to draw even if she was not directly informed of her husband's malaise. A man could also have his leave stopped.[29] Thomas Walter McIndoe, 12th Middlesex, vividly remembered that:

> When we arrived in France a memo was issued by Lord Kitchener … it said that in recent months quite a number of the expeditionary force had rendered themselves not fit for service in contracting venereal disease. This must stop forthwith as the war office take a very poor view of this *in view of the number* (author's italics)… The note said that a man's wife or relatives would be notified if anyone rendered themselves unfit in this way'.[30]

The phrase 'in view of the numbers' adds an interesting dimension; whether or not it was used, for McIndoe and others the belief was that it was the scale of infection that concerned the authorities, not the moral implications of having contracted it.

Punishment, economic or social, affected all ranks in some way in the early war years, as the 'temporary gentleman', Denis Wheatley, was chagrined to discover:

> It was not the discomfort of the disease alone which made me so cautious, but an iniquitous decree that … Anyone who reported sick with VD automatically had

---

27 Coppard, *Machine Gun*, p. 57.
28 IWM 67/52/1, Butlin, J. H., *'Letters'*, May 1917.
29 Gibbons, *Roll On*, p. 163. IWM Sound Archive, No. 8231, Lovegrove.
30 IWM Sound Archive, No. 568 reel 3, McIndoe, Thomas Walter, 12th Middlesex.

his leave to England – theoretically a fortnight in every four months – stopped. The consequence was that thousands of men did not report their misfortune with the results that the disease worked its way into their testicles and bladder and they suffered from the affliction for the rest of their lives.[31]

At least the War Office did not inform the officer's wife but the following anecdote of Harry Taylor, a NCO of the South Staffs, is illustrative of the effects of ignorance and active concealment on the statistical returns. He was asking for sick reports while on three days 'rest' out of line (1915) and checking an incoming draft:

> Barley asked, 'are you Orderly Corporal Harry? Do you know anything about VD?'.
> This question took me by surprise ... I don't know much about it but I can tell you if you got it. I took a look and there was no doubt about it ... [On the following day] ... I halted them [eight in total on sick parade] in front of ... our MO. "I have one man who thinks he has gonorrhoea"... Next day the order came, full battalion parade in loose dress at 10.00 for medical inspection with no absentees allowed ... Captain Lane, the MO, went along the line and examined every man. Eleven men [from a total draft of 50] from the new draft were found to be infected and were isolated ... till they could be sent back to Rouen to the appropriate hospital.[32]

Of specific interest here is, firstly, the fact that the first man reporting his problem was unsure of his condition; secondly, that 11 others were either ignorant of having the disease or were choosing to conceal their problem; and finally, that 22 per cent of the men were infected.

Sometimes it appears that concealment was connived at, perhaps because of the associated shame, while a man obtained a private cure. Patently, this option would only have been open to an officer with finance for private medicine, and leave available to arrange it. Officers suffering VD were sometimes able to persuade a considerate medical officer to treat them privately at the front. Crozier's story illustrates the obviously 'matter of a fact' and routine nature of these instances, and indeed the semi-official understanding of his plight afforded the officer by his peers:

> the medical officer comes into the mess... 'Young Rochdale has venereal, gonorrhoea, in fact, he's in an awful stew. He's engaged to be married. If I send him down to the venereal hospital it is sure to get out at home where he is ... He can be got fairly right in ten days. If he goes to Amiens to one of these French doctors

---

31 McPherson (ed.), *Medical Services,* pp. 123-25; Wheatley, *Temporary Gentleman,* p. 152; and Gibbons, *Roll On,* p. 163.
32 IWM Sound Archive, No. 6617, reel 3, Taylor, Harry, NCO 1/6th South Staffs.

for three or four days and gets a cure – at a price – he may be all right; he could come back with the dope and treat himself'... I say: 'I will see what can be done, leave it to me'. After dinner I see the Colonel ... 'We don't go in for 10 days: do you mind if I let him go at the first opportunity and give him a pass?' 'Certainly, Crozier, certainly,' assented the C.O. Rochdale returned in 10 days' time and took his place in his platoon – cured.[33]

One assumes this case never appeared in any official statistics. Others, perhaps less well-off or less-well connected, made recourse to the mail order 'quack' cures advertised in the press.

That concealment and attempts at self-cure were prevalent, at least on the home front, was suggested by the 1916 Royal Commission on Venereal Diseases report: 'The fear of disgrace and the consequent desire for concealment necessarily render the sufferer from venereal disease specially liable to attempt self-treatment, or to entrust his treatment to persons who are in no way qualified to deal with the disease'.[34] There was a history of sufferers seeking either self-cures or quack remedies as an earlier Local Government report had discovered, with 'the upper classes resorting to quacks as readily as the poor',[35] and Indian Army soldiers were found by the censors to be sending home for medicines. If a soldier managed to keep his condition quiet he avoided the threat of having leave or pay stopped, and family informed of the reason. But concealment from diligent MOs was not always possible, and the disease could simply become too advanced to hide.[36]

Possibly the most poignant understatement of figures is due to those who, with morale at rock bottom, chose death rather than admit their shame. They remained anonymous. The number of men who went over the top bravely, but for suicidal reasons, can never be quantified but there are sufficient reports of it to suggest it was not uncommon, including this from Fischer and Dubois: 'The reason for his long absence [from home] was because he had contracted syphilis from a prostitute and, after a period during which he deliberately sought death, he finally submitted to medical treatment'.[37] Others found the death they sought, as infantryman Trafford of 1/9th Battalion Kings Liverpool Regiment recounted:

> This sergeant had got it, a Welshman he was ... we were going over the top... [he] says, "you lads, I want to go over first, you hold back until I go over. I don't

---

33 Crozier, *Brass Hat*, pp. 80-1, see also Holmes, *Tommy*, p. 484: 'Officers suffering VD were sometimes able to persuade a considerate medical officer to treat them privately'.
34 TNA: CAB 24/162, Final Report of the Royal Commission on Venereal Diseases, Reports, XVI (1916).
35 Hall, *Hidden Anxieties*, p. 35, citing the Local Government 'Report as to the practice of Medicine and Surgery by Unqualified Persons' (1910).
36 IWM Sound Archive, No. 9875, Ashurst, G., 2nd Bn Lancashire Fusiliers.
37 Fischer and Dubois, *Sexual Life*, p. 152.

want to go home. I've got, you know … I don't want to give it the wife [sic]". However, to cut a long story short we let him get over. He hadn't gone far and he got it; he was killed, you know. "If I don't get killed", he said, "I'll have to do myself in. I can't go home like this. I've got it bad … I haven't reported it" … he killed himself.[38]

Hiscock provides evidence of two more men who preferred not to leave it to chance whether or not their number was on a German bullet, preferring to take their own lives rather than return home and face their families.[39]

That suffering from venereal disease could bring a man so low as to want to kill himself was known to both the military and the politicians. Joseph Ward, the New Zealand Minister of Finance, noted that 'as a matter of fact, we heard of cases when we were in France the other day, of men who had deliberately gone over the top with the intention of not coming back in consequence of suffering from this terrible disease to which we are referring'.[40]

Although there is no official confirmation, at least one reliable witness claims that the army allowed a form of 'Samaritans' service to prevent suicides. The real result of the system were camps full of men just about on the edge of suicide. Gibbons claims not only to have talked a man out of killing himself while working as a stretcher bearer at the Cherry Hinton hospital near Cambridge, but also to have met an 'elderly lawyer', too old for active service but having taken on the 'self-imposed charge of acting as a sort of anti-suicide squad to those VD camps and hospitals … Night after night, for three years, he had been visiting this hospital or that'.[41] It was perhaps because the army realised that its 'retribution' policy of informing the man's family was directly and permanently costing them soldiers in a way that VD only temporarily did, and perhaps, more importantly, that it was having a negative effect on morale, that around 1916 it changed tack and quietly dropped this practice. It is even claimed that it was as a direct result of reaction to the suicide of a Major whose wife had been informed.[42]

Finally, it is interesting to speculate why the army, who it must be assumed were aware of the level of statistical misreporting that was occurring within the VD figures, were prepared to accept it. Given the problems it had historically had in defending regulated brothels, it is perhaps unsurprising that it would not have been anxious to see the figures inflated. This might have provoked the same level of controversy in the UK that, in 1918, high infection rates were causing in the dominions. Irrespective

---

38   IWM Sound Archive, No. 24540, reel 2, Richard Trafford, 1/9th Bn Kings Liverpool Regt.
39   Hiscock, *Bells of Hell*, pp. 14, 90.
40   TNA: WO 32/11404, Minutes of the Inter-Allied Conference on Venereal Disease (1917).
41   Gibbons, *Roll On Next War*, p. 16.
42   Harrison, M. 'The British Army and the problems of Venereal Disease in France and Egypt during the First World War', *Medical History* 39 (1995), pp. 139-40.

Entanglements

"COME ON, BERT, IT'S SAFER IN THE TRENCHES"

Predatory women might lead to many problems, including venereal disease. (Courtesy Mark Warby. ©2015 Estate of Barbara Bruce Littlejohn)

of the reasons, this wartime acceptance of the statistics laid the foundations for the future and has biased the discussion of sex and the soldier since.

Whatever the cause of understatement of VD infection figures, we have to conclude that the base number normally accepted for infection rates is too low and therefore any contention that the figures are indicative of a correspondingly low level of sexual activity needs qualification. Firstly, all sources underestimate the rate and, secondly, and much more fundamentally, using it as a comparative statistic is logically on uncertain ground.

The statistics, by definition, only include those admitted for treatment. Men had union with uninfected women. While VD in the community was high with as many of 10% infected (and higher in the later years of the war, corresponding with increases in military infections),[43] neither 100 per cent of the population, nor even 100 per cent of 'amateur' or clandestine prostitutes were infected. Further, an infected woman might not pass the disease on to everyone she came into contact with: 'I had to take this man … to a house where he had caught VD … And so this man identified the woman and it turned out the 12 men from his battalion had been with this woman and this man was the only one who had it', remembered Private Stagg of the RAMC.[44] One contemporary study estimated that as low as three percent of unprotected sex led to VD.

The army allowed its soldiers to use the French system of regulated brothels mostly to control the spread of VD. While it could not guarantee the safety of these brothels, had every sexual contact resulted in an infection then the entire rationale for their existence would have crumbled. It is a more logical conclusion that infection rates from the brothels were low and that the VD infection rate corresponds more closely with the level of unregulated rather than regulated sex. This indeed was an argument advanced by supporters of the 'lamps' when answering criticisms of the brothel during the Imperial Conference in 1917. According to MacPherson, the one brothel which yielded some statistical evidence (Rouen) was visited by 171,000 men in its first year and there were only 242 reported cases of VD.[45]

Regulated brothels were just one of many initiatives by which the army hoped to keep the troops healthy while keeping them happy. These initiatives either provided effective protection directly or ensured that the soldier protected himself when having intercourse. The most ubiquitous were the regular lectures and written warnings. The former were not always treated as seriously as they might have been as Kings Own Liverpool private Edmund Williams happily remembered: 'The only lecture I remember was given by brigade's bishop … at the conclusion he said, "remember for 5 minutes of pleasure you'll get a lifetime's misery" … the sergeant major got up and said, "how the hell do you make it last 5 minutes"!'.[46] More effective was the policing

---

43   Royal Commission on Venereal Diseases. 1916. Cited in Cassel, *Secret Plague,* p. 137.
44   IWM Sound Archive, No. 8764, reel 4, Stagg.
45   TNA: WO 32/11404. Macpherson *et al.* (eds), *Medical Services: Diseases of the War,* pp. 135.
46   IWM Sound Archive, No.10604, reel 5, Williams.

and removal of infected clandestine prostitutes from areas where there were soldiers to be tempted. Further, while initially a policy confined to ANZACs, increasingly all soldiers were provided with condoms and other prophylactic kits as the war wore on and, albeit often still unofficially and unsystematically, the Director General of the Army Medical Service could tell the 1917 Imperial Conference on VD that some 130,000 prophylactic tubes 'had been distributed with good effect'.[47] Local girls probably also supplied them, and the troops were often 'mollycoddled' by paternalistic officers. Presuming the efficacy of these measures, only a small proportion of those having sex would actually have caught the disease. Tozer records one specific success where education had delivered a 'one hundred-percent fit battalion',[48] and there is other evidence of similar successes in keeping the men free of disease.[49] The men might thus have been active sexually without leaving a trace.

Even the most biased observers were aware of the magnitude of sexual activity both on active service and on leave. Speaking of the average British soldier, a Chaplain, Shaw could note:

> In fact, taking the number of those who have been medically treated for certain complaints contracted on Active Service as only a small proportion of those who have actually given way to temptation, then the full number of offenders must be very large.[50]

Shaw could not quantify it but another observer, albeit in a different theatre of war, was able through analysis of VD infections to put the pursuit of sex more definitely at somewhere between 33 per cent and 50 per cent of all troops. This estimate is contained in an unsolicited letter received by Lord Derby from Sir George Riddell during the height of the 1917-18 controversy over the use of red lamps. It also provides another indication of the army's implicit attitude towards sex, in this case as evidenced by the promotion of prophylactics:

> I have just received a letter from the Army Doctor at Port Said, which may be of interest to you. He says: In August of this year a permanent camp of rest was formed at Port Said for the mounted corps of the EEF [Egyptian Expeditionary Force] … these troops had been fighting for more than 12 months: many had had no leave during that period and no relief from the monotony of the desert … if any troops were likely to indulge in excess, it would likely be men who have endured such conditions.

47 TNA: WO 32/11404.
48 Tozer, Bazil, *The Story of a Terrible Life* (London: T. Werner Laurie Ltd, 1929), p. 198.
49 Crozier, *Brass Hat*, pp. 64-7.
50 Shaw, K. E. *Jottings from the Front* (London: Allen & Unwin, 1918), p. 36: for similar observations see also Charles Plater (ed.) *Catholic soldiers by Sixty Chaplains and Many Others* (London: Longmans & Co., 1919), pp. 70-88.

The doctor continued that he had monitored venereal disease infections, finding only 19 cases amongst 9282 men of all ranks that remained in the camp.

> I have reason to believe that the majority, if not all, of those infected failed to make use of the prophylactic treatment provided, owing to their being under the influence of drink ... The numbers availing themselves of prophylaxis have been 4580, or approximately 50 per cent of the men attending the camp. It seems reasonable that possibly one third have made use of the treatment on more than one occasions; or in other words, that (say) one-third only of the total visitors at the camp have had sexual relations with women during their stay at Port Said.[51]

The key figures here are the doctor's estimate that fifty percent of the men were apparently considering sexual activity, and thirty-three percent acted upon it. Less than one percent of those appeared as VD statistics; significantly more men had sex than the VD figures would indicate. Although this is reporting the behaviour of a battalion in a different theatre to the Western Front, where environmental influences may have made a difference, it nevertheless adds to the evidence of relatively promiscuous behaviour. Unfortunately, the identity of the battalion is not recorded so its movements cannot be mapped, but it is highly likely that such behaviour would have been transferred to the Western Front with the battalion.

One alternative way of measuring activity is to look at the supply side of the equation. In subsequent chapters we will examine this, looking first at non-venal contacts, then at prostitution and try to assess the size of that 'industry'. It is sufficient to note here, however, anecdotal reports of demand out-stripping supply, despite the numbers of unregulated prostitutes and ubiquity of regulated brothels. Further, near contemporary accounts report a renaissance of a regulated brothel sector that had been dying out in the years preceding the war,[52] as part of the strategy to contain the growth in unregulated clandestines.[53] One such brothel, opened for British troops in the base camp of Granville Ste Honorine, was to become the focus of a 1918 controversy. The large number of barracks and convalescent hospitals at Granville had already led to the opening of one regulated brothel in May 1917, but an increase in 'clandestines' a year later saw the Mayor writing to the French Minister of War in June to inform him of the opening of another:

> Aussi j'authorisai immediatement la creation d'une seconde maison de tolerance, la commune n'en possedant qu'une, ce que je considerai absolument insuffisant

---

51 TNA: WO 32/5597.
52 See Corbin, Alain, *Women for Hire: Prostitution and Sexuality in France after 1850* (Harvard: Harvard University Press, 1990), and Blizzard, Dr Leon, *Les Maisons de prosititution de Paris pedant la guerre.* (Poitiers: Societé Française d'Imprimerie, 1922), p. 3.
53 Grayzel, Susan, 'Mothers, Marraines, and Prostitutes: Morale and Morality in the First World War in France', *International History Review* 19 (1997), p. 81.

pour le nombre tres important de troupes … campées et canonnnées sur notre territoire.[54]

What this investigation into VD and related statistics frustratingly illustrates is that it is impossible to enumerate sexual activity with any accuracy over proscribed periods let alone the whole war. But despite this the scale becomes apparent; to put it in crude perspective many more men were, for example, hospitalised by the 'friendly' fire of sexual activity than there were by the enemy's gas attacks. Tellingly, the story behind the latter is better known than that of the former. However flawed the statistics, they at least provide a baseline and add considerably to a qualitative picture otherwise painted merely by inference, deduction and speculation. Whatever weakness inherent in the figures, in combination with the stories recounted by individuals such information as we have is indicative of the prevalence of sex in many soldier's lives. It is an activity that cannot be ignored and because of its widespread incidence it is of as much importance in the question of morale as it is of general descriptive interest.

There is another frustrating aspect to these statistics; however much they point to previously unquestioned levels of sexual activity, they tell us nothing of who was involved other than the basic fact that Dominion troops suffered more than their Imperial comrades and that activity was apparently greater in one year over another. The oral and written histories of individuals point to sex being an 'across the board' activity but sadly the statistics provide no further pointers to whether the pursuit of sex was influenced by class, age, religious belief or even the geographic origin of the man. We cannot segment the market for sex, so to speak. Neither can the allegations of some memorialists be substantiated that officers were more active in pursuit than the rank and file – though having both time and money may lead to that conclusion – or that the 'Taffy' was more inclined to licentious behaviour than the 'Jock' or 'Tyke'. It really is the pity of war in this context that any hospital records that might have broken down admissions by military or social variable do not exist, and that even partial answers to any of the above questions might only now be discovered by the Herculean task of analysing individual service records.

We are left with the unscientific finding that sexually-related activities were not only important to the 'everyman' soldier but prevalent throughout the period. On the evidence to hand, demand was not apparently predicated on any pre-war socio-economic variable. Conversely, as we'll see in the following chapter, 'Everyman' shared a distinct pre-war moral code that would have perversely indicated that he would have been indisposed to promiscuous activity. This being so, Herschfeld's contention that there was a 'social breakdown' has some foundation and that on the Western Front morals were sacrificed in favour of morale.

54 TNA: WO 32/5597.

4

'It's Not Something a Gentleman Talks About':
The soldier and his moral code

The Army and political establishment were under no illusion when they initially despatched the seasoned troops of the regular army onto the continent, that sex would inevitably rear its head. History, especially that of the relatively recent Boer War and that of those regiments serving in the far flung corners of Empire, especially India, provided sufficient examples of what was likely to occur. Consideration of what might be required to satiate a man's sexual desires was, however, way down on the list of priorities, especially given the received wisdom that it was to be 'all over by Christmas'. Even Kitchener, a Commander-in Chief unconvinced as to the war's brevity, was nevertheless content to issue his famed injunction to the troops was that they should 'avoid any intimacy' with the locals.[1] 'He may as well not have bothered for all the notice we took …' wrote Frank Richards, who summed up the attitude of the BEF regulars.

In August 1914, the initial BEF comprised approximately 247,400 career regulars. Who were they?[2]

If the officers in the Victorian army were society's elite, the enlisted men were its dregs. The majority of the rank and file was from the bottom end of the social hierarchy. Baynes found that 'the average soldiers of the 2nd Scottish Rifles sprang [from] … the real lower class of the industrial cities'.[3] Despite improvements in conditions, the army as a career was still considered by the majority almost as a 'distress occupation', the last resort of the destitute. Although this was slowly changing, some estimates put the number of men recruited from the unemployed as high as 90 per cent.[4] This description may be over harsh but is useful as a comparison with later recruits.

---

1 See George, *Lord Kitchener*, Volume III, p. 27.
2 For a fuller analysis of the BEF, see Spiers, E., 'The Regular Army in 1914', in Beckett and Simpson (eds), *Nation*, pp. 37-62.
3 Baynes, *Morale*, p. 6.
4 Reader, W. J., *At Duty's Call: A Study in Obsolete Patriotism* (Manchester: MUP, 1988), p. 6; Spiers, 'The Regular Army in 1914', pp. 45-7.

So what defined the regular soldiers' attitudes to morals? Their traditional proclivity to take sex where they found was noted by Carrington: 'One of the oldest jokes that British soldiers make about themselves is to refute the accusation that they are "brutal and licentious". "No inclination to be one, and no opportunity to be the other", they say, and so the truth slips out'.[5]

Further indications are provided by Flexner, who noted that recruiting was in the bar and brothel from the ranks of 'the derelict and adventurous', and by Sir George Scott, COC India in 1888, who pointedly remarked that, 'our soldiers come from a class on which the prudential motives operating against immoral conduct have little effect'.[6] Baynes, examining the relationship between morals and morale, noted that 'the average man in 1914 would have said [morals meant] refraining from extra-marital sex, swearing and drinking'. These, while not the sole ones, 'loomed large in men's minds'.[7] However,

> most soldiers were ready to have sexual intercourse with almost any woman whenever they could … sex was a primitive business untroubled by pangs of conscience. The men rarely had any scruples about it at all: they looked on every woman as fair game.[8]

Denis Winter likewise opined that 'the infantry were largely working class men and it was part of the working class ethic that good health required a regular lay',[9] this generalisation applied more to the lower working classes (the unskilled, and traditional army recruit) rather than to the higher working classes who, as we shall see, made up more of Kitchener's army.

It is doubtful whether the social purity movements of the time had much impact on the regular soldier who, by nature of his being a member of a virtually closed caste, would have been somewhat shielded from their influence. Further, although the army had introduced reforms, including changes to marriage policy and leisure provision from the late Victorian period that would have had some impact on both sexual activities and demand, they were limited.[10]

Battalions were also regularly rotated: most regulars would have seen action in a posting somewhere in the Empire. Despite the demise of the 'official' regulated brothel at home in England, following the repeal of the Contagious Diseases Acts in 1885, regulated prostitution was, *de facto*, still a part of life in virtually every garrison

---

5 Carrington, *Soldier*, p. 180.
6 Both quotes cited from Hyam, *Empire and Sexuality*, p. 122.
7 Baynes, *Morale*, p. 6.
8 Ibid., pp. 213-14. Gibbs, Philip, *The Soul of War* (London: W. Heinemann, 1915, repr., 1938), p. 310, suggests certain regiments were 'worse' than others: 'Highlands and Lowlands … rather crude in their advances to girls of decent up-bringing'.
9 Winter, Denis, *Death's Men*, p. 151.
10 See Trustram, *Women*, for a full analysis of the changes effected with regard to marriage.

ALL THROUGH WALKING WITH A SOLDIER

The regular soldier's reputation was well established. (Author's collection)

overseas and in none more so than the Indian Army where the bulk of the overseas army served.

The officer class in this regular army was from the opposite end of the scale, being drawn from the upper middle class, landed gentry and aristocracy: in 1912, 59 per cent of officers were middle class, 32 per cent landed gentry, 9 per cent aristocracy. Having attended the right school was of paramount importance.[11] 'For its officers, the army preferred gentlemen to professionals … leadership was an attribute of birth; not something to be learned … Because he was a gentleman the officer was beyond reproach … [and] operated according to code of practice universally accepted'.[12] R. C. Money, commissioned into the 2nd Cameronians before the war, recalled that:

> we were, I suppose, very innocent by modern standards … right was right and wrong was wrong and the Ten Commandments were an admirable guide. There was no obsession with sex, drink and drugs. The approach to sex was perfectly normal, while the horror of VD very real. A 'homosexual' was a bugger and

---

11 For an indication of what comprised the 'right' school, see Razzell, P. E., 'Social Origins of Officers in the Indian and British Home Army, 1758-1962', *British J. Sociology* 14 (1963), p. 258; Simpson, Keith 'The Officers', in Beckett and Simpson (eds), *Nation*, pp. 63-98; Simkins, *Kitchener's Army*, p. 19.
12 De Groot, *Blighty*, p 35.

beyond the Pale. A drunk was a drunk and quite useless. A coward was not someone with a 'complex' (we would not have known what it was!) but just a despicable creature. Drugs were unheard of, and I personally never heard of a lesbian until I was over forty. Frugality, austerity and self-control were then perfectly acceptable. We believed in honour, patriotism, self-sacrifice and duty, and we clearly understood what was meant by 'being a gentleman'.[13]

This 'self-control' did not, however, lead exclusively to sex (outside of marriage) being totally cut from the lives of all officers. One of the perceived benefits of serving overseas was being free of the censorious gaze of home and, living alongside officers who held their sexual urges strongly in check, were another group who indulged freely in sex, heterosexual and homosexual. Officers indulged in extra-marital affairs with the wives of brother officers (though a heinous 'moral' crime)[14] and 'fraternised' with locals, though some certainly held to the philosophy of 'whor[ing] it out to the end' as one officer prosaically put it.[15]

The original BEF was virtually destroyed as a single body by December 1914, though individual 'old soldiers' survived, with new recruits coalescing into a unit around them or trained by them, and others transferred from various outposts of the Empire. Thus, 'old soldiers', 'out since Mons', or relics of the British Indian Army and other colonial postings, could be found right through the war years, though in diminishing numbers, in battalions where the bulk of the men were raw recruits. Importantly, they had some influence on the morals of the next waves of recruits and that these men could be looked up to, their stories enthralling their newer comrades and their behaviour aped, is evident in memoirs.[16] As well as their undoubted fighting experience, aspects of their soldiering past – such as brothel visits (army-sanctioned or otherwise) and drinking – were passed on to some if not all. It is probable that habits acquired in India would have transferred to France, and that the influence of Indian Army veterans on newer recruits could be pervasive. It could, however, work the other way and 'old soldiers' actually act as a deterrent: 'Lot of the regulars used to visit the brothels … I saw enough of it at Gallipoli … a lot of them got disease, especially those from India [British regulars] so it put me off', told Bird, a driver in the RFA.[17] Certainly the strength of their wider cultural influence, however, is evidenced in army slang used along the Western Front, *dekko, blighty, cushy, char, base-wallah*, etc., and they passed information on to newer colleagues in a variety of other ways

---

13 Simpson, '*Officers*', p. 68 (from a questionnaire used by Simpson).
14 Masters, John, *Bugles and a Tiger* (London: Michael Joseph, 1956), p. 153.
15 Hyam, *Empire and Sexuality*, pp. 208-14.
16 Kipling, Rudyard, *The New Army in Training* (London: Macmillan, 1915) p. 12.
17 IWM Sound Archive, No. 10656 reel 8, Bird. See also Giles E. M. Eyre, *Somme Harvest*, pp. 29-31; T. S. Hope, *Winding Road*, p. 16.

like sprinkling curry powder over their meat and urinating in boots at night to make them easier for route marches.[18]

Retired officers seeped back in (as 'dugouts') both to train the new armies and, if not too old, to command field units. Their attitudes would have set up a certain framework for the men they commanded and they were, as described by Gibbs, 'some strange fellows', including 'old soldiers who had served in India, Egypt and South Africa … purple-faced old fellows … and young bloods who had once "gone through the Guards" before spending their weekends at Brighton with little ladies from the Gaiety chorus…'.[19] Crozier was in no doubt as to the influence of a senior officer on an inexperienced new recruit:

> Many a bad old captain ruins his subalterns in the company mess, and in clubs, by his example, his conversation, behaviour with women, and drinking habits generally. We know it is it sad but almost inevitable.[20]

Following the demise of the 'old contemptibles', the army looked in several directions for reinforcements. Reservists and 'time-served' regulars were recalled to the colours to replenish home-based battalions that were as much as 40 per cent understrength. Many were like the Welshman, Richards, who would have initially welcomed the prospect of a French adventure as 'a bit of a lark', a short-term escape from domesticity and the chance for a reprise of their earlier life.

This was to be a source throughout the war as manpower crisis hit with increasing regularity and, as upper age limits were raised and physical fitness parameters slackened, the 'dugout' became a feature of every battalion.

Immediate replenishment for the regular army, and then for the initial cohort of the First New Army, was found from a number of other sources than just reservists. Firstly, Territorials (at least those who first consented to overseas service) replaced the regular army troops who were in turn redeployed to France from overseas garrisons. Secondly, there was a general rush to enlist from those who traditionally made up the army: the unemployed, the uneducated and the young, all needing work as industry contracted.

Territorial units, formed by the reorganisation of 1907 by combining Yeomanry, Militia and Volunteer units, had 'shadowed' the regular peacetime army. As with the regular army, the majority of officers came from the same upper middle-class stock, with public schools (many having had Officer Training Corps) supplying them. It is largely this stock who were to gain the slightly disparaging epithet 'temporary gentlemen'. The differences between the culture of the regular army and that of the Territorials were few, traditionally having been drawn from the same demographic

---

18 Priestley, J.B., *Margin Released* (London: Heinemann 1962, repr., 1962), p. 88.
19 See Gibbs, *Soul of War*, p. 311, for a vivid description of these 'strange fellows'.
20 Crozier, *Brass Hat*, pp. 106-7.

pool. The social composition of some of the rank and file, especially at the war's beginning, can be read from one officer's conclusion that the 42nd Territorial Division had 'picked up any loafer or corner boy they could find to make up the numbers'. Where this general social profile existed, their moral position would probably have initially been similar to that of their regular army contemporaries. Not all Territorials were recruited from the lower ranks of society, however, and there were some that were socially exclusive, reflecting the moral position of the skilled and middle classes from which they were drawn. As the war progressed, territorial battalions also attracted Kitchener volunteers, who felt these battalions offered a quicker route to the battlefield than the new armies.

It is tempting to assume, indeed argue, that all of the sexual activity from late 1914 onward could be placed at the door of the regular and those of his social class, who although a fine solder was, as Wellington had famously described, the 'scum of the earth' enlisting for drink and to escape civilian responsibilities and mores. But the argument does not hold; apart from the basic fact that the 'Old Contemptibles' numbered a fraction of their August 1914 strength, the scale of activity is too great, and the reports across too wide a spectrum for it to be solely attributed to one segment of the army.

Secondly, while undoubtedly many of the lower industrial and rural classes continued to enlist as rank and file in the Regulars and Territorials, the bulk of new recruits for Kitchener's New Armies comprised a broad, if statistically unrepresentative, cross-section of Edwardian Britain and Ireland.

The war began with a massive and unprecedented wave of enthusiasm and, by Christmas 1915, Kitchener's volunteers would amount to 2,466,719 men.[21] These can be divided into two basic groups: the smaller number from the public schools and grammar schools, most of whom became officers though not all took a commission, and those from the rest of society who made up the ranks. With almost unimaginable speed, the social composition of the army had changed beyond recognition.[22] The army that was recruited from August 1914 to the end of the war no longer simply represented the two opposing ends of British society; the aristocracy and the underclass. Rather, it represented a complete socio-demographic cross-section of males from the teens to the sixties, from all corners of the British Isles, and included first, second and third-generation colonials. Over 20 times larger, it recruited citizens who had never before seen military service and for whom it was neither a career choice nor a social lifeboat. It recruited the educated, the religious, the temperate; it recruited from worker groups never previously considered military material. It cast its net throughout the Empire's Anglo-Saxon colonies, and beyond; it was constantly recruiting throughout the period, forever changing the acceptable parameters in terms

---

21 Simkins, *Kitchener's Army*, p. 70; also Winter, *The Great War*, pp. 34-5.
22 Simkins, *Kitchener's Army*, p. 71.

of age, physical fitness and even size. Importantly, in the context of sexual behaviour, it recruited married men. Ultimately, moreover, it even recruited women.[23]

What nobody in authority anticipated was how far the vast new citizen armies following the pre-war regulars of the BEF 'out' to France would emulate the behaviour of their more experienced comrades. This applied not only towards matters sexual, but also included such 'vices' as gambling, drinking and the use of 'colourful' language. They might be forgiven; traditionally bound to a much greater degree by the conventions of society than were their lower-working class comrades, the peace-time morals of this class gave no indication of the change in behaviour that occurred when they swapped flannels for khaki.

This represents perhaps the biggest conundrum of all. Attitudes are generally precursors and predictors of behaviour; yet apparently strongly-held morals and ethical codes etched deep into the Edwardian psyche crumbled on contact with a new environment, leading to totally unpredicted behaviour.

A starting point in understanding the dimension of this conundrum is an overview of the Edwardian moral landscape. The vast majority of the population, irrespective of class, subscribed and, with the occasional lapse adhered to an ethically-based and non-dogmatic form of Christianity, one that espoused an identifiable moral code. Transmitted through a variety of channels including Sunday schools, youth associations, grammar and public schools, and contemporary literature, the main tenets of the code were of personal abstention from drink, bad language, gambling and sexual vice – the exact environment men were to find in the army. In peace-time self-control and restraint were the order of the day. This would not only describe the men of Britain but largely also those of the Dominions. For the ruling classes, especially those of the Mother country, it was the concept of service that took the central place in their moral compass though, of course, the other tenets were essential components.

With particular regard to sexual morals, we can generalise but with caveats; the Edwardian era was witnessing the beginnings of change in virtually every aspect of life. One commentator has described is a 'Turn of Mind'[24] and analysis is complicated as attitudes were undergoing change, and doing so in differing ways and speeds in each social class. The colonies, too, exhibited a different set of variables though sharing the same core ethics. Also, while there was a broad acceptance of what constituted moral sexual behaviour within the majority of society, there were significant divergences at the peripheries, those colonised for example by the 'thinking libertine' and the 'dissolute', both of whom favoured free or 'wild-love' though for quite different reasons. In Britain there were also subtle differences exhibited between the skilled-working classes and middle-classes (with courtship rules and conventions, for

---

23 See Winter, J., *Great War and British People* (London: Macmillan 1985) for a full analysis of social, age and occupational composition of the army recruited from 1914.
24 Hynes, Samuel, *The Edwardian Turn of Mind* (Princeton: Princeton University Press, 1975).

example), and even differences within classes themselves, for example between those of industrialised and rural areas. Prostitution was acceptable in some industrialised working class communities and relatively permissive customs regarding pre-marital intercourse could be found in some rural areas.

Booth, founder of the Salvation Army, had found in his contemporary survey of London's working classes that, 'With the lower classes premarital relations are very common ... I do not know how far upwards in the social scale this view of morality extends, but I believe it to constitute one of the clearest lines of demarcation between upper and lower in the working class'.[25] The war's impact was probably to spread promiscuity from the lower classes upwards.

Interestingly, if lower working class morals were seen to be 'loose', there were those at the other end of the social scale, elements of the aristocracy and upper middle classes, whose lives were also marked by a similarly relaxed code. Pornography, for example, had long been the preserve of the rich, at least until technology delivered cheaper print and photographic imagery. 'High-class' brothels existed, catering to the more perverse sexual needs. In high society, adultery was hardly concealed: there were some high-profile divorce cases, and peers of the realm, and indeed royalty, were implicated in homosexual scandals, most notably, of course, in the Oscar Wilde case.

Whether at the high or low end of society, this socially-perceived 'immoral' behaviour was, however, evident only in a minority and sexual attitudes tended to be more conservative with the most sexually conservative inhabiting the broad centre of British society. As Carrington recognised when writing his memoir:

> If I had lived a little higher in the social scale I might have met promiscuous groups in the fashionable world ... I think I should have found in the working class a healthier, more natural, approach to sexual conduct. What I have to offer is a single case study with the suggestion, made after a varied life, that it was typical of the Englishmen in the middle ranks of society.[26]

What were the attitudes of the 'middle ranks'? Broadly they would very much have been influenced by those held by the previous generation; Victorian conventions still stood.[27] Inculcated by the writings of medical practitioners, the church and their schooling, sex was viewed as something solely to be had within marriage, a guilt-ridden experience practiced only when reproductive need dictated. Uncontrolled passions presented moral and physical dangers, with the enslavement to the senses promising the horrible fate of Dorian Grey, or worse.

---

25   Booth, *Life and Labour in London*, cited in Thompson, Paul, *The Edwardians: The Remaking of British Society* (London: Paladin, 1979), p. 76; see Priestley, *Margin*, p. 61, describing his Bradford upbringing.
26   Carrington, *Soldier*, p. 178.
27   Marwick, *The Deluge: British Society and the First World War* (London: Bodley Head, 1965), pp. 105-13; Hall, *Hidden Anxieties*, p. 13.

Fornication with prostitutes was unacceptable, as was masturbation, and even involuntary nocturnal emissions were suspect. It is doubtful there would have been any general use of hard core pornography though cheap illustrated papers, filled with advertisements for everything from VD remedies to 'French pornography by post', were selling 400,000 copies a week and there was a craze for innuendo-laden postcards. This, however, was really no more than a precursor of today's 'red top' tabloid titillation. Generally speaking, they would have had a fundamentally conservative attitude to a wide range of sexual issues of the day, including marriage and family planning; birth control was contentious or at least sensitive. In so far as there was any real thinking about sex, it would have been more about preserving a status quo or, where thought necessary, a return to high Victorian morality to ensure the preservation of the racial superiority considered as essential to the maintenance of Britain's empire and her position in the world.

For the young educated at a public school, or grammar school, and destined for an army commission, indoctrination into the defining code of 'muscular Christianity' was the norm. Exemplified in literature by lawyer and author Thomas Hughes in *Tom Brown at Oxford*, and in Baden Powell's *Scouting for Boys* (1908), it was described as 'manliness'; this code valued attributes including honour, duty, sacrifice, honesty, physical strength and endurance, with the soul of a Christian knight. Formal sex education, as such, was non-existent. Poor lads; they were imbued with guilt, often repressing thoughts of sex totally and blighting their adult years. One observer of the Edwardians even claimed that 'married or not, (they) were having less sexual intercourse [than earlier generations] ... victims of self-denial'. [28]

The morals of significant other sectors of that 'broad middle' were further influenced from the 1880s onward by the reactionary forces of the powerful social purity movement (which also spread to Canada and Australasia), and much can be understood about how the man in the trench initially felt about sex by examining the attitudes and campaigns of the social purists. Organisations, like the White Cross Societies and the Alliance of Honour, made a lot of noise attracting a large membership, and managed, through applying local political pressure at key times and places, to have brothels closed down, music hall licenses revoked, pubs purged of prostitutes, offensive mutascopes removed from public places and books banned. Far from the image sometimes projected of a Britain as an immoral society pullulating with sexual vice, it was largely the opposite. The number of divorces, for example, was comparatively very low given the size of the population, partly due to the state of the Law, and partly due to social stigma, though bigamy was not unheard of. Illegitimate births had generally, if not in every social segment, diminished since the mid-nineteenth century. Even visible prostitution had declined from its mid-Victorian period to the point at which purity campaigner could claim 'London today ... is an open-air cathedral'; had he looked harder, however, he may well have found a reasonable numbers of prostitutes

---

28 Thompson, *Edwardians*, p. 78

figuratively 'hiding in the crypt' having been driven underground, or hidden from view.

It would have perhaps been unnatural had all vice was successfully repressed; at least some parts of society demanded it, or had differing definitions of what 'vice' constituted, and the Victorian double standard, whereby a man might indulge but a woman not, was still being observed.

Perhaps the social purity movement was simply putting its finger in the dyke and the fringe activities were early indications of a gradually evolving attitude change yet to flow outward from the 'innovators'. Perhaps, too, public display of morals were a veneer and it was 'outward respectability' that was important.[29] Writing of middle-class moral views of the time, Hynes comments with the somewhat sweeping generalisation that they 'were a contradictory mixture of public propriety and private indulgence ...'.[30] Novelist J. B. Priestley hints of such hypocrisy existing in his northern home town:

> An ultra-respectable suburb like ours, I began to see, had too many badly divided men, all heavily solemn and frock-coated on a Sunday morning, too coarsely raffish, well away from their families, on a Saturday night. Managers who were obdurate if the mill girls wanted another shilling a week could be found in distant pubs turning the prettiest and weakest of them into tarts.[31]

Self-denial and repression, perhaps wrongly perceived as self-control, might ironically have led to an underlying sexual frustration.[32] If this is true, and even if affecting a small part of society, then perhaps the sexual activity that exploded both on the home front and in France was not the result of an erosion of morals, but a simple release from constraints; a dam bursting in a time of change. The inherent sexuality buried in everyone, but socially repressed or suppressed, rose to the surface in extraordinary times. It is an interpretation favoured by Hirschfeld and others. The war environment was not the reason *per se* for a change of morals but simply fostered and made easier a tendency already there. As Lord Moran held, 'war ... merely exaggerates the good and evil that are in us, till it is plain for all to read; it cannot change, it exposes'.[33]

Whether sexually repressed or simply holding strong convictions, the great mass of the men in Kitchener's Army came exactly from what Carrington called the 'middle ranks of society'. At the time of enlisting their outlook reflected the broad strands of Edwardian opinion and morals. Despite the possible indicators of what the future might hold, generally speaking most of the rank and file who went off to fight the

---

29 Snape, *God*, pp. 20-28.
30 Hynes, *Edwardian Turn of Mind*, p. 7.
31 Priestly, *Margin*, p. 60
32 Thompson, *Edwardians*, p. 78.
33 Moran, Lord, *The Anatomy of Courage* (London: Constable, 1945), p. 170.

European war, especially over the first years, were, if not physically carrying the banners and flags of the social purity movement, aware that they were flying above their heads.

Bourne has defined the army as being an 'overwhelmingly working-class, urban army ... The British working man in uniform'.[34] Ascribing a particular class definition is notoriously difficult given the problems of deciding whether class is determined by employment, financial status, education, housing stock, or even self-referential criteria such as manners, clothing or moral outlook. This was anyway a period of class instability, particularly for the perennially blurred gradations between the working class and the middle class, but the bulk of Kitchener's Army would fall into a range between middle class and semi-skilled worker, with a bias towards the latter. This would comprise approximately seventy-five per cent of the population. The composition of a section of a battalion raised in Durham is indicative of the class by occupational mix: three teachers, three chemists, one builder, three clerks, one tram driver.[35] There were extremes at either end of the scale. As one Scottish Kitchener officer remarked, reflecting some of the extreme social elements within the new armies, 'the finest officers and training couldn't make saints of men straight from the Falkirk High Street and south side of Glasgow'.[36] Oxford-educated J. Staniforth was distressed to find that his unit consisted of 'tramps' who were 'drunk ... seedy, lousy, unshaven' and 'given to smoking, spitting, quarrelling, making water all over the room ... hiccupping and vomiting'.[37] Staniforth was unlucky. Had he joined an appropriate Pals Battalion, one raised amongst his peers, he would probably have found a lot more in common with his fellow recruits. The 10th (Service) Battalion of the Royal Fusiliers which was later referred to as the 'Stockbrokers' Battalion', and 7th Battalion, Royal Dublin Fusiliers, for example, drew from both the professional and labouring classes. The former was known as the 'Toffs among the Toughs' and included 450 students from University College Dublin and 869 from Trinity College.

The moral make-up of Kitchener's army reflected the broad sectors of society from which it was drawn, not those of the social extremes, sharing generally uniform attitudes towards sex. Cutting across strict class delineations and in terms of attitude and morals, as opposed to just social habits, the general consensus would have been to think of themselves as 'decent' and of 'being from good homes'. This is how the soldiers describe their comrades time and time again, even if lurking amidst the 'decent chaps' were inevitably thieves, villains, bigamists, fornicators, cowards and cheats.

---

34 Bourne, J., 'The British Working Man in Arms', in Cecil and Liddle (eds), *Facing Armageddon*, p. 336.
35 Ibid., p. 25. IWM Sound Archive, No. 9751, reel 6, Frank Raine, NCO 18th BN Durham Light Infantry; Hughes, 'New Armies', in Beckett and Simpson, *Nation at Arms*, p. 105 for examples of other battalions.
36 Spiers, E.M., 'The Scottish Soldier at War', in Cecil and Liddle (eds), *Facing Amageddon*, p. 321, citing 2nd Lt Gillespie, A.D., *Letters from Flanders* (London: Smith Elder, 1916).
37 De Groot, *Blighty*, p. 162.

It is probable that, despite making up less than twenty per cent of the population, until 1916 the army would have been comprised of many church goers; largely because many volunteers were signing up as part of a 'crusade' against the German 'horde'. They would have been influenced by the many Christian revival movements that were a feature of both pre-war years and indeed the early war years.[38]

It is also pertinent to note that there was strong initial recruitment from both Irish Roman Catholic and Protestant communities, and large numbers of non-conformists, representing most, if not all, sects. In all probability, this was an army of relatively innocent 'white knights', modern crusaders with a definite set of ethics and strong moral code. Not generally a cynical group of men, their relative sexual innocence and crusading was often captured in their own words:

> In the workaday world we were being subjected [mid-1915] to a great deal of war propaganda – anti-German of course. Likened to the Huns of Attila, the stories of rape by German soldiers nearly all had to do with nuns as their victims, and in our puritanical, sex tabooed atmosphere, this was difficult to appreciate. Much more easily understood by we youngsters were those about babies being waved around on bayonets.[39]

When coming across 'naughtiness' in France they were often initially discomfited by what they saw. As RFC member Thomas Armstrong recalled:

> From some of our battery positions one could go back into a little town and go to an estaminet [for breakfast] … a young officer came in with a girl and sat at a table beside me. 'Fini with me?' she said. And that shocked me very much … I was green and innocent and romantic I suppose.[40]

Private Goodman of the 2/1st London Field Ambulance reveals the depth of his own discomfort and indicated the general moral position felt by many of his class and background in describing during an interview for the IWM how:

> I had quite a number of difficult duties [referring venereal disease cases] … the colonel used to send me to investigate … one of these dreadful places [note: he is referring to a brothel or similar] … *you can please yourself whether you want to put this on the tape* … what we, and the troops were upset about was this … when I went to St Pol once … to investigate one of these dreadful places … almost across the road was a place frequented by WACs … our own girls and they knew

---

38 Snape, *God*, p. 139.
39 Taylor, F. A. J., *The Bottom of the Barrel* (London: Regency, 1978), p. 14.
40 IWM Sound Archive, No. 9758, reel 2, Sir Thomas Armstrong, RFC.

what was going on … very unpleasant … *goes very much against the grain, doesn't it* [author's italics].[41]

With this initial contingent containing a goodly number of committed church-goers, influenced by the Christian revivalist movements, one way of understanding the general attitudes of the average man who made up the volunteer force of 1914 and 1915 is to focus on what those 'flags and banners' of the social purity movement stood for and against. Eight individual targets can be seen as generally in the movement's sights: the Contagious Diseases Acts as 'the symbols of state-regulated prostitution'; soliciting and the age of consent (both effectively aimed at driving out prostitution); homosexuality; masturbation and schoolboy sex; incest; pornography; and nude bathing. It is again pertinent to note that the fight against these was wrapped up in a general 'Christian' lifestyle that would also often have meant temperance, forswearing of obscenity, blasphemy and abstinence from gambling.

These movements, with their large active membership throughout the country, sold millions of books and pamphlets which would have inculcated in many future soldiers a set of moral values. In theory, traditional pastimes familiar to soldiery, including sexual, would not have been considered acceptable. A spokesman for the National Vigilance Society could claim 'public opinion in South Wales and notably the Rhondda Valley had entirely changed for the better with regard to the whole moral question and that was entirely due to the work done by our South Wales branch'. The miners of South Wales contributed more than 150,000 men to Pals battalions. We cannot know, however, whether once in France they remained Christian 'crusaders', or became Saint-Mandé's 'typical Taffy, short, dark ebullient and religious, although his piety did not prevent him from going into all the brothels he could find'.[42]

If the activities of the NVA and others had an impact on the morals of the men marching off to France, what of its impact on the morals of the officer class? The first and probably most noteworthy fact is the extreme youth of the subalterns, many mere schoolboys sent straight from England, without any war experience, to take charge of as hard-bitten and experienced old sweats as one could imagine – and it was in life as well as war that they lacked experience. As with the regular army, officers for Kitchener's armies were initially largely recruited from the public schools and universities. The Haldane reforms of 1906 onward had established that schools and universities should introduce Officer Training Corps. This meant that, when needed, the army could count on recruits having basic military training, an idea of army culture, and most importantly, the right sort of leadership characteristics: these were most definitely 'Christian' and based on physical fitness. By Edwardian times the Headmasters Conference had become a pivotal constituency in the purity lobby, and

---

41 IWM Sound Archive, 9398, reel 5, Goodman.
42 Saint-Mandé, *War, Wine and Women*, p. 379.

'moral' education very definitely part of the curriculum, ensuring that the impact and influence of the purity movement remained strong throughout the period.

Officers were not confined to public school and university graduates, given both the high numbers required and the attrition rate. Traditional social backgrounds widened, and pips were worn by the middle classes, who were acknowledged as 'temporary gentlemen'. This was especially true of Pals battalions, where those who had been managers and supervisors of the men enlisting in the industrial areas tended to become their officers on enlisting themselves, and those of the rural battalions being from the gentry and professional classes.

'Temporary gentlemen' brought modified attitudes into the army: 'a pre-war regular officer of the 1st Royal Berkshire Regiment … was shocked to hear "these queer Yorkshire lads" boasting about embracing girls in public whilst wearing uniform, and the fact that other officers saw nothing wrong with such behaviour'.[43] However, in terms of overall morals there was initially little difference to those exhibited by the traditional officer class and the new 'breed' tended to conform to the existing attitudes as teaching and discipline in the ever-widening state secondary schools tended to ape that of the public schools.

Many men of this large initial influx into Kitchener's armies were dead by mid-1916, following the battle of the Somme. Battalions were broken up and survivors melded into the general body of the army. One outcome was the loss of social pressures associated within the original enlisting peer group, perhaps a factor leading to a revised moral outlook from this period onward.

Toward the end of 1915, with inadequate numbers now volunteering, the Derby Scheme was introduced, with some 840,000 single men and 1.35 million married men attesting their willingness to serve. This final attempt to save the principle of voluntary enlistment, however, proved to be a temporary response to the continuing manpower shortage and led inexorably towards full-scale conscription, with the attestation process merely forming the initial basis for determining who should join and when.

There is a compelling argument for considering these latterly recruited troops as a segment distinct from the earlier 'Kitchener men', with different attitudes and predispositions toward sexual activity. Firstly, their demographic would have been different. Although likely to have been from the same social class, there were more married and older men finding their way to the front, especially after the full introduction of conscription, despite Asquith's promise to the contrary. The proportion of active church-goers would have been declining, for 'death, wounding, transfer and reorganization destroyed the original character of many units that had once harboured strong religious cultures'.[44] These differences will all have affected their propensity to take advantage of any sexual services on offer; at least this was thought to be the case by a

---

43 Simpson, 'Officers', p. 76.
44 Snape, God, pp. 167-68.

number of the younger recruits who often seemed to think that it was more difficult for a man who had tasted the apple to resist further temptation.: 'It was an older man's thing', thought Raynor Taylor of the Glamorgan Yeomanry. [45]

Further, there were probably more men from the unskilled working classes than the skilled, as a result of the workings of the recruitment boards and skilled men asking to be considered as being in a 'reserved occupation'. As noted earlier, the unskilled working class traditionally displayed a different attitude towards sexual morals and may have been more predisposed to taking advantage of the opportunities. Certainly, this class did not live by the same middle-class rules governing matrimony, as the Executive Committee of the National Relief Fund had already discovered with the earlier working-class intake. As Marwick described it, 'they discovered a whole underworld of irregular conjugal relationships'.[46]

In addition to the men's own demographic differences, there was also an important environmental change taking place: as the war progressed there were social changes on the home front, a 'live for now' feeling. Private Harry Blunt, Machine Gun Corps, recalled an overall attitude change in the young women of his local town and how 'Girls used to wait at the railway station every Saturday to see who was coming home'.[47] The 'khaki fever' reportedly infecting Britain's young women at the beginning of the war was a precursor of the wider atmosphere of freer sexual behaviour evident throughout the home front during the whole war period.[48] There was a sudden increase in sexual opportunity that not even the moral police could contain, and this can only have had the impact of contributing to the general loosening of morals of the man eventually donning the uniform. Equally, the conditions on the actual front would have evolved. There would have been more opportunities for vice at the ever-growing base camps, with the number of displaced females turning to prostitution expanding. It is perhaps unsurprising that from early 1917 there was a rising concern about the declining morals of the soldiers with several church-led initiatives and investigations taking place.

The final wave of recruitment lasted from late 1917 through to the war's end. Though once again, non-manual workers bore a disproportionately higher share, recruiters scraped the bottom of the barrel in terms of the age of the conscripted. As a result, this

---

45   IWM Sound Archive, No. 9876, Cyril George Dennys, officer, 212 Siege Bty RGA 1917-19; No. 8868, reel 6, William Holmes, Pte, 12th Bn London Regt; No. 1111, Raynor Taylor, Pte Glamorgan Yeomanry. Similar feelings about older men having lower morals is also evidenced in comments of use of pornography, see No. 9343, reel 2, Gordon Davis, Pte 22nd Bn Royal Fusiliers 1915-17 and RFC 1917-18.
46   Marwick, *Deluge*, p. 107.
47   See Thompson, *Edwardians*, p. 267. See also IWM Sound Archive, no. 645, reel 1, Harry Blunt, Pte Machine Gun Corps. See also Marwick, *Deluge*, pp. 105-9, for fuller discussion of changes in wartime sexual morality.
48   Woollacott, 'Khaki Fever', pp. 325-47.

segment is distinguished by the fact that almost half the infantrymen were nineteen or younger.[49]

Would the attitude and morals of these final recruits have been any different from those joining earlier? It is certainly possible. On the one hand, social purity education had not stopped reaching out to the young. The controversy over increasing civilian VD rates, not to mention personal experience, may well have heightened the fears of those reaching maturity on the home front, from 1914, and steered them away from casual sexual encounters. Conversely, perhaps, the general moral loosening evident in society might have counter-balanced this.[50] Some of the conscripts were now very young, and large numbers of them would certainly have been socially innocent, with some so immature as to be able to put sexual concerns to one side. Harry Wells, a private in 17th and 23rd Battalion Royal Fusiliers, records that 'I was too young to worry about sex', and William Smathers of the 2nd Battalion Kings Liverpool Regiment was 'not bothered, more interested in football then'.[51]

It is interesting that the rates for venereal disease in the army increased during 1918, and while this could conceivably have been the outcome of a home-based epidemic, with men being infected on leave rather than in France, it suggests that sexual activity in general increased and might reflect a more relaxed attitude towards sex within the last conscripted intakes into the army. This increase was despite the increasing precautions being taken against the spread of venereal disease amongst the soldiery both at home and at the front, including the passing of the controversial DORA Regulation 40 which restricted contact between diseased women and men in uniform, the maintenance of regulated brothels, the control and removal of 'clandestine' prostitutes in France, and the increasing use of prophylactics.

The difference for the 1918 recruit was the changed nature of the fighting and the attendant sexual opportunities that followed. After the great reverses of March and April, the tide turned against the Germans. The war once again became mobile, with a forward momentum which lasted until the Armistice. Those attached to various HQs, providing support functions, in the heavy artillery, or fortunate enough to be with reserve battalions stationed behind the lines, would have found the regulated brothels functioning and accessible, despite the pressure on the army at home to have them closed. There would also have been some, though limited, possibilities of contact with nurses, VADs, and the newly formed WAACs, even if mostly restricted to officers and 'base-wallahs'. Closer to the front, clandestine prostitution would have been evident

---

49 For conscription statistics, see *Statistics of the Military Effort of the British Empire During the Great War, 1914-1920* (London: HMSO, 1922), pp. 364-70. Also see Winter, *The Great War*, pp. 39-48.

50 Robb, George *British Culture and the First World War* (New York: Palgrave, 2002), pp. 46-61. See also two oral reminiscences which provide an indication of the changed moral circumstances of the period: IWM Sound Archive, No. 4228, Shuttleworth, and No. 11712, reel 4, Ernie Rhodes, 8th Reserve Bn and 16th Bn Manchester Regt.

51 IWM Sound Archive, No. 22740, Wells; No.10769, Smathers; similarly No. 9751, Raine.

across the battlefield,[52] Corday noting in early 1918 that 'moral laxity appears to have increased ... especially under the pressure of necessity, which seems to have transformed many women into temporary prostitutes'.[53] Some genuine fraternisation was also possible with civilians.[54] For front-line infantry in one of the active divisions, and with no leave, sex would, however, have been of the auto-erotic kind,[55] with heterosexual sex only available once the British soldier became a member of the 'occupying army' in liberated Belgium. For example, those serving in the post-war period on the Rhine and in liberated Belgium were to enjoy relationships with local women.[56]

The preceding analysis of the British citizen army brings us back to the basic conundrum underlying sex and the soldier. It is clear that after the demise of the old regular army the prevailing attitudes of the majority of civilian-soldiers taking the King's shilling would have been morally conservative. The men considered themselves to have been of high moral character and fortitude, believing in cleanliness 'in mind and deed'. Specifically, when it came to matters of sexual behaviour and choice, their attitude and predisposition towards casual and especially venal sex, and towards pornography and auto-eroticism, suggest that sex of this nature would either not be important, or simply would not take place; self-control would be the guiding principle. Yet, the wide-ranging sexual activity that took place was too great an amount for it to have been limited to only those from the social peripheries. The autobiographical writings and oral reminiscences further illustrate the widespread nature of sexual episodes with accounts covering officers and rankers from every recruitment period, from front and back-line units, and from wide geographical recruitment regions.

The moral codes of a diffused Christianity, school warnings, the rare fatherly talks, peer group approbation, Kitchener's exhortations, and innocence were all forgotten. What must have taken place, therefore, between the act of signing up and the entry into the French boudoir, the purchase of titillating pornography, or a discreet fumble, was a fairly fundamental change in attitude. Morals were sacrificed for morale. As we'll see, it was army life in general, and army life in France, that was responsible for this fundamental change in attitude and subsequent behaviour. And this change caught most unaware and unprepared, leading to an unplanned *ad hoc* response from both civilian and military authorities and in turn causing all manner of dilemmas and practical problems.

---

52 See also TNA: WO 154/77.
53 Corday, Michel, *The Paris Front: An Unpublished Diary: 1914-1918* (New York: E.P. Dutton & Co., 1934), Jan. 1918, p. 306.
54 See Hiscock, *Bells of Hell*, p. 128.
55 Ibid., p. 76. Hiscock, who was in this final call-up, is frank about this aspect.
56 See Wheeler, Victor, *The 5th Battalion in No Man's Land* (Ontario: CEF Books, 2000), p. 272, and IWM Sound Archive, No. 9420, Arthur Gillman, Pte 2/2nd London Regt (Royal Fusiliers), for examples of sexual opportunities presenting themselves to advancing soldiers.

La Vie Parisienne's illustrations made astute and accurate observations of life outside the war zone. Their caption reads; 'The Little lady, with frantic admiration and recognition, "Then it's true, my little Tommy, that your miserable little army has three million fellows like you…"'. And over the four years of 'occupation' many little Tommies would be stealing away from a French boudoir. (Author's collection)

5

The Road to Hell:
From morals to morale

In the years leading to the bonfire of certainties that was to be the Great War, sexual propriety was dominant: 'There cannot be any doubt that as a whole this was a time of striking sexual restraint', argues Thompson.[1] But self-restraint was to go up in flames as the soldiers' pre-war moral outlook changed to one which made sexual licentiousness more likely and for the soldiers, in Eksteins memorable phrase, to consider 'themselves privileged citizens in relation to, among other things, morality'.[2]

It is remarkable that attitudes towards sex changed to the degree they did, even if such changes proved to be only for 'the duration'.[3] Cognitive theory recognises that people hold on to existing attitudes, even being prepared to twist new sensory stimuli, or knowledge, to fit their existing beliefs, rather than change. Yet they did change. Contemporary observers, such as Crozier, acknowledged this:

> As there are in the ranks of the British Army some of the finest middle and lower-middle class stock in the kingdom, is it not surprising that young men find themselves in this strange queue [outside the red lamp], who would, in times of peace, have hesitated to line up outside a music hall?[4]

It might have been expected that the church, or one of the many associative organisations that were active on the Front, might have acted more of a buttress against moral collapse, while also contributing to general morale. While an existing moral code and the religious upbringing of some soldiers could have had a lasting impact on preserving attitudes (as Sidney Taylor of the RFA remarked, 'the upbringing we'd

---

1   Thompson, *The Edwardians*, p. 77.
2   Eksteins, Modris, *Rites of Spring: the Great War and Birth of the Modern Age* (London: Doubleday, 1989), p. 223.
3   FO 141/466/2 – Part I, Report of the Cairo Purification Committee, Cairo, 1916, 14.
4   Crozier, *A Brass Hat,* p. 127.

had [Methodist] just cut that out'[5]), one Catholic chaplain, perhaps exhibiting prejudices inherent in the centuries-old antagonism between the religions, disagreed. He responded to a 1917 church survey of the frequency of moral lapses among the troops with the following indictment; 'I prefer the recording Angel to say how "frequent" are moral falls among non-Catholic soldiers. They have a lower standard, far lower, then we have, and some absolutely no standard at all', while another claimed, 'the average non-Catholic is frankly and practically a sense-utilitarian'.[6] There are 'none so blind'…; in truth, the Catholic soldier was himself far from pure of thought, mind or action. Even Catholic chaplains, generally closer in the line to their flock than chaplains of other denominations, were just as ineffective as their counterparts in stiffening moral fibre.

The role of the church in the lives of the soldiers, however, as distinct from the role of religion *per se*, remains a contested one. There can be little doubt that in initially keeping Chaplains away from the front line, the church squandered an opportunity and that the soldiers distanced themselves from their chaplains. Despite year on year increases that saw thousands of chaplains being dispatched to the Western Front to provide comfort and solace,[7] many soldiers believed, with some justification, that army authorities were more interested in the chaplains getting across a message of the moral rightness of the war rather than stiffening general morals; propaganda rather than spiritual guidance and comfort.[8]

While individual padres might try to bolster the soldiers' moral fibre in an *ad hoc* manner at the Front, at a generic level the soldiers' Church, however, seems to have had little to say to the soldier in France itself, though it commented from the pulpit at home. At times it joined the general agitation for brothel closures but concerns were mostly manifested in reports submitted by padres, visiting church dignitaries and quasi-religious organisations like the YMCA.[9] While some bemoaned the lack of sexual morals, many turned a blind eye and, when commenting on the situation in France for home consumption, being somewhat 'economical with the truth' there was patently an element of propaganda involved.[10]

The truth of the matter concerning morality on the Western Front was such that the Church could hardly comment; there was already sufficient ambiguity over the right or wrongs of taking life. An individual would have found it difficult to relate

---

5   IWM Sound Archive, 10615, Taylor.
6   Plater, *Catholic Soldiers*, pp. 74, 86.
7   For a full discussion on religion see MacKenzie, S. P., 'Morale and the Cause. The Campaign to Shape the Outlook of Soldiers in the British Expeditionary Force, 1914–1918', *Canadian Journal of History* 25 (1990), p. 23. Snape, *God*, pp. 89-90.
8   See also Graham, *Private,* re. padres allowing MOs to dictate sexual policy and ch. 1 above, n.10.
9   See for example, Cains, D. S. *The Army and Religion; an Enquiry into the Religious Life of the nation* (1919); Also, Plater, *Catholic Soldiers*, p. 110.
10   Tiplady, *The Cross at the Front:* p. 83; Also Snape, *God*, p. 157, n. 105.

to – and hold onto – other, lesser moral constraints when breaking one of the most sacred and fundamental of Judeo-Christian tenets, 'thou shalt not kill'. One indicator of this was perhaps the less-than-total respect that soldiers often showed towards the organised church. Many men, who had virtually deserted institutionalised religion if not some sort of faith, treated most things the church said with outright cynicism. This overall lack of respect is evidenced in a couple of widely believed 'latrine rumours'. The first was that padres were themselves in unholy communion with locals and, secondly, that there was a special VD ward in Le Havre reserved for them. There is no evidence to support either report, but they were readily believed by the soldiers.[11] Whether true or apocryphal, reports of priests who had fallen from grace are measures of a deeper malaise. It was the perception that moral certainties no longer existed that is the crucial point.

There undoubtedly were individual padres who cared for the moral welfare of their flock, and the ranks themselves contained a leavening of ordained men, to whom the men looked for moral guidance, as they did to their officers, but they were not always around to provide or stimulate conscience when needed.[12] Often, when they were, their presence was unwelcome. Sergeant Ashurst of the 2nd Battalion Lancashire Fusiliers, remembered the moral policing of a house of ill-repute. The padre's disgust and dressing down of the men led to removal of leave privileges, taking away what would have been seen as a welcome break from the trenches. This seemingly unique example of soldiers being 'crimed' for using an estaminet brothel – 'He reduced our time in the town', complained Ashworth – would probably not have made him, or his church, popular.[13]

The role of the church representative was thus often reduced to presiding over burials, giving support to medical teams, hearing occasional battlefield confessions, and presiding over unpopular church parades where attendance was often obligatory and where they treated the men to a moral justification for the war. In these contexts they certainly could do little to stem the erosion of pre-war moral attitudes.[14]

It might also be thought that the tentacles of 'the salvation industry', which proliferated at the front, might have had a restraining influence on troop behaviour. One of the main objectives of the multitudinous Church Army, Salvation Army and YMCA funded canteens and clubs was to provide an alternative to sin. While they undoubtedly could provide a successful diversionary alternative to brothel visits, and perhaps bolster the faith of the already committed Christian, they were probably not successful missionaries and soldiers' positive memories recalled tea, biscuits and letter writing

---

11   Wheatley, *Officer*, p. 152; Robert Graves, *Goodbye*, p. 207; IWM Sound Archive, No. 8764, reel 4, Stagg:Frank Richards, *Old Soldiers*, p. 59.
12   Snape, *God*, p. 148.
13   IWM Sound Archive, No. 9875, reel 5, Ashurst.
14   For a contemporary account of the soldiers' attitude to the established church, see Hankey, Donald, *A Student in Arms* (London: Andrew Melrose, 1917), Ch. 15.

a rather than the sometimes resented religious zeal.[15] A credible witness, Donald Hankey – a young soldier and a pre-war denizen of the Oxford and Bermondsey Mission – illustrates how any inadequacy of the facilities led directly to the alternative of sex, and how morals could be forgone for the sake of morale:

> Fifteen months ago I was a private quartered in a camp near A— ... The tent was damp, gloomy, and cold. The YMCA tent and the Canteen tent were crowded. One wandered off to the town ... And if a fellow ran up against 'a bit of skirt' he was generally just in the mood to follow it wherever it might lead.[16]

The numerous organisations, who made the moral welfare of the soldier their concern, tended to concentrate on the problems of prostitution among men on leave rather than actively policing the general moral climate overseas (at least until a scandal erupted in 1918 over the running of the brothels in Cayeux-sur-Mer). Many soldiers anyway gave them short shrift, and if individuals felt inclined to proselytise, attitudes such as Denis Wheatley's probably kept them quiet:

> This organisation was another product of the influential old women who formed the unofficial Purity League ... The object of this operation was to prevent men coming on leave from the Front from spending a night in the great big wicked capital with a girl.[17]

Some would argue that the church and similar institutions were fighting a losing battle from the start with the very nature of war leading to moral breakdown. Fischer and Dubois offer a quasi-Freudian explanation:

> It is a characteristic feature of all wars that the combatants follow their sexual instinct without restraint, even when, in private life, they are strictly moral. The lust for killing goes parallel with sexual lust, which may manifest itself either in rape or merely in reckless promiscuity, for love and death – creation and destruction – are psychologically inseparable allies.[18]

Some literary-minded former combatants saw sex simply as the direct antithesis of the killing and violence,[19] while for Cloete, it was almost a Darwinian urge:

---

15 See Brugger, S., *Australians and Egypt, 1914-1919* (Melbourne: MUP, 1980), pp. 65-7, Wheeler, *The 50th Battalion in No-man's Land* (Ontario: CEF Books, 2000), p. 272.
16 Hankey, *Student in Arms*, p. 55.
17 Wheatley, *Temporary Gentleman*, p. 203.
18 Fischer, and Dubois, *Sexual Life*, p. 48.
19 Manning, *Her Privates We*, p. 55.

> There is always talk of increased immorality, loss of virtue and the lowering of standards in war. But it is not that morals get worse, merely that the pressure against the restraints of what we describe as morals increases in a direct ratio to the losses in the field, in a frantic race to replace the dead … I was an organ of reproduction to be used before it was destroyed. This force was operating all round me as it has round every soldier in every war.[20]

Whether the average soldier would have worried himself with such complexities as to his motives, is doubtful. While it was the 'viciousness' of day-to-day army life that assaulted the individual's attitude toward swearing and blasphemy, gambling, stealing, alcohol and sex, with the vices and taboos of civvy street paradoxically the traditional stuff of soldiering, of more immediate and pressing concern for most would have been the broader moral challenges of the war itself. Some men were easily conditioned to accept army morality, as the very fact of being in the army seemed to abrogate them from all moral responsibilities:

> [To] the new recruit who had common health and good-humour, all his maturity's worries and burdens seemed, by some magical change, to have dropped from him; no difficult choices had to be made any longer; hardly a moral chart to be conned; no one had finances to mind; fate was … not even his own.[21]

If such 'vices' were seen to serve to uphold a soldier's morale it is unsurprising that both the individual and the army would find excuses to discount them. Indeed there appeared to be no moral ambiguity. Apart from gambling, which the army expressly prohibited though with little effect, all other vices were in practice condoned. There was no case to answer for bad language, unless it was part of insubordination to a superior, and all ranks swore and blasphemed freely. Crude and 'lusty' songs were the fuel that kept a division marching 40 miles with full pack. One does not read of men being hauled over the coals for vulgar, obscene or sexually-explicit backchat with local women folk. Stealing was sanitised as 'winning' unless it was from one's immediate comrades, or was obviously looting (though looting from the dead was condoned). Drinking alcohol was not only permitted, but so ingrained as to be a problem. R. C. Sherriff's *Journey's End* with its strikingly authentic retelling of the pressures of trench existence memorably introduces the young captain who is gradually losing control through alcohol.[22] As for sex, the soldier was not castigated for immorality, but carelessness if he caught 'venereal'.

---

20 Cloete, *A Victorian Son*, p. 258.
21 Montague, C. E., *Disenchantment* (London: Chatto & Windus, 1924), p. 6.
22 Sherriff, R. C. *Journey's End* (London: Victor Gollancz, 1929).

Charles Carrington wrote: 'Part of the attraction of soldiering was the unspoken assumption that on active service soldiers were released from the taboos of civil life'.[23] It was inevitable, that in this febrile environment, the soldiers learned to conform to a behavioural pattern that they perceived both as normal and expected of them, and then to do so without attendant moral guilt: 'The army tends to give one an unmoral [sic] outlook on life and we do things here that we wouldn't dream of doing in civil life', claimed Kiwi Rifleman Maloney [24]. An element of male 'bonding' may also have been evident with sexual activity considered a sign of masculinity. Some may have seen it as a necessary 'proof' of their masculinity. Conformity meant following behaviours perceived as the cultural norm of the organisation as Graves reported: 'Young officers, at this period [1917], were expected, as someone has noted in his war-memoirs, to be roistering blades over wine and women. These ten did their best.'[25] It was a strong man who resisted and kept his own counsel, and this in part explains the ungrudging respect that one reads of those who did not succumb. Certainly the pressure to conform would have been intense, as Canadian officer Wheeler found:

> Some of the signallers seemed puzzled that I did not cuss, smoke, drink … or show much interest in les Mesdemoiselles. *'There must be something wrong'*, was the consensus. Accordingly, one of their number, winsome signaller Johnny Rickert, was delegated to approach me with the simple (alas, profound) question, 'Wheeler, are you *natural?*'.[26]

Many individuals, especially when new to the military environment, would have initially wrestled with their conscience as they met with a range of perceived moral challenges. 'Another great pain which is suffered is in learning to be impure', wrote Guardsman Graham: 'the grief in the secret places of the heart when you first begin to swear, when you first say indecent things … The pang is repeated when he first gives

---

23   Carrington, *Soldier*, p. 180.
24   Cited in Boyack, *Behind the Lines*, p. 134. For the absolving effects of contrition among Catholics see Plater (ed.), *Catholic Soldiers*. Ch. IV.
25   Edmonds, Charles, *A Subaltern's War* (London: Peter Davies 1922, Anthony Mott repr., 1986), p. 101. See also Graves, *Goodbye*, p. 195 and Bourke, *Dismembering the Male*, pp. 128-31 for a further interpretations of army 'conditioning'.
26   Wheeler, *50th Battalion*, p. 67; see also Aldington, Richard, *Death of a Hero* (London: Chatto & Windus, 1929*)*, pp. 32, 226, for similar alienation by a character. Interestingly, Makepeace contends that such pressure to conform was not always overt with the occasional reported incidents of soldiers not consummating sexual act at brothels proving they had individual choice. Makepeace, C., 'Punters and Their Prostitutes: British Soldiers, Masculinity and *Maisons Tolerees* in the First World War', in Arnold, John H. and Brady, S., (eds) *What is Masculinity? Historical Dynamics from Antiquity to the Contemporary World* (Palgrave Macmillan, 2011), p. 416. These are individual cases, however, with explanations varying from will-power to lack of money and they do not disprove the broader contention that peer pressure would have been immense.

Peronne was certainly not Eden, nor the offer of sex the first moral collapse, but this scene could very well have illustrated the young and innocent T.S. Hope's Peronne experience (see chapter six). Official war artist, William Orpen's allegorical painting, 'Adam and Eve at Peronne'.

way to drink, and if he succumbs, *as so many inevitably do* [author's italics] to sexual temptation and if he falls for the wrong sort of girl'.[27]

Losing control in one area would not necessarily lead to a wholesale capitulation but it was a difficult task to hold on to all existing behavioural norms and for many, once new mores were accepted, it was 'in for a penny, in for a pound', a policy taken to its extreme perhaps by soldiers drinking themselves to oblivion, seeking out aphrodisiac pills,[28] marrying locals bigamously,[29] stealing from billets and betting all on the *Crown and Anchor* board. The soldier was quickly conditioned into the new social order by a combination of official ambivalence, the all-pervading atmosphere and by those immediately around him.

The army's official policy towards sex was looked at in a previous chapter, but understanding the soldiers' perceptions of that policy is as important. It was this that provided the framework for the development of personal attitudes. For the average soldier, the army took more than just a benign view: by tolerating brothels it colluded, promoted, and inevitably inculcated an acceptance of a behavioural norm among sections of the troops. The padres who were surveyed by Plater in 1917 were convinced that moral standards were lowered because of 'the lack of moral sense pervading the Army' and the 'vicious surroundings', especially at the base camps.[30] Dixon expressed it thus:

> I do not feel called upon to apologise … [for] the topsy-turvy world of the battlefronts, where values were totally different … in which woman is something to be used as – who first said it? – the relaxation of the warrior![31]

Trench gossip must have been responsible for all sorts of wild tales that would at the time have been perfectly credible to a soldier who genuinely believed that the army had a policy of encouraging sex, or at the least 'turning a blind eye'. Two tales in the Imperial War Museum's oral collection exemplify this. One concerns an officer reputedly given a week's special leave to 'cure' sex-starvation.[32] Another, recounted by an officer of the RAMC in 1974, is of importing girls 'of great repute' from London brothels to work in France as a remedy for 'undiagnosed psychiatric' illnesses at the instigation of a 'famous psychologist'. The latter is even more improbable given the

---

27   Graham, *Private*, p. 67.
28   IWM Sound Archive, No. 737, reel 10, Fred Dixon, trooper Surrey Yeomanry.
29   Dinesen VC, *Merry Hell!*, p. 178. Also Bird, Will R., *Ghosts Have Warm Hands: a Memoir of the Great War, 1916-1919* (Toronto: Clarke, Irwin, 1968, CEF Books edn, 2000), p. 85.
30   Plater (ed.) *Catholic Soldiers*, pp. 70-88.
31   IWM 92/36/1, Dixon, '*The Wheels of Darkness*', pp. 56-8. See also Burrage, *War is War*, p. 27.
32   IWM Sound Archive, No. 9876, Dennys.

attention this example of 'white slaving' would probably have received from social purity organisations.[33]

What is remarkable about these quotations is that, despite their total improbability, they did apparently have contemporary credibility, demonstrating the men's interpretation of the army's attitude to sex. It was a confusing time of mixed messages. Examples include men given a financial reward for a job well done and time off to spend it in well-known, vicious back areas;[34] tales of men marched by officers to the red light district as an explicit reward for battle performance;[35] stories of men handed out protective 'packets' following lectures on the dangers of venereal disease and advice to avoid women. Three soldiers were given 300 francs and a day off in Amiens as a reward for their part in the attack on Malakoff Farm: 'What an experience; never forget it', enthused Henry Rogers, Private, 2/7th Sherwood Foresters, writing of the day off rather then the attack!. Thomas Dinesen VC was in no doubt of the moral double standard being practised:

> Three times now we have been listening to long, serious lectures about VD … how the Empire expected every man to do his duty, keep his path clean and not risk health and future during these hard times. Nevertheless, the doctor knows that every man means to do exactly the reverse, and he is therefore sensible enough to supply us with the proper disinfectants, together with minute directions for their use.[36]

This training was something the men got used to throughout their army career. The VD lecture was ubiquitous; they heard it at their initial training camp, again before going out to France, and again before periods of leave. It was the same theme: if you are going to indulge, indulge carefully, 'or else'.

The assault on the individual's attitude to sexual matters was encountered on a day-to-day basis from the day of enlistment. A recruit was often introduced to the promise of women early on in his new career. Indeed, there was sometimes even an implicit suggestion of the sexual rewards to be accrued by the victorious as an inducement to enlist. A young recruit remembered that:

> In this atmosphere [crowds gathering around a well-dressed marching band] … a recruiting address was given, and on the platform some beautiful ladies who, as their part in the war effort, were prepared to give every man a kiss who joined up. This then was the path which eventually led me straight to hell itself.[37]

---

33 IWM Sound Archive, No. 378, reel 3, Maberly Squire Esler, officer RAMC.
34 IWM Sound Archive, No. 19072, Henry Rogers, Pte 2/7th Sherwood Foresters.
35 Tucker, John F., *Johnny Get Your Gun* (London: Kimber, 1978), p. 25.
36 Dinesen, *Merry Hell!*, p. 65.
37 Lofthouse, 18th DLI (Bantam), quoted in Allinson, Sidney, *The Bantams* (London: Howard Baker, 1981*)* p. 83.

There is a suggestion of this being the start of sexual adventure, and the double meaning of 'hell', implying both the fighting and the outcome of sliding morals. The promise of sex, or of being attractive to women, was exploited in a variety of other ways. If a man were brave enough he would enjoy the 'spoils'; a coward would not.[38]

On enlisting, the men found themselves in training camps where they would be inducted into military life and mores, often by regulars or by 'old soldiers' and 'dugouts'. Kipling, among others, was aware of the possible 'bad influence' that such trainers might have. On his 1915 visit to the training camps, he conversed with the training sergeants:

> 'Were they good men?' I asked.
> 'Yes. Verra good. Who's to mislead 'em?' said he.
> 'Old soldiers?'
> 'Ay, there might have been a few such in the beginning, but they'd be more useful in the Special Reserve Battalions'.[39]

In the reserve battalions, there would have been no fear of corrupting innocence, as they comprised men already well-versed in military life.

The new recruits, especially this immense mass of citizens responding to Kitchener's call, certainly learned all about sex, gambling, drink, swearing and crudity even before they had left training camp. In a letter to his wife from training camp at Aldershot, Colin C. Stanley said of a lecture that 'it was hot'.[40] Gibbs at the Woolwich training school for artillery summed his experience up as 'Bad smells, bad beer, bad women, bad language!'.[41] For Arthur Baxter, a private in the 51st Machine Gun Corps, sexual opportunity presented itself immediately outside the gates of his Bradford camp: 'We came out that night and I'll guarantee there must have been 100 women waiting, sweet, you could pick your like … because I expect their husbands must have been in the army'.[42] J. Williamson, found a similar situation at Burly training camp. Prostitutes could not be avoided: they were attracted to the barracks gate by the prospect of trade. The GOCs at Portsmouth and Plymouth, for example, were much exercised by the rate of venereal disease in their commands, the latter reporting that an 'ill lit stretch of road near the barracks and huts enabled prostitutes to solicit'.[43] Some new soldiers

38 Carrington, *Soldier*, pp. 180-2.
39 Kipling, *The New Army*, p. 12.
40 IWM 84/52/1, C. S. Stanley, 'Diary' (unpubl.); Gibbs, A. Hamilton, *Gun Fodder: the Diary of Four Years of War* (Boston: Little, Brown, c.1919. Naval & Military repr.), p. 7; IWM Sound Archive, No. 9346, reel 4, A. Baxter, Pte, 51st Machine Gun Corps.
41 Gibbs, *Gun Fodder*, p. 7.
42 Baxter, IWM Sound Archive, No.9346, reel 4. See also No. 1948, J. Williamson.
43 Beckett, p. 19, 'The Territorial Force', Beckett and Simpson (eds), *A Nation in Arms*.

were morally confused by the military mind: 'I wonder why they are allowed to hang about the streets here at the barracks at all,' mused one.[44]

Some officers took their role of training new recruits to be somewhat wider than the obligatory lecture on venereal disease. Realistic officers, like Crozier, knew that they had innocents within their charge, often straight from the classroom of the public and grammar schools, where sex education had often been confined to the dangers of masturbation:

> The Sex question played a large part in my training syllabus both of officers and men ... I was able, by arrangement with a medical officer, to ensure that every officer, N.C.O. and rifleman was instructed in sexual [sic] and had access to disinfectants after indulgence in sexual intercourse ... .[45]

Similarly, young subalterns were introduced to the ways of the world by their superiors in a more practical manner. It would have taken some strength of character for a younger man not to have followed his superior's lead, especially if the older or more senior man were the power behind arranging an 'educational' field trip. According to Powell, of the Royal Flying Corps:

> We'd get into cars and go off to local towns ... where ... most of the boys learned a lot more about life than they would have ever have done in civilian life ... we used to go to estaminets ... which I believe is called a brothel, so although they were young in years it wasn't long before they were worldly-wise men.[46]

Wheatley, writing at much the same time, tells of how an older officer (in his early 40s) led the younger officers on missions to look for women.[47]

This initial experience or education in sexual matters was not confined to England. Soldiers enlisting in Ireland, Canada and Australia were receiving similar introductions, both formally and informally.[48] And many British Territorials, ANZACs, and even the Indian Army, were also to receive an education in Egypt, an epicentre of carnal delight, before they were posted to the Western Front. For many, Cairo represented something equivalent to an immersion course in immorality with its notorious Wazir district inevitably becoming a magnet for the curious, the adventurous, the disbelieving, and in some cases the downright foolhardy. It would have been the first time that even the relatively sophisticated from Sydney and Auckland, let

---

44   Dinesen, *Merry Hell!*, p. 57.
45   Crozier, *Brass Hat*, pp. 64-7.
46   IWM Sound Archive, No. 87, reel 6, Frederick J. Powell, Officer and Chief Flying Instructor, RFC.
47   Wheatley, *Temporary Gentleman*, p. 82.
48   See Lucy, John F., *There's a Devil in the Drum* (London: Faber & Faber, 1938, Naval & Military, 1993), p. 40 for Ireland.

alone the wide-eyed farm boys from the outback, would have been exposed to such open sexual sewers. Moral innocence died here even before it died physically on the beaches of Gallipoli. The frank account of Read illustrates the universal importance of being shown the ropes by an older or more experienced soldier while in Cairo.[49] Acknowledging these experiences is important because they made the men more likely to avail themselves of opportunities when they arrived on the Western Front.

The initial assault on morals was not simply confined to the army itself. Sometimes it was billets that provided an unexpected classroom with their increased opportunities for sexual adventure. Women whose husbands and fathers had left home to join up were sometimes over-friendly with those billeted on them and the men more likely to take advantage, being away from the traditional moral and social restraints imposed by home and neighbours.[50] Hosts equally had to be wary of the young soldiers, especially if they had young daughters,[51] and not surprisingly some communities took early evasive action by 'locking up' those daughters.[52] Poor Johnny Tucker found that the inhabitants of Saffron Walden also kept their daughters out of sight; 'We hardly saw a young girl all the time we were there'.

Outside the billet environment, another danger that faced the newly uniformed soldiers in the early days of the war was the so-called 'khaki fever'. This was an epidemic reported to affect mostly very young girls, often between the ages of 13 and 16, who suddenly found the attraction of a man in uniform irresistible. Despite the relatively short-lived nature of the original manifestation of khaki fever, the soldier in uniform became something of a sex symbol among some women as the war progressed, notably those munitions factory and other female workers enjoying their sexual liberation. All in all, they added to the home front environment characterised by looser sexual behaviour.[53]

---

49 Read, I.L., *Of Those We Loved: A Narrative 1914-1919 Remembered and Illustrated* (Bishop Auckland: Pentland Press, 1994), p. 312.
50 Simkins, 'Soldiers and Civilians: billeting in Britain and France', in Beckett and Simpson (eds), *A Nation in Arms*, p. 172; and Priestley, *Margin Released*, p. 95.
51 Graves, *Goodbye,* p. 64.
52 Simkins, 'Soldiers and Civilians', p. 173 where L.Cpl Ernest Sheard is reported as recalling that the 'the Ilkley people, especially the mothers, had formed a league, its object being to keep the girls away from the soldiers'. Pte John Tucker noted: Tucker, *Johnny*, p. 17.
53 'Looser morals' on the home front are debated by Thompson, *Edwardians*, pp. 267-9 and Marwick, *The Deluge*, pp. 105-13. For a description and analysis, see Woollacott, Angela., 'Khaki Fever and its control: Gender, Class, Age and Sexual Morality on the British Home-Front in the First World War', *J. Contemporary Hist.* 29 (1994). For a wider analysis of the role of women police in controlling prostitution as well as general morals, see Levine, Philippa, "Walking the Streets in a Way No Decent Woman should": Women Police in World War One', *J. Modern Hist.* 66 (1994), pp. 34-78. See also Swanson, Chris and Smith, James, *Soldiers in East Grinstead* http://www.spartacus.schoolnet.co.uk/FWWcamps.EG.htm, accessed on 18 June 2010.

The army's moral ambiguity, and the worldly ways that recruits were learning even before embarkation to France, chipped away at moral certainties.[54] The next damaging attack on personal morals would be the language they would hear in the barrack-room, and it is difficult to over-emphasise the impact of this 'dirty talk' on many soldiers. What made it so toxic was the combination of the most commonly talked subject, sex, with the language used to describe it. Swearing, obscenities and blasphemy were the order of the day and could affect a man's longer term outlook and views[55] irrespective of rank or status: 'Their language is equal to the purest Billingsgate', noted Shaw, a front line chaplain in 1917,[56] but the rot even affected men of the cloth, 'Every one of us in the Battalion swore heartily, and even some padres'.[57]

Kitchener's volunteers – 'decent men' – were those whose daily utterances in civilian life were governed by an Edwardian propriety, in part reinforced by the social purity movements, in which language and manners 'maketh man'. While basic expletives would have been commonplace in some segments of the community, the majority both believed and feared that crossing the line to obscene talk led to a loss of sexual control and continence.[58] Guardsman Stephen Graham outlined the potentially damaging nature of the issue: 'Inevitably you say and think such things which are obscene and brutal and many go and do the sort of things they think and say'.[59] It was a slippery slope from thought to deed.

Not all found this a one-way slope. For some stronger characters perhaps its very ubiquity removed its corrupting power and some younger soldiers simply found it educational. It promoted curiosity:

> Older men … talked … openly … didn't embarrass us, made us more curious, very curious indeed … some of the blokes telling us the story of their exploits it was quite funny … It was an older man's thing … but some younger ones did … well, you'd just reached the age where you started feeling your oats a bit, you know.[60]

For some, this curiosity led directly to the brothel.[61]

---

54 Brugger, *Australians and Egypt*, p. 47.
55 Gibbons, *Roll on*, p. 18.
56 Shaw, *Jottings*, p. 19.
57 Andrews, W. L., *Haunting Years: The Commentaries of a War Territorial* (London: Hutchinson, 1930, Naval & Military repr., 2001), p. 216.
58 Bristow, *Vice and Vigilance*, pp. 200-25.
59 Graham, *Private*, p. 40; also IWM Sound Archive, No. 10168, reel 2, Donald Price, 20th and 30th Royal Fusiliers; IWM, P246, P. H. Jones, '*Diary*', 24-25 Oct.; Smith, *Four Years on the Western Front*, p. 253. Also, in literature, Hodson, James Lansdale, *Grey Dawn–Red Night* (London: Victor Gollancz, 1929), p. 148,
60 IWM Sound Archive, No.11113, Taylor.
61 Hope, *Winding Road*, p. 91.

Tilsley, Hiscock, Manning *et al.*, all had experience of the trench conversation as the confessional where men would confide in each other,[62] even intimate details of home life.[63] 'Conversation turned *inevitably* to what is now called "sex"', admitted one soldier later in his life. Another light-heartedly remembered ascribing 'this customary talk of women at breakfast, dinner and tea [as] the secret of the magnificent digestive abilities of our war-time army'. It was the sexual act, rather than sexual relationships, which was the dominant topic. 'What did we talk about? Anything and everything. Women particularly. Sole topic of conversation actually … they had a name for all the locals … "Nel, Swansea Sal"… the names the troops gave them'.[64]

The sex-laden conversations were not limited to the 'other ranks'. Artillery officer, Harry Siepmann sat disgustedly on a train listening to his fellow officers: 'There were seven officers in the compartment … the conversation started on the war in general … then the reminiscences settled down, as they nearly always do, to the shadier and more disgusting self-revelations, lasciviously exchanged'.[65]

There is no doubt that these conversations could for some be dispiriting and disgust those forced to listen. It would have been difficult to avoid them in the close confines of the military. Recounting a night in a mess, Siepmann also illustrated how, for some, such conversations were far from morale-boosting: 'They retell their more revolting stories with conscious pride, and Morgan outbids them with vulgarities from India. They are too much for me. The Mess is sometimes like a tap-room: even in working hours. And my soul sickens'.[66] Again, the point is made that it would have taken a great deal of moral courage and strength of character not to be changed by this constant drip-feeding of obscenity.

Coarse, lewd and obscene language was also the stuff of the marching song, the concert party and the estaminet sing-a-long.[67] It is important to note that their function was to remind, and to divert thoughts from other concerns. Dinesen remembered 'the best of the lot is the everlasting and ever-varying song, *Mademoiselle from Armentiers* [sic] … Our imagination pictures the continuation of the song in lusty and vivid colouring'.[68] 'Some of the songs were recherché obscene', admitted Guardsman Graham, 'I have never come across such bestiality in any language … that might make a devil's hair erect'.[69] Inevitably, there was a level of moral ambiguity involved illustrated nicely by a humorous story recounted concerning Haig's attitude to one of

---

62 Dorgeles called the trenches 'this huge confessional', cited in Ekstein, *Rites,* p. 209.
63 Tilsley, W. V., *Other Ranks* (London: Cobden Saunderson, undated), p. 18.
64 IWM Sound Archive, No. 22739, reel 2, McCormack; see also Read, *Those We Loved,* p. 333: Hope, *Winding Road,* pp. 68-9, and p. 83:
65 Siepmann, H., *Echo of the Guns* (London: Robert Hale, 1987), p. 58.
66 Ibid., p. 106; and Mark VII (pseud. Plowman, Max), *A Subaltern on the Somme* (London: J. M. Dent & Sons, 1927, Naval & Military repr., undated), p 17.
67 Edmonds, *Subaltern's War,* p. 93.
68 Dinesen, *Merry Hell!,* p. 103.
69 Graham, *Private in the Guards,* p. 40.

the more popular yet vulgar marching songs, *Do yer balls hang low?* 'I like the tune, he said, but you must know that in any circumstances the words are inexcusable!'.[70]

Tilsley quotes the lyrics to another where the last line would have been especially pertinent. The traditional elements of English folk song with the chorus, 'Iddy I-ay, Iddy I-ay, Iddy I-ay' and the subject 'Riley's daughter', made more relevant to time and place with the lines, 'I'd like to kiss old Riley's daughter … Jig-a-jig-jig *très bon*!'[71] Since the songs were often a parody of popular ones back home, perhaps their corrupted lyrics can be taken as a rejection of old attitudes. It might be argued, too, that the words such as those of Tilsley's sergeant, were an unguarded projection of inner thoughts, and as such provide more evidence of the attitudes commanding the trenches: 'Sergeant Orrell came along humming to the tune of "God send you back to me", "God send a WAAC to me!"'.[72]

Once the initial moral affront of obscenity in conversation and songs wore off they undoubtedly had a positive impact on morale. Not only did they help men get through arduous marches but helped them recover sanity when they came out of the line. However, spontaneity was the key. Forced repetition of crude songs could meet with the same rejection that was earlier noted when men were forced marched to a brothel as Burrage remembered:

> He [an officer] was foul-mouthed and used to encourage the men to sing smutty songs on the march because I suppose he thought it promoted high spirits. I was no prude and liked singing them myself when the spirit moved me, but I objected to organized obscenity.[73]

The talk and songs needed to be seen as a gentle challenge to authority, not owned by it.

Jokes functioned in the same way. They diverted a man's mind both from home and from the rigours of army, temporarily boosting his morale and in some way providing an alternative to sex. Coppard and Carrington both bear testimony to this: 'It is appropriate to mention here that the telling of risqué stories was an important feature of trench life',[74] in that 'a compensation was found for sex-starvation in the recourse to bawdy jokes and rhymes, of which there was a never-failing supply'.[75] Like so many aspects of army life, however, the inherent moral ambiguities were always present. For infantry officer Douie, sheltering in a dugout during a barrage, the silence in which men were quietly and inwardly praying was broken 'appropriately by the padre,

---

70 See Macdonald, *Somme* (London: Michael Joseph, 1983, repr., 1993), pp. 206-08.
71 Tilsley, *Other Ranks*, p. 121.
72 Ibid. p. 18.
73 Burrage, *War is War*, p. 200
74 Coppard, *Machine Gun*, p. 87.
75 Carrington, *Soldier*, p. 184.

who, in a manner devoid of all concern, commenced a story which to my regret, I feel unable to place on record'.[76]

Sometimes, in the sexually charged environment, it was news from home that could push a man over the edge, and a soldier's attitude and behaviour might be affected by news of a wife or girlfriend's infidelities, real or imagined.[77] Marriages broke up under the strain of war and 'married men [who'd] lost their wives and that sort of thing ... were absolutely terrific just for women', witnessed Private Shuttleworth while serving as pensions and allowances clerk.[78]

Boredom, too, might lead the man to stray. 'So frightful is boredom that men were tempted to take to drink, to look around for unattached women, to gamble at cards', reported Philip Gibbs.[79] Eventually, perhaps it was simply a question how long rather than whether a man could hang on to his principles. The longer a man served and the more he was exposed to the insidious influences, the more desensitised he became and the greater the likelihood of his accepting the inevitability of it all. A sense of predestination forged in many men the sense that 'you only live once, so live for today'. Sherwood Eddy, an American Protestant missionary and secretary of the American YMCA, was in no doubt that time had an attritional effect:

> At the beginning of the war in 1914 there was talk of a religious revival in the various countries. The churches for a time were filled. The opening of the war drove men to God. With the passing months, which have now dragged into years, many of the high ideals have gradually been lowered or lost.[80]

His comments applied as much to the Tommy as to the Doughboy of the American Expeditionary Forces (AEF). As one soldier put it: 'Tomorrow we may be dead. The world is shot to pieces. Nothing matters. There are no ten commandments. Let 'er go!'.[81] It was noted later by Fischer and Dubois from a more civilian angle that 'self-control is not only weakened but almost completely eliminated, perhaps on the account of the subconscious thought, logical enough when death is omnipresent, that "tomorrow may be too late"'.[82]

---

76 Douie, Charles *The Weary Road* (London: John Murray, 1929, Naval & Military repr., 2001), p. 116.
77 IWM Sound Archive, No. 4228, Shuttleworth, Pte. F.; Taylor, *The Bottom of the Barrel*, p. 93, and IWM Sound Archive, No. 22745, Ted Rimmer, Pte South Lancs Regt, for reactions to 'Dear John' letters.
78 IWM Sound Archive, No. 10615, Sidney Taylor, Pte 250 Coy, RFA.
79 Gibbs, P., *Realities of War* I (2 vols, London: W. Heinemann, 1920, repr., 1938), p. 129.
80 Eddy, *With Our Soldiers*, p. 62
81 Harrison, Charles, Yale, *Generals Die in Bed*, (London: William Morrow, 1930, repr. Annick 2002), p. 93.
82 Fischer and Dubois, *Sexual Life*, p. 57.

I. L. Read found himself in a miner's home doubling as estaminet and a billet outside Vermelles in 1916. He and his two fellow soldiers were soon in romantic relationships with three French refugees from Lens who were helping in the estaminet: 'So started the first of what, in latter days, we used to designate 'the better nights' – a night which compensated us for all the mud of the Hohenzollern: much more than that – a night such as I had vaguely pictured ... I told our colonel that I didn't want to die just then, as I hadn't started to live – in the fullest sense of the word'. Here was the realisation it seemed of a legitimate youthful longing rudely interrupted and stifled by more than two years of war.[83]

Such feelings pervade memoirs, diaries and oral records.[84] A philosophy of *carpe diem* overrode moral concerns: 'Damn it, you're men, aren't you? Let's be merry while we can; who knows the next time we go up the line we may all go sky-high!'.[85] The feeling could not be put more cogently than by the RFA driver, Lawson: 'When you knew you might be killed the next day you didn't have any compunction'.[86] Lord Moran, in his classic account of courage, admitted that the feeling was universal, leading to a loss of self-control; 'Many officers on leave came to think they were entitled to a degree of licence they had not dreamed of taking before they went to France. This was their last chance to get something out of life while it lasted'. In terms of morals, 'most men just relaxed the discipline of their own lives'.[87]

One all-pervasive factor influencing behaviour of every kind was the consumption of alcohol. In this army alcohol had many uses: as a warmer at dawn stand-to; as a provider of pre-attack 'Dutch courage'; to increase aggressiveness; for parties and celebrations in well-stocked officers' messes and dugouts; and even as a 'recreational drug' for the rank and file – if they could afford it. There can be little doubt that the consumption of alcohol led to the overcoming of individual inhibitions and, if taken to excess, to the loss of personal control. 'For a soldier the taboos [affecting courtship and sex] no longer existed,' found Carrington: 'Nothing prevented an approach to the other world of the women who "did", except a fastidious timidity'.[88] Alcohol certainly helped overcome that timidity.

Amongst the few 'surveys' carried out on the Western Front this, by the American YMCA, is most instructive:

---

83   Read, I.L., *Those We Loved*, pp. 234-7.
84   Hope, *Winding Road*, p. 17; Douie, *Weary Road*, p. 219; Marks, T. Penrose, *The Laughter Goes from Life: In the trenches of the First World War* (London: Kimber, 1977), p. 75; Plowman, *Subaltern*, pp. 208-9. For fictional accounts see also Blaker, Richard, *Medal Without Bar* (London: Hodder & Stoughton, 1930); Bennett, Arnold, *Pretty Lady* (London: Cassell and Co. 1918), p. 14, and most powerfully, Williamson, Henry, *The Patriot's Progress* (London: Geoffrey Bles, 1930, Sphere reprint), pp. 134-35.
85   Hope, *Winding Road*, p. 91.
86   IWM Sound Archive, No. 24882, reel 2, Lawson.
87   Moran, Wilson C., *The Anatomy of Courage*, p. 53. See also Wheatley, *Temporary Gentleman*, p. 153.
88   Carrington, *Soldier*, pp. 180-2.

Among the men in the venereal hospitals of France are musicians, artists, teachers, educated and refined boys from some of the best homes, and in another camp we find several hundred officers and several members of the nobility. What was the cause of their downfall? A questionnaire replied to by several hundred of them revealed the fact that six per cent attributed their downfall to curiosity, ten per cent to ignorance, claiming that they had never been adequately warned by the medical authorities, 13 per cent to loss of home influences and lack of leave, 33 per cent to drink and the loss of self-control due to intoxication, while the largest number of all, or 38 per cent, attributed it to uncontrolled passion when they were unconverted or had no higher power in their lives to enable them to withstand temptation.[89]

Leaving aside the happy coincidence of the YMCA finding a lack of religion being a factor, drink is blamed for a third of moral lapses.

While there is no record of an equivalent survey conducted amongst British troops, qualitative evidence demonstrates that alcohol undoubtedly went hand-in-hand with the potential slide in moral behaviour. Not many men had taken the pledge, though there were exceptions. Drink was the main escape route from both the daily horror and the boredom, but it was also the handmaiden of venal sex and was served in both estaminets and brothels. Where there was drink, there were women. Its effects were known to the men, to the women – who were encouraged by their employers to get the men to drink – to the politicians who made the laws, and to the army.

In 1915, François Dulom had opened his study of prostitution in France, 'La Prostitution dans les Débits', with this poem about the estaminet:

Chez les débitants de liqueurs et de bière
Que l'on peut voir danser avec la garnison
Ces fameuses catins à la vie ordinaire
Qui sont de notre armée un terrible poison.[90]

Alcohol created an atmosphere that encouraged prostitution, 'poisoned' soldiers and threatened to undermine the 'physical, material and moral health of the society'. By enabling soldiers to meet prostitutes, bars and cafes were 'even more contrary to military discipline than to the health of the troops'. Dulom asked the state to punish those 'who provide asylum to women leading a bad life', or who are reputed to do so, and by implication the owners of the bars.[91] Despite anxieties, and some *ad hoc* attempts to

---

89   Eddy, *With our Soldiers*, ch. VI.
90   'It's the home of dealers of liquors and beers/That one can see dancing with the garrison/The famous harlots of everyday life/Who are a terrible poison for the army', cited in Corbin, *Women for Hire: Prostitution and Sexuality*, p. 331 and in Grayzel, 'Mothers, Marraines, and Prostitutes, p. 77.
91   Ibid.

restrict drink sales to certain times in the regulated brothels, it was not until October 1917 that prostitutes were forbidden by law to enter bars and cafes, and the formal link between alcohol and prostitution was challenged.

Perhaps the final key to the question of what led to attitude change was the wider geographic and cultural context in which the soldier found himself. France was patently not England, nor was it Canada or Australia, nor India. The soldiers found themselves in a different cultural milieu (to be discussed in a following chapter), where, when outside of the narrow confines of the day-to-day army existence, opportunity presented itself in a way it never had at home and a man was exposed to a greater range of sexual temptations.[92]

Despite the pressures exerted by their environment, there were inevitably a significant percentage of men who did not visit prostitutes, have local liaisons either in France or while on leave, or consume pornography. Many men held on to their pre-war beliefs despite the onslaught of circumstance. So what then were the factors that held a man back?

Sometimes simple moral repugnance or naivety were decisive, as these two soldier recalled: 'I don't know whether I should record it … we were out at Béthune and I do remember being horrified to see a queue outside as if it was a cinema … I wasn't of an age … I thought it a rather disgusting thing'.[93] Another soldier added, 'I'd never been into one of those … seeing [someone like] your father queuing up … well, gor [sic] blimey!'[94] On occasions, the repugnance was not moral but based on physical revulsion either of the woman, the place of work, or other aspects of the situation. John Cordy simply found it distasteful to be involved with the same woman as his colleagues.[95]

Soldiers, conscious of their desires, were also wont to believe that the army somehow controlled them. Tea being laced with all sorts of concoctions such as bromide to keep sexual desires under control was one myth.[96] But a shortage or absence of women near the line would certainly have thwarted temptation and, similarly, limited free time would have restricted both fraternisation and brothel visits. There were also those too young to have any experience in the arts of courtship and seduction, others consciously wishing to remain chaste.[97] Without doubt, there were those young and emotionally immature boys who had yet to discover sex as an alternative to football or other boyish interests. Some too, had not left their homoerotic public school-days

---

92   Hankey, *Student in Arms*, p. 58: 'immorality is rife. There is more abroad than at home'.
93   IWM Sound Archive, No. 9552, reel 13, Farrer, Basil
94   IWM Sound Archive, No. 11029, Bretton, Harry RFA, Pte.
95   Saint-Mandé, *War, Wine and Women* (1931, repr., 2003), p. 313. Tilsley, *Other Ranks*, p. 264. IWM 86/30/1, Cordy, John, '*My Memories*', unpaginated.
96   Taylor, *Bottom of the Barrel*, p. 112. Also a letter (by L. H. Field), quoted in Coppard, *Machine Gun*, appendix; and similar suspicions, see Tilsley, *Other Ranks*, p. 19.
97   IWM 87/51/1, Will H. Bowyer, 'Letters' to his girlfriend Dorothy claimed war 'delayed his maturity'; other examples, Graves, *Goodbye*, p. 151; and Dinesen, *Merry Hell!*, p. 185.

Perils of War—and of Popularity
Old Bill wishes now that he had never gone into that café on the Boulevard des Italiennes

Out of the line, and especially in the back areas, soldiers had few problems in meeting women. In fact, it was often the case of 'fighting them off'. (Courtesy Mark Warby. ©2015 Estate of Barbara Bruce Littlejohn)

behind, whilst others preferred male companionship.[98] Some were simply too tired to take advantage of a situation and preferred to sleep.[99] There were also those for whom the very act of war was the opposite of an aphrodisiac, and those who suppressed, or even sublimated, their desires.

The greatest barrier, however, was fear of catching a sexually transmitted disease. This encompassed fears relating to health, punishment and social shame, ingrained moral repugnance, the strength of the bond with a wife or sweetheart, and the moral protection of a peer group. The army and civilian educators did a superb job when it came to terrifying the individual over the likely consequences of sex with 'dirty' women.[100] As previously noted, lectures were frequent, their content graphic, and their message unambiguous. VD was a horrible disease causing long-term health problems.

---

98 A view partially fostered by Fussell, Paul, *The Great War and Modern Memory* (Oxford: OUP, 1975), ch. VIII, especially pp. 272-79. See also Parker, Peter, *Ackerley: The Life of J. R. Ackerley* (New York: Farrar, Straus, Giroux, 1989), p. 21.
99 IWM 88/27/1, McKechnie, 'Reminiscences'.
100 Cloete, *Victorian Son*, p. 207.

The Road to Hell: From morals to morale 119

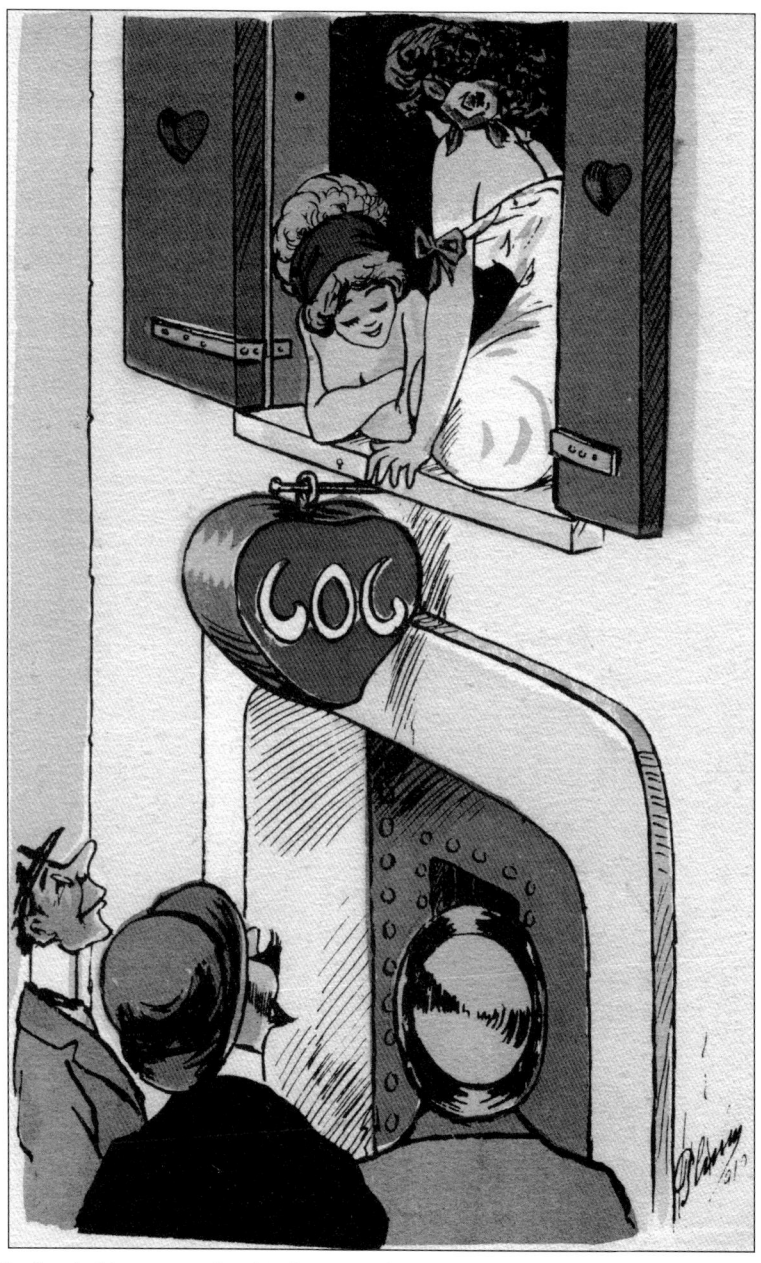

The brothel house number '606' was a coded message with the number referring to 'compound 606', a drug called salvarsan, developed in the early 1900s to treat syphilis. The number identified a 'safe' house. In reality, the girls were forbidden to show themselves at the windows. (Postcard courtesy: Stephen Likosky collection)

Even when the army (and the politicians) eventually accepted the requirement for introducing prophylactic precautions, and even after the Salvarsan cure for syphilis became known, fear was still relied upon as the main weapon. 'I never went in [to a brothel] other than the once as I was so scared of VD … the very thought of it terrified me!' admitted infantry NCO Lane. [101] In fact, 'most people were frightened of it'.[102] Conversely, however, the army appeared to have a done a good job of convincing some that the regulated brothels were safe. In so doing, it removed barriers to their use.[103]

Other men were warned off, having come into direct contact with sufferers and recoiling from the impact of the disease.[104] For F. A. J. Taylor, who served in the RFC, 19th City of London Regiment (St. Pancras Rifles) and the 2nd Worcestershire Regiment, a residue of civilian morality, and the fear of VD he had seen close up, kept him faithful to his girl at home, at least initially:

> Amongst the female staff at the hotel was a very pretty waitress … I nearly lost my virginity amongst the sand dunes but I was saved by my puritanical inhibitions and the fear of sex put into me by my guard duty at the VD hospital at Chiseldon.[105]

Even those prepared to risk disease through contacts with 'amateurs', were scared of the social opprobrium. There was no hiding from the general disgrace, whether as a member of the rank and file or an officer, with T.H. Brown of the Kings Own Liverpool Regiment confirming that 'it was looked down on, once you got that VD', and Stagg adding that 'you wouldn't be liked [having VD]'. But the physical punishments wielded by the military on the rank and file were often the greater deterrent and the social injustice was still heartfelt by soldiers like John Henry Boon nearly 70-years later: 'If a man met a foul woman … his wife's pay and subsistence was stopped and she was destitute … can you imagine anything more dastardly.[106]

Donald Hankey, writing in 1916, recognised the link between boredom and immorality and the importance of providing alternative pursuits for the men. He proselytised for the YMCA but nevertheless saw several other factors as being important in the battle to keep morale high:

---

101 IWM Sound Archive, No. 22739, McCormack. Also No. 24546, Brown, T. H., Pte 18th King's Liverpool Regt: 'We had a big lecture by the medical men before we left it didn't really worry us very much as your mind was set on avoiding danger' and No. 568, reel 3, McIndoe, Thomas Walter, 12th Middlesex Regt.
102 IWM Sound Archive, No. 7257, Lane, C. J., NCO 7th Bn Bedford Regt..
103 IWM Sound Archive, No. 6678, Alban; No. 9544, Bromley, NCO Army Service Corps; No. 24539.
104 IWM Sound Archive No. 10168, Price, D. 20th and 30th Royal Fusiliers.
105 Taylor, *Bottom of the Barrel*, p. 155.
106 IWM Sound Archive, No. 9476, reel 4, Boon, John Henry, air mechanic HQ Fienvillers Chateau. See also No. 17 24546, Brown. And No. 8764, Stagg.

> Let us be frank about this. What a doctor might call the 'appetites', and a padre the 'lusts' of the body, hold dominion over the average man, whether civilian or soldier, unless they are counteracted by a stronger power ... These are the four powers which are stronger than 'the flesh' – the zest of a quest, religion, hero-worship, and the love of a good woman. If a man is not possessed by one of these he will be immoral ... The moral of this is, double your subscriptions to the YMCA, Church huts, soldiers' clubs, or whatever organisation you fancy![107]

Some men were protected from 'contact' by Hankey's 'hero'. These might occasionally be padres but were more often the fatherly, older NCOs, or members of a peer group who gave tacit support. This was certainly the case with the young Private Sidney Taylor: 'the man in charge of us, our corporal [was] an ex-naval man, and he knew the ways of the world and he kept a very strict eye on us and he would not allow anything and we didn't know what a red lamp was'.[108] Sometimes, however, the warning was more explicit; 'If you wanted a woman go to the red lamp where they were looked after, don't take the ordinary prostitute', was advice Taylor remembered receiving from his sergeant.[109] Private Gordon Davis of the Royal Fusiliers was lucky; he survived the war along with four friends from home. This enabled them to offer each other continued protection and support particularly in avoiding the temptations of easy vice.[110]

Hankey observed that love and respect for someone at home was an important factor in keeping many men on the straight and narrow. Marriage was seen as a tie that bound.[111] As Subaltern Hamilton Gibbs found, a loved one could be an inspiration; 'we clung to our chastity because of one woman with us every hour in our hearts whom we meant to marry if ever we came out of this hell'.[112] And for some men, like Tom Bromley, a N.C.O in the Army Service Corps, this meant sticking to conventions regarding pre-marital sex, 'I thought that if I had expected my wife to be a virgin when I married her, she should expect the same as me'.[113]

Understandably, someone with Hankey's perspective on life would not immediately see it, but, while some men would never be prepared to pay,[114] for others, the lack of money and inability to pay was a strong influence in keeping them moral. Conversely, if British soldiers had had more money, then those indulging might have done so more often, as Private Hill of the Rifle Brigade tacitly admitted: 'What it cost us? About

---

107 Hankey, *Student in Arms*, pp. 58-60.
108 IWM Sound Archive, No. 9476, reel 4, Boon.
109 IWM Sound Archive, No. 10615, Taylor.
110 IWM Sound Archive, No. 9343, reel 2, Davies.
111 IWM Sound Archive, No. 6678, reel 2, Alban. IWM 82/3/1, Mudd, 'Letters to Wife', unpaginated.
112 Gibbs, *Gun Fodder*, p. 144.
113 IWM Sound Archive, No. 9544, Bromley.
114 Cloete, *Victorian Son*, p. 207.

5 francs, I think. Of course we were all young, no responsibilities. Nobody to worry about. It was nice to have a night out … but you couldn't have many nights out on seven bob a week!'[115] Read remembered going 'down to Rouen' where they 'sampled the flesh-pots as thoroughly as we could … until funds ran low again'.[116]

Ironically, for some, looking back in old age, it was a great regret that lack of money had denied them opportunity, 'I've never been in one, and I can say with my hand on my heart, I wish I had now' admitted one old soldier.[117] It is interesting, too, that many of the younger, single men, whom one might assume to have been the most active sexually, and the least worried about disease or social concerns, thought that sex was for older or perhaps married men only. It seems that pre-marital rather than extra-marital sex was the concern for artilleryman Taylor: 'Now me and my brother weren't married so it didn't enter our minds'.[118]

The majority of Edwardian civilians were morally 'decent' on first entering the army, or at least professed to be such. However, the evidence of actual behaviour during the war illustrates that moral attitudes changed as a result of the environmental factors they encountered, and the ways in which the individual processed and internalised those new experiences.

The new 'amateur' soldier faced a corrosive moral environment from almost the day of his enlistment. Traditional bulwarks to upholding his civilian morality, were for many and to all practical purposes *in absentia*. The army itself sent out conflicting and ambiguous messages as to what was and was not acceptable in terms of appropriate behaviour. While some men did manage to adhere to a set of principles that had defined a civilian existence, or at least retain an element of them, many more found it hard to resist the range of factors that conspired to erode a man's pre-war manners and morals. Chief amongst these was alcohol, but general coarseness of language, peer group influence, the easy availability of sex, a *'carpe diem'* mentality and simple boredom all played a role to a greater or lesser extent. If there was one factor that promoted sexual continence it was the fear of catching venereal disease but even that fear was undermined by the existence of the red lamp with its apparent army seal of approval.

In the final analysis, the British soldier faced the harshest wartime conditions. Amidst the constant death and destruction that surrounded him is it no surprise that past moral certainties gave way to a 'live for now' philosophy in the constant fight to sustain morale. For many the final truth was that:

---

115 IWM Sound Archive, No. 24539, reel 2, Hill; No. 9418, Ashby, John, Pte 2nd and 5th Battalion; No. 9431, reel 5, Grunwell, George, Pte West Yorks Regt.
116 Read, *Of Those We Loved*, p. 337.
117 IWM Sound Archive No. 11113, Taylor. Similar sentiments are to be found in No. 10115, Bigwood; No. 11581, reel 13, Hopthrow, Harry, NCO Signals; No. 10168, Price.
118 IWM Sound Archive No. 10615, Taylor.

doubtless when a man has died in battle it does not matter whether he knew who Shakespeare was or whether he was a customer of the woman who lurketh at the corner. He is sped … .

Given this, many understandably emulated Guardsman Graham's approach that it was 'to hell with it and the Devil take the hindmost!'[119]

---

119 Graham, *Private*, p. 171.

6

'Volez vous couches avec moi?':
Fraternisation with the local population

Siege warfare meant that the soldier was often living side-by-side with local people for an extended time. He slept and rested in billets found amongst the civilian population, was entertained in local cafes and shopped in local towns and villages. Inevitably, this meant coming into contact with local women, and offered the possibility of relationships developing, sometimes leading to romance or to sexual activity that did not cost him financially, at least not directly.[1]

It was these encounters, where the hand of the fair maid was won without recourse to obvious payment, and took more of the form of friendship (sexual or otherwise), that not only presented the least challenge to morals but also had a greater impact on morale.

We are faced with one great challenge when reading soldier accounts of fraternisation; discriminating between relationships that were truly freely formed between soldiers and the local populace, and those that were in reality forced or of a pecuniary nature. In war zones, or in situations where the local economy is dislocated, where women have to trade their bodies as there is little else to trade or where there is no work to be had, prostitution becomes a semantic term.[2] The lives of the women investigated by the journalist Philip Gibbs in towns and villages newly liberated from the Germans were no different from those of the women trying to survive on the allies' side, employing the same survival techniques:

---

1   A detailed account of the wider relationship between troops and civilians can be found in Gibson, K. Craig, *Behind the Front: British Soldiers and French Civilians, 1914-1918 (Studies in the Social and Cultural History of Modern Warfare)* (Cambridge: Cambridge University Press, 2014).
2   Flexner, A., *Prostitution in Europe: The Regulation of Prostitution in Europe* (New York: American Social Hygiene Association, 1915), p. 12. See also Rhoades, Michelle, '"There are No Safe Women": Prostitution in France during the Great War', *Proceedings of the Western Society for French History* 27 (1999).

Fraternisation with the local population 125

It is a long way to "Scheveningen"

"Cross-Fire"

Tommy's continental amours were the subject of comic speculation as these postcards illustrate. These were probably produced post-war for purchase by day-trippers to Ostend and depict the 'plight' of interned British soldiers (from the Naval Brigade sent to Antwerp in 1914). Note the play on 'It's a long way to Tipperary'! (Courtesy: Anthony Gracier collection)

[the German occupiers] had not misused the women ... But many women shrugged their shoulders when I questioned them about this, and said, 'They no need to use violence in their way of love-making. There were many volunteers'. They rubbed their thumbs and fingers together as though touching money, and said 'you understand?'.[3]

In strict terms perhaps, the female who, rather than accept direct payment, exchanges sex for a tin of bully beef is a prostitute, as is the maid in a Paris leave hotel described as giving supplementary services for higher tips. Farm girls too might supplement their meagre wages with the occasional sex-for-money exchange. But many women must have been 'amateurs' indulging in 'wayside promiscuity'. That is, women who would not have considered themselves as prostitutes at all but who would occasionally accept money, souvenirs, nights out and food in return for favours. They may even have regarded the men as 'temporary boyfriends'. Percy Clare, a private in the 7th East Surrey Regiment, had no doubts that there was a definite distinction between the hardened prostitute of the towns and the girls that the soldiers found in the villages behind their lines. These girls had very mixed motives, including genuine sympathy and probably liking for the men they gave themselves to. It is obvious that even if there was a commercial transaction, the girls did not define themselves as prostitutes, and, perhaps more importantly from the consideration of morale, they were not considered as such by the men. Clare's comments are revealing because he was himself not 'a customer', believing in marital fidelity. His views have an objectivity where those of others might be considered self-justifying:

> Although a girl would always yield her body to our boys, she did not do so solely and only for money or other gain; there was a certain strange sympathy with, and response to, the need of our own men away from their wives for years at a time and 'women-starved' for months. At any rate whatever her motives she did not like to be handled roughly or disrespectfully and have it rubbed in that she was paid. There was all the difference between these French peasant girls and women and the prostitutes of the towns. Whatever these girls were, and they were just natural, simple minded, affectionate or good-natured creatures generally, they were most emphatically not prostitutes.[4]

The town girls described by Cloete who were 'suspended in the limbo of war', and went with officers in return for the things they could not afford to buy themselves, should also be considered in the same light.[5] There were, however, women whose motives were more biased towards the strictly mercenary. Patently, differentiating fraternisa-

---

3   Gibbs, *Realities of War*, p. 416.
4   IWM 06/48/1, Clare, Percy, '*Reminiscences,* 1916-1918', unpaginated, book three.
5   Cloete, S, *How Young they Died*, p. 55.

tion from prostitution becomes easier where there was a quoted tariff, or where the initial meeting place was one favoured by the professional prostitute. In unpublished letters in the IWM, Butlin wrote to a friend in England of a sexual adventure:[6]

> 29.01.17 (6th Dorset Reg. France)
> On Sunday I went into Rouen … The place was absolutely chock full of girls some pretty, some pretty awful. I saw one in particular about 6.30 pm who was most awfully pretty and looked different from the painted type with which we are all familiar … on the next day I had a pretty good time and took her to Rouen for dinner … Her name is Jubilette and she is only eighteen … By this time I got to know her pretty well and was very much in love with her. I went by invitation to her house last night at 8 o'clock and stayed with her till 7 o'clock this morning …

The early part of this letter suggests he may well have been in a café known for prostitutes, that is, the 'painted type with which we are all familiar'. She also patently lives in her own house or apartment, possibly unusual for a girl of just eighteen unless a prostitute. However, his later proclamations of love and his gushing description suggest she may not have been – although men have, of course, been known to fall as heavily for a 'harlot' as the girl next door. This ambiguity, however, presents the historian with a problem. One has to weigh up the likelihood from the account given whether the sexual 'adventure' was genuinely fraternisation or was in reality paid for sex, even if not explicitly described as such.

Determining the writer's veracity demands appreciation of the context, not only of the incident itself and where it occurred, but relating it to the moral climate that existed on the Western Front. Tozer, for example, suggests that as prostitutes were very largely recruited from 'amongst maidservants, certainly in the towns; in the country there is so much free love that prostitution for payment is much less common'.[7] In the following much bowdlerised account written by the Welshman, Frank Richards, the girls were probably exchanging favours in return for a good night out. This assumption is based on Richards character as he does not shirk from admitting the use of prostitutes elsewhere:

> The RSM's batman invited me to spend an enjoyable evening … [with] two charming young ladies who were refugees from one of the villages closer to the line … I spent one of the most enjoyable nights that I ever spent in France. It hadn't cost Nutty a cent.[8]

---

6   IWM 67/52/1, Butlin, J. H., letter collection.
7   Tozer, *Terrible Life*, p. 143.
8   Richards, *Old Soldiers*, p. 98.

The nature of 'the two young ladies who we picked up' on another escapade is more ambiguous, as no consideration for services is mentioned. Richards describes how they 'proved true daughters of France', and one can infer from Richards' general stories that a pecuniary aspect to their amorous nature accorded them this epithet.[9]

In the following episode the key to accepting there was no monetary exchange lies in understanding the moral climate of the time, the restrained description of the episode, the absence of other episodes in the same source, and the soldier's own incredulity. This Field Artillery gunner, intent on visiting Amiens Cathedral, was waylaid by a young girl who invited him into her house to meet the rest of the family and enjoy coffee and cognac:

> We had been there quite some time when the young woman took my hand and beckoned me upstairs. Off I went innocently into her bedroom where she started to undress. I was, of course, a little discomforted but not too drunk to know what was expected of me. I enjoyed my first woman and lost my virginity. I will never understand why it happened but I shall never regret it.[10]

The soldier does not disguise his joy over this unambiguously morale-boosting incident.

A further complication, or ambiguity, arises out of the fact that a woman might be a prostitute on one occasion, but give herself in a non-mercenary way on another. A story recounted by an Australian soldier, W. H. Downing, in a biography otherwise devoid of sexual reference tells of two serving girls from an estaminet patently treating officers as 'work' while he and a companion, both other ranks, as boyfriends. Interestingly, in this instance, the soldiers' morale is boosted not by the conquest *per se*, but by the undisguised joy of feeling they have 'got one over' on some officers.[11]

It might be argued that a good definition of what constituted prostitution would be that given by the soldiers themselves. Certainly, use of the pejorative 'whore' tends to place the woman described as such being in the realm of the 'vicious' or hardened prostitute, rather than of the casual or occasional type. Use of this descriptor may also provide an indication of the individual soldier's view of prostitution. It might be morally acceptable to exchange a meal, or even the proverbial tin of bully beef for sexual favours, this being viewed as 'fraternisation' in its widest sense, but beyond the pale if it involved a straight monetary transaction.

Whatever, discriminating between the self-defined prostitute, the girl who offered sex in exchange for some kind of remuneration, and those who offered it freely, whether out of sympathy of the soldier or to satisfy their own sexual needs, is difficult. This

---

9   Ibid., p. 13.
10 W. J. M. Gnr., RFA mss recollection, PHL Archives, cited in Liddle, Peter H., *The Soldier's War, 1914-1918* (Dorset: Blandford Press, 1988).
11 Downing, W. H., *To The Last Ridge* (London: Grub Street, 2002), pp. 150, 154.

Fraternisation with the local population 129

The shared attraction between soldier and locals is satirised in this *La Vie Parisienne* cover illustration entitled 'L'Entente Cordiale', and equally celebrated in a widely-sold postcard. (Author's collection)

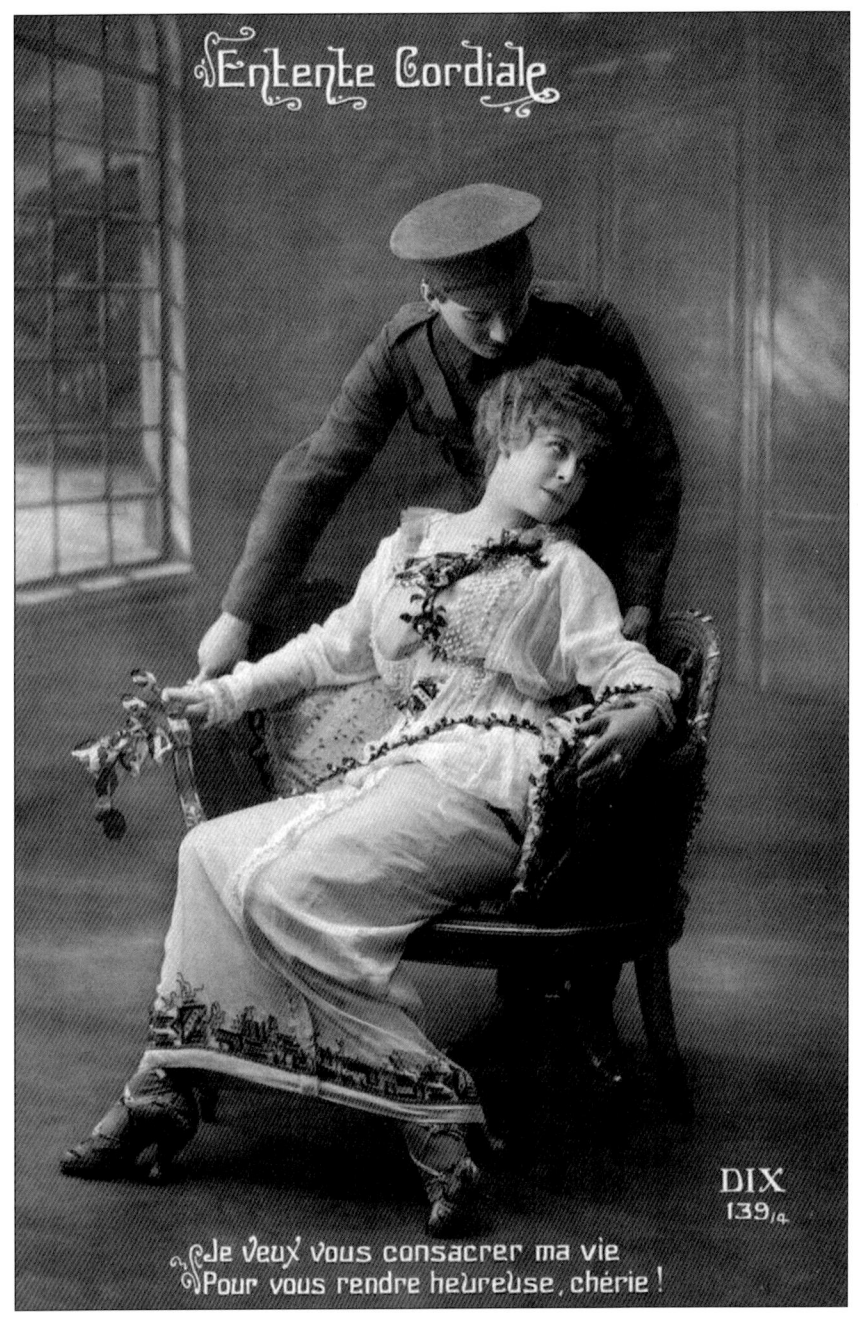

'I want to devote my life to you to make you happy, dear'. Seductive words that could be attributable to either or both parties. (Author's collection)

is not only a problem facing the modern historian but also one that regularly faced the soldier as Carrol Cairstairs illustrates, recounting his disappointment in finding a woman he assumes to be genuinely flirting is for sale; 'I saw a very pretty girl near the cathedral. One did not expect to "pick-up" someone so early in the morning – that kind was not about'. She gave him an address but when he went there later discovered it is was an unregistered brothel, 'I remonstrated with her. She was a different class.' Her excuse must have been one offered by many in those times: 'Voyons, Monsieur, il faut gagner de l'argent lors qu'on peut'.[12]

This tale of disappointment not only argues for the fact that 'picking up' appears to have been a fairly regular occurrence – if not at that time of day – but further illustrates that seduction rather than payment was more meaningful in boosting morale.

There can be no doubt that relatively easy fraternisation between soldier and civilian was anticipated by the authorities. Lord Kitchener's famed and often quoted message reminded every soldier who crossed to France that:

> In this new experience you may find temptations both in wine and women. You must should avoid any intimacy.[13]

The advice was regarded with a certain amount of cynicism by the recipients, with many men eagerly anticipating the opportunities they might find for carnal adventure. Pre-war stereotypes created fantasies, not only of Paris as a sort of 'gigantic brothel where women wore nothing but underwear and extra-long silk stockings',[14] but in general of a 'different system of taboos about sex'.[15] In reality, however, even for those with an interest in sexual conquest, the opportunities for achieving it were bound to be challenging across the disrupted 'zones of occupation'[16], with usual 'life as normal' activities constrained by military regulation, the business of fighting, and the demographic imbalance.[17] Certainly, as the war dragged on and became increasingly more destructive, a picture emerges of front line regions often devoid of women. It is not unusual to find men writing of being so estranged that when they did come back

---

12 Carstairs, Carroll, *A Generation Missing* (London: W. Heinemann, 1930, Stevenage: Strong Oak repr., 1989), pp. 161-62.
13 George, *Life of Lord Kitchener*, Vol. III, p. 27.
14 Boyack, *Behind the Lines*, p. 125.
15 Lewis, Cecil *Sagittarius Rising* (London: Peter Davies, 1936; Harmondsworth: Penguin Classics reprint edition 2014), p. 74.
16 Contemporary descriptions are of abandoned villages by the thousand; Young, R. J. (ed), *Under Siege: Portraits of Civilian Life in France during World War I* (Oxford: Berghahn Books: 2000), pp. 92, 104.
17 Fraser, Donald *The Journal of Private Fraser, 1914-1918*, ed. R. H. Roy (Victoria, B.C: Sono Nis, 1985, CEF Books repr.,1998), p. 190. In Bollezeele (Northern France). Carrington, p. 186.

into contact with women they found them almost alien; W.L. Andrews thought their high-pitched voices reminded him of 'screaming monkeys'.[18]

Where there were women, there were practical brakes on fraternisation, such as the lack of free time in which to indulge in sex. This could especially be the case for those unlucky segments of the 'poor bloody infantry', whose battalions were more regularly rotated to the front line than others. But even when out of the line, nominally 'resting', all troops were kept busy with training, route marches, miscellaneous labouring tasks or sporting activities designed to keep them fit and distracted. As a Leicester infantryman noted:

> The phrase 'six day's rest' was really a snare and delusion. In the imagination … one had visions of binges in Baileul, razzles in Reninghelst, and perchance passion in Poperinghe. But in reality 'six day's rest' was an entirely different affair.[19]

His alliterative skills are poetic reminders of the soldier's traditional and timeless love of wine and women. But more prosaically he goes on to describe 'rest' as comprised of parades, working parties and drill. Some biographies even suggest that fatigues during rest were specifically designed as a barrier to fraternisation though the broader picture of an army wishing to preserve morale suggests this may be too cynical a view.[20]

These were times where men's only option was the hardened prostitute, regulated or otherwise, but whatever the practical barriers, and despite the sometimes self-imposed discipline or the hurdles of circumstance, a not inconsiderable number of soldiers 'got lucky' with the local population. Carrington suggests as much:

> Front-line soldiers rarely got farther from their units than walking distance … There was no regular leave for the day or for the weekend in France, so that visits to the towns were rare pleasures. Yet they occurred: occasionally, once or twice a year when you were out in rest, brigade might get the loan of a few lorries and run an excursion to Amiens or Boulogne, from which the lucky ones would return at midnight, not too drunk, and boasting of their sexual adventures.[21]

Though the occasional trip out of the line like this one was probably too rushed to allow real social contact with women, and 'adventures' were most likely of the paid-for kind, this would not have been exclusively so as other accounts have indicated. Ronald Marsden of the 104th brigade (Lancashire Fusiliers) reported one particular instance

---

18 Andrews, *Haunting Years*, p. 199.
19 Milne, J., *Footprints of the 14th Leicester Regiment, August 1914 to November 1918* (Leicester: Edgar Backus, 1935).
20 Cuddeford, D. W. J., *And All For What? Some wartime experiences* (London: Heath Cranton, 1933, Naval & Military repr., 2004), p. 79.
21 Carrington, *Soldier*, p. 182.

of *carpe diem* following a nerve-sapping spell in the front line: 'Lads who had been too tongue-tied to so much as say 'hello' to a girl before were dragging them off into the woods after five minutes acquaintance... From all the threshing in the bushes, I'd say there must be a fair number of people with English blood in their veins near Corbie to this day!'[22]

It was undoubtedly the case that a determined Lothario, especially one in a non-infantry role, could find 'wild sex' (defined then as being that outside of the regulated brothel) even if it presented a greater challenge than visiting a prostitute: 'I can always pick up a bit of skirt when I fancy it and for nixes, even in this bloody country where they charge you for the very air you breathe', boasted Bob Mariner VC, serving in Lens in 1915.[23]

One way of determining the likelihood of a reported relationship being true fraternisation is to look at where it took place. While the whole Western Front is often described as one vast 'zone of occupation', it can be subdivided. Differing potential for civilian–military contacts occurred in each of these subdivisions. Cloete provided a useful template for delineating the zones, and a context for examining the scope and nature of fraternisation. He describes the occupied region as being divided into three zones, and places women and sexual activity in two of them. There was:

> The line where there were only fighting men, the next zone that was semi-immune to shellfire, with the ancillary services, Army Service Corps, casualty clearing stations, horse lines, and possibly some heavy guns. There were also some civilians and one could buy food, wine and women – women whose cupidity was stronger than their fear; and finally the back areas peopled by old people, cripples, children and virtuous women.[24]

Although with most regulated army brothels in the main back areas, it was hardly one of completely 'virtuous women'!

Inevitably, sexual activity in these zones would have changed with the ebb and flow of the war. The picture painted of deserted villages is always time-specific; a village denuded of life in 1916 might still have been populated in 1915. 'Public women' whom the mayor of Boesinghe requested to have moved by the Gendamerie National in February 1915 would probably have left of their own accord long before the 1917 battle laid waste to this village to the north-west of Ypres.[25] The many reported amours taking place in Amiens would not have been in evidence from March 1918,

---

22 Allinson, *Bantams*, p. 215.
23 Eyre, *Somme Harvest*, pp. 29-31. See also IWM Sound Archive, No. 24882, Lawson.
24 Cloete, *A Victorian Son*, p. 244.
25 Richsarchief Brugge, Archif de Panne, Onbezert, No. 21185/488: Bestuiteven en Onzendrieven 1914-1918: Consolidated report of the Colonel, Commander of the Belgian Territorial National Guard in the zone occupied by the allied armies, to the (assistant) General of the General Headquarters of the Belgian Army, 21 Feb. 1915, No. 1359.

134   They Didn't Want to Die Virgins

Entitled 'La Peche', *La Vie Parisienne* once again brilliantly captures the flirting game played out by the hunters and the hunted. (Author's collection)

when fighting reached the city, though Orpen notes the speed with which the 'early birds' returned to the city once peacefully reoccupied.[26] It is also probable that the women of particular areas may have been more inclined to promiscuous behaviour than others. Those who lived closer to billets, rest areas, railheads and main supply

26   Orpen, Sir William, *An Onlooker in France, 1917-1919* (London: Williams & Norgate, 1921, Dodo repr.), p. 85.

towns would have been more exposed to moral challenges. Possibly even different regions and villages may have had their own moral micro-climates.[27] At certain times, and in certain environments, local culture and tradition put constraints on how openly an affair might be conducted: 'It was most unusual for a French [or Belgian] girl to openly accompany a British soldier anywhere in France; the priests in many places forbade it and it always led to gossip', wrote Rifleman Smith, adding that: 'only once … I actually walked alone in a big town with a female … such a thing was usually not done'.[28] Smith's experiences are contradicted by other soldiers who found considerably more freedom of movement.[29]

Cloete's first zone, the forward zone, 'of young men and guns', was virtually devoid of women though occasional sexual opportunities did apparently arise right up to the line, with girls offering themselves in ruined buildings. John Gibbons found 'vice of a sort to be had … [but] … not in any appetising form'.[30] It is probable that in the war's first winter, when trenches were close to, or even ran through, villages, and shelling was not as violent as it was later to become, there was close contact with the local population. Soldiers tell of women in these forward towns and villages with Carrington, for example, finding 'Armentières … a quiet sector and mademoiselles [sic] were still to be found living in the town in 1915, within a mile or two of the Germans'.[31] Interestingly, as one must assume some common denominators amongst the women on each side of the line, less than five miles away lay occupied Lille, a city the Germans came to regard as 'the chief seat of prostitution … and "wild love"… with many of the women belonging to the better classes'.[32]

Any local women left in these villages and small towns would be hugely outnumbered by the men in khaki, 'there might be two hundred men to three or four women … I do not think that the males won easy victories in the sexual contest', remembered Carrington.[33]

It is debatable whether any contact made here between troops and women could be referred to as fraternisation, other than perhaps at the very beginning of the war. The ladies Cloete found in the very front line of Ypres in late 1916 'were generally girls *of a sort* [author's italics] … and some officers went with them'.[34] That said, Gibbs did find women of another sort close to the sound of guns mixing freely with the soldier boys:

27 Graves, *Goodbye*, p. 169; Macintyre, *Foreign Field*, p. 139, and Junger, Ernst, *The Storm of Steel* (NY: Zimmerman & Zimmerman, 1985), pp. 111, 119.
28 A. Rifleman, *Four Years*, p. 124.
29 See Blunden, Edmund, *Undertones of War* (London: R. Cobden-Sanderson, 1928; Harmondsworth: Penguin repr., 2000), p.103.
30 Gibbons, *Roll on*, p. 54.
31 Carrington, *Soldier*, p. 91.
32 Hirschfeld, *Sexual History*, p. 156.
33 Carrington, *Soldier*, p. 185. Also, IWM Sound Archive, No. 20, reel 3, Holdstock, Henry Thomas, driver/kite balloonist. Plater, *Catholic Soldiers*, p. 71.
34 Cloete, *Victorian Son*, p. 224.

> I saw lightly wounded girls [in Loos in 1915, post-bombardment] ... with bandaged heads and hands ... they gathered around the British soldiers ... and clasped their arms, or leaned against their shoulders. They had known these men before. They were their sweethearts. In those foul little mining towns the British troops liked their billets, because of the girls there. London boys, and Scots, 'kept company' with pretty slatterns who stole their badges for keep-sakes and taught them a base patois of French, and had a smudge of tears on their cheeks when the boys went away for a spell in the ditches of death.[35]

The use of the word 'sweetheart', and what appear to Gibbs as signs of genuine affection, suggests, echoing Percy Clare, these are not prostitutes *per se*, though the epithet 'slattern' probably suggests looser morals than the somewhat moralistic Gibbs might have preferred to see. These sort of situations could only be morale-building and one imagines the soldiers looking forward to returning to the same billets, as was often the case, having completed their turn in the line.

Describing Arras just before the 1917 big push, Cuddeford found, however, that it was only the most resilient, or mercenary, who stayed when the fighting started,[36] but a 'business as normal' philosophy was apparent in other towns and villages along the front, especially over the first few years of war.[37] While one might expect occasional women to be found at the front, one would not expect to read of any physically in the trenches themselves. Remarkably, however, there are a few reported instances. James Cole, Pte, 1st Devonshire and 2nd Bn Middlesex who fought at Neuve Chappelle in 1915 witnessed 'a couple of women ran across from German lines to British lines during initial bombardment. Germans had had them in the trenches with them'.[38] Orpen found 'three French girls, all dressed up, silk stockings and crimped hair ... standing over the dead Tommies, asking if you [sic] would not like a "little love?"', outside St Quentin in October 1918.[39] There is a suggestion by Gibbs that, possibly in quieter spots, local girls were willing to visit the trenches even if forbidden: 'Here one might sport with Amaryllis in the shade, *but for the fact that country wenches were not allowed into the dugouts and trenches*'.[40] And Chapman records actual instances of sexual activity taking place in the front line; '"You've no idea what a long time it takes to brush this chalk off a black silk dress" remarked one 19-year-old swashbuckler'.[41] It is impossible to know whether any contact at the front came at a price, but common sense dictates that it probably did, a conclusion also reached by Baynes:

---

35   Gibbs, *Realities*, I, pp. 147-8.
36   Cuddeford, *And All For What?*, p.117.
37   A Rifleman (pseud. Smith), *Four Years*, p. 197.
38   IWM Sound Archive, No. 24876.
39   Orpen, *Onlooker*, p. 92.
40   Gibbs, *Realities*, I, p. 117.
41   Chapman, Guy, *A Passionate Prodigality* (London: I. Nicholson & Watson, 1933, Buchan & Enright repr., 1985), p. 258.

Sex given for nothing on the basis of affection was unlikely to come the way of the soldier once the War had settled down into its static pattern ... The only soldiers in France who had a chance of making love to a French girl were those who [sic] duties kept then far behind the line.[42]

They did not have to go that far behind the lines and opportunity increased in direct proportion to the number of miles behind the line the soldier found himself.

It is in the second zone, Cloete's 'zone of vin rouge, omelettes, whores and harpies', that the levels of fraternisation increased and the men had more time to seek morale-boosting diversions.[43] This zone, in terms of size, would have stretched from just a few miles from the front to the more easily identifiable rear where GHQ and Brigade HQs might be positioned. It was here that life continued, if not quite as normal, then at least with some semblance of normality. Here were to be found billets, estaminets, functioning villages and larger towns with shops, rest and recreation areas – including venues for concert parties – bathing facilities, hospitals and stores. It was here that soldiers were also exposed to the charms of local professionals in the ubiquitous unregulated brothels. As Williamson noted, his pilgrim arrived at camp after a long march to find the 'women waiting outside'.[44] The railhead towns, St Omer, Steenvoord, Bailleul, Poperinghe and Béthune were in the second zone, as were myriad small villages and hamlets, recorded in the APM returns, from where local, venereal-diseased women had to be removed: 'All local life went on to within about three of four miles of the front line', reported W.A. Groom somewhat obliquely.[45]

That is not to say, however, that it was normal in terms of the demographic mix, or that there was not a shortage of women. Chapman reinforces what Carrington noted above commenting on the gender imbalance, but equally gives a hint as to the 'sport' enjoyed:

> It had about two hundred active inhabitants, of whom five or six were buxom young peasant women ... every month, a hundred sex-hungry officers descended upon Toutencourt to attend a refresher course at the Fifth Army Infantry School, and by the third day it was generally known that one of the five or six girls was remarkably pretty, a slim, black-eyed darling called Yvonne ... At least thirty officers a month, many of them ... skilful hunters, gave as much concentrated attention to the pursuit of Yvonne as they did to the study of tactics ...'.[46]

---

42 Baynes, *Morale*, p. 212.
43 Cloete, *How Young They Died*, p. 92.
44 Williamson, *Patriot's Progress*, pp. 44-5.
45 W. H. A. Groom, *Poor Bloody Infantry* (London: Kimber, 1976, Picardy edn, 1976), p. 46.
46 Chapman, *Passionate Prodigality*, p. 185.

At least, in this second zone a large number of soldiers were able to see and talk to women who were not prostitutes, and where there was perhaps real fraternisation between troops and locals. In the early years, before villages behind the lines were completely destroyed and inhabitants evacuated, relationships between the soldier and the local population could get remarkably close. 'An amazing feature to me', noted infantryman Russell, 'was the coolness with which the troops made use of the villagers' homes. It seemed as though every house was open to them'.[47] Indeed, men were simply trying to re-create a semblance of home life as they had known it. Inevitably, it was often a small step to intimacy and the men soon found themselves diverted from matters military to matters amorous. Vera Brittain's subaltern fiancé wrote of having to finish a letter as he had 'to go off and make his men practise hand grenades etc., since they were inclined to be lazy and prefer flirtation with a pretty girl in a cottage nearby'.[48]

The needs of the British troops who passed through Flanders and Picardy were no different to those of the German men who, as Hirschfeld illustrates, enjoyed wide-ranging contacts with the local civilians.[49] But relationships were more easily formed by the troops in the zones of occupation than in the occupied territories; 'our men were there as friends and allies and a woman will do a lot for love that nothing will force her to do otherwise', observed Percy Clare.[50] Other than language, there were fewer social barriers to overcome because they came as protectors, allies and liberators, sharing the lives of the inhabitants rather than determining them (though there was inevitably a feeling amongst some that it was an occupation in the true sense of the word).[51]

The longer a man served, the greater the range of opportunities he experienced for rubbing up against the locals. In the early years, British soldiers effectively substituted for absent family males. Andrews told of meeting a young French farmer's daughter near Festubert, in 1915, who brought them coffee. Her familiarity with British soldiers was apparent: 'She spoke soldier's English, and there were inevitably swear words in it: profanation of such sweet, pretty lips was inevitable ... "I love the Jocks – damn nice, you Jocks"'.[52] In this environment, the more determined soldiers could find ample opportunities for casual sex with willing girls. Indeed, Gerald Brenan, an officer in

---

47 Russell, Henry, *Slaves of the War Lords* (London, 1928: Naval & Military repr., undated), p. 25.
48 Brittain, Vera, *Chronicle of Youth: Great War diary, 1913-1917*, ed. Alan Bishop with Terry Smart (1981, 2000 edn), p. 202.
49 Hirschfeld, *Sexual History*, p. 156; Macintyre, *Foreign Field* where the entire story is built around such a liaison.
50 IWM 06/48/1, Clare, '*Reminiscences*', unpaginated diary, book three.
51 Tombs & Tombs, *That Sweet Enemy: the History of a Love-Hate Relationship* (London: Random House, 2009), p. 478. Corday also noted the increased activity throughout the French-held sector, Corday, *The Paris Front*, p. 173 (June 1916); IWM 06/48/1, Clare, '*Reminiscences*', unpaginated, book three.
52 Andrews, *Haunting Years*, p. 115; Hankey, *Student in Arms*, pp. 230-1.

the 1/5th Gloucestershire Regiment, slept with a peasant girl at Merris only three days after arriving in France, in 1915,[53] and the soldiers own trench newspapers, like the celebrated *Wipers Times* and the Canadian's *Dead Horse Corner Gazette*, contain cryptic references to what appear to be consummated relationships.[54]

The full extent of the fraternisation and social intermixing that went on in this zone, can be inferred from the occasional wistful reflection of a soldier's written reminiscences, like this of Rifleman Smith:

> La Gorgue, that town where we had had such fine times, was now in German hands. Every man's thoughts flew to some damsel or other in that once happy little township. Some went to Madeline, the girl at our billet there; some recalled the saucy puss at the favourite estaminet and other scintillating beauties … My own thoughts turned to Erma, my especial favourite … she wrote to me afterwards to say that she and so many others had fled a day or so before, when the town was heavily shelled.[55]

It is not simply a single soldier that had found companionship but 'every man'. Lieutenant William Morgan, a Welsh tunneller with the 175th Coy, Royal Engineers who, as photographs in a following chapter illustrate, also frequented the Blue Lamps, found a love that lasted long after the war. Despite his family discouraging him from marrying his French sweetheart, Renée, he continued to write to her many years after the war and even through the Second World War. A more humorous incident, which illustrates the relative freedom of movement available to soldiers in these villages and their expectation of finding local women to chase, came from subaltern Arthur Behrend:

> During our stay, the silence of the village (Morchies) was shattered one night by an uproar so violent that I picked up my revolver and roused the nearest N.C.O … We ran out and had our greatest laugh for months. The centre of the disturbance was a drunken gunner of Toc I; in the moonlight he had mistaken the local priest for a girl. Since the priest was wearing his cassock and the time was long past midnight it struck me, if not him, that the mistake was understandable.[56]

---

53 Brenan, Gerald, *A Life of One's Own: Childhood and Youth* (London: Hamish Hamilton, 1962).
54 Cambridge University Library, WR422: The *Wipers Times*, facsimile edition, No. 3, 1 and *New Church Times* No. 2 Vol.1. See also the *Dead Horse Corner Gazette* (4th Bn Canadian Contingent Oct. 1915, No. 1), under heading, 'Our Thirst for Knowledge', p. 5 and *Minden* magazine, August 1916.
55 Rifleman, *Four Years*, p. 333.
56 Behrend, A., *As from Kemmel Hill. An adjutant in France and Flanders, 1917 and 1918* (London: Eyre & Sottiswood, 1963), p. 44.

Finally, there was Cloete's third zone, 'the place of virtuous women': nurses, VADs, FANYs, middle-class volunteers like Lady Angela Forbes, who ran the café at Étaples training camp, and local townswomen. Not all were truly 'virtuous',[57] and, more importantly for the soldier, in this zone came were to be found both the tolerated brothel – readily accessible – and the unregulated prostitute.

Typically, it was one such town (perhaps Abbeville, Amiens, Le Havre, Boulogne or Rouen) in which Edwin Vaughan first found himself on arrival in France. Indeed, his conversation with his driver gives a good indication of life and opportunities available in a back area: 'He told me about the locality ... [I] was confused by his references to the estaminets the men frequented, the girls they met, and the cushy time they were having'.[58] Few infantry soldiers were in this zone, other than those on rest or convalescing, or those attached to staff or taking messages to them. Fraternisation was between the officers, locals and, in the latter stages of the war, female service personnel. War was a long way away for the men enjoying these local charms: 'in Boulogne I came across ... Bob ... now doing a staff job ... having the time of his life on his present job [with] one of the smartest fillies in Boulogne, who was the goods in every way' wrote an admiring Crozier.[59] Paris might be regarded in the same category. Though readily accessible only to officers and ANZAC troops on leave, it was a major source of sexual adventure, as many memoirs testify.[60]

Three other zones are not described by Cloete but are equally important in any discussion of fraternisation. Firstly, there was German-occupied territory, where any fraternisation between local and British soldier was of a desperate kind, involving concealment from the enemy. Any soldier living here was one who had either been cut off during the initial retreat of 1914, or who had escaped from a prison camp. As Macintyre has written, some soldiers left behind the line fraternised to the point of becoming husbands of locals in attempts to integrate and 'disappear'.[61]

Secondly, in the closing stages of the war as allied troops pushed towards the Rhine, liberating towns and villages en route, another zone opened up. Here troops enjoyed the time-honoured favours bestowed on liberators, 'to the victors the rewards'.

---

57 The controversy over the morals of nurses, WAAFs, VADs and other females in official roles, is discussed in Mitchell, D., *Monstrous Regiment* (New York: MacMillan 1965), pp. 222-9; Crozier, *Brass Hat*, p. 178. See also Edvane Price (pseud. Helen Zenna Smith), *Not So Quiet; Stepdaughters of War* (London: Albert E. Marriott, 1930, NY: Feminist Press edn.), fiction based on a female ambulance driver's diary.
58 Vaughan, Edwin Campion, *Some Desperate Glory: The Diary of a Young Officer, 1917* (London: Warne, 1981, New York: Henry Holt, 1988), p. 8.
59 Richards, *Old Soldiers*, p. 158; Dunn, Capt J. C., *The War the Infantry Knew, 1914-1919* (London: P. S. King, 1938, Abacus repr., 1994).), p 352; Gibbs, *Realities*, II, p. 327; Douie, *The Weary Road*, p. 207, and Crozier, *Brass Hat*, p. 255 on his time in Boulogne with WAAF staff.
60 Graham, *Private*, p. 222; Becker, J. H., *Silhouettes of the Great War: The Memoir of John Harold Becker* (Ontario: CEF Books, 2001), p. 101; Read, *Of Those We Loved*, p. 330.
61 Macintyre, Ben, *A Foreign Field, p. 27*

As the troops advanced and liberated areas of previously German-held territory, they encountered 'friendly' natives. Canadian infantry officer, Wheeler, recounted one episode where an opportunity arose in a billet: 'my hostess ... craving a mite of physical gratification ... [after] four long years under difficult, brutal and humiliating conditions – deprived of the normal and natural love'.[62] His morals precluded taking advantage of the situation. One can only speculate whether this would have been the general response. Third, reference must be made – for the sake of completeness – to the fraternisation that occurred in the immediate post-war years, with the British army camped throughout eastern Belgium, the Ardennes and in Germany itself. Despite the enmity of the war years, relationships did develop between the British soldier and neighbourhood girls which perhaps may have been the result of a lack of eligible local young men.

These zones represented the geographical context in which troops could enjoy a measure of sex often with no direct financial cost. Of equal importance, however, is an understanding of the moral context in which sex took place. What was the traditional attitude of the local population he encountered? To what extent did this allow for, or promote, casual or romantic relationships?

The soldiers certainly found a freer moral atmosphere in both France and Flanders than they were used to. In France, local manners and morality tended to depend, as they had in Britain, on traditional class and gender roles and possibly also on geographic location, for example differing between urban and rural areas. James McMillan holds that there was a general moral double standard not unlike in Britain, which:

> in the bourgeois ethic ... social convention prescribed chastity for daughters and fidelity for wives ...[while] boys and men were assumed to indulge in both pre-marital and extra-marital sexual relations.[63]

Middle-class girls were deliberately kept in ignorance of the world outside their home and treated as decorative ornament. 'In the years before the First World War', argues McMillan, 'there seems every reason to suppose that the aim of preserving the chastity of the bourgeois girl was successfully accomplished'.[64]

The soldier was, however, largely living in a region dominated by the rural and industrial working class, where daughters enjoyed a good deal of freedom of movement and sexual opportunity. Amongst these classes, extra-marital affairs were not unknown, and sex outside of marriage was not particularly condemned even when leading to childbirth. 'Villaret had a long and fairly broad-minded history of illegitimacy ... but there is no evidence to suggest that the village folk were markedly

---

62 Wheeler, *The 50th Battalion*, p. 272.
63 McMillan, James F., *Housewife or Harlot: the Place of Women in French Society, 1870-1940* (New York: St. Martin's, 1981), p. 16.
64 Ibid., p. 20.

more promiscuous than those of any other rural community',[65] argues Macintyre in his study of British soldiers caught behind the lines following the 1914 retreat from Mons. 'There was a village saying, much repeated: "God said behave, but he didn't say how"'.[66]

It was working-class girls who traditionally provided the labour force for the *maison de tolérance* and were considered fair game for seduction by their betters. A tradition of 'fallen women' perhaps helps explain both the number of opportunities for casual sex and the apparent proliferation of clandestine and amateur prostitutes.

Prostitution was quite literally tolerated, with even small villages and towns having their red lamps, though in decline in the immediate years leading to the war. Visits were conducted openly and not in the furtive manner of a visit to a suppressed brothel in Britain. Schoolboys were the most regular patrons of the brothels as the eve of departure for military service was another recognised occasion for the *rite de passage* of male sexual initiation.

Interestingly, an apparent dichotomy existed in French sexual culture that pervaded all social groups between upholding a moral code whilst at the same time being patriotic and producing children. This arose from the eugenic fear that the falling birth rate was weakening the country. With a government effectively prepared to subsidise the production of children with social benefits, and with husbands and local boys away at war, there was an ample pool of sexually compliant women for soldiers to chase and perhaps less social opprobrium toward illegitimacy than there otherwise would have been. Chaplain Shaw could:

> never forget meeting one morning in a village street a young girl and her mother. The daughter, who was about 17 years old, was carrying a baby, and she quite unabashed volunteered the statement that the little one was a 'piccaninny souvenir' at which her mother laughed heartily.[67]

Ironically, there had been less illegitimacy in pre-war France than in Britain where French couples generally had fewer children, but married earlier and had them sooner and then practised contraception, and thinks Tombs, possibly had more frequent sex.[68] Their acceptance of contraception was more open than in Britain, where it was still controversial and often equated with immorality. This would back up Crozier's contention that a supply was often on-hand in the soldiers' billets.

---

65 Macintyre, *Foreign Field*, pp. 138-40.
66 Ibid., p. 117.
67 Shaw, *Jottings*, p. 37; for other British babies see Wheeler, *50th Battalion*, p. 68; Corday, *Paris Front*, pp. 167-8, May 1916.
68 Tombs and Tombs, *That Sweet Enemy*, p. 447, n. 4.

Whatever the state of pre-war morals, there is little doubt that the war stimulated desires as well as loosened social constraints amongst the local French women, though Crozier's painting of the scene is perhaps a little too vivid:

> women were excited to sexual frenzy by the constant imminence of danger, and when the acrid smell of bursting shell acted as a powerful aphrodisiac ... women, discarded the code of virtue that had governed their whole lives, and abandoned themselves.[69]

But undoubtedly, the large number of female refugees, orphans and widows (actual or temporarily separated from their husbands), living transient lives far from the gaze of those who might normally have censured their actions, led to a further loosening of morals. The young lady that the young infantry soldier Hiscock encountered was not unique in her attitude: 'the local Alice "was at it again". She was young ... her father had been killed and her mother didn't care what she did. She didn't, she told me, fuck for money if it was with a British troop, but just for the hell of it'.[70]

Fraternisation existed across all social classes, not simply between the transient or lower-class women and the troops; contemporary observers like the journalist Corday observed that 'Women are leading fast lives from one end of the social scale to the other' and adultery was 'common'.[71] French wives and girlfriends found themselves with, in the words of James McMillan, 'uncustomary opportunities for enjoyment'.[72] Officers were often welcomed into middle-class homes, relationships developed across social lines and, though time out of the line was short, some men had regular girlfriends rather than brief encounters. However, the middle-class attitude to their daughters' sexual upbringing (they were supposed to be virgin brides) explains both the protective attitude and the ambivalence one observes when, having invited British soldiers into their homes, they were upset when they seduced their daughters.[73]

Sometimes, however, the object of the soldier's desire would remain tantalisingly out of reach, because the girls kept to a moral code, either enforced or voluntary. Infantry private, Bird sadly commented: 'Near Béthune at Noel le Mines, she cottoned on to me ... she was a good looking girl but she had a very strict father and he looked after his daughter so no hanky-panky'.[74]

The situation in Flanders was somewhat different. The British-held line was considerably shorter than that of France. With most of the country being under German occupation, and the front line being effectively only a few miles from the border with

---

69 Ibid., p. 55. The same is said of World War Two in Beevor, A., *Berlin: The downfall* (London: Penguin Viking, 2002), p. 282.
70 Hiscock, Eric, *The Bells of Hell*, pp. 88-9.
71 Corday, *Paris Front*, pp. 81, 184, 203.
72 McMillan, *Housewife or Harlot*, p. 19.
73 Gibbs, *Realities*, Vol. II, p. 282.
74 IWM Sound Archive, No.10656, reel 8, Bird.

France, the troops came into contact with both the truly local Flemish community though billeting, and with the temporary visitors who swamped the region.[75] Contact between the traditionally working class population, with occupations dominated by farming, brewing and lace-making, the occupying soldier was not completely harmonious with a certain level of antipathy evident on both sides.[76]

Local contacts, too, would have been constrained by the highly Catholic nature of the community and the firm grip that local priests held on their congregations. This is not to say that fraternisation did not occur, but that it was far less likely to be open and the interface with women other than the recognised prostitute, more likely to come through points of general commercial contact such as the shop or estaminet. Despite this context, it would seem from the limited evidence still extant that the soldiers of all races held a fascination for the local women. 'A Belgian, man or woman, especially the latter' noted Father Benoot, 'is an admirer of the exotic, and all, or nearly all, understand with pleasure and honour the attractiveness of the brave soldiers of our allies'.[77]

Local priests viewed the practical issue of soldier/civilian relationships with distinctly mixed feelings. For the diary-keeping priest Achiel Van Walleghem, the problem lay more in the seductive powers of the soldiers, rather than the virtue of the local maidens:

> Alas, so many young daughters in Dikkebus and surroundings who behave scandalously. Some are flaunting their virtue, others, alas, let themselves be seduced by cunning and deceptive language, by the shiny uniform of the officers and most of all by their money. Yes, our women are exposed to so many dangers. The soldiers seek them out and give them money, rings and bracelets.[78]

It was not that fraternisation generally was frowned upon, or that soldiers were the sole reason for its instigation. In a sermon, reported in the *De Poperingsche Keikop* of 15 December 1917, the priest, Auguste Benoot, railed against the changes in morals that had followed war. 'We have to admit that we lost our edge, both civilians and soldiers'. For Father Benoot, sections of his parish had 'shaken off their old Christian conviction in order to adopt a modern one' and 'pathetically fallen into moral misery'. Unlike Father Van Walleghem, the blame is not that of the Tommy who has 'the right to go conquer the soul and heart of the women of Poperinghe; they are after all human

---

75 Denhooven, Domeniek, 'Living Apart together; Belgium civilians and non-white troops and workers in war time Flanders', in Santanu Das (ed.), *Race, Empire and First World War Writing*, (New York: Cambridge. University Press, 2011), pp. 143-57.
76 For general relationships see the fictional, Mottram, R. H., *The Spanish Farm Trilogy* (London: Chatto & Windus 1928, repr., 1930).
77 Poperinghe Town Council Archive. *De Poperingsche Keikop* magazine.
78 Flanders Fields documentation centre, Diary of Achiel Van Walleghem, 26 May 1916 (hereafter Van Walleghem diary).

beings like us and fighting for a spot of soil of our beloved Motherland', but rather 'those Poperinghe Misses … [who] … have adopted the bad habits of the big cities'. Indeed, it is simply the open flaunting of themselves that concerned Father Benoot, 'there wouldn't even be a single reprimand … if they would behave themselves appropriately towards their fellow citizens'.[79]

This somewhat ambivalent relationship between soldier and civilian is not unsurprising. In truth, the soldiers were as guilty as the local girls in terms of who was taking the initiative and the soldiers' behaviour was seemingly not as chivalrous as it might have been. Echoing Darrow's contention that the men often expected the local women to be readily available at a price, council officials at Coxyde were moved to complain to the Governor of West Flanders, that 'it hasn't been long since a married woman was tempted by soldiers, while getting angry flatly refused an advance of 20 francs, replying to them that she had her husband with her'.[80] And the *De Poperingsche Keikop* carried a damning report of the insensitivity of a '*jam potten*' (Tommy) who made inappropriate sexual remarks to young girls in a procession to their first communion.[81]

These two particular accounts illustrate that the soldier's general attitude toward his French and Belgian neighbours would to some degree determine the level and type of fraternisation. Initially this attitude was defined by his expectations, his prejudices and his first experiences of a strange land.

The average British man was not well-travelled: other than perhaps a 'wakes week' holiday in a comparatively local coastal resort, he would probably have lived and died within ten miles of where he was born. His image of France was thus a heady mix of distilled historical and political views, misinformation and the salacious, much of which came from travellers' tales and 'yellow books'. "French" came to be used in colloquial English to mean sexually explicit and 'the ordinary English lad from the not very educated classes had grown up in a sort of national tradition of French immorality, the Moulin Rouge, champagne and all that'.[82] It was immediately apparent to soldiers crossing the Channel, even if stereotypes were not immediately confirmed, that the French and Flemish cultures were different, and the locals did not share their Anglo-Saxon lifestyle or moral code. 'Strange people, these Frenchies, when judged by our own standard of morals',[83] found T.S. Hope whose view was the commonly expressed sentiment of the average ranker. 'They thought nothing', noted Private Burrage, 'of recommending their female friends and relatives for a purpose which, if specifically named, would bring a blush of shame to the cheek of Innocence'.[84] British

---

79 Poperinghe archive: *De Poperingsche Keikop*.
80 Richsarchief Brugge, Archif de Panne, Onbezert, file 11/3 Venerische Zicktern and Regle meitering Prositution, 1914-18, 6 Mar. 1915.
81 Poperinghe archive.: *De Poperingsche Keikop*, 15 Sept 1918.
82 Gibbons, *Roll on Next War*, p. 87.
83 Hope, *Winding Road*, p. 67.
84 Burrage, *War is War*, p. 43.

officers, perhaps having visited France, or at least having a higher general education, may not have been quite so shocked but they too would have been aware of differences.

Soldiers' memoirs are littered with stories concerning their initial discomfort and embarrassment at French openness, especially with breaches of privacy when at daily ablutions in billets or camp. This is typical:

> At one of the camps near a village behind Arras we had some rather embarrassing visitors. Our latrine as the usual deep trench surmounted by a pole supported by trestles, the area being screened by canvas. Two or three young women would arrive from the village and walk along the seated occupants selling chocolate from trays hung from their shoulders. This they did quite unconcernedly, joining in with the inevitable banter.[85]

Unsurprisingly, the general environment created by war and its attendant hardships, in an already economically poor and perhaps culturally challenging region, did not always provide the most auspicious of contexts in which a sexual frisson might develop. Andrews colourfully illustrates this telling of a time when he was billeted in a loft where two, every poor seamstresses lived; 'One night as I was returning to the billet and the wind tore a rough newspaper that was their only bedroom window and I caught a glimpse of the pair, naked, sitting side by side on the bed, searching their vests for lice.[86]

It was new to find people not bathing, and dirty, to find women wearing no underwear, or to see them naked in fields, or to see women urinating openly, or going into men's urinals, and for some it was off-putting. 'The French peasant women are far from civilised', complained Canadian officer Becker in a letter home.[87] Tommy could be equally unimpressed: 'They were not, speaking generally, of the cleanest type by any means', wrote John Jackson.

To some extent, the soldier's attitude towards the Flemish was coloured by his distrust of a people that spoke something that sounded suspiciously like German, who were popularly supposed to favour the enemy and who were suspected of wholesale spying. The soldiers' prejudices were perhaps also the result of their experiences of dealing with the Flemish when buying food, drink and souvenirs. They often found their mercenary attitude grasping and felt they were being fleeced. Infantryman Jackson spoke for many, commenting: 'I cannot say we were very much impressed with either the town or the people ... and their main object in life just then, seemed

---

85   Tucker, J. F., *Johnny Get Your Gun*, pp. 108, 137. For embarrassing stories about billets, see Cuddeford, *All For What?*, p. 129; Bird, *Ghosts*, p. 16; IWM Sound Archive, No. 11376, reel 5, Field, Laurie, Pte, Oxs and Bucks LI.
86   Andrews, *Haunting Years*, p. 190.
87   Becker, *Silhouettes*, p. 240 and Jackson, John, *Private 12768: Memoir of a Tommy* (Stroud: Tempus, 2004), p. 58.

to be to make as much money as possible, out of the *soldat Anglais*',[88] and 'frequently showing unmistakeable dislike of the British soldier'.[89]

The different outlook that the locals apparently had towards sex and sexually related matters, if not the 'shamelessness' that was a feature of daily life, came as a shock to men from a country still largely bound by high-Victorian moral ideals, enforced in some sections of the community by an active social purity movement.[90] 'The moral outlook of the country where he is stationed is different from that of his own land; he is often billeted on people whose morals are distinctly lax', commented army chaplain, Shaw, reflecting the views even of many ordinary, non-religious soldiers.[91] Clare, for example, was shocked by his landlady's contention that having an affair though married was of no consequence – *'san fairy ann'* – and decided that 'The French of course is (sic) a very amorous nation and the peasantry have a different code of morals altogether than we; they cannot be judged by our standards'. There seemed to be a dichotomy between the ideals of an apparently highly religious people and their daily life:

> The seeming piety of the French home with all its sacred pictures and relics was rather puzzling to the Tommy, but he realised that it did not make any difference to character, and that the religiously minded girl was as accessible to his love-making as if she had no religion.[92]

Inevitably, there were some who simply did not enjoy the familiarity they initially found in the French, but once accustomed to these cultural differences – which often took some time – most men took their experiences light-heartedly and without offence, not allowing them to become a barrier. Montague noted: 'The British soldier's incorrigible propensity, wherever he may be, [was] to form virtuous attachment. "Love, unfoiled in the war", as Sophocles says'.[93] One reads everywhere of this 'virtuous attachment'. It is evidenced in soldiers helping farmers' wives get in the harvests, in officers assisting the younger daughters of billets with English lessons,[94] in helping locals to compose letters,[95] or in acting as protector from 'predators', or in helping to sort out compensation claims with relevant authorities.[96]

---

88 Ibid., p. 58.
89 A Rifleman (pseud. Smith), p. 77, and for further unflattering quotations, see pp. 78, 98; Tucker, *Johnny*, p. 108; IWM 06/48/1, Clare, '*Reminiscences*', book three, unpaginated.
90 Clare ibid., unnumbered page.
91 Shaw, *Jottings*, pp. 36-9.
92 Graham, *Private*, p. 180.
93 Montague, *Disenchantment*, p. 144.
94 Gibbs, *Realities*, II, pp. 281-2.
95 Dunn, *War the Infantry Knew*, 5 Dec. [1915]; also Manning, *Her Privates We*, p. 121.
96 Mottram, *Spanish Farm*, where it forms a central plot line.

Once the men had overcome their cultural prejudices, or grown accustomed to the environment, their attention naturally turned to evaluating the women as sexual partners. While for many, the women were an exotic attraction, for others the local women were simply unappealing, and this formed a natural barrier to anything other than the most basic social intercourse even when it was the local girls who initiated the foreplay. Chapman found himself 'billeted in houses presided over by grim slatterns of repellent aspect but of amorous nature'.[97] Another soldier found the 'average Flemish female is an unattractive sight, attired in unbecoming clothes and sabots'. He described the occupants of a farm billet, comprising:

> 'His wife ... an old hag with a sallow complexion ... Juliette [the daughter] ... a wench of some three and twenty summers, portly, ungainly, and not by any means handsome – the sort of sight in curling pins that puts you off your breakfast'.[98]

It was not only the Flemish who were found wanting. The French peasant too was not always considered particularly alluring: 'We spent a night at Merville ... its womenfolk – the dirtiest slatterns we had seen in France', recalled the Welsh officer, Griffiths.[99] Burrage was unlikely to forge any relationships with local peasants whom he disparaged as 'genial ... [but] dirty and obscene. They had the manners, morals and habits of tame monkeys'. And for some men the local women compared unfavourably with those they had left behind. 'I gazed at that bevy of pretty girls' wrote one soldier coming into Victoria station on leave, 'and, as I thought of the Flemish maidens, odious comparisons arose in my mind'.[100] Similar comparisons were made by Harry Siepmann,[101] and Holdstock, a balloonist, remembered that 'if there was any thought of immorality in men's minds once you had a good look at them [local women] and compared them with the girls we'd left at home, there was no attraction at all'.[102]

That said, a poor comparison with the girls at home did not always mean abstinence, and anyway favourable comments were much more common in the soldiers' accounts. There was a definite preference for the French girls with whom, by happy circumstance and dint of the geography of occupation, they would inevitably have greater contact. Even soldiers who found the Flemish 'odious', like Rifleman Smith, had a different view when exposed to the French: 'For some days we remained at Tattinhem ... where ... very nice looking French girls were among the delights of civilisation'.[103]

---

97 Chapman, *Passionate Prodigality*, p. 110.
98 A Rifleman (pseud. Smith), *Four Years*, p. 89.
99 Griffiths, Wyn, *Up To Mametz* (London: Faber & Faber, 1931, Seven House edn, 1981), p. 169; Burrage, *War is War*, p. 43.
100 A Rifleman (pseud. Smith), *Four Years*, p. 114.
101 Siepmann, *Echo*, p. 52.
102 IWM Sound Archive, No. 20, reel 3, Holdstock.
103 A Rifleman (pseud. Smith), *Four Years*, p. 71.

It is also probable that the relative attractiveness of the women increased, the longer men were away from their own families and morale needed a boost. Amongst the very human range of motives for sleeping with them was that they simply substituted for missed loved ones, as Graves discovered: 'I had a letter to censor the other day, written by a lance-corporal to his wife. He said that French girls were nice to sleep with, so she shouldn't worry on his account, but that he far preferred sleeping with her and missed her a great deal.'[104]

Undoubtedly there were girls and women of the zones of occupation for whom the arrival of foreign troops promised excitement and replacements for their own missing men. Percy Clare observed, 'It must be remembered too that all the men folk other than children and grand folk were away at the war and so that the women were the more ready to accept the attentions of our men'.[105] It is important to note that, in many instances, the women took the initiative and they encouraged the men. This was not confined only to those trying to sell sex: 'if one has to blame Tommy for misdemeanour, then equal blame must be attached to the womenfolk – for it is in most cases six of one and half a dozen of another'.[106] We have already seen how this was seen as a feature of the behaviour of the Flemish girls. Attitudes and behaviour towards their foreign allies across the occupied zones varied from amused interest through to overt desire. Private Tucker remembered an incident near Watten, France, in autumn 1915 with:

> a very good looking French girl of about 20 ... She was rather flirtatious and made a dead set on me ... kissing me and inviting us into her cottage where her mother was sitting ... her young brother was sent to the village for a tot of rum ... we were given coffee and rum and shown photographs of her finance who was away in the army. She stole one of my photographs and would not give it back, and asked me to come to sleep at the cottage that night.[107]

In another part of the line, Dixon also found that much of the flirting came from impressionable young girls they met, and it required self-control not to let one thing lead to another:

> There was one house in Zeggers ... occupied by a family of *père et mère, et une très jolie fille*, their daughter. This pretty young lady was 16 years of age, but older than her years – war is a great educator and matures the young quickly ... She

---

104 Graves, *Goodbye*, p. 97. See also Carstairs, *Generation Missing*, p. 184.
105 IWM 06/48/1, Clare, '*Reminiscences*', book three, unpaginated.
106 Shaw, *Jottings*, pp. 36-9. See also Mottram, *Through the Menin Gate* for a good example of a love affair stimulated and led by the female.
107 Tucker, *Johnny*, p. 31; and B. Adams, *Nothing of Importance: A Record of Eight Months at the Front with a Welsh Battalion, October 1915 to June 1916* (London: Methuen, 1917), p. 258. Also, IWM P185, Runcie, '*Territorial Mob*', unpub. account, pp. 84-5.

knew how to kiss, that little lady, in spite of her tender years. I did not attempt any further intimacies – I was still young and chivalrous, and, although the little minx led me on to an extent which might have justified it, I felt that to 'seduce' her would be taking a wrong advantage of her parent's hospitality.[108]

Allied soldiers of every character found themselves the objects of interest from virtually the moment of their arrival: 'The French overwhelmed us ... barely gave us room to form up ... and the women kissed us with alarming freedom' found John Lucy arriving with the regular BEF in August 1914.[109] The local Poperinghe musician, Albert Baert, noted that the local girls showed a preference for the soldiers over the indigenous male.[110] There was, perhaps, some preference shown to officers over men, probably due to class distinctions, snobbery, or just the fact that officers were more likely to speak French. They also, of course, enjoyed more leave opportunities and had better billets. Perhaps the girls were themselves looking for a better 'prospect': 'A peculiar thing about the French peasants was that they imagined the English to be wealthy and that we all had servants at home' thought Johnny Tucker.[111]

The more exotic soldier, made so either by dress or colour, was often particularly popular. Few women, for example, can have seen kilted regiments before, and the novelty excited and intrigued them. The first Highland regiments of the BEF were so popular that they had to be billeted behind school railings for their own good. The curiosity of the ladies of the town was piqued by the speculation of what was worn under the kilt with much ribald fun and entertainment was inevitably enjoyed by the wearers in helping the ladies find out!

Indeed, there appears to have been little colour or religious prejudice – certainly less than the non-white soldier may have found if stationed in the UK itself where he was virtually isolated to prevent local contacts developing.[112] Indian, Caribbean, Maori, Chinese Labour Corps, and the French Army's own African and North African troops, all enjoyed local amours, each finding the other equally exotic. 'The ladies here are very nice and bestow their favours freely', wrote Balwent Singh to Pandrit Chet Ram in Amritsar, from France in October 1915.[113] Corday noted in his diary that in the north the Indian troops, 'who are very handsome, are forming families', and later that 'A camp of Indian troops has been pestered by women, who are so insistent that

---

108 IWM 92/36/1, Dixon, *'Wheels of Darkness'*, p. 105.
109 Lucy, *Devil in the Drum*, p. 81,
110 Poperinghe Archive: Dairy of Albert Baert.
111 Tucker, *Johnny*, p. 31.
112 For discussion of this, see Levine, Philippa, 'Battle Colors: Race, Sex and Colonial Soldiery in World War', *Journal of Woman's History* 8 (1998), pp. 104-30; Howe, D. Glenford, 'Military-Civilian Intercourse, Prostitution and Venereal Disease amongst Black Soldiers in the Great War', *Journal of Caribbean History* 31 (1997), pp. 88-102.
113 Omissi, David, *Indian Voices of the Great War* (London: Macmillan, 1999), p. 114.

measures have had to be introduced to curb their ardour'.[114] In Flanders, Denhooven notes how the 'exotic' coloured troops were viewed with a mixture of fear and romance by one particular educated woman.[115]

This appeal of the exotic was, incidentally, not confined to the women of France and Flanders. Dunn, a medical officer in the Royal Welch, and a generally respected and reliable witness, contends that WAACs' 'fascination for abnormal and erotic males', in this case Maoris, was the cause of rioting at Étaples.[116]

As for the women, aware of their potential failings, and like females throughout every time and culture, they understood the importance of making themselves attractive to the visiting soldier. Private Holmes found that they:

> know how to make the best of themselves … putting all their colour on their faces It was an art with them and every girl you met was beautiful. She looked beautiful. Even if she hadn't been a real beauty she'd have made herself [so].[117]

Siepmann noted how the women wore fashions 'that caught the eye and were meant to … Each one was coquettish and winsome by premeditation'.[118] In Flanders the behaviour of the young ladies of Poperinghe moved the local priest to note with a degree of concern;

> In one word, everything is permissible: translucent stockings, short skirts, open-necked blouses, etc. No trick is forgotten to appear pleasant, to make oneself attractive to the soldiers of Douglas Haig.[119]

Whether it was love or just sex they sought, there were inevitable consequences. The general promiscuity of both locals and visitors was soon evidenced by the children of every hue and eye-colour who started appearing on the street and in the homes and orphanages of the occupied areas. 'It's not surprising several soldier's children have been born already' noted the Belgian priest, Van Walleghem.[120] Canadian, John McKendrick Hughes, reported of being told by one woman of a sister who had had

---

114 Corday, *Paris Front*, p. 46, Jan. 1915 and p. 189, Aug. 1916. See also Fogarty, R., 'Race, Sex, Fear and Loathing', iHerzog (ed.), *Brutality and Desire*, pp. 59-90.
115 Denhooven, 'Living Apart together', p.151.
116 Dunn, *War the Infantry Knew*, p. 389,
117 IWM Sound Archive, No. 8868, reel 6, Holmes, William, Pte, 12th Bn London Regt.; see Junger, *Storm of Steel*, pp. 111-12.
118 Siepmann, *Echo,* p. 52.
119 Poperinghe Archives. Sermon of Auguste Benoot, *De Poperingsche Keikop*, 15 Dec. 1917.
120 Flanders Field Museum, Ieper, Van Walleghem Diary, 26 May 1916. See also Burrage *War is War*, p. 90: p. 90. Hughes, McKendrick, *The Unwanted*, p. 48., Also Richards, *Old Soldiers*, p. 30; Saint-Mandé, *Wine*, p. 248; IWM 06/48/1, Clare, '*Reminiscences*', book three, unpaginated; Corday, *Paris Front*, p. 193 for Aug. 1916 and pp. 167-68 for May 1916.

a child by an English officer. Burrage met 'One lady in an estaminet [with] a fine fat baby which she proudly displayed with two words of explanation: "Souvenir – Canadian"'. Both Robert Graves and Frank Richards mention children whose skin colour suggested African and Indian fathers. So widespread became the phenomena that the subject soon provided the lyrics for one of the soldier's more enduring popular songs:

> *Apres la guerre fini,*
> *Tous les soldas parties,*
> *Mademoiselle avec piccanini*
> *Souvenir des Anglais*

War babies presented both something of an embarrassment and a dilemma, especially for the French authorities. This applied both to the German-occupied areas, where fraternisation was with the enemy, as well as in the zones of occupation.[121] It also presented problems for wives having to explain additions to the family to returning *poilu*.[122] Inevitably, there is evidence of illegal abortions being carried out by those colloquially know in Flanders as '*angel makers*'.[123]

There were those, too, who had given their affections, perhaps even bodies, to the incoming troops, but when the troops departed were left with a bitter taste of betrayal. Gibbs, in conversation with a lady in Amiens, discovered an embarrassing level of alleged disingenuousness; young English officers promising much but inevitably leaving with ne'er a backward glance and the judgement that 'When the English army goes away from France it will leave many bitter memories because of that'.[124]

'Many young women, who are in the English zone', summarised one French report on civilian morale, 'write to English soldiers ... who have left the area, as if engaged'.[125] Determining that relations between soldiers and local women had become 'too close', another cited a correspondent who was convinced that the English would 'be the cause of much unhappiness and [many] ruined relationships after this cursed war'.[126] Naturally, some residents were unhappy with the situation and criticised the authorities for not putting a stop to the 'debauchery of women and troops

---

121 For the problems caused by German offspring, see Harris, Ruth, 'Children of the Barbarian', *Past and Present* 141 (1993), pp. 170-206 and Macintyre, *Foreign Field*, pp. 138-40.
122 Reboux, Paul, *La Guerre Inconnue,* quoted in Fischer and Dubois, *Sexual Life,* p. 143.
123 Denise de Weerdt, *De vrouwen van de Eerste Wereldoorlog* (Ghent: Amsab, 1993), p. 303.
124 Gibbs, *Realities*, II, pp. 281-2.
125 Archives de 'l'armee de terre, Chateau de Vincennes (ATT): AAT/16 N 1472, rapport, 28 aout-1 septembre 1916, Commission de Controle. Dunkerque, no. 77.
126 AAT/16 N 1472, rapport, 9-15 septembre 1916, Dunkerque, no. 107.

of all nationalities'.[127] As we have seen, however, it was often the girls themselves who were doing the chasing and were not to be put off despite the individual soldier's attempt to end an affair. In the words of Fusilier Officer Davies:

> I met one woman who I couldn't get rid of … she heard we were in Arras and was coming up to see me, so I asked my second in command … to write and say unfortunately I'd been killed … she wrote asking if there were any effects she could have as a souvenir [and then] she started writing to him, however it faded out![128]

Another infantryman, Eachus, introduces the duplicity, intrigue and tenacity that *affaires de coeur* might involve. The story is interesting in that, although anecdotal, it also further illustrates how liaisons between the military and civilian populations were widespread and how one woman could sustain the morale of multiple men:

> It is true that there have been quite a large number of marriages contracted between the 'lily' and the 'rose' in addition to the vast number of unsolemnised unions also. A case in point I may relate with accuracy … The man is married, but the girl is unaware of the fact and believes she will eventually go to England with her fiancé (that word fiancé covers a great deal of sin). She followed him from place to place … she has always managed to find him wherever he has gone and stayed with him attached to the British Army. This is a very good representation of what in various ways occurs daily out here and is not exaggerated, but on the contrary quite the reverse. The story is only half completed for the girl has reiterated several times that if Monsieur leaves her, she will follow him and shoot him with a revolver, or throw vitriol over him, although she is herself a wrong one, for in conversation she has told me of her many amours with British Officers at Béthune, Boulogne and Paris, she also writes to one officer now whose mistress she has been and whose address she says is at Bristol. Ah, well, 'c'est la guerre'.[129]

Undoubtedly, war gave opportunities for deceit on both sides of the gender divide and the wonder is that the *crime passionnel* did not make regular headlines. Such stories, however, simply do not surface unless they reach the level where officialdom is involved, and the veil of secrecy is forcibly lifted in reaction to scandal.

---

127 AAT/16 N 1540, raport, 18 fevrier 1918 cited K. C. Gibson, 'Through French Eyes: the BEF and the records of the French postal censor', *History Workshop Journal* 55 (Spring 2003), p. 181.
128 IWM Sound Archive, No. 9750 reel 11, Davis, Jim, NCO 12th Bn Royal Fusiliers/officer 8th/9th Royal Fusiliers; also Read, *Of Those We Loved*, pp. 414-15.
129 IWM 01/51/1, Eachus, S. T., 'Memoirs' (unpubl.), p. 39; see also Dunn, *War the Infantry Knew*, p. 365, 9 July [1917].

On the other hand, and more markedly, the popularity of the troops was often greeted by sadness when they marched away. For the older generation, these young men were reminders of their own sons and husbands who were fighting on a distant front, many Tommies were invited in to enjoy almost family life, but for the young women it was perhaps a sentimental farewell to lovers. When they left, found Gibbs, 'women kissed, and cried in spite of the laughter, and joked in a queer jargon English-French'. Sections of the Indian Army departed in similar circumstances.[130]

If generally soldiers and the local female population were favourably disposed towards each other what were the attitudes of those of absent husbands, and the church in France and how did that affect any potential intimacy that might develop?

Understandably the most interested parties were the absent husbands. The *poilu's* attitude to the Tommy was not always one of respect; British contributions to the war effort were felt at time to have been less than sufficient. Within this general context, some French soldiers were undoubtedly also resentful of *les Anglais*, who had more money and were regarded as more smartly uniformed. Fear of infidelity among women at home was obsessive in all armies, and – for the French, for most of the war – the most suspected seducers were the British. One postcard writer from inside the zone of occupation vented his anger to a correspondent:

> More women arrested at the English camp. And not whores, you can be sure; married women … What a blow for their husbands, when they find out … they should have their heads shaved.[131]

In some sections of society, it was considered shameful for married women to be seen with British soldiers, and indignant neighbours sometimes had offenders arrested as prostitutes. Sometimes, however, this was simply the result of local politics or long-standing disagreements between neighbours.[132]

The French or Belgian male did not always have to be absent for jealousies to occur and for the *entente cordiale* between the allies to break down. There are accounts, for example, of fights breaking out in estaminets when the troops found themselves using the same facilities as the locals. And no doubt the French defended the reputations of their women. British soldiers were aware that their presence was a cause of jealousy. Taylor recounted an episode in a Boulogne hotel where jealousies reached a boiling point with an exchange of blows between erstwhile allies.[133] But intriguingly, there

---

130 Gibb, *Realities,* II, p. 105; Omissi, *Indian Voices*, p. 215.
131 Tombs & Tombs, *That Sweet Enemy,* pp. 480-81, also citing Rousseau, Frederic, *La Guerre Censurée* (Paris: Editions du Seuil, 1999).
132 Ibid., p. 481. See also letter dated 6 Apr. 1915 to Governor, West Flanders, *Eerste Wereldoolog* file, Richsarchief Brugge, Archif de Panne.
133 : Hankey, *Student in Arms,* p. 232, and Taylor, *Bottom of the Barrel,* p. 153.

seems to have been both an acceptance and complicity at times with, as Clare found, infidelities 'not regarded by them as it would be by the majority of our people'.[134]

The French church also took an interest in its parishioners' sexual affairs with the British. The local curés in some areas forbade women from 'openly accompany[ing] a British soldier anywhere in France'.[135] With regard to casual relationships, Graves asserted that '"*Peut-être après la guerre*" [was] the stock answer that the Pas de Calais girls were ordered by their priests to give to Allied soldiers who asked for a "promenade, mademoiselle?"' But he also said, 'It was seldom given, I heard, except for the purpose of bargaining'.[136] Some soldiers felt too that the concern of the French priests for the local girls' welfare had more to do with self-interest than saving them from moral degradation. The Canadian, Will Bird, recounted being told by a local that:

> You waste your time [in his interest in a village girl]. That is the priest's girl … she sleep with him. It is a great honour for her. And she has been with him since January … He changes every two or three months for a new one.[137]

The Belgian church, or at least such that remained in the unconquered lands, had, as previously noted, equally mixed feelings. It was not a dislike of the soldier *per se*, but as with their French counterparts, priests worried about the effects on morals, especially those of the younger girls who might succumb to a local version of 'khaki fever'.

Inevitably, there were also those who had little or no desire to mix, finding the sometimes ribald and coarse soldiers a trial and imposition. The British soldiers' lack of cultural awareness and insensitivities must have seemed particularly boorish to the local population at times. Rude sallies of doubtful wit at the expense of the womenfolk, young and old, who stood at cottage doors as troops passed could cause the inhabitant to 'gesticulate wildly with virtuous indignation', remembered I. L. Read.[138] Burrage, too, felt that although generally speaking, the indecent gestures were not resented 'the few pure and fastidious women must have suffered torments'.[139] On the whole, though, if sections of the people of Belgium and France were antipathetic, the cause was more often the damage the soldiers did to farms and billets and the consequent economic loss.[140]

The act of courtship was morale-boosting without it necessarily leading to sexual congress, but if there was one factor that seems to have determined how far

---

134 IWM 06/48/1, Clare, '*Reminiscences*', book three, unpaginated.
135 A Rifleman (pseud. Smith), *Four Years*, p. 80.
136 Graves, *Goodbye*, p. 207.
137 Bird, *Ghosts*, p. 40.
138 Read, *Of Those We Loved*, p. 228; and Gibbons, *Roll on*, p. 87.
139 Burrage (Ex-Private X) *War is War*, p. 47.
140 This is captured well in Mottram's *Spanish Farm*, and more formally in Gibson, 'The British Army, French Farmers and the war on the Western Front, 1914-1918', *Past and Present* 180 (2003), pp. 175-239.

fraternisation progressed towards establishing a carnal relationship, it would be either side's ability to speak the other's language. Difficulties in communication discouraged the forging of any real relationships, as some soldiers remembered:

> I didn't have a French girlfriend 'didn't have enough French [language] for that
> ...
> *Interviewer:* Did anyone find French girlfriend?
> I don't think so ... inability to speak French was a problem in developing relationships of any kind.[141]

Certainly, those soldiers who spoke French (few had any Flemish) found any barriers to moving from polite social greeting (or suggestive pidgin banter), to intimate relationships less difficult to overcome. It was often easier for officers, whose education had provided them with at least some language skills, than it was for the ranker who had no prior knowledge. Men with the ability to communicate were often found helping colleagues further their amorous intentions in a variety of ways, from accompanying them to the brothels[142] to composing or translating their love letters.

Many of the soldiers' diaries or letters contain a smattering of French words or Anglicised versions. The phrases they thought important are a good indication of the sort if conversations they hoped to enjoy. This list is from the diary of Stanley Mills serving with the AIF:

Etre-vous libre le dimanche?	Are you free this Sunday?
Ou demeurez-vous?	Where do you live?
Combien de soeurs avez-vous?	How many sisters have you?
Serez-vous libre demain soir?	Will you be here tomorrow evening?[143]

The man who spoke French was thus at a distinct advantage. One soldier tells of developing a relationship while first out of the line on rest at Le Bizet in December 1914. It was consummated later when returning to the same billet: 'I could do very well then, me, at French, I'll tell you, with the girls or anybody else ... I could get along very nicely'.[144]

---

141 IWM Sound Archive, No. 12575, reel 1, Stammers, A. C., driver ASC; and see also Higgins C. F. No. 9884, reel 19.
142 IWM Sound Archive, No. 9544, Bromley: 'For Corporal Simmonds ... I ... translated into French his billets-doux to the daughter at the big farm where we had stayed at Wascherville', Smith, *Four Years*, p. 128. See also Lucy, *Devil*, p. 89.
143 Fellows, Carol, *Love and War: Stories of the War Brides from the Great War to Vietnam* (Sydney: Bantam, 2002), p. 49.
144 IWM Sound Archive, No. 9875, reel 5, Ashurst. See also Read, *Of Those We Loved*, pp. 333-5, for an illustration of the advantages of speaking the language; also Boyack, *Behind the Lines*, p. 138.

Speaking the local language delivered more prosaic benefits than 'owning two languages is to have two souls' as *La Vie Parisienne* poetically observed in the title of this print. Interestingly, the advert on the wall behind guarantees 'success', implicitly for the local in attracting the ANZAC officer. (Author's collection)

The war novels of ex-soldiers are full of stories of encounters that progressed to full-blown relationships, largely because of the storyteller's or central character's ability to speak French. Even given the possibility of their accounts being 'sexed up', there are so many episodes across so many novels, that one has to accept the likelihood that many of these 'fictional' incidents were based either on fact, observation or credible reportage. Those who couldn't converse suffered the inevitable outcome and could only harbour regrets.

Such was the advantage of speaking the language, and such was the demand for having a certain vocabulary that enterprising publishers cashed in and printed self-help texts – sometimes to the moral fury of the French. In an attempt to buttress, as well as defend, morality for French women, in late 1917, the *Conseil National des Femmes Françaises* subsection on morality launched an energetic attack on what it called an 'almost pornographic' pamphlet found in the possession of a British soldier, entitled 'Five Minutes Conversation with Young Ladies', and described as 'one of the most infamous productions' designed to 'facilitate vice by foreign men'. The pamphlets were attacked on two fronts: for the damage it would do to the French by encouraging Allied soldiers to vice, and for angering American, Canadian and British women who sent their men to defend French women and expected them to come home 'morally and physically pure'.[145] But phrase books were what the soldier wanted since they gave the soldier all the language-skills required for the purpose needed:

> This Irishman [*writes one officer meeting another on leave in Paris*] has acquired a smattering of French which he was airing to me with much pride and an atrocious accent. The phrases were of one kind 'Vous ets tres gentile mamsell!' [sic] 'Vouli-vu promenade avec moi?' [sic] and 'Embrassez-moi veet' [sic], were the most polished ones.[146]

Nevertheless, while speaking French was an obvious advantage, it was not an absolute prerequisite. Either the universal language of love or simple gesticulation was often adequate substitute as Percy Clare observed: 'Such a small thing as language was no bar to a Tommy intent on engaging a lady's affections be she old or young!'.[147]

It was not only the soldier who tried to learn to communicate. He often found he was an unpaid language teacher to the local community, though perhaps interest was feigned merely to have an excuse for meeting. Private Tucker discovered this: 'there was another young girl who, armed with a French-English phrase book asked me to sit on the platform with her and study this together, but we both soon became bored and wandered off'.[148] Normally, at street level, most English that had been learned was either slang or what might help the speaker sell something. As the drafts of soldier marched through cobbled streets, school French made tentative contact with the working language. The first hint of local English came from gamins who ran alongside

---

145 Quoted in Susan Grayzel, 'Mothers, Marraines, and Prostitutes, Morale and Morality in the First World War in France', *International History Review* 19 (1997), pp. 77-8.
146 Rifleman, *Four Years*, p. 72.
147 Hodson, *Grey Dawn–Red Night*, p. 218; Eyre, *Somme Harvest*, pp. 29-31; Shaw, *Jottings*, p. 54.; Gibbons, *Roll on*, p. 54. For the usefulness of sign language IWM 06/48/1, Percy Clare, 'Reminiscences 1916-1918', unpaginated,
148 Tucker, *Johnny*, p. 31; also Blunden, *Undertones*, p. 147.

shrilly proffering the blandishments of their sisters in exchange for English cigarettes. 'Jig-a-jig with my sister, mister?' litters the accounts of scores of old soldiers.[149]

Inevitably, pidgin caused plenty of unfortunate misunderstandings. This lighthearted account taken from Manning's novel, *'Her Privates We'*, must surely have had its roots in reality. It should remind us that the majority of relationships were not sexual and would have been 'proper' and platonic, with great offence being caused to those whose propriety might have been questioned. Returning to a billet he has previously used, the madame welcomed him. He returns the greeting:

> Glad to be back, *compris? Cushy avec mademoiselle.*' The expression on her face … passed very rapidly from astonishment to indignation and from indignation to wrath. Before Corporal Greenstreet realised what was about to happen, she had swung a muscular arm, and landed a terrific box on his ear … *'Madame … "cushy" est un mot d'argot militaire que veut dire doux, confortable, tout ce qu'il y a de plus commode … calmez-vous … que sentiments très respectueux.*[150]

Whether the conversations and meetings took place with fluency in either language, in pidgin, or through gestures, they did so: flirting could always be helped along with small gifts, always with the hope of it leading further: 'The local people strolled around … Some cap badges were parted with, and some rendezvous for next day were given that evening'.[151] The gifts, the cap badges, given to the 'French ladies that they had been walking [with]' often had their desired effect for the flirtatious soldier, as the redoubtable Richards attests there was reciprocation, and 'in some cases [they] also left other souvenirs which would either be a blessing or curse to the ladies concerned'.[152]

Most liaisons were inevitably short, but sometimes the temporary relationship became permanent and occasionally marriage followed.[153] One estimate of the number of marriages is as low as 51, but this is based on the limited evidence of one English-speaking church in Boulogne. New Zealander Private Quartermain wrote home:

> In the town there is a notice board for a sort of public announcement of engagements … ['Promises of Marriage' the wording has it]. And one of the recent ones bears the name of a French girl, and a British soldier … and a New Zealander. I don't know the chap, but I nearly burst when I read the successive words 'Soldats [sic] Ambulancer, Nouvelle Zealande.

---

149 French, Anthony, *Gone for a Soldier* (Kineton: Roundwood Press, 1972), p. 26.
150 Manning, *Her Privates We*, p. 115.
151 Dunn, *War*, p. 19.
152 Richards, *Old Soldiers*, p. 14.
153 Bell, P. M. H., *France and Britain, 1900-1940: Entente and Estrangement* (Harlow: Longman, 1996), p. 99.

Whether it was the novelty of the thing, or that the author did not feel that local girls were the marrying kind, will never be known.[154] But there are other reports and after the war men both took brides home and also returned to the Western Front to marry and settle with women they had met during the war years. It was not uncommon as late as the 1960s to meet gardeners employed by the Commonwealth War Grave Commission who had followed the latter route. One of the daughters of the famed Poperinghe estaminet, *A la Poupée,* Marie Louise, married a Captain Jack Reynolds, and followed him to England, while Major-General I. G. Adcock, who had written home to his Mother that she should not 'be surprised if I bring a Belgium girl home as a souvenir' did eventually married locally, staying behind in France for a few years before returning to his native Australia with a French wife.[155] Another Australian NCO, Andrew Anderson, found his wife-to-be, Louise, in a billet near Rouen in mid-1916. While they too eventually returned to Australia after the war, the army had not made it easy for the marriage to take place; 'I have been rather unlucky re my marriage … the General Officer commanding the lines of communication area would not allow Loulou to stay in the war zone (once we were married) which meant she would have to go away'. [156]

Possibly a greater number of marriages might have taken place had the army's view been more positive. The peacetime tradition of limiting wives in the regiment appears to have been continued in wartime. Though the following example is from the experiences of the Canadian Expeditionary Force, because the Canadian Divisions were so integrated into the normal British Army structure, it is indicative of the general situation. We read that: 'Another Sergeant's appeal was that he be permitted to marry a pretty Belgian *mademoiselle* with whom he had fallen passionately in love. RSM Blake properly (at the time) refused the request of the amorous Sergeant'.[157] Of interest here is not only the army attitude to marriage but that the soldier had the time and opportunity to fall 'passionately in love' and this applied to soldiers of every colour. While the white authorities were determined to prevent dark-skinned races from defiling European women it did not appear to bother the New Zealand Maori. For other cultural groups, such as the Indians, inter-racial or inter-faith marriage was taboo, even if there were plenty of potential willing local partners as Jai Singh of the 6th Cavalry implied, writing to a friend that 'I should like to marry in France, but I am afraid the family would be ashamed. You can marry very fine girls if you like'. [158]

Taboo or not, Abdul Ali 6th Cavalry France, writing to his Punjab-based friend to Rissaldar Farz Ali Kahn tells of a great scandal caused by a marriage: 'There was an extraordinary affair in the regiment yesterday, although there have been similar

---

154 Boyack, *Behind the Lines,* p. 34.
155 AWM L/12/11/2122 '*Letters From the Front'.*
156 Fellows, *Love & War,* p. 62.
157 Wheeler, *50th Battalion,* p. 86.
158 Omissi, Indian Voices, p. 331.

cases before in other regiments. Mahomed Khan, the lance dafadah, is engaged to a Frenchwoman on the understanding that he becomes a Christian. The marriage ceremony is to take place in two or three days. We have all done our best to prevent it, but all has been in vain. You can judge the state of affairs when it has got to the length of our marrying Frenchwomen'.[159] In this case the reluctant lance dafadah found that even out of the front line one could still face a shotgun if a local girl was made pregnant!

What the girls themselves saw in these marriages is open to conjecture. Their motive was perhaps love, but in some instances it was basic economic security. No doubt many marriages made in haste were likely to be repented at leisure, as Crozier attests in his report of the young officer who married an apparent prostitute, was disinherited, and after the war banished to the colonies: 'There are dozens of cases of this sort for which the war is alone to blame'.[160]

Just as many affairs did not end in marriage, with participants unable to bridge the cultural gap, or simply unwilling to make the sacrifice of relocation. As Mottram wrote of his fictional couple, the only thing in common was the war. 'The War removed, they had absolutely no means of contact'. Their case 'was not isolated. It was national'.[161]

There can be little doubt, however, that during the conflict itself, love was given and taken freely on an *ad hoc* basis in all of the varied zones of occupation, even if any ensuing physical sex often incurred an indirect cost. This was one war in which fraternisation replaced the usual wartime practices of rape and treating women as a spoil of battle. The open cultural and social context, coupled with the length and static nature of the occupation ensured that this was inevitable: 'matters adjust themselves … women like a man to fetch and carry and to run after children … and the soldiers … want a woman around to give heed to their grumbling'.[162]

The best witnesses are naturally the soldiers themselves and, even if they were loathe to commit themselves formally, the breadth of their sexual activities slips out in the reminiscences, the reported banter, the jokes and even the songs of the period. Perhaps there is none so illustrative of what the 'boys got up to' than the words of 'advice' contained in a song popularised by the music hall veterans, Flanagan and Allen, and sung as the sons of the Western Front veterans marched off to fight in France again a generation later:

If a little grey-haired lady asks 'How's your Father'?
That's Mademoiselle from Armentiers [sic]

---

159 Ibid., p. 279.
160 Crozier, *Brass Hat*, pp. 106-7.
161 Mottram, *Spanish Farm*, p. 233.
162 See Young, *Under Siege*, p. 56 for *New York Times* citation 5 Dec.1915; Corday, *Paris Front*, p. 81, May 1915.

7

A Moral 'No Man's land': The billet

Borrowing VC winner, Bob Mariner's phrase, Tommy would rub up against a bit of skirt most often in his billets and in the ubiquitous estaminets, but he also met women in a whole range of other less obvious locations, both formal and informal, planned and accidental; by the roadside, when shopping, in the volunteer canteens and on fatigues where facilities were shared with the local civilian.

There was also a compensation in being wounded; he would be nursed back to health by apparent angels, and perhaps enjoy further convalescence in the company of the fairer sex. The women spoke the same language, even if there were other barriers. Although relationships were most often the stuff of erotic fantasy – and suggestive postcards played on this – there can be no doubt of the morale-boosting nature of coming into contact with a 'rose of no man's land'. Cloethe memorably describes the impact: 'The sound of their starched skirts and woman's voices was like the sound of running water to a man dying of thirst.' [1]

Women serving in France attracted some controversy with accusations of promiscuous behavior and there were occasional scandals concerning VADS and WAACs who were send home pregnant, though the numbers bandied about were much inflated and in reality it seems few actually were. Many of these stories may well have emanated from inter-service rivalries and jealousies but the more credible Crozier, for example, told of the many liaisons he witnessed between young women and senior officers in Boulogne. It was commonly felt that officers were the quarry rather than humble rankers but the Royal Welch Fusiliers medical officer, Dunn, found no such social barriers: 'In Abbeyville I saw WAACs for the first time. If they don't speak to officers they seek and find ample solace with other ranks'. Helen Zena Smith's 'Not So Quiet', a fictionalized account of an ambulance driver's experiences, is sometimes found to be the source of the more controversial revelations, but being based on what are claimed to be 'real diaries, since lost' this remains suspect testimony.

---

1   Cloete, *Victorian Son*, p. 244.

One might be incredulous over reports of physical intimacy between patient and nurses within the hospital itself but Hiscock relates a story of a young British nurse who had a sexual encounter with a patient in a bed next to him in a hospital in Boulogne: 'The next morning she put the screens around Vanners's bed and Sister or anyone else passing might imagine that the occupants was having a tricky private blanket bath. …. Maud hadn't been with Vanner long when I heard girlish gigglings …. It ended with a gasp of pleasure from Nurse Maud'. Hiscock is not alone in in having witnessed such alleged behaviour. [2]

What are more readily believable are the numerous accounts of men who met the nurses outside of the immediate clinical context despite the fact that nurses were not always allowed total freedom of movement, even when off duty; one account has them 'in hutments caged in with barbed wire.' It is not uncommon to discover accounts of healthy, or recovering soldiers enjoying the company of off-duty nurses, I.L. Read captured the atmosphere of one of the larger base hospitals:

> 'Most afternoons and not a few evenings found us in the company of nurses from the great field hospital nearby at Wimereux, now occupying what, in happier days, had been the casino and its extensive grounds… They were jolly girls from various voluntary nursing services – St John, British Red Cross or V.A.D – generally either with a brother, a finance or even husband, serving somewhere….. (It was) a very pleasant change to sit on the dunes or cliffs (with them) on a warm afternoon and chat … on two occasions [we had] a mixed foresome dinner in Wimereux. But, like all good things, the fortnight … came to an end'. [3]

Hiscock told of a similar chance meeting, but with a nurse. The episode not only demonstrates that the impetus might come from the woman but more importantly, the wistful tone of his memory illustrates not only his long-remembered yearning for female company but the tremendous morale boost it injected:

> On one of my wanderings I came across Maud sitting on an Army blanket between two dunes and to my surprise she asked me to stop and sit down beside her… she stirred something in me that hadn't been stirred for a long time…. As the sun moved slowly and down across the sky Maud and I, with Maud in command, forgot war and troop trains full of wounding men, forgot green identification cables with D.I markings on them, forgot imminent Field Courts Martial, and enjoyed each other. Collegiates on American campuses, some years later, were to call what we did … 'deep petting'. It was nothing new. What we

---

2   Read, *Of those we Loved*, p. 396.
3   Cloete, *Victorian Son*, p. 244.

did that afternoon in wartime was discover that Adam and Eve's disease – loneliness – could be assuaged.'[4]

Time out of the line at convalescence camps provided greater opportunity for meeting French women, sometimes those that worked at the camp, but more often simply local girls whom the soldier might meet while taking a convalescent stroll. George Ashurst, a private in the 2nd Bn Lancs, found himself recovering from trench foot in Boulogne, where: 'we met these girls … we had a jolly good time and I saw them every day, there was nothing to stop me'.[5]

Naturally, whether it was with the few girls from home, or with the local women, time and opportunity were as much a variable as morals in determining whether the meeting, wherever it occurring, lead to casual sex, a recognizable relationship, or merely fed a fantasy to be enjoyed at some future private moment. Ashurst's opportunity arose because he was settled in one location for an extended time.

Exploring the soldier's memories of other less immediately obvious meeting locations, where something other than blatant prostitution might develop, provides interesting and often unexpected detail on daily life behind the lines.

The local rail station was often a place targeted by both sexes and where apparently more than train carriages coupled. Inevitably, it was prostitutes who made the most of the flow of traffic passing through stations en route to the front, but at some of the quieter railheads there were encounters not based on a financial arrangement. The sexually prolific Lawson recounted the first of his many conquests as happening:

> when we going up the line in a cattle truck. We stopped at a station and some French girls there and some of the chaps started to maul the girls and they were very pretty, so I had a row with one [of the chaps] … eventually having rescued the girl … started doing [it] on the platform … well it was a grass verge really… she was a nice girl.[6]

Lawson is a fascinating if somewhat unsavoury witness and sexual predator: in his apparently open and honest interview he lists his conquests, experiences and other opportunistic one-off sexual adventures in a variety of situations as well as admitting regular brothel visits and liaisons with individual prostitutes.

One fairly common opportunity for soldiers to meet and flirt with local girls was when they were out of the line, mostly in Cloete's second zone of occupation, relaxing beside rivers, streams and canals, bathing, swimming, or fishing. The scenes described are almost pastoral, certainly some are comic. All are illustrative of the culturally different environment that the soldier was exposed to – quite literally, in the case

---

4 Hiscock, *Bells of Hell*, p. 50
5 IWM Sound Archive, No. 9875, reel 7, Ashurst.
6 IWM Sound Archive, No. 24882, reel 2, Lawson.

of bathing parties where local girls might gather to watch the boys wash naked in the streams and canals, often much to Tommy's embarrassment.[7] Occasionally, as Canadian Will Bird remembered, the girls stripped off themselves and joined the boys in the canal.

It was not only these *ad hoc, al fresco* opportunities to see the disrobed young men that the girls found so alluring. Many soldier baths were in converted breweries where the old beer vats, not always totally out of view, provided the washing facilities. Soldiers would often be taken by battalion to these and directed *en masse* though the sequence of disrobing, bathing and redressing (usually in replacement ill-fitting but cleaner uniforms). Norman Edwards of the Gloucesters remembered the baths at Pont St Neep Brewery where 'up on the hill to the left of us was a bridge ... on which the village maidens foregathered because they would see us walking across practically naked'.[8] Was this any more than curiosity or teasing on the part of the women? Other evidence in similar circumstances suggests that, once the barriers were down, it was a short step to active flirtation with either side being the instigators.

Communal baths, which were in part staffed by local women, provided another context. When Corporal Grey was placed in charge of a communal bath with a staff of 44 men and 58 women, he found he had quite problem on his hands: 'The boys upstairs in the drying and sorting room take some watching I can tell you as their work interacts with that of the girls', and P.H.Jones found at another work placement 'the place was overflowing with girls who were not exactly bashful.'[9]

Any normal activity in civilian areas could lead to some level of intercourse with a local girl and soldiers were not slow to exploit any situation. Dixon had 'dim memories of a certain establishment [in Béthune] we called "Le Mouchoir Shop", or in English, "The handkerchief shop", which we patronised because of two ravishingly pretty girls behind the counter', and where to 'exchange airy badinage with two such delightful creatures once in a while was a most delightful change from an all-masculine society'.[10] Vaughan, too, recalled shopping forays as a time for meeting the opposite sex. These appear to be quite genuine shops, not the 'pretext shops' that were often a cover for prostitution.[11]

Perhaps the most colourful of incidents resulting from a shopping expedition happened to T. S. Hope. Hope and his colleague were shopping while on leave in Peronne (in November 1917) where the initiative was taken by the lady owner and her friend, whose husbands were away at the front. The invitation led to sexual adventure,

---

7 Kelly, R. B. Talbot, *A Subaltern's Odyssey: memoirs of the Great War*, (London: Kimber, 1980), p. 104. Not all soldiers were unembarrassed: See Rifleman, *Four Years*, p. 73.
8 IWM Sound Archive, No. 14932, reel 4, Edwards.
9 Cited in Boyack, *Behind*, p. 129. See also Runcie, 'Territorial Mob', p. 85 for story of 'forward' and flirtatious French girls in a gas mask assembly factory in Abbeyville, 1916. IWM P246, Jones, P. H., 'Diary', p. 198.
10 IWM 92/36/1, Dixon, 'Wheels', p. 58.
11 Vaughan, *Some Desperate Glory*, p. 36.

and the description provides an interesting insight into both the women's attitudes and the reaction of the naive young soldier.[12] The painting, *Adam and Eve at Peronne*, by war artist, William Orpen, could almost have been inspired by the story.

Though the soldier might have met a member of the opposite sex while shopping, 'walking out', or on rarer occasions at shared social events such as the cinema or army sports day; the army horse show to which prominent locals were invited, is good example of the army function as a meeting place, though this was mostly enjoyed by officers. Repeated social contact, however, was the key to a blossoming relationship. Extended contact was most commonly experienced in the billet and estaminet where familiarity often bred longing rather than contempt. The greatest opportunities occurred where the soldiers lived or were entertained: in billets and estaminets.

Billets inhabited an ambiguous moral 'no-man's land', with sexual adventures being either the 'wild sex' or 'free love' kind, sometimes paid-for but with girls who would not necessarily have considered themselves as prostitutes. Given this, an examination of billet life provides further evidence of the sexual *milieu* and the prevalence of opportunity outside the regulated brothel. As one would expect, free from immediate danger, and allowed to enjoy at least a modicum of normality, the billets were generally a place of high morale, despite the actual living conditions being basic.

The billet and the estaminet were sufficiently recognisable as locations for romance and relationships to provide R. H. Mottram with the basis of a complete plot for one of the novels in his *Spanish Farm Trilogy*, where he follows the culturally doomed relationship between Madeleine and the English Officer, Skene. On publication, the book was hailed as one of the greatest novels to have come out of the conflict and one of the most authentic. It is a mystery why this, and indeed several other remarkable works are not currently in popular print.

Percy Clare confirms the billet's status and throws an interesting light on the inhabitants' attitudes:

> Of course, in the villages in which we billeted the women wished to be kind to our men and were willing, too willing, to oblige, but it must be remembered that our men were there as friends and allies and a woman will do a lot with for love that nothing will force her to do otherwise.[13]

How often billets gave rise to amorous adventures can never be measured but Clare was certain that 'abundant opportunities … were afforded in these little villages where our men were billeted'.[14] If he survived any length of time on the Western Front, the soldier would often find himself in the same towns and villages, even the same billets

---

12   Hope, *Winding Road*, pp. 196-97, 202-03.
13   IWM 06/48/1, Clare, '*Reminiscences*', unpaginated, book three.
14   Ibid,.

Billets provided potential for sex and romance for all combatants as this German postcard illustrates. (Author's collection)

on successive tours of duty, giving rise to familiarity and intimacy.[15] 'When the same troops quarter in the same village for a long time', observed a French postal censor, 'relations become quite good'. Good relations, wrote another censor, 'mostly come from the fact that the same unit stay[s] a long time or always return[s] to the same billets'.[16] The soldiers were well aware of their potential. Billet adventures often began for Kitchener's army long before it had even left England, and gave many a taste of the possibilities that might be open to them once in France.[17] For Crozier, the billet played a central role in the lowering of moral standards, not just overseas, but back in Britain, too: 'The habits acquired in the billets of France and Flanders … are spread rapidly to Mayfair and Whitechapel and all places in-between'. Echoing one of the soldier's excuses for promiscuity – the uncertainty of continued existence – he writes:

> 'Why not,' they argue, 'the war is long, life is short, it cannot now be too sweet, let it be as sweet as possible.' This free love in billets is understandable – the women and girls were generally clean … in the billets the girls see to it that preventatives are used, for their own protection, and, in fact, often keep a stock of requisites for the purpose of safety and profit.[18]

It was not a one-way street. Young girls in the family, or perhaps refugees working in the billet, would have seen the soldiers as a source of fun and adventure, not always profit. Behrend told of a time when obtaining a billet was proving difficult. Though the madame of the house protested over the soldiers being billeted on her, her daughter had a different view: 'Jeanette winked at me and smiled and pouted and danced on her toes'.[19]

Families, finding themselves overrun with young men were, not unnaturally, protective of their daughters. Writing in 1916 of experiences gained in the region of the Somme, one soldier, knowing his own kind well, understood their predicament:

> The French people are not hospitable to English troops … Yet I can picture their angle … You have to be very charitable before you open your house too gladly to officers who are a little lousy, usually none too well-bred, and sometimes anxious to seduce your servants.[20]

---

15   Becker, *Silhouettes of the Great War*, p. 63.
16   Gibson, Craig,'Through French Eyes', *History. Workshop Journal* 55 (2003), p.179. French postal censors reports, 1916.
17   Read, *Of Those We Loved* (1994), p. 229.
18   Crozier, *Brass Hat*, p. 73.
19   Behrend, *Kemmel Hill*, p 113.
20   Plowman, *Subaltern*, p. 106 and Noakes, F. E., *The Distant Drum, A Memoir of a Guardsman in the Great War* (N.p.: Private printing, 1952; Barnsley: Frontline Books facsimile 2010), p. 92.

As Guardsman F.E. Noakes admitted, 'we ... often, I fear, 'ruined' their daughters (not always without encouragement)'.

The longer the stay, the greater the likelihood that a real relationship might develop. Such relationships could settle into domesticity almost of the kind a soldier might find at home. 'All right to tell you about my girlfriend?' asked one Imperial War Museum interviewee tentatively;

> At Westoutré, just back from front line ... I went to a billet ... there was a lovely girl about 20 ... she used to do everything for me ... she'd clean the mud off my uniform, make me coffee ... make me sandwiches when we'd go back [to the trenches] ... this went on several months.[21]

The fact that the interviewee referred to his 'girlfriend' as he recounted this episode suggests it was more than a simple monetary arrangement.

Another of Lawson's less bashful accounts (though he was quick to add the caveat that his wife did not know of his French adventures!) remembered some 'lovely billets' including the one where 'I used to take my washing to when we were out of the line and we did it over the ironing'. The description of the female as a 'civvy girl' by a soldier not ashamed to admit to using the services of prostitutes, again suggests this was not a relationship based on payment. The same soldier admits to having had several relationships in both official and unofficial billets (this being where the soldier found his own sleeping quarters rather than waiting for the official billeting allocation): 'The best one was the last one ... Fernand ... This girl was really fond of me'.[22]

In France and Belgium, billeting the troops was necessary mostly in the second and third zones of occupation.[23] Although the army used tents and temporary buildings, the sheer number of men stationed on the continent, and their constant movement between the rear areas and the front line, meant that civilian habitations had to be commandeered as shelter. Billeting officers negotiated direct with people for the number they could house, based on fixed pay rates. Troop rotation in and out of the line and reserve meant that the individual soldier would see many types of billet, with varying levels of comfort. They included estaminets, individual houses (such as miners' homes around Lens) and even chateaux. In deserted and bombed-out villages, cellars and coal-holes passed muster, and, where they were part of the geology (Arras for example, and later Vimy), caves or underground caverns were used. These billets might house a platoon, company, or even a battalion for a single night on a break from a march, or for extended periods while in reserve.

---

21 IWM Sound Archive, No. 9339, reel 15, Holbroke.
22 IWM Sound Archive, No. 24882, reel 2, Lawson.
23 For an account of the billeting process, see Simkins, Peter, 'Soldiers and Civilians: billeting in Britain and France', in Beckett and Simpson (eds), *A Nation in Arms*, p. 179.

Most of the line held by the British cut across fields and through small agricultural villages, resulting in the farm becoming the most common form of billet.[24] Officers and NCOs slept in the house, often several to a room, while the men slept in barns or outhouses.

The large number of men billeted at any one time in a farm gave any one individual a challenge in establishing relationships with the women living or working there. But it was patently not impossible. As was discussed earlier, rural morals could be very different. For the urban soldier the farms brought many young men closer to nature than they had ever been, even providing the rudiments of a sex education for some:

> On one or two other occasions it was curious to observe a young woman encouraging and actually assisting a bull in the mating process. This kind of thing was perhaps to be expected as in many instances their able bodied men were absent from the farms on war service, although French women on the whole seemed much closer to mother nature than their English cousins.[25]

These rural sights and sounds may well have kindled, if not inflamed, passions. They certainly gave cause for much ribaldry, and such stories again demonstrate the power of sexually-related conversations or incidents to lighten moods and improve morale:

> We had a farm billet near Busseboom where a farm girl had the unenviable task of preparing food for their cattle each morning before we were up. This poor Belgian lass had to stride over our blanket-covered recumbent bodies to get to the cutting machine in the corner of the barn ... Her fresh coloured sunburned face would redden as she guessed the nature of some of the remarks called out to her.[26]

That some farm girls did had relationships with the troops is undeniable. A mixture of local moral ambivalence, mercenary motives (the public subsidy for maternity, if not direct payment) and sheer pleasure was a powerful one. Wheeler recounts what must have been a fairly typical experience, given his statement that it did not faze his 'more sophisticated buddies':

> Another chap had been doing his best to 'violate' *une jolie mademoiselle* in the hayloft ... mademoiselle's shrieks almost burst our eardrums. I looked up and saw her clothes in a state of disarray and her hair dishevelled, as if she had been,

---

24 For an excellent description of a typical farm billet, see Becker, *Silhouettes*, pp. 63, 92.
25 Tucker, *Johnny*, p. 112.
26 Taylor, *Bottom*, pp. 95-6.

or was about to be raped … I was aghast that her plight was ignored, but my more sophisticated buddies recognised her feigned resistance![27]

That this level of intimacy was by no means unusual is also confirmed by Rifleman Woods, Queens Westminster Rifles:

> The farm was run by a widow and her three daughters, all good-looking. The Sergeant slept in the farmhouse and after two days I found out that my two mates had fixed up with two of the daughters to sleep with them leaving the youngest for me.[28]

Another liaison, reported without irony, was that of an army meteorologist whose farm billeting 'led to an idyllic love affair in a pastoral setting. All was shattered in an instant when the girl was blown to bits by the explosion of a shell'.[29]

Inevitably, the sex was not always based on romance. It was not unusual for the daughters of the farm to make themselves available for money and there are references both in diaries and letters to the younger boys of the household, too young for military service, virtually pimping their sisters.[30]

However, the overriding fact remains that heterosexual relationships developed with regularity on these farms throughout the war. As ever, quantifying them presents challenges. It is difficult to imagine, however, that the girls whose adventures were quoted above slept only with those particular soldiers, and only on these reported occasions. A few sexually active girls could have provided sexual opportunity for a relatively large number of young men.

Where the line cut through or was close to larger urban areas, billeting tended to be in private homes, as it did at railheads and base camps. Even the smallest householder could supplement his or her income by taking in soldiers, as Bird shows in his account of being billeted in a miner's cottage on the edge of the Lens battlefield. These were very basic two-up, two-down dwellings. They provided another opportunity for non-pecuniary liaisons to develop; the size of the home often meant that there was little privacy for the soldier or family and that proximity worked to break down barriers. Bird was much disconcerted by the site of his entire coal mining billet family taking their baths of the table at which he sat trying to compose a letter home but an even greater level of discomfort must have been felt by the Indian soldier, writing to his Punjabi home from France 1917, and intimating that he was present during love-making by members of his billet family.[31]

---

27 Wheeler, *The 50th Battalion*, p. 68.
28 Liddle, *The Soldier's War*, p. 59.
29 Ibid.
30 Hope, *Winding Road*, p. 68; Tilsley *Other Ranks*, p. 16. Cloete, *How Young*, p. 153.
31 Bird, *Ghosts*, p. 16. See also Omissi, *Indian Voices*, p. 208.

Be this as it may, home billets were a world away from the trenches. They were where the young soldier could experience some normality again and, once rested, other youthful preoccupations came quickly to dominate their thoughts and lives. Sex was never far away from 'top of mind'. With many home billets populated by desirable, younger women trust and familiarity developed, and both officers and men found opportunities for dalliances with willing partners. General Crozier not only reported free love as common in this situation, but found little morally wrong with it[32] though he was probably in the minority in turning down a proffered opportunity. Graves reported that:

> The officers of another company had just been telling me how they had slept in the same room with a woman and her daughter. They had tossed for the mother because the daughter was a "yellow-looking scaly little thing like a lizard".[33]

Inviting attractive young officers into the home was popular in some areas. There may have been some prestige, or social cachet, in billeting these young men, especially for the provincial middle classes. Perhaps there was even a hope of a catch being made, as Gibbs discovered with soldiers stationed in Amiens and billeted in private houses. Naturally, where young girls were part of the family relationships and intimacy could develop: 'In my own circle of friends', said a lady of Amiens, 'I know of 18 girls who were engaged to English officers'.[34] The reported numbers involved is illuminating and indicative both of how widespread fraternisation was during certain periods, with officers probably enjoying the most opportunities. Blunden, a man typical of his generation and class, described occasions that must have been almost surreal for men who were either just returned from the front line, or about to return to it. The interesting aspect here, however, is the implication that one of his brother officers was perhaps guilty of taking advantage of the girl's feelings, though to what end one will now never know:

> Evenings were spent in the drawing room [of a local chateau], where the widower's young daughters would sing and talk sweetly; the younger of them, pale with an illness, was in love with another officer who on some business like mine was billeted in the house. I did not think he was in love with her; but I will not go into that aspect.[35]

The constant fear of 'sweet sorrow' and forced parting probably added an almost Shakespearian intensity to the romance and it is easy to see how false promises might easily be made. The scene was undoubtedly repeated time and time again:[36] Edwardian

---

32 Crozier, *Brass Hat*, pp. 72-4.
33 Graves, *Goodbye*, p. 103, and Chapman, *A Passionate Prodigality*, pp. 25-6.
34 Gibbs, *Realities* II, pp. 281-2.
35 Blunden, *Undertones*, p. 35.
36 Manning, *Her Privates We*, p. 121 and Dunn, *War the Infantry Knew*, p. 169.

manners, discretion and the censor have robbed the historian of more evidence, but observers such as Gibbs have left sufficient references to hint at the frequency of these temporary amours: 'For a time letters arrived, eagerly waited for by the girls with aching hearts. Then picture postcards with a line or two of affectionate greeting. Then nothing … in spite of all the letters addressed to them'.[37] Sometimes, it was not simply callous disregard, or a 'love 'em and leave 'em attitude', which prevented lovers from writing. Many could not return even if they had wanted to. In yet other cases the uncontrollable army machine determined the soldier's every move, and under the iron rod of military discipline, the opportunity to pay a social call simply did not arise. Leave, especially for the other ranks, was scarce (sometimes a few brief weeks in 18 months service) and the time, especially for imperial troops, too valuable to use in any other way than to get back to see loved ones in Blighty. There was, at the end of it, little free will involved in being in Kitchener's Army once the initial volunteering was done:

> Dobbie announced that the countryside hereabouts was familiar to him … he became quiet and I surmised, there was a lady in the background somewhere … we marched by the signpost for Voleringckhove [sic], keeping to the main road. Dobbie looked at the distant village longingly; what a fine billet it had been! He relapsed in temporary silence, his thoughts no doubt of his girl friend here.[38]

Here, the longed-for opportunity of revisiting obviously better times was thwarted, but the pull of love, or sex, was strong, strong enough for men to risk punishment, even to face the prospect of a firing squad for desertion. Memoirs tell of men 'lorry-hopping' to get visit local towns behind their lines, and of others 'disappearing' for a few hours to enjoy female company. This Australian soldier's perhaps apocryphal tale is a good example:

> It was a bitterly cold night near a small Somme village, probably Harronville, and the sentry was not in the best of humour when an Australian Bluey approached him. Though the village was out of bounds Bluey decided to risk the sentry in order to see a girl who lived within the prohibited area.
> 'Halt, who goes there!' shouted the sentry.
> Bluey walked up to him until the end of the bayonet touched the middle of his tunic. 'Look here,', he said, 'I've got a mother in heaven, a father in hell and a bonzer girl in this here village, and I'm going to see one of them tonight. Now, it is for you to say which one.'
> Bluey saw his girl.[39]

---

37 Gibbs, *Realities* II, pp. 281-2.
38 Read, *Of Those We Loved*, p. 392.
39 Laffin, John, *On the Western Front* (Stroud: Sutton, 1997), p. 110.

In most cases, while love and romance played their part, many relationships developed in the household billet were necessarily temporary and based on physical sex, both for the soldier and the local offering the billet. Rowarth is openly crude in his description, but he gets to the point:

> I made friends with the family ... sharing our rations, cigs with them. I know for sure that some of my mates ... were having it off with some of the young girls and married women ... and when I asked them about the men who were away fighting, while they were having it every night and day with our Irishmen, replied they will never know because a slice is never missed off a cut loaf.[40]

The surviving evidence highlights that billets provided a happy hunting ground for both sexes. Rising birth rates in areas where the husbands were away at the front can only be explained by these relationships. While sometimes there was an exchange of money, in many cases sexual adventure flowed serendipitously from the coming together of two young people consummating natural desires.[41] These relationships were patently known to the army command and accepted provided that they did not compromise the soldier's health, or be the cause of antagonism between locals and the military, in which case the girl was removed.

We have yet to examine estaminets as a meeting place; there is a reason. There is some ambiguity concerning how far these billet relationships were financially driven, even though they provide undeniable evidence that Tommy's sexual contacts were commonplace rather than isolated. The position of the estaminet in this sexual landscape is less controversial. While some 'innocent' liaison's certainly developed (we only have to remember the case of the bewitching Ginger, the youngest daughter at Poperinghe's popular estaminet, *A La Poupee*), on balance, and given its pre-war history, unions formed in the estaminet were mostly of a venal type. Given this, an in-depth examination of the estaminet is included in the following survey of sexual activities *about* which there *is* no ambiguity: the use of regulated and unregulated prostitution.

---

40 IWM 80/40/1, Rowarth, '*Misfit Soldier*', p. 19, and Allison, *Bantams*, p. 106, quoting Frank Heath 17th Bn. Also Eyre, *Somme Harvest*, pp. 29-31.
41 Macintyre, *Foreign Field* (2002), pp. 138-40. See Adams, *Nothing*, p. 258, for an account of true love.

Duty before Pleasure

"Well, if yer thinks yer ought to, I'll lend yer this bit o' mistletoe o' mine"

The situations parodied in Bairnsfather's cartoons would have been instantly recognisable to the troops on the Western Front. (Courtesy Mark Warby. ©2015 Estate of Barbara Bruce Littlejohn)

The Ideal and the Real.
What we should like to see at our billets—
and (inset) what we do see.

Despite Bairnsfather's intimation of a gap between the dream and the reality, there was an allure and the girls of the billets often provided romance and sex. (Courtesy Mark Warby. ©2015 Estate of Barbara Bruce Littlejohn)

8

A Red Lamp to Guide Mars to Venus: Regulated prostitution

'Generally the men paid for what they had, and paid dearly'[1] believed Burrage, but individual experiences do not tell the complete story; every man had his own story. On the supply side, the regulated sector varied from quite literally factory-scale production to the cottage industry. The individual soldier 'client' paid for sex with women who worked in the regulated brothel sector and with 'clandestine' or the oxymoronic 'amateur prostitutes' who worked outside of the direct control of the army or local authorities. That money, or even gifts in lieu of cash, passed hands was not always the case as we have seen, but when francs were a prerequisite, the sex workers' fees varied considerably. Like any marketplace, it was governed by the laws of supply and demand and by recognised and accepted industrial practices.

It is intriguing that outside Alain Corbin's ground-breaking work on the pre-war regulation of prostitution in France, little else of note has been produced on the subject. The pity is that Corbin did not extend his analysis through the war years as he would have found that the declining industry of his researches was given a new lease of life by the influx of millions of sex-starved troops from across the globe.[2] What the soldiers (and their High Commands) found on arrival in France was a recognised structure of regulated prostitution which they gratefully took full advantage of. Unlike the Germans, the allies had no Herschfeld to record some of the finer details; nor apparently did Tommy use his box-Brownie as prolifically as Fritz in recording this aspect of his war. Thankfully, some of the less reticent Tommies left behind very vivid and colourful oral recollections, and occasionally reports worthy of the best tabloid investigative reporter. From these we are able to describe, albeit with great gaps and the help of speculation, the size, structure and economics of an industry. We

1 Ex-Private X (pseud. A. M. Burrage), *War is War* (1930), p. 47.
2 See Corbin, A, *Women for Hire: Prostitution,* for the history of regulation. For a general history of prostitution in the Victorian era, see Harsin, Jill, *Policing Prostitution in nineteenth-century Paris* (1985) and McMillan, James, F., *France and Women, 1789-1914* (London: Routledge, 2000), and Rhoades, "No Safe Women", *Proceedings of the Western Society for French History* 27.

are also able to learn something of the individual worker, the environment and the nature of the service she delivered.

The traditional French attitude to prostitution (at least throughout the nineteenth century) was that it was an unavoidable issue. 'Prostitutes are as inevitable, where men live together in large concentrations, as drains or refuse dumps ... they contribute to the maintenance of social order and harmony'.[3]

Venal sex provided an outlet for social and immoral vices, it kept marriages going, it was the source of initiation for the youths, and allowed men – who traditionally married late – to sow their wild oats. On several levels, prostitution was a recognised and acceptable 'job'; there was no disgrace, for example, attached to those women, the *femmes gallantes*, who practised high-class prostitution, or those who were 'kept women'. They were part of the social order. In fact, in most contemporary studies they were not even included in any classification of prostitutes, nor indeed were women who supplemented their wages occasionally through selling themselves. The concern of this period was that the women of the lower orders who, by alternating between periods of prostitution and periods of 'normality', presented a potential 'moral, social, sanitary, and political' threat to the social order. The most dangerous of these threats was the sanitary: their potential for spreading venereal disease. Of all diseases that can effect mankind, and can have repercussions on society, it was felt that there was none more serious, more dangerous, and more feared than syphilis.

It was how the issue of venereal disease could be dealt with that concerned the French, rather than controlling prostitution *per se*. The solution, effectively introduced in the mid-1800s, was the regulation of 'common' prostitution, isolating, marginalising and tracking the women by confining them in literally 'closed' houses and regulating their movement. These were the *maisons de tolérance*. It was concept that found favour with, and was adopted, at least to some extent, by the British Army.

Originally, they were designed to be completely closed houses, part of a wider closed system that included medical inspection facilities and special hospitals for women with venereal disease. They were tightly regulated by the local 'vice' police, as were the girls working in them. Once a girl decided on entering this particular closed order, and it was a voluntary decision, she was effectively legal, and issued with a card to prove it, but subjected to tight rules and regulations. These included regular medical inspections, prescribed hours of business and standard fees. The *maisons* took venal sex off the streets and placed it in a clinical environment, and, in theory, in a specially designated area of the town or city. Within this context, venal sex could be completely regulated by the state, and in this way not only would a 'sink' for society's vices be provided, but also the much-feared venereal disease would be controlled, and socially unavoidable, but morally suspect, paid-for sex made would be made safe for clients. Any description of these closed houses makes them seem like virtual prisons, but they

---

3   Corbin, *Women*, p. 4, quoting Parent Dachelet.

were initially popular with some 'working women', as they provided an element of security and certain basic comforts, almost – comparatively – a life of luxury.

The cantonment system established in India by the British Army bears a close resemblance to this with its system of controls, medical inspections and 'lock hospitals'.[4] Unlike the one-size-fits-all model of the British Indian version, civilian *maisons de tolérance* in France were established almost on market segment principles, with variations appealing to differing socio-economic groups and sexual tastes. The army officers' exclusive access to 'blue lamps' was part of this tradition. Although their locations and purpose were generally obvious and widely known within the community, some discretion was observed; technically, windows had to be shuttered and the women were prohibited from exhibiting themselves. Further, *Maisons* were not allowed free rein to market themselves – with 'advertising' limited to a red (or blue) lamp, a prominently displayed large house number (sometimes a coded reference to the delights on offer within), or an occasional handbill – but they were considered above-board, legal, commercial ventures, in which respectable bourgeois people might invest, and which clients could visit without shame and with some assurance of general cleanliness. The many, usually humorous postcards depicting scenes both within and outside the brothels bear witness to their general acceptance and in their early incarnations they were popular and partially effective at achieving the aims of their founders.

Maisons de tolérance were part of the social fabric wherever local ordinances gave them licence. In varying degrees and at differing times the *maison* fulfilled many social functions; it was a meeting place for the male bourgeoise of the small towns lacking in other entertainments, it could quite simply be a place of passing entertainment for tourists or pilgrims who wanted to 'get away from it all', perhaps experiencing something new in their sexual life, it could be purely functional or a mecca of eroticism, and at the basic level it was simply a source of sex for all those deprived of such in the area.

Regulation of prostitutes was not confined to the *maison*. It was further extended to include women who might work outside of the licenced *maison de tolérance* but still submit themselves to its regime of medical inspection. These *filles soumises* joined the other registered and card-carrying sisterhood of tolerated prostitutes.

Despite the grand designs of the regulationalists, prostitution inevitably proved impossible to corral and limit in this fashion. Unregulated prostitution proved difficult to stamp out. In addition other factors conspired to undermine the efficacy of the system. As the century progressed, and attitudes towards prostitution and indeed towards women changed, this virtual imprisonment of the women was increasingly questioned. Its critics also questioned its very efficacy in controlling venereal disease and found fault with the system, including inevitably the 'vice' police who controlled it. The concept was further challenged by changes in the social and built environment; town planners (led by Haussmann in his grand design for Paris) swept away

---

4   For a description see Hyam, *Empire,* pp. 121-7; Balhatchet, *Race,* p. 80.

Even though this French postcard is meant as a humorous comment on aggressive prostitutes and naïve soldiers, it is easy to see why young British soldiers might find the atmosphere intimidating. (Courtesy: Stephen Likosky)

French postcard entitled 'The Lust' captures the spirit of the maison de tolerance. Note the black prostitute, popular in some areas and mentioned as being found in one Calais brothel by a Tommy. (Courtesy: Stephen Likosky)

the geographical areas where *maisons* had been concentrated; recruitment of workers for the *maisons* became increasingly difficult; and above all, there were changes in the pattern of demand. Men were no longer satisfied with sex served in this clinical way and sought a less controlled, more 'romantic' alternative.

Thus the latter half of the nineteenth century saw the gradual decline, though not eradication, of the enclosed house and a corresponding growth in other forms of prostitution. Despite the threat of imprisonment, the unregistered army of '*filles insoumises*' saw steady expansion and this evolutionary change speeded up in the decades immediately preceding the war with many differing formats vying to service and exploit the market for venal sex.

Inevitably, the coming of war in 1914 had a massive impact on the demand for prostitutes. This war had one overarching unique aspect; unlike prior wars that largely saw soldiers passing relatively quickly through towns and regions according to the ebb and flow of battle (and as indeed happened over the first four months of 1914), once stalemate had set in by December of the first year the war became a quasi-medieval siege war – and stayed that way for over three years. Behind the trench battlements, the war zones of both sides were flooded with testosterone-fuelled young men who, when not actually engaged in killing each other, had the common enemy of time to kill. Additionally, prolonged war also meant that leave had to be introduced. Since travel was difficult and many could not return home in their allotted leave times, they took the leave locally, swelling the ranks of the bored and sexually frustrated. And they had at least some money in their pockets, with nothing to spend it one other than alcohol and vice. A number of variables influenced the supply side, seeing it grow considerably to meet this new expanded demand. A mass of displaced refugees, the geographic redeployment of existing prostitutes, the entry into the market of new opportunists, their morals loosened by the war, all swelled the ranks of the clandestine venal army. And even the declining *maisons de tolérance* took on a new lease of life as entrepreneurs sensed quick profits. The *maisons* of Paris provide a superb illustration of the ability and speed of adaptation of the business model to the exigencies of the moment. As German troops neared Paris in August-September 1914, *maisons* closed and Paris emptied. French victory in meeting the Germans on the Marne and forcing them back, gave the owners the confidence not only to return to the capital and reopen, but to expand, even opening new branches. There are reports of the most prescient and strategically perceptive *maisons* offering their girls English lessons! The 'oldest' profession proving, as it often does, to be the slickest.

Out of the existing *maisons* grew the first of the BEF army brothels with the British often simply inheriting (and sometimes sharing) the French army establishments. This regulated army brothel existed almost exclusively in Cloete's third zone of occupation: the back areas and base camps. Unofficial brothels and other forms of clandestine prostitution were to be found in the second and third zone, as well as almost at the front line.

This environment of venality was, for most if not all individual soldiers, often a shocking and unrecognisable new world. Naturally, prostitution existed back home, but brothels *per se*, which a generation before had been fairly conspicuous and openly used, had since been suppressed or where existing at all, forced into operating under a variety of guises. Any that clung on illegally would certainly not have been considered either reputable or attractive. 'The Gallic outlook on one particular subject shocked the unsophisticated Islander', recounted Captain Dunn of the Royal Welch:

> it was alien to his upbringing to hear the decent materfamilias of his billet recommend as a respectable resort a house with discreetly curtained windows, in a side street: it held "Billet stores" the French troops had left behind.[5]

Those of a more upper-class background, some of whom might even have had pre-war experience of France, or had served in a British overseas garrison, probably had a somewhat better idea of what to expect as Charles Carrington confirmed:

> In France, as we well knew, there was a different system of taboos about sex, so that it was no surprise to find the town of Le Havre wide open. It had a red light

5   Dunn, *War the Infantry Knew*, p. 161.

Wartime French humour magazine, *La Rire*, captures a crowd of Poilu's being turned away from a shared brothel as two smug-faced Tommies leave. There is an implicit joke over the British having precedence, referring back to the 1745 Battle of Fontenoy. On a wall behind the madam can be seen a sign, 'The Establishment is closed at 8 clock for British troops'; a kilted soldier is seen slipping in. (Courtesy: Anthony Langley)

district with well-advertised brothels on two scales of payment, first-class for officers and second-class for other ranks.[6]

To the soldier predisposed towards buying sex, and to those for whom the old moral certainties were disappearing fast, the promise of sampling the women of France in comparative safety, and seemingly with the army's implicit blessing, must have seemed like being offered the forbidden fruit but without the cost. The contrast with the comparatively repressed atmosphere of home was liberating to some, intriguing to many and, as time on the front progressed, promised adventures to be looked forward to, remembered and recounted with glee to those of his peer group, if not to those at home. 'We have heard a lot about these brothels. They are a constant topic of conversation in the trenches and billets', recorded the young and excited T.S. Hope.[7]

That the individual soldier is comparatively silent in his reminiscences on the subject of visits to any prostitute is the result of a moral dilemma inculcated during his upbringing. Hope, who had speculated with friends on the French brothel's almost legendary existence, could only with difficulty admit to having visited one: 'Don't know if I should mention this, but here goes – I've seen the inside of a "red lamp"'.[8]

Not all would necessarily have gone to a brothel with intent to use its services. Many claim, probably legitimately, that they went to see brothels out of curiosity. But, as Hope admitted, 'the opportunity to visit one … [had] never [before] presented itself to us, and now it has we are torn between a desire to satisfy our curiosity and the natural loathing we feel towards something we have been taught is shameful and degrading.'[9]

'Natural loathing', however, caused initial restraint even in this new permissive world. Succumbing to temptation could also lead to a heavier price than the initial payment, as Gibbs noted: 'A little love … a little laughter – alluring words to boys out of one battle, expecting another … and then up a little dark stairway to a lamp-lit room … Presently this poor boy would be stricken with disease and wish himself dead'.[10]

In their memoirs, soldiers tell of accompanying companions to a brothel, leaving the friend to his enjoyment while they excuse themselves before getting in too deeply.[11] Private Lewis, of the Royal Warwicks, whom we have met before denying he ever saw a woman on the front, is typical; 'I only went in to have a look round. Of course I'd got no money or nothing'. Is it classic Freudian masking behaviour, projecting their

---

6   Carrington, *Soldier,* pp. 180-82.
7   Hope, *Winding Road,* p. 91.
8   Ibid., p. 86.
9   Ibid., p. 95. Hope describes himself and friends as 'sightseers'.
10 Gibbs, *Realities* II, pp. 278-9.
11 Mark VII, *Subaltern,* p. 108; Lewis, *The Colonel's Runner.* http://www.hellfire-corner.demon.co.uk/runner.htm.

deeply felt immoral experiences onto an imaginary third party, or claiming themselves absent? We can never now know.

Whatever their initial qualms, for many, as has been argued, morale soon took the place of morals. Once the primary fear of catching venereal disease was removed, and a boy or man had time and money, then the brothel visit became an easier decision: 'I visited [the red lamps] myself, once or twice; we all did! They always told us if you want some fun go into these places', admitted W. Hill, Pte, 8th Bn Rifle Bde.[12] Unfortunately, Hill's interviewer did not ask who the 'they' doing the recommending were.

Unsurprisingly, given the age and immaturity of many recruits, there was often a complete ignorance of what they might find, even in those coming from the larger cities of home. Dubliner John William Rowarth's naivety was such that discovering payment was required came as surprise. And John Laffey told of one young recruit who believed the teasing girls of one establishment that they were all sisters.[13] An 18-year old Londoner, Bob (Bert) Chaney, noticed a long queue of soldiers standing in two-by-two order with no inkling of the reason:

> Thinking there might be a concert or cinema … I asked what was going on. 'A bit of grumble and grunt,' I was told, 'only costs two francs'. Puzzled, I asked what that meant. 'Cor blimey, lad. Didn't they learn me anything at all where you come from?' They thought me a proper mug. Fancy a lad like me, and a Cockney at that, not knowing what that mean – and I didn't know what a red lamp stood for? These places, I was told, were not for young lads like me, but for married men who were missing their wives.[14]

Hope admitted, 'So far I have had no dealings with women outside my own family, and girls to me are a sacred sex composing [sic] all that's good and clean. The stories regarding women of the army brothels I have never really believed, and now that I am in contact with the real thing I have no way of dealing with it'.[15]

Such was the 'culture shock' that many lads did not get beyond the door. Mundy, an NCO in the 1st Ox and Bucks, took one look and decided, 'I ain't going in there … there's girls sitting in there with only a bit of lace on … so we never went in'.[16] If they did, that first encounter could be both intimidating and unsuccessful, despite a readiness to experiment, sometimes affecting their ability even to do what was expected of them. However far this initial contact took them, it was a vividly remembered

12 IWM Sound Archive, No. 24539, Hill, Pte, 8th Bn Rifle Bde.
13 IWM 80/40/1, Rowarth, *Misfit Soldier*, p. 17: also Laffin, *Western Front*, p. 79.
14 IWM 77/47/1, Chaney, Bert, *'A Lad Goes To War'*, unpublished journal. For similar accounts see Hope, *Winding Road*, p. 96; Michael Moynihan (ed.), *People at War, 1914-18* (Newton Abbot: David & Charles, 1973), p. 107.
15 Hope, *Winding Road,* p. 91.
16 IWM Sound Archive, No. 5868, reel 2, Mundy.

experience[17] and initial failure or reticence did not necessarily put a man off future visits. Inevitably, the ever-ready Lawson was one repeat client, 'I went once or twice afterwards, and it was alright'.[18] Once the Rubicon had been crossed, the initial trepidation removed, brothel-visiting could become a habit for some soldiers.[19]

On the evidence of many eyewitness reports it appears that demand for sexual services often outstripped supply, with lines forming outside the brothels and long waits for those who joined them. The veterans remembered long queues, with men both quietly and in party atmosphere waiting their turn, regularly numbering more than 150 men and sometimes double that. It reminded them of scenes back home, but there the queues were for music halls.[20] The fact that the long lines could contain men from throughout Britain, as well as the Empire, often made as big an impact.[21] And for some finding themselves amidst grizzled old soldiers, survivors 'out since Mons', made them feel more soldierly themselves.[22]

What were the brothels like? And what was the soldier's assessment of them after he had crossed whatever threshold had initially kept him out? There are a number of memoirs that have left graphic descriptions of both the basic British Army brothel and what appear to be *maisons de tolérance* (i.e. regulated), or at least privately-run brothels, and from these it is apparent that the army brothel was often a basic, sordid affair. Burrage described one thus; 'The interior was rather like that of a non-conformist meeting house and never before or since have I seen commercialized vice made to look so unattractive'.[23] Cloete describes and dismisses them summarily: 'In the men's brothels they queued up and no man got more than 5 minutes with a girl. For officers things were not so bad but the difference was only one of degree … I never went. It was like eating off someone else's plate'.[24]

The most graphic, if not to say pornographic account, is related by Rowarth. The description, though long and explicit, is worth quoting as it contains all the main descriptive elements, the queues, the lack of anything remotely romantic, the girls flimsily-dressed and flirtatious, the bare and basic décor, the indignity of the inspection

17   IWM Sound Archive, No. 24546, Brown, Pte, 18th King's Liverpool Regt; No. 10168, Price, Donald, 20th and 30th Royal Fusiliers, 1915.
18   IWM Sound Archive, No. 24882, reel 2, Lawson. See also IWM 80/40/1, Rowarth, *Misfit Soldier*, p. 28.
19   Burrage, *War is War*, p. 27; Coppard, *Machine Gun*, pp. 157-59.
20   'stairs were lined with them', Ashurst, IWM Sound Archive, No. 9875; 'At least 150', Graves, *Goodbye*, p. 104; 'more than 150', Coppard, *Machine Gun*, pp. 156-7; Williamson, *Patriot's Progress*, pp. 134-5; '300', Harrison, *Generals*, p. 97; IWM Sound Archive, No. 24882, Lawson, '100s to go'.
21   Stuart Cloete, *How Young*, pp. 55-7.
22   IWM Sound Archive, No. 24546, Brown, Pte, 18th King's Liverpool Regt.
23   Burrage, *War is War*, p. 27.
24   Cloete, *Victorian Son*, p. 207. See also IWM, P185, Runcie, '*Territorial Mob*', p. 185 and IWM, P126, A. Surfleet, '*Blue Chevrons*' (unpubl. memoir), p. 126, for further examples of reasons why men did not use brothels.

and post-sex washing, the plainness of the female but her assumed 'health', the speed of events (which must have been a huge let down after perhaps hours of queuing), and the workmanlike exchange of payment:

> It was at this training camp [Étaples] I had my second whore. Noticing a long line of soldiers lined up outside some huts, and making enquiries was told it was the camp brothel. The whores were clean and free from the pox, they were examined by our own doctors and not allowed in if they were found dirty … the queue moved slowly when we was almost at the door … standing in front of the usual old lady cock examiner. Opening my fly pulling out my thing, I noticed her hands were dirty. I must have passed the examination she held up five fingers and said francs. A young girl came and led me by the hand to a very small room … the dirty looking girl only had a stretcher with a sheet and blanket. My whore was in a hurry, taking off a kind of slip … lay without any clothes on, she said 'hurry up others are waiting', all this in very broken English, it took me a while to unbutton my tunic, undo my braces, take off my pants and long underpants … I got the shock of my life, I was finished before I started. Finished, the girl washed her business said, 'you were very quick and very good'. I was hustled out of the door and on to the street, the queue I thought longer than when I went, I was told their [sic] was about 6 or 7 girls employed to cater for our carnal needs, the officers and NCOs had their own private brothels.[25]

The veracity of Rowarth's description is backed up by others. George Ashurst's equally frank oral account stresses the sordid and hurried nature of his visit, though adding the concern of the woman in ensuring a measure of basic hygiene.[26] A very similar (but fictionalised) picture is painted by Aldington in the excellent '*Death of A Hero*',[27] whose fiction, like most written by those who served, accurately mirrors fact. Coppard's brothel was the red lamp at Béthune, its *modus operandi* differing only in that it was in the town rather than at the actual camp, and it had a bar attached – as had many privately-operated, town-based brothels. Unlike the army brothel, there were no MPs ensuring with bayonet and butt that there was no line jumping but as with others, this brothel employed civilian 'bouncers'. Despite his unflattering description, Coppard was not put off by the nature of the visit and was one of those who enjoyed unnumbered repeat visits, though he was 'particular not to get any disease'.[28]

Lawson, recalled that brothels had 'opening times from 4 pm to midnight' but 'expensive at 10 francs'. Some accounts have the army brothel closing much earlier at 8pm so perhaps Lawson is describing the private *maisons*. Whichever, the experience

---

25   IWM 80/40/1, Rowarth, *Misfit Soldier*, p. 29.
26   IWM Sound Archive, No. 9875, reel 5, Ashurst.
27   Aldington, *Death of a Hero*, p. 293.
28   Coppard, *Machine Gun*, pp. 56-7.

was rushed at 10 minutes' activity, 'non stop … 100s of troops arrived to go… Madam took the money. She was a horror … she would more or less time you, make sure you spent some money drinking'.[29] It was a very well-oiled conveyor belt as the soldier-clients testified:

> Soldiers are constantly coming and going, each new arrival being confronted by one of the damsels and bombarded with invitations … Every now and again one goes arm-in-arm with a man to the bar. Money is passed over the counter, and they disappear into the bedrooms. A slip of a girl in a pale green wrap seems to be doing a roaring trade. Already she has had three customers since we arrived and seems likely to get a fourth.[30]

Every aspect of the regulated brothel was strictly controlled, with the girls subject to an inspection regime that attempted to keep them free from disease. It is impossible to say just how successful this was and it undoubtedly would have varied over the course of the war, depending on such variables as the frequency of inspection, and experience and proficiency of the doctors concerned. However it achieved its ends, the army patently did a good job in promoting their relative health merits over those of the competition. The soldiers themselves believed them safe: 'mostly I think those places were properly regulated and there was little or no risk of contracting VD in those. It was in the other places where they picked it up', thought Tom Bromley, an NCO in the ASC.[31] And Private Alban of the Royal Ordinance Corps was equally confident believing that: '… not many chaps got into trouble, get venereal or anything … going to these places … they were quite safe … inspected every week or fortnight by doctors'.[32]

At some brothels, condoms were available, though this does not appear to have been habitual policy, at least not until the final year of the war and then only with some dominion troops.[33] There is some evidence to suggest that some men either had their own suppliers or relied on other prophylactics. The trenches proved a good school, however: 'Men in trenches … talk about being with women and talk about gonorrhoea, how you get it, how you avoid it', remembered Wilf Wallworth, an NCO in the 7th Bn South Lancs.[34]

While there are photographs of sex workers in German brothels, there are few of the women who serviced the men of the British and Dominion army. Bearing in mind

---

29 IWM Sound Archive, No. 24882, Lawson.
30 Hope, *Winding Road*, pp. 93-5.
31 IWM Sound Archive, No. 9544, Bromley; also No. 6678, reel 2, Alban. No. 22740, Wells: 'the girls were inspected every day … the licensed places were fairly safe'; No. 11047, reel 4, Dixon:
32 IWM Sound Archive, No. 24539, Hill.
33 IWM Sound Archive, No. 24882, Lawson.
34 IWM Sound Archive, No. 22748, Wallworth.

the adage that 'beauty lies in the eye of the beholder', one struggles to find a report of a good-looking girl at any of the army places. Lieutenant William Morgan's photographs of what are probably the women of a 'Blue Lamp' are possibly unique and while these particular women have an allure, the men's written and remembered opinions of the women are far from complimentary; the girls were variously described as being very low class, unwashed, an unhealthy-looking lot, a dull sickly colour, no beauties either in face or body, common,[35] and perhaps the most off-putting description, from Burrage, of their being, 'worn and hideous, with death's heads instead of faces'.[36] To a young private Chaney 'they looked like disapproving mothers watching with distaste the antics of their young offspring'.[37] Many more uncomplimentary descriptions are to be found in the fiction of the period but, as previously noted, with many of the authors themselves formerly front-line soldiers the descriptions may well have been drawn from life.[38]

Despite the unappealing descriptions, either desperation or the occasional rose amidst the thorns apparently brought men back. In Lawson's wide experience he inevitably found, 'some prostitutes were very nice. I picked the youngest ones every time I could because some were repulsive, great big fat lumps'.[39] He also remembered, rather incredibly, an experience in the middle of an area that was 'hot' in more ways than one. In a rare confirmation of Hirschfeld's view of the intimate connection between war and libido, he recounted how: 'one time we should have been evacuated ... during the retreat, shells were falling and I went to bed with madam ... and the shells were pounding down'.[40] It is unclear whether this was one of his many claimed girlfriends or a prostitute.

Some men were patently less choosy than others, feeling that the absence of health risk over-ruled aesthetic considerations. Hope reports a conversation between two of his colleagues in a Calais red lamp: 'Hell, what do you want for five francs? Cleopatra? Damn it, they're all clean and that's about as much as a good soldier should want'.[41] It would seem that most of the girls whatever their age, shape or size were either French (though not always native of the district) or, occasionally, Belgian refugees. The fact that the soldiers only ever refer to 'French women' tends to support this, though there are some intriguing references to more 'exotic' imports. At one brothel in Calais a soldier recalled an incident with 'a little black girl, Nigerian or something, real black

---

35 IWM Sound Archive, No. 24546, Brown; No. 9875, reel 5, Ashurst; IWM, P185, Runcie, *Territorial Mob*.
36 Ex-Private X (Burrage), *War is War*, p. 27.
37 IWM 77/47/1, Chaney, *Journal*.
38 Aldington, *Death of a Hero*, p. 293; Williamson, *Patriot's Progress*, pp. 144-51; Hanley, J., *The German Prisoner* (New York: Exile Books, repr., 1923), p. 73.
39 IWM Sound Archive, No. 24882, Lawson: See also H. E. L. Mellersh, *Schoolboy into War* (London: Kimber, 1978), pp. 148-49.
40 IWM Sound Archive, No. 24882, Lawson.
41 Hope, *Winding Road*, pp. 93-5.

girl'.[42] She is unlikely to have been 'Nigerian' but could well have been from one of the French African colonies. Black women were quite commonly found in the brothels as evidenced by their depiction on numerous cartoon postcards.

Whatever the nationality or ethnicity, however, it seems that there was little difference between the allure of women recruited for service in the lower standard of public *maisons de tolérance* than for the army version. The author of the article in the *Shield*, the Journal of the Association for Moral and Social Hygiene, was not too far from the truth in describing the atmosphere as sordid and the transaction mechanical. It would have been degrading to most men once they had gotten over the excitement and trepidation of the initial visit. But, having bitten of the apple, there would have been no turning back and inevitably the path from the regulated brothel led to the door of the clandestine. The presumption that regulated prostitution had a direct link with the growth of the unregulated kind, was a core argument against the provision of the lamps for those who fought their existence.[43]

The officers had their own brothels, 'Blue Lamps'; fewer in number, discreet, and seemingly of a higher standard in just about every aspect. Some, boasting pianos, areas of comfortable seating and paintings hanging on the walls, provided both the appearance and comforts of clubs rather than the Spartan facilities experienced by the ranks. Photographs taken by Welsh soldier, Lieutenant William Morgan, of the 175th Company of the Royal Engineers – a tunnelling unit – provide probably the only visual record of a 'Blue Lamp'. The officer at the piano, the club-like, 'comfy chair' atmosphere, albeit makeshift, and the pages of *La Vie Parisienne* pinned to the walls provide a unique glimpse of the moral-boosting normality these places could offer a soldier. As much as the subject itself, Morgan's willingness to capture the scene on film, and the similar willingness of his fellow officers to be photographed, captures the relative innocence of the place.

Price, rather than pips on a shoulder, seems to have acted as the 'entry qualification', though Percy Clare and others claimed that other ranks were officially restrained from going to the designated officers' brothels; 'at the large towns special facilities and resorts were allotted to officers and put "out of bounds" to the men. The registered houses under Police and Health Officers ("Red Lamps") were those intended for the men'.[44] If this accusation of enforced segregation be true, it once again suggests the army exercised a level of control over a brothel's workings and connived at its officers using them. The idea of differing establishments for different social classes was not without precedent: it had been a common feature of peacetime *maisons*. It is highly unlikely that some *maisons* merely had two doors leading into the same interior, where once inside no deference was made to rank, as one trench myth repeated by Coppard

---

42 IWM Sound Archive, No. 14599, reel 4, Hall.
43 'British Troops in France', *Journal of the Association for Moral and Social Hygiene*, 'British Troops in France: provision of Tolerated Brothels', *The Shield*, 3rd series, 1916-17, p. 397.
44 IWM 06/48/1, Percy Clare, '*Reminiscences*', p. 9.

These rare photographs taken by Lieutenant William Morgan, illustrates how the officer 'Blue Lamps' were usually more club-like in their atmosphere. Note, too, the ubiquitous Kirchner pin-ups on the walls. (Courtesy: Jonathan & Fran Gluck, descendants of William Morgan)

promulgated![45] It would certainly have been bad for morale, for both men and officers, had they had to share, undermining both respect and discipline. 'Captain [Robert] Graves has mentioned a Blue Lamp establishment for officers, but I never thought of officers in that connexion, and I don't remember seeing a Blue Lamp', remembered Private Jim Davis who thought that 'brothels pandered mostly for the troops'.[46]

45 Coppard, *Machine Gun*, p. 56.
46 IWM Sound Archive, No. 9750, reel 11 and 12, Jim Davis.

These photographs, taken by Lieutenant William Morgan, are very probably of the girls who worked in the 'Blue Lamp' he visited. Such women would have been of a better class than those working at the Red Lamps frequented by the other ranks. (Courtesy: Jonathan & Fran Gluck, descendants of William Morgan)

Graves was not too impressed with what was on offer for fellow officers, though avoiding the lamps himself:

> I commanded a draft of ten young officers. Three of them got venereal disease at the Rouen Blue Lamp. They were strictly brought-up Welsh boys of the professional classes, had never hitherto visited a brothel and knew nothing of prophylactics. One of them shared a hut with me. He came in very late and very drunk one night, from the Drapeau Blanc, woke me up and began telling me about his experiences ... I said irritably, and in some disgust: 'The Drapeau Blanc? Then I hope to God you washed yourself'.[47]

It is interesting that he makes a point of mentioning their social position; sex had no class barriers and brothels attracted soldiers from across a wide social spectrum. Moral ties were loosened, as we have seen, no matter what the social or religious background. Unlike the establishments frequented by the lower orders, the officers' facilities offered some comforts and an experience seemingly more in line with 'customisation' than production line. Queues were not something to be seen outside a Blue Lamp. If the establishments were 'healthy' then, as R. G. Dixon recounts, the officers might become regular visitors, having favourite girls and treating the brothel as something of a club. Of a Blue Lamp that he visited on a number of occasions in Dunkerque that was almost certainly a regulated *maison de tolérance*, he wrote:

> There was one reserved for officers, in the Rue de something-or-other in the suburb of Rosendale, I remember the house had a paved courtyard at the back, with rectangular lily-pool in the centre. Here you might stroll, or sit and drink a bottle of wine with your very scantily clad companion – they all sported exceedingly gauzy shifts decorated with ribbon and lace, and not a stitch underneath ... She couldn't speak a word of English.[48]

Better-quality establishments existed in most back towns of any size, especially if they were home to some staff HQ or popular with officers taking leave. Towns easily in reach of the line, like Amiens, could attract officers when simply off-duty, though most often visits appear to have been taken while on leave, rather than on rest. Officers, however, enjoyed a great deal more leave than other ranks. This, perhaps, kept their activities away from the gossip of the men. Denis Wheatley, in his frank memoirs, talks candidly of several visits he made to what appear to be brothels of a more luxurious type, one in Rouen, and one in Amiens, where he found:

---

47 Graves, *Goodbye*, p. 195.
48 IWM 92/36/1, Dixon, *Wheels of Darkness*, p. 55.

All the main streets were crowded with figures in khaki and French girls plying a lucrative trade ... and a most luxurious brothel ... It functioned at all hours and the Madam took me to an eight-sided room, the walls and ceiling of which were entirely covered with mirrors ... we breakfasted off an omelette, melon and champagne.[49]

What is particularly illuminating is Wheatley's use of the plural: 'There were also brothels: the best was Madame Prudhomme's'.[50] Gibbs found the base-wallahs and staffs of Boulogne in similarly well-appointed places.[51] Private Percy Clare's officer Rawson, was, like Wheatley, a habitué of such places, finding them in Amiens, Arras and Warloy; Clare tells of him 'away all the afternoon and most of the evening visiting his French ladylove and having a bath in her "flat"'. The existence of the bath suggests a better class of place.[52]

Perhaps the level of quality, and the range of services offered, is best illustrated by Philip Zeigler's account of the future King Edward VIII. The Prince of Wales was with fellow officers at a brothel in Calais in May 1916, watching, but not touching, naked prostitutes as they struck exotic poses. The young Prince, then aged 21, echoed the sentiments of many of his contemporaries on their first visit to such a place and found it 'a perfectly filthy and revolting sight, but interesting for me as it was my first insight into these things!' Later that year, however, his equerries 'handed him over to a skilful French prostitute called Paulette in Amiens, where he lost his virginity'.[53] Prince or pauper, 'no one wanted to die a virgin'.[54]

Some higher-end brothels still followed the pre-war model of offering more varied entertainments. Where the troops commonly found this was in the brothels they 'liberated' from the enemy following the German withdrawal to the Hindenburg Line, and later when the troops moved into Belgium and they themselves became an occupying army on the Rhine. In the brothels they inherited, the new nationality of the customer was never an issue for the working women. Neither was offering a more varied type of service. The *'Tableau vivant'*, for example, was a static sexual scene that the clients viewed from behind a screen or darkened window. A particular recollection one higher-ranking officer could not 'put out of my mind' was of a 17-year old prostitute showing him a small room that was fitted out for 'torture'; the flagellation of German officers by the girls. Evidence of brothels in occupied France catering for similar tastes during the war itself is also found in Hirschfeld.[55]

49 Dennis Wheatley, *Temporary Gentleman*, p. 153.
50 Ibid., p. 185.
51 Gibbs, *Realities* II, p. 327.
52 IWM 06/48/1, Clare, *Reminiscences*, p. 9.
53 Zeigler, Philip, *King Edward VIII; The Official Biography* (London: Collins 1990), p. 79.
54 Graves, *Goodbye*, p. 195.
55 IWM Sound Archive, No. 13717, Gee, Charles H., Lt Col, 9th Bn Durham Light Infantry. A similar story is told in No. 9955, reel 18, Calvert, Horace, Pte, 1/6th Bn West

Photographs taken of 'Tableaux Vivants' often offered in high class brothels would be turned into erotic postcards and sold to the soldiers. 'Satisfies 'is lust, I s'pose'. (Courtesy: Stephen Likosky)

Brothels were ubiquitous and, reflecting what were effectively free market conditions, catered for every demand, including those of the overseas troops and Chinese Labour Corps. Whether these establishments were kept exclusively for non-white use is unclear. What is certain, however, is that reflecting the general racist attitudes of the time, the non-whites were kept well away from those brothels used by the white troops.[56]

While it is difficult to quantify statistically the number of brothels (either army controlled or private *maisons*) active on the Western Front at any one time, there is sufficient information extant to be able to at least undertake a basic analysis of the economics of the brothel industry. Their number add to the argument that the soldiers' sexual activities were more varied than has been previously acknowledged.

Yorks and Hussars. See also Hirschfeld, *Sexual History*, p. 151.
56 Levine, 'Battle Colors', *Journal of Women's History* 8 (1998), p. 110; Jeffery Greenhut, 'Race, Sex and War: The impact of Race and Sex on Morale and Health Services for the Indian Corps on the Western Front 1916', *Military Affairs* 45 (1981), p. 73.

The financial size of the venal economy illustrates that it was an industry; even at the time its ramifications could neither have been ignored nor overlooked.

It is known that each base camp had a semi-institutionalised red lamp. Their establishment and operation depended on the ebb and flow of war, the number of girls available and 'healthy' (as the army so coyly referred to those who were disease-free) at any one time, and the state of public opinion back home. Nearby towns of any size offered multiple private brothels, and of varying sizes and standards, both regulated and unregulated. These grew or declined in number according to local police action (and sometimes military pressure), according to the sanitary arrangements, the movement of troops and the legality of their operation. The laws, as well as military policy, also changed over the period. For example, a change in law prohibiting the sale of alcohol in 1917 effectively made some choose between supplying women or drink.

As demonstrated, the French had no qualms about opening new brothels throughout the war, nor about closing those that flouted the regulations. The fluidity of the situation explains why official French statistics are hard to find. The soldiers' own memoirs identify the following locations as having at least one tolerated or base-camp brothel: Amiens, Le Havre, Étaples, Béthune, Calais, Rouen, Hedsin, Warploy, Harfleur, Abbeville, Armentières, Amiens, St Omer, Doullens, Dunkerque, Boulogne and Cayeux sur Mer. To these must be added those of the recuperation stations and back-area camps and some of indeterminate status like that of Poperinghe. The brothels of Paris would require their own study being numbered in the hundreds; however, these would only have been available to officers and to the ANZAC troops who were permitted to take leave in Paris. It has to be noted, too, that the known or publicised brothel was not an isolated place. Indeed, such was demand that there were often multiple establishments located in a 'red lamp area' and soldiers shopped around before deciding on where to spend their money as Mellersh recalled.[57] Bromley remembered the many brothels, though it alone in remembering 'green lamps':

> The larger towns had the red light areas ... there were brothels in Rouen. In Abbeyville [sic] there were two, a red lamp and a green [sic] lamp. I don't know what the difference was because they were both brothels. In any case the word brothel was not used, they were called 'knocking shops'. In St Omer there were two, No. 1 and No. 4.[58]

George Ashurst found it quiet in one section of the line, 'but when you got to Armentiers [sic] ... phew, dear me, what a hell of a difference'.[59] The function of these back areas was evident whatever the colour of their lamps, or how they were colloquially referred to, as Canadian Will Bird noted: 'We went to the town [Le Havre] one

---

57 Mellersh, *Schoolboy*, pp. 148-49.
58 IWM Sound Archive, No. 9544, Bromley.
59 IWM Sound Archive, No. 9875, reel 6, Ashurst.

This postcard captures the spirit of the notorious 'Breda' district of Paris but similar streets existed in Amiens, Calais, St Omer, Le Havre, Poperinghe, Boulogne and many other base camp areas. (Courtesy: Stephen Likosky)

evening, a long walk, and found it organised to separate the soldier from his money with the least possible effort'.⁶⁰ The Harve town pass (see illustration), with its list of locations open and closed to the soldier visiting the town, provides a striking indication of the number of establishments there could be. Today's visitor to certain areas of Bangkok or Taipei would provide the nearest contemporary experience of what was presented to the soldier on a night out.

The army allegedly kept such neighbourhoods in-bounds even after the general ban on visiting *maisons de tolérance* had been passed in March 1918. The *Shield* could claim, 'We have it on good authority that in Havre these words were printed on the back of soldiers' leave passes "— St.* is not out of bounds", — St.* being the street where the tolerated brothels are situated'.⁶¹ This was not quite true, as the illustration of the notorious pass shows; the army lists those that were out of bounds, entry to others was allowable by default. What the pass list demonstrates is the high number of brothels that the army knew of and this was only a fraction of those operating.

Within two years of the start of 1915, 137 new regulated *maisons* had opened in 35 towns throughout France, most, naturally located near the Front.⁶² Brothels might be opened at the request of the military, or the local inhabitants. Parisian-based civilian diarist, Michael Corday recorded that in one unnamed town 'The local GOC received a deputation from the worthy burghers begging him to open a brothel, since the troops were pestering all their wives and daughters. So he opened one'⁶³ The mayor of Cayeux appealed for a second *maison* on the grounds that the one existing town brothel could not cope with the soldiers' demand and hence they were corrupting the morals of young wives and daughters of Poilus away at the front.

The biggest problem in estimating the number of establishments, however, is that there is enormous difficulty in defining the term 'brothel'. It refers to *maisons de tolérance* registered by French authorities but, as we will see below, estaminets, disused hotels, wine-shops and even the back rooms of innocent retailers doubled as unregistered and unregulated brothels (defined here as places where multiple girls worked at the same time). Winter argues that many of the front-line soldiers would not have had access to the red lamps: 'The flesh trade can be exaggerated. For most of the front-line men the biggest town they ever knew was a semi-deserted village with a few cellars and perhaps a wrecked cottage producing eggs and chips for the men'⁶⁴ – this discounts the fact that such a cottage might have been doubling as an unregulated brothel, serving sex in addition to food.

60 Bird, *Ghosts*, p. 7; IWM Sound Archive, No. 11047, reel 4, Dixon: 'rouge lamps in Béthune'.
61 'British Troops in France', *The Shield*, p. 396.
62 Harrison, 'The British Army and the problems of Venereal Disease', p. 142. This figure probably includes those situated in solely French controlled areas not exclusively serving the soldiers on the British-held Western Front.
63 Corday, *The Paris Front*, p. 254, May 1917.
64 Winter, *Death's Men*, p. 152.

PASS.

ARMY FORM W. 3105

No.	No.
Regiment	Regiment
Regtl. No.	
Rank	No .... Rank .... Name ....
Name	has permission to be absent from his quarters, from
Date from	
to	to
Commanding	for the purpose of proceeding to
Station	Station
Date	Date
	Commanding.

THE FOLLOWING CAFES, LOCALITIES, ETC., ARE PLACED PERMANENTLY "OUT OF BOUNDS" BY BASE STANDING ORDERS, PART I., Order 24.

French Cafes, Estaminets, or establishments where wine, beer, etc., are sold in Havre and vicinity are "Out of Bounds" for British Troops except between the hours of 12 noon and 2 p.m. and between 6 p.m. and 8 p.m.

Belgian Hutments South of Rue Christophe-Colomb and West of the Old Fort Hutments.
The racecourse near Docks Rest Camp.
The small jumping course in the Forest de Montgeon.
The Town of Montivilliers.
Hôtel des Voyageurs, Harfleur.
All the parts of the R.E. Inclined Railway that are fenced in, except for men actually employed on work in connection with the Tramway, men wishing to cross the line must use the openings provided.
Fort de Frileuse, behind the Canadian Veterinary Hospital, and immediately N.E. of Molon Brickyard.
The road running along the Sea and Beach between the Southern extremity of the Boulevard de Graville and the Southern extremity of Rue de la Grève, INCLUDING THE BUVETTE BELLEVUE.
The House of M. Catelain, close to the R.A.M.C. Officers' Mess, Quai d'Escale.
The houses at the Western end of the Base Ordnance Depot and South of the La Floride Battery Road.
The Cafe de New York, 5. Quai Videcoq.
Cafe, 7, Quai Videcoq.
Cafe, 15, Quai Videcoq.
Cafe, 33, Quai Notre-Dame.
Cafe, 35, Quai Notre-Dame.
The entire Area bounded by and including the QUAI LAMBLARDIE, QUAI CASIMIR-DELAVIGNE, QUAI DE L'ILE, QUAI DES CASERNES, except that the RUE DU GENERAL-FAID-HERBE may be used as a thoroughfare, BUT ALL CAFES in this Street are out of Bounds, except the Brasserie Schuster and the Friture Parisienne.
The Sailors' Rest in the Casimir-Delavigne is also "In Bounds," but N.C.Os. and men are only permitted to enter this Quai by the Rue du General Faid-herbe end.

The Quai de Malakoff and the Quai d'Escale.
The landing stage of the Quai de Southampton from which the Southampton steamers start.
Cafe des Allies, near Rouelles Halt.
Cafe, 404, Boulevard Sadi Carnot.
Cafe, "Bar Maritime," 19, Rue des Galions.
"Ferme de la Breque," entrance to 9 to 19 Camps.
"Hotel Brunet," 35, Rue Diequemare.
Cafe, "Maupas," 20, Rue Piedfort.
Cafe, 91, Rue Chantiers, Graville.
No. 82, Rue d'Eglise.
Cafe, "Oriental Bar," 8, Place des Halles Centrales.
Cafe, "de Bearn," 5, de la Comedie.
Cafe, "Maxim Bar," 10, Rue Moliere.
Cafe, "Bar Lyrique," 12, Rue Moliere.
Cafe, "L'Operette," 14, Rue Moliere.
Cafe debit 42, Rue Racine.
Cafe, "Friture," 40, Rue des Remparts.
Cafe debit (Hendier), 412, Rue de Chantiers.
The House of Mlle. Gautheron, 22, Rue Jean Hachette.
Estaminet (Albert), near Cinder City, on the Canal Road.
The house adjoining the LAZARET, near Bassin à Petrole and all buildings inside the La Floride Battery.
The area bounded by the RUE DE PARIS, QUAI ALEXANDRA III, PLACE DE ARSENAL, QUAI VIDECOQ, QUAI NOTRE-DAME, and QUAI DE SOUTHAMPTON, except the direct thoroughfare from Place Richelieu to the Quai de Southampton, via Rue Jean Mace, and Rue des Galions, which is "In Bounds" from 9 p.m. till 8 p.m. only. The Cafes fronting on the streets and quays forming the boundaries in this area are not out of bounds, except those specially mentioned.

N.B.—A list of all Cafes, etc., Temporarily "Out of Bounds" will be issued to all Units on the 1st of each month by the A.P.M.

British Soldiers are prohibited from going on board any ship in the Port of Havre, or on any barge on the Canals, except on duty.

Soldiers found in any of the above will be severely punished.

ARMY PRINTING AND STATIONERY SERVICES. B. 288. 400000. 8/17.

The notorious 'Le Cayeux' pass issued to soldiers enjoying Harve town leave in 1917. The number of banned cafes and localities gives some idea of the huge number of brothels (presumably both regulated and unregulated) operating in this one town. (TNA WO/150/8)

Examining the likely usage of an individual brothel is illuminating, though establishing the level of business transacted over the period is even harder to achieve than establishing the number of brothels, there being too many variables. Employing certain known facts about their operation with a little speculation, however, can provide a better understanding and estimate of the amount of soldier sex than using the simple VD treatment figures as a measure.

An imagined hypothetical investor of the period, approached by someone selling him a business or investment opportunity, would probably have been presented with a business analysis somewhat similar to the following. Tolerated brothels had between six and twenty girls working as part of the establishment at any one time. It is documented that the one at Cayeux sur Mer contained fifteen women.[65] The number of clients serviced in a day would vary day-by-day depending on the opening hours. The camp brothel had restricted hours from 18.00 to 20.00, but other town *maisons* were restricted often only in when they might also serve alcohol, though troops might themselves be banned from visiting outside of certain hours. Where the service provided was basic, i.e. sex at the end of a queue, as John Rowarth had experienced it, the throughput would have been quicker than when the client had the opportunity to drink and make some form of choice. Even given these variations, sources claim that the girls serviced between 15 and 30 clients a day, but 'During times of great pressure', writes Dr Lacassangne, 'some women received from sixty to eighty consecutive visits'. Of course these figures were exceptional but from twenty to thirty consecutive contacts may be taken as a fair average. Yves Guyot estimates the number of clients received by one inmate could at times mount of fifteen, twenty, or even twenty-five a day.[66] According to Dr Leon Blizzard, writing just two-years after the war's end, women in war-time Paris brothels worked 18 hours a day, serving 50 to 60 men and earned 400 to 500 francs a day.[67] Some women were so productive that they earned themsleves the sobriquet *'mitrailleuse'* (the machine gun). At the other extreme, Rhoades quotes another contemporary report claiming one particular, provinces-based woman as seeing between ten to fifteen men per day, 'almost all soldiers'.

It has been suggested that an average of 360 men a day visited the house in Cayeux which contained 15 women.[68] That is an average of 24 men per woman a day. Unfortunately, there is no record of how long the facility remained open. It serviced the nearby convalescence hospital which housed 7000 men at any one time. It would have taken the girls less than three weeks at that level of throughput to service the entire population. The fact that one of the main objections of locals to the existence of the brothel was the long lines of soldiers continually outside adds weight to the argument that it was indeed well-used. Winter was possibly referring to the Cayeux brothel when he stated 'The red lamp … at Rouen was visited by 171,000 men in its first year'.[69] This figure supports the above analysis.

65   TNA: WO 32/5597.
66   Corbin, *Women*, p. 81.
67   Ibid., Blizzard, L., *Les Maisons de prostitution de Paris pedant la guerre* (1922), p. 3. Rousseau, *La Guerre Censurée*, p. 316. Rhoades, '"There are No Safe Women", *Proceedings of the Western Society for French History* 27, p. 46.
68   'British Troops in France', *The Shield*, p. 397.
69   Winter, *Death's Men*, pp. 150-2. Harrison, 'The British Army and Problems of Venereal Disease' cites Paul Faivre, *Prophylaxie et de Police Sanitaire* (1917), TNA: WO 32/5597, as his source.

Battalions had a nominal strength of approximately 1000 men. When they came out of the line after an engagement they were much depleted with sometimes approaching half that number, but even at full strength it would take just a day and a half to satisfy the complete regiment. The long queues outside the establishment, featuring in witness accounts, would in all probability have been a single battalion taking its turn. But with a standard four-day rotation served in the reserve, the girls would have had sufficient time to welcome multiple visits.

The girls certainly worked hard, and their 'lifespan', if not cut short because of disease, was between two weeks and a month at most. If, as Graves claimed, a girl serviced a battalion a week it was no wonder that 'three weeks was the usual limit' to their working life at any one establishment. [70] Bert Chaney tells of the girls being so worn out at the end of the day, and unable to walk that cars had to be provided for them.[71] Even if these stories are apocryphal, they confirm how busy the average soldier believed them to be. It is not clear whether the women 'retired' completely after one stint or worked in rotation with other girls, or transferred to another brothel. In peacetime Corbin found that the girls were often rotated between *maisons de tolérance* in different areas of the country by procuring agents, earning what was a small fortune during their stint in each establishment:

> The girls rose at eight o'clock. By half past eight they [there were eight of them] had to be at the estaminet [in Amiens] for the British soldiers were at that hour already arriving in crowds from the neighbouring districts, where they were resting. Work lasted until midday, was resumed at one-thirty and continued until eight pm. The clients came into the estaminet one by one, made a rapid choice – for drinking was prohibited – and before 'going upstairs' paid the fee to the proprietress, then handed the girl her 'little present', and carried out a quick coitus … the soldiers were generous … gave a girl twenty or thirty francs … At eight pm the house closed down. Sleeping in was prohibited … The work was tiring, but it was lucrative. Each girl made at least three hundred francs a day … the good earners easily reached six thousand francs a week.[72]

Brothels were kept in constant use, with prostitutes replenished by detachments from a seemingly inexhaustible supply of volunteers. The available figures provide an interesting and indicative, if not statistically valid, picture of the financial rewards of such 'productivity'. Taking just 15 of the named brothels to which this research has found direct reference, and multiplying these by 10 girls working in each, at an average of 20 visits per day, produces a figure of 3000 men served daily. Taking into allowance

---

70 Graves, *Goodbye*, p. 104.
71 IWM 77/47/1, Bert Chaney, 'A Lad Goes to War', unpaginated.
72 Fischer and Dubois, *Sexual Life*, p. 329; Winter, *Death's Men*, p. 151; Graves, *Goodbye*, p. 104.

days off during battles, temporary close-downs and simply slow days, 200 active days a year allows for 600,000 men per annum being serviced in just this small sample. If the Cayeux productivity estimates are used, the figure exceeds one million for just fifteen identified brothels. Such highly speculative projections such as these can, of course, only be used with extreme caution but whatever the real figure, these estimates once again illustrate that the scale of sexual encounters, and thus their impact on the general soldiery, cannot be lightly dismissed or ignored.

Lawson, with the experience of a discerning and regular client, quite correctly described brothels as 'big business'.[73] It is instructive to estimate the daily turnover if only to illustrate that this was truly an organised and 'industrialised' activity, mirroring the industrialised nature of this war. The cost to the soldier varied; at the lower end it was a 'tribute of two francs from each candidate; one franc for madam, one franc for the dame'.[74] At the upper end, Lawson remembered clearly that they were 'expensive at ten francs'; others quote in sterling at 6*d* or one shilling, but the majority, including Leo Cormack, George Ashurst and W. Hill, remember five francs.[75] Blue Lamps charged a higher price for a higher quality of service and environment, and because their target market could afford to pay more. Graves, believing the cost to have been 10 francs was probably basing his information on what fellow officers had told him. We cannot know how the revenue was split between the actual sex-worker and the owner of the premises but as the latter paid all operating expenses, and provided both the legality and safety, it can be assumed that the former would have been unlikely to have received fifty-percent in every operation. The number of women reportedly available for the work would also have acted to have kept their personal fees down.

This price survey is important in that it illustrates that an individual's sexual activity was constrained as much by economics as by the availability of women and the morals of the individual. Donald Price of the 30th Royal Fusiliers remembered thwarted desires; 'how much you got?'... 'only got a 6*d*'...'that's no good, it's a shilling' whereas Read remembered savouring the flesh-pots until our funds ran out'.

There are several reasons why soldiers' memories of the price differ, other than perhaps fading memory or confusion over currency conversion rates. It is probable that the army establishments had their rate regulated, while privately-owned but tolerated *maisons* would have had more freedom in price setting. As Tom Bromley, and NCO in the ASC, recalled 'if you wanted to go with one of them you make [sic] your wishes known and go and there's a bit of negotiating about the fee'.[76] As in any competitive business model, they certainly responded to the factors impacting on the elasticity of demand: a common complaint was that rates apparently always rose when

73 IWM Sound Archive, No. 24882, Lawson, R. H.
74 Coppard, *Machine Gun*, pp. 56-7.
75 IWM Sound Archive, No. 9875, reel 8, Ashurst; No. 24539, reel 2, Hill'; Graves, *Goodbye*, p. 104, quotes 10 francs.
76 IWM Sound Archive, No. 9544, Bromley; and also No. 10168, Price:

the higher-paid Dominion troops were in town. At least one soldier, in this case Leo McCormack of the Royal Field Artillery, ruefully remembered that the rates of the prettiest girls certainly went up: 'Young women got the Australians; the older women got the British. The Aussies had the money'.[77]

As we have seen, the servicing of clients was extremely fast, with various tricks of the trade to ensure speedy resolution: 'they'd have one thin petticoat on to give you the feeling straight away', was how Lawson remembered it.[78] The experience was rushed at ten minutes, with activity 'Non-stop'. With opening hours between 16.00 and midnight and allowing an average of four clients an hour, with a break of an hour, a girl could potentially process up to 35 clients a shift. Even if one uses the lower figure of 20 clients per day as used in earlier analysis, at five francs a client, a day's takings could be in excess of 100 francs per girl. With brothels housing anywhere between five and 20 girls, a single establishment could turn over between 500 francs and 2000 francs, excluding any takings from alcohol and related items.

Even with operating costs that included rent, security and payment for the medical inspections, both the house and the individual girls were making money at an extraordinary rate. The individual girls would not have had to work long before they could retire, though it seems that not all were particularly prudent with their earnings and some worked until literally worn out, 'Retired, pale but proud' as Graves memorably put it.[79]

Unsurprisingly, there was no shortage of investors wanting to get into this market. Our hypothetical investor could not have failed to have been impressed with the potential returns on investment offered. With so much at stake, and nothing on record about how or from whom a 'franchise' for a red lamp was obtained, it would be surprising if there was no corruption in the process, though without any further evidence of the workings of the industry, this aspect of business history must remain tantalisingly out of reach.

So far only the tolerated brothel has been described, but in major towns other forms of prostitution were allowed, adding to the supply of available women. It had been traditional in France for some women to register with the authorities, subjecting themselves to an examination regime and work the streets, or operate from home, as individual *filles soumises*. It is impossible to estimate the number choosing this role but, in all probability, given the lucrative earnings potential of the brothel and competition from the unregulated street prostitute, it would not have been the most favoured option. There is anecdotal evidence from the soldiers, however, to suggest that at least some of this type were active. Leo McCormack, tells of 'certain well-known women,

---

77 IWM Sound Archive, No. 22739, McCormack.
78 IWM Sound Archive, No. 24882, Lawson.
79 Graves, *Goodbye*, p. 104.

Regulated prostitution 203

Legally, women were forbidden to appear at the windows but such soliciting was prevalent. The house number '69' suggests exotic 'French practices'. (Courtesy: Stephen Likosky)

like Tina of Bailleul'.[80] The fact that she was well-known and plying her trade without being 'removed' implies she was 'regulated'. Perhaps others, like the woman Priestley discovered outside Rouen in 1918, were too old or too ugly to work other than at the basest of levels.[81]

The situation was different in West Flanders, that area of Belgium occupied by the allies. The army's objective, as elsewhere in the military zones of occupation, was to attempt to control the spread of disease and there was no moral sanction intended. However, reflecting both local cultural sensitivities and the high concentration of refugees,[82] attempts to introduce an effective regulatory system failed, though not for the want of trying. One major barrier to the registration would have been the refusal to admit the existence of prostitution at all in a Catholic country where the church, and particularly the priests, retained great moral authority. This will have led to a great deal of hypocrisy, shown for example by the use of the less value-laden terms of 'bad girls' and 'fornication sisters' as generic terms for prostitutes.

In theory, however, the women had little choice but to register as individual 'public women' if they were openly to follow their professions. There were no 'official' army-controlled red or blue lamps *per se*, from which they could work, although there were seemingly establishments where a number of women might work together and at least 'be known' to the authorities. Interestingly, the Belgian attitude to prostitutes was much more paternalistic, perhaps making allowance for the fact that many of the women were prostituting themselves out of hardship and would presumably wish to return to the respectable community once circumstances allowed. The recommendation, sent from a government health inspector to the Minister of the Interior when the system was first established in 1915, that health inspections should 'be facilitated with discretion … either at their home or in our facility … In order not to hurt the feelings and dignity of the families of which one of the members may have erred'[83] is indicative of this approach.

The Department of Health further recommended that female nurses and, if possible, doctors should be employed to undertake both the regular inspections and deliver treatment because 'a female doctor will instil greater confidence in the examination' and presumably make the women less reticent in registering.[84] This was a far cry from the insensitive and chauvinistic way that inspection regimes had been set up in Britain and France in the past and, in addition to allowing the women a measure

---

80 IWM Sound Archive, No. 8945, reel 5, Greener, Martin, Officer 9th Bn Durham Light Infantry.
81 J. B. Priestley, *Margin Released*, p. 125.
82 An indication of the number of refugees is provided in Dendooven, 'Living apart together', in Santanu Das (ed.), *Race, Empire*, p. 144.
83 Provinciaal Archief West-Flanderen, Brugge, File Eerste Wereldoorlog, Minutes of a meeting between 'HR Inspector, Ministry of Interior (Belgium)' and Military Authorities at Belgium GHQ, De Panne, 7 Feb. 1915.
84 Ibid.

of self-respect, was perhaps also a way of heading-off an anticipated negative reaction from anti-regulation campaigners. Whether this plea had any success is unknown, but it would seem likely that few female doctors, or nurses, prepared to be diverted to this task from treating wounded soldiers, would have been available so close to the front.

The regulations, introduced in each of the civilian-administered areas over a three-month period from February to April 1916, probably, as argued earlier, at the behest or at least with the encouragement of British and French military authorities, were, on paper, fairly proscriptive. The women could either volunteer themselves for registration or be 'denounced' as prostitutes. Once being recognised as such there were placed on a list, kept by local police but seemingly open to the military police to view, and issued with what was effectively a pass book. They were bound to report for weekly medical inspections and the book, containing their full details, was to be 'stamped' by the inspecting doctor.

If there were records held of these inspections by the local police and Department of Health they are seemingly no longer extant. Indeed, local hypocrisy might even have meant that no such records were ever kept. However, if records were initially maintained, it is highly possible that they would have been destroyed following the war, especially if they contained the names of local women trying to return to respectability. In the absence of data, no conclusions can be drawn over either the number or demographic background of the women who were prepared to be identified as regulated prostitutes.

It is also highly likely, given local ambivalence to prostitution, that with the exception of denunciation and removal, the rules were never fully enforced. This was a regulation in theory rather than in practice. The Poperinghe town council, in a reply to what must obviously have been an official memo asking why they had not implemented the new regulations (which had anyway taken them longer than any other local administration to even publish), could answer, straight-faced, that there were no public girls in Poperinghe.[85] This would have been a difficult stance to have taken for long with the Groote Markt noted for its officers' cafes, and the *Petit Paris* neighbourhood located just behind it being well-known for catering to the troops' carnal needs. There are several other indicators of the town council's purposeful blindness. By way of their being specifically singled out and banned, several articles in the regulation point to the existence of considerable soliciting activity. The local gendamerie also appear to have been less than enthusiastic in wanting to implement the regulations, at times claiming they were powerless when it came to stopping prostitution in private houses, and there was even a suspicion that some girls were sheltered by the police in return for favours.[86]

---

85 Richsarchief Brugge, Archif de Panne, Eerste Wereldoolog file, separate letter dated 26 Apr. 1916 from acting Mayor to the civilian Governor, De Panne.
86 Ibid., handwritten, unsigned letter, 6 Mar. 1915, to the civilian Governor.

Given this context, one can understand the frustration expressed in some Divisional APM reports from the Flanders region over the apparent lack of speed in following up on denunciations and ridding the locale of 'dangerous' women.

Whether the sex trade was openly sanctioned and directly controlled by the authorities, or merely overseen with a light-touch, it is apparent that both regulated brothels and individual women were easily found by those having an interest in finding them, with the immutable laws of supply and demand governing their number and operation. Regulated and tolerated forms of prostitution played a key part in supplying the soldiers' sexual needs throughout the war. Further, the army wanted to protect the system, despite doubts that it was not as efficacious at controlling the spread of disease as might be claimed. When the political clamour surrounding the increasing rate of VD among dominion troops, combined with the growth of prostitution on the home front, forced the government to take action, banning the *maisons* through new regulations under the Defence of the Realm Act in early 1918, the army establishment fought the measure. Even Haig was against closure, predicting a rise in unregulated prostitution and growth in VD.[87] They also knew they would never enforce it, especially if the French military establishment would not co-operate. They were right: there is evidence to show that the brothels scattered across the occupied lands in virtually every town or village where the army made camp, continued to be used by soldiers right up to the end of the war and beyond.[88]

For many British soldiers, the red and blue lamps provided a welcome respite from both the boredom and the rigours of the battlefield. Although the ambience was basic, their working girls rarely attractive, and the cost often prohibitive, they were popular with the troops. It was not simply the ease with which they were found, nor the army's complicity in helping find them that made them attractive. The soldiers genuinely believed them to be safe: a quick release of sexual pressures that would not result in months of sickness and possible social disgrace.

Despite the number of establishments, their general accessibility and the productivity of the individual women, however, from the evidence of reported queues there was an insufficient number to meet demand. The VD figures also argue this. In theory, if all sexual activity was confined to that between 'punter' and regulated and healthy sex worker VD should have decreased, not increased.

Patently, in their relative frustration and driven either by economics or unavailability, soldiers looked elsewhere for that boost to their morale. Fortunately for the Tommy, he did not have to search too hard to find substitute product. With – to appropriately borrow a concept from the business world – the barriers to market entry being very low, it was very easy for would-be suppliers to literally get into the game. The result was the parallel existence of unregistered prostitutes in absolutely vast numbers.

---

87 TNA: WO 32/5597: Letter, March 1918.
88 Corbin, *Women*, pp. 39-42.

9

Following the Drum: Unregulated prostitution

Regulated prostitution provided the basic service to assuage the soldiers' sexual needs but 'clandestine', 'wayside' or 'amateur' venality – the epithets are used by the military of the time to describe women who were not working as recognised, regulated, full-time prostitutes – probably out-weighed, or, at the very least, matched it. The disruption of the peacetime economy and the displacement of a large number of women whose partners were themselves serving at the front led to a massive rise in the number of women selling sex.

Despite the efforts of the military and civilian police the sheer scale of the refugee problem made control difficult. In a report on the situation of controlling refuge families in Flanders, addressed to the civilian Governor of the Province of West Flanders, the author told of one family where the 'girls devote themselves to soldiers in the private rooms of the villa where they live together', and despairingly added there are 'all sorts of similar cases too long to describe'. And it was only those women with venereal disease they were concerned about but remove one infected woman and another soon took her place.

The prevalence of unregulated prostitution is witnessed in countless memoirs such as Percy Clare's, as is the ease with which the soldiers found them: 'both officers and men knew where the "Circe's Cup of Pleasure" could be obtained, and any girl in the villages would oblige' he wrote.[1] Not only did soldiers use unregulated prostitutes, arguably they enjoyed it much more. Most memories of sex with amateurs are positive and the girls are described in more alluring terms than their regulated counterparts; Lawson boasted that 'I had some nice civvy girls', and J. Wedderburn-Maxwell an Officer in RFA recalled a 'Snappy little tart'.[2]

The unregistered prostitute came in many guises and worked in many different ways. She was a barmaid at an estaminet, tea shop, wine bar or beer hall (popular

---

1   IWM 06/48/1, Clare, *Reminiscences*, book three, Aug. 1917.
2   IWM Sound Archive, No. 24882, reel 2, Lawson: No. 9146, J. Wedderburn-Maxwell, Officer 45th, 1st and 36th Batteries RFA.

That Provost-Marshal Feeling

A sensation only to be had at a Base—in other words, a base sensation

The threat of the Provost Marshal was actually not a great discouragement to finding available women, and officers were only really at risk of censure if bringing disrespect to the uniform. (Courtesy Mark Warby. ©2015 Estate of Barbara Bruce Littlejohn)

in the Nord region). She worked in informal, unregistered brothels of varying sizes, from single rooms in private houses to converted small hotels. She worked in retail, sometimes selling gloves or, during the war, souvenirs, as well as an hour with herself in a back room. She was a common street-walker, lurking in doorways and down darkened alleys, 'speaking their part in innuendoes, revealing themselves only under [the] cloak of darkness' as Hope found.[3] She waited outside garrisons and base camps, or even offered herself *al fresco* beside the canal, the arms dump, the railway station or anywhere she might find a client willing to take her. Clare provides an example of the breadth and unexpectedness of opportunity recounting the time he took an officer's washing to a 'peasant's cottage' and the young woman invited him upstairs to stay with her.[4] And finally, she was the 'amateur' who worked occasionally from home and was not always immediately recognised or recognisable as a prostitute. Together they are often described or categorised as 'clandestine' prostitutes. The soldier was their natural quarry.

Somewhat ironically, the registered brothel, instead of channelling and containing men's desires to that one place, was partly responsible for the growth of unregulated prostitution. There were simply not enough of them, or too far back behind the lines[5] and although there was some suggestion that men found the atmosphere of the regulated establishments sordid, and the transaction too degrading, the brothel arguably gave men a taste for 'vice'. Rather than the degradation of the circumstances leading men to eschew sexual indulgence altogether, these establishments encouraged the men to seek the same indulgence in more aesthetic surroundings, with prostitutes who were not subject to any form of regular medical examination or licensing.[6]

If quantifying regulated sex presents problems, then these are minor compared with quantifying the unregulated. It flourished right across the occupied lands, and the term includes everything from the girls in the estaminet brothel to those who waited beside the canal or at railway stations. According to Corbin, this indiscriminate, street walking, clandestine prostitutes outnumbered those registered by six to one in peacetime, with the war multiplying their numbers considerably.[7] A fair description would be that they were ubiquitous, though, as Gilfoyle notes in his study of historical prostitution, 'one must recognise the inherent empirical limits for such studies … the obstacles in identifying the precise populations of prostitutes … Precision is impossible, maybe even pointless'.[8]

The French authorities certainly showed concern, as traditional confidence in male abilities to discriminate between types of women evaporated. An official government

3   Hope, *Winding Road*, p. 94.
4   IWM 06/48/1, Clare, *Reminiscences*, book three, Aug. 1917.
5   Hirschfeld, *Sexual History*, p. 156.
6   Hall, *Hidden Anxieties*, pp. 49-50.
7   Corbin, *Women*, pp. 140-41, for other statistical evidence.
8   Gilfoyle, Thomas, 'Prostitutes in History: From Parables to Metaphors of Modernity', *American Historical Review* 104 (1999), p. 138.

memorandum warned that 'Feminine prostitution has spread so much that it is now impossible to mark out precise limits … unregulated prostitution has developed in such proportions that it is impossible to say where it starts and where it finishes'.[9] Military doctors, concerned about the spread of VD, argued that the problem lay in telling which women on the street might infect a man:

> [you] can meet them everywhere by day; in the form of, for example, either as elegant women out for a stroll on the boulevard, or as what passes for workers, a package in their hands … in the *brasseries à inviteuses*, the *spectacles*, the aisle of the theatre, in public bars, cafes, the café-concerts … in perfume boutique, or in curio shop, in the back of a boutique created for a completely different industry, as well as in all these *maison de tolérance*.[10]

Whatever their number, the British soldier became aware of their existence virtually on landing in France. When landing at Boulogne, there was already a reception party awaiting their arrival. Clarence Walter Jarman, a private in the 7th Royal West Surrey Regiment, was astounded by the 'kids [who] came running up asking you to go with their sisters … little boys running along grabbing your hand, "come cushy with my sister" … that was the first time I'd ever experienced anything like it'.[11] The reception grew in size and seeming ferocity as they moved inland as he discovered:

> At St Martin's camp in Boulogne [July 1915], under canvas, where our main job was keeping the prostitutes out of the tents; they were shocking … hordes of them. And there was youngsters running along the side of the regiment advertising their sisters.[12]

'You want jig-a-jig with my sister' was a very common offer.

Who were these girls? Certainly some were professionals who preferred to take their chances and work outside the tolerated system. In the larger cities some may even have previously worked within a tolerated brothel but no longer wished to subject themselves to the rigours of bi-monthly inspection. Corbin shows that this movement between closed house and street was common practice before the war. Some would have been girls who had relocated from other regions. The majority, however, were refugees or local women forced into prostitution as their financial support disappeared to the battlefield, death or prisoner of war camp. Others were simply young women

---

9   SHAT 9N 968 suppl. Pautrier, report Oct. 1917, cited in Rhoades, '"There are no Safe Women"', p. 47.
10 Ibid., p. 47.
11 IWM Sound Archive, No. 10168, reel 4, Price.
12 IWM Sound Archive, No. 12925, Jarman, Clarence Walter, private 7th Bn. Royal West Surrey Regt. Other examples, Chapman, *Passionate Prodigality*, pp. 16-17; Graves, *Goodbye*, p. 79; Hope, *Winding Road*, p. 88.

('flappers') chasing the uniform and making some money into the bargain. There are few reliable estimates of the number of persons displaced, swelling the ranks of refugees but Dendooven estimates that refuges may have accounted for 45 per cent of the population of West Flanders during the war years.[13]

Hirschfeld contends that 'More than four-fifths of the occasional prostitutes whom the police had under their control were married women and mothers of from three to eight children. Their husbands gone either to the front or captivity, or dead, they were driven into the arms of the enemy soldiers, not by any pleasure in vice but by the cry of their children for bread'. As for the unmarried occasional prostitutes, they were recruited almost exclusively from jobless servants, factory girls and seamstresses. The more factories and business establishments were shut down the greater the number of unemployed grew, the more did the mass of occasional prostitutes increase.[14]

With no other means of sustaining themselves, sex work became a survival necessity. In the vast majority of cases, women entered into these relationships driven by the indescribable misery and suffering that reigned in the occupied area. Where the Four Horsemen of the Apocalypse tore over all the fertile fields stamping out all life, necessity drove the French women, who had been robbed of their husbands, to sell their bodies. With anger and disgust, a *poilu* summed up his feelings in a postcard censored by the French authorities:

> The rich, with their money, can afford pleasure, happiness, base and ignominious passions. Every day in the most sumptuous and famous cafes, women can be seen selling themselves to strangers for a few Louis: British, American or others … and don't think it is for love.[15]

What cannot be ascertained, however, is exactly what price they put on their bodies. Being clandestine or amateur almost certainly meant that the rate was less than that of the regulated brothel and sex might be bartered for food – 'beauty taking stores as a tribute' as Dunn poetically put it – as well as paid for in cash. It is a sad but unavoidable fact that for some desperate women, having sex was the only way for them and their families to eat. Eustace Booth, an ASC motorcycle dispatch rider, noted that 'the girls would do anything for a tin of bully beef' and Leonard Stagg, an RAMC private, confirmed how extensive this trade was:

13 Dendooven, '*Living Apart Together*', pp. 143-57.
14 Hirschfeld, *Sexual History*, ch. 9., Prostitution behind the lines.
15 Gibson, C., 'Through French Eyes', *History Workshop Journal* 55 (2003), p. 181.

You know the tins of bully beef we had? Well, at one place there was a place called bully beef island and some of the chappies would save a tin of bully beef and go there and get their enjoyment for a tin of bully beef.[16]

Given that we find many soldiers claiming not to have used the brothels because of their high cost, it may perhaps be deduced that the army was correct in arguing that most venereal disease was contracted through the unregulated girls. The French authorities, alarmed at the increase of venereal disease that this massive increase in unregulated prostitution brought in its train through 1916 and 1917, did what they could to curb the clandestines. They passed a variety of laws forbidding soliciting near railway stations, banning alcohol from sale where women were selling themselves and tightening up on police surveillance. The tide of clandestine and amateur prostitutes reportedly continued to rise, however.[17]

Some contemporary observers felt that certain laws actually promoted vice rather than acting as a prohibitor. Dr. Leon Blizzard attributed the growth of unregulated vice to mid-war regulations forbidding the restaurants and café from serving alcohol to soldiers and women, and requiring them to close at nine: 'If soldiers and women could not go out in public, what else was there to distract oneself with besides sex?'.[18]

The estaminets – a combination of café, restaurant and bar – were smoke-filled havens from the war, where men talked, joked, sang sentimental and coarse songs, occasionally fought each other, and perhaps found temporary solace in the arms of a woman. Somewhat appropriately, the word 'estaminet' appears to be of French derivation but borrowed from Spain and initially designating a cabaret which provided prostitutes.

Estaminets were regulated – if not all formally licensed – and policed by the military police as well as the local gendarmerie. They ranged from the formal, with mass seating around large tables, to the 'front room' of a house. Some might have several rooms, and be large enough to separate officers from men, or diners from drinkers. Some became *de facto* officers' clubs, while others were frequented only by other ranks. Some had simple accommodation for rent by the night. Many doubled as billets, and many more as brothels. They could be located in a permanent structure (which had perhaps been a simple cafe before the war), or in a farmhouse kitchen temporarily turned into an estaminet to capitalise on troop movements, or in *ad hoc*, roadside sheds that lasted until closed down by the authorities for some infringement or other of an agreed operating code. Others simply disappeared with the tide of war.

16   IWM Sound Archive, No. 8764, reel 4, Stagg; No. 9263, reel 2, Booth, Eustace Russell. Dunn, *War*, p. 189.
17   Grayzel, 'Mothers, Marraines, and Prostitutes', *International History Review* 19 (1997), p. 78.
18   Blizzard, *Les Maisons de Prostitution de Paris pendant la Guerre*, p. 25.

As with brothels, establishing a definition of what constituted an estaminet, as opposed to a basic *shebeen* (an often illicit drinking den), is difficult and thus presents a challenge estimating how many existed at any one time. It would, though, have run into many hundreds up and down the line, with some very close to the front. The 5th Division APM, stationed south of Ypres in early 1917, estimated there were over 500 in his section alone.[19] Perhaps the only definition possible is one which recognises their ability to provide the soldier with a cheap meal (often the ubiquitous egg and chips), warmth, the company of fellow soldiers, and alcohol in the form of vin blanc, cheap champagne and weak beer.

Indeed, selling beer and wine proved a lucrative business and many inhabitants 'dug in' at homes and shops near the front, despite the obvious dangers from stray shells and the prospect of a German breakthrough. The trade offered a better prospect than the unknown future facing a displaced refugee.

Lieutenant-Colonel Jarvis, the Assistant Provost Marshal, 2nd Canadian Division, for an area near Poperinghe, undertook a census of estaminets in the rural Westoutré area. In an area less than 3 kilometres at its nearest point behind the front line, he discovered: 'every second house in Locre, Dranoutré, Westoutré, etc., apparently has a licence to sell beer and wine and this trade seems to be a recognised "side line" by the average householder'. In January 1916 there were a reported 39 in Westoutré alone (not counting sellers without licences) and in Caestre, Nord region, he discovered one house in every five to be an estaminet.[20] Further down the line, in France and in war zone urban areas, the situation was much the same as Max Plowman recorded:

> In the town itself [Laventie, February 1917], although certain houses were in ruins, most of the civilians carried on, the estaminets and shops doing a roaring trade. It reminded me of Ploegsteert in its complete disregard of a war being in progress close at hand'.[21]

Poperinghe, the largest town in the Divisional area, had numerous estaminets, many quite literally becoming famed brand names. There was *Cyril's*, the *Savoy Restaurant*, *Skindles*, the *Four Crowns*, *Take Five*, and *What 'opes?* catering for officers, and many more smaller establishments that catered for the troops. They sold fish and chips, scrambled egg, tea and biscuits, coffee and cake, and the occasional tot of rum. Liaisons made in these were more likely to have been of the non-venal kind, but, as noted, in the *Petit Paris* area estaminets and brothels catered for more carnal needs. In these the girls were not local but from refugee families that had fled from other parts of Belgium down to this area behind the front line.

19   See TNA: PRO 154/112
20   TNA: WO 154/77.
21   Mark VII (pseud. Max Plowman), *Subaltern*, p. 197.

The larger estaminet establishments were sometimes similar to the *maisons* in the manner of their operation. It is possible that the soldiers' memories are sometimes mistaken, labelling somewhere an estaminet when it was an unregulated brothel that also sold food and alcohol.[22] What characterised many estaminets, other than providing food and drink, was that they were family affairs. Most estaminets were run by women, often mother and daughter combinations, or by the owner with refugee help. The women soon became a focus of attention for the troops, who eulogised their charms. They became the stuff of dreams for the men. Some almost passed into legend.

Soldiers' comments and stories illustrated their general importance to morale: William Holmes, 12 Bn London Regt, fondly remembered the 'girls always gaily dressed … food was good … atmosphere was such a wonderful change it was like Christmas day'.[23] Percy Clare wistfully recollected, 'a village with plenty of estaminets where '*beaucoup vin rouge ou blanc*' and '*café avec rum*' could be procured and with plenty of pretty girls to make love to. No girls were ugly to us boys straight from the blood, mud, stench and filth of the trenches'.[24]

A male environment ruled, and the girls working there would have had to put up with all sorts of lewdness and suggestiveness, not all of it as witty or as harmless as the following banter:

> A buxom barmaid peered at his shoulder flashes, and expertly identified the 35th Division [Bantam Division]. Having overheard his men address him as 'Sir', she remarked, 'Your Officers are very small'. 'Yes, madam', replied Tich gravely, 'But we have big privates'. His word brought the house down in a bellow of laughter and became the Division's joke thereafter.[25]

Although there were estaminets that stuck to such innocent pursuits as providing egg and chips, a large number were as active in satisfying the soldier's other hungers as the more instantly recognisable brothels. Such places were ubiquitous. 'Not all estaminets were bad. Not all girls in a village were purchasable though most certainly were. You could have as much or as little as you liked' remembered Clare.[26] Few actually needed to advertise themselves with a lamp of any colour. The soldier was capable of finding them without much help but always appreciated the recommendation of his comrades as Hope recalled; 'And if you want a good thing,' a gunner yells after us, "take the small one in the blue garters, she's a peach"'.[27]

---

22   IWM, Sound Archive, No. 9875, reel 8, Ashurst, describes an obvious brothel, with rooms off a bar, as an estaminet.
23   IWM Sound Archive, No. 8868, reel 6, Holmes.
24   IWM 06/48/1, Clare, *Reminiscences*, unnumbered page.
25   Allinson, *Bantams*, p. 203.
26   IWM 06/48/1, Clare, *Reminiscences*, unpaginated, Book Three, Aug.1917.
27   Hope, *Winding Road*, p. 91.

It was certainly a case of *Inky Pinky Parlez-Vous* for the soldiers from all allied armies who frequented these places, and who literally found that the 'landlord had a daughter fair' to be either flirted with or hired.[28] That many required money rather than seduction is apparent. Though identified as a brothel by Private Lewis, the following description of this establishment with its music, food, and family involvement marks it as an estaminet:

> There was one place what was a brothel – they was all a-dancing, our soldiers. This bloke as owned the brothel – they were his two daughters that was supplying all the soldiers … This place was about ten mile behind the front line – there was civilians in them places. I asked this bloke who the girls was. He says 'They're the Gaffer's daughters.' And he was a-serving … while they was doing their stuff.[29]

Inevitably not all the women were memorable beauties: 'Slatternly women' or 'flashy looking girls in the estaminets who offered themselves for cash on the line … riddled with VD most of them', were more likely to be the norm as Clothe discovered.[30] Some soldiers, however, found them acceptable, as one philosophically put it: 'Well, you can't have everthink [sic], so you've got to be content with what you got'.[31]

Plied with drink, the soldier's moral resistance (and often taste and discrimination) crumbled, and they became easy targets for the prostitutes who worked the estaminet. As Hirschfeld noted, the estaminets enjoyed more freedom from inspection regimes: 'it is clear that the real breeding place of prostitution in the West was the notorious estaminet … This was true on both sides, the only difference being that the estaminets in the allied territory enjoyed more freedom'.[32] This sector was regulated by the authorities only in ensuring it complied with the appropriate alcohol licences. Prostitution itself was not illegal (until the change of laws in 1917) and was tolerated in the liberal rather than legal sense, provided the girls were healthy, and there was no obvious threat to military law and order. The opportunity of closing down estaminets that flouted their liquor licence was often taken, however, thereby removing places from where the girls could operate. The APM of the 2nd Canadian Division, Jarvis, knew many of these places to be bases for prostitution and on several occasions he had to remove, or hospitalise, infected women or those who were causing a nuisance. The APM of the 3rd Australian Division had the same problem.[33] The following

---

28 Becker, *Silhouettes*, p. 63; Boyack, *Behind*, p. 128; Voigt, F. A., *Combed Out* (London: Jonathan Cape, 1929), p. 56.
29 Lewis, *Colonel's Runner*, Manning, *Her Privates We*, pp. 69-71 for fictional portrayal.
30 Cloete, *How Young*, p. 104.
31 Manning, *Middle Parts*, p. 46.
32 Hirschfeld, *Sexual History*, ch. 9, p. 162.
33 TNA: WO 154/77: 'House at Outtusteen [sic] and estaminet au Point du Jour, placed out-of-bounds on 21st and 27th January 1918 respectively (infectious disease), reported by ADMS as safe and reopened accordingly'.

estaminets were identified as brothels evidenced by VD returns from July to October 1917: 'estaminet au Point du Jour. Estaminet and farm at Henneveux'. Initially placed out-of-bounds (due to infectious disease) once reported by ADMS as safe again they were reopened accordingly.

Corbin is in no doubt that the barmaids in the vast majority of French pre-war drinking places were prostitutes. This applied not only to the establishments recognised as estaminets, but also to the beer-drinking halls and wine shops where shop owners employed unregistered prostitutes in order to compete with other establishments, tempt their clientele and to sell their products more easily. Usually young prostitutes worked, helping the owner to serve drinks. Although the practice was effectively outlawed by changes in the laws of 1896, only a brake was placed on the extension of this practice. For the soldiers, they exerted a certain charm over the more overt form of prostitution found in a brothel. And of course, the "barmaids" were a great deal cheaper than the regulated girls.

With a tradition of barmaids doubling up as prostitutes, it was perhaps inevitable and natural that estaminets and shebeens took on this double role as *de facto* brothels during the war years though some did so more openly than others. For example, Cloethe remembered the 'tea shop' that served more than tea, 'a café that turned out to be a brothel',[34] and Canadian Private Frazer the case of the best hotel in town, '*Les Quatre Saurs Amantes* ... a near brothel at the time', with 'a very suitable name'.[35]. Father Achiel Van Walleghem, parish priest of Dickebusch, noted in his diary:

> Nowadays it's not the inns that are the worst, but the houses where one orders coffee. The inns are only open for 4 hours per day, they are very crowded and time and circumstances don't allow for evil. However, those coffee houses are open all day, there are almost always a small number of soldiers keeping themselves busy, and there is plenty of time and opportunity for evil.[36]

Not all of the estaminets that operated this way were instantly identifiable as providing services other than food and drink. There was a great deal of subterfuge as Dunn gleefully recounted:

> It is told of our dour Scotch Commander in Chief ... [he] stopped at [an estaminet on a breezy height, the well-named 'Au Bon Air'] ... the highest on the Amiens road, to enjoy the beauty of the scene while he ate his sandwich lunch. After finishing, he looked at the house, humble as any other wayside estaminet ... everyone but he knew that half a dozen daintily appointed rooms lay behind that in which he sat. The house was owned by a notorious Parisienne who had

---

34 See TNA: WO 154/8, APM Report I X Corps.
35 Cloete, *Victorian Son*, pp. 210, 283; Fraser, *Journal of Private Fraser*, p. 230.
36 Flanders Field Museum document centre, Diary of Achiel Van Walleghem, 11 July 1915.

CONFIDENTIAL.   PARTICULARS OF VENEREAL DISEASE.

It must be impressed on the patient that information given will be treated as confidential and used only for the purpose of ensuring that the woman concerned undergoes proper treatment and does not meanwhile have the opportunity of infecting other soldiers.

A.
1. Formation.   2. Unit.

3. Number, rank and name.

4. Disease, (if Syphilis state Primary or Secondary).

5. Date reported sick.

B.
6. Date first signs of the disease became apparent.

7. When and where contracted.

8. Can the patient identify the woman.

9. What is her name and address.

If the patient cannot identify :-

10. Did he meet the woman in a licensed house.

11. Can he describe it, or its position or locality.

12. Where did he meet her, town, street or locality.

C.
13. Where did they go to.

14. Did he pay her.

15. Her description and dress.

16. Could she speak English (well or badly).

17. Did he meet her more than once.

18. Does he know anyone else who knows her, if so who.

If the patient says he does not know when and where he contracted the disease :-

19. When and where did he last have connection with a woman.

```
    20. Can he give any particulars about her.
D.
    21. Has he had Venereal disease before, if so when and where.

    22. Where treated.
    ─────────────────────────────────────────────
        Date ............    Signature of Interrogator ....................

                                E.
A.P.M., IX Corps.
----------------
            Arrangements have been made for this man to be
        (a) evacuated, as he cannot identify anyone.
        (b) transferred to No.42 Stationary Hospital, AMIENS.
                            No.30 General Hospital, CALAIS.
                            No. 1 Stationary Hospital, ROUEN.

                    ............................
    to identify the woman, please forward this paper to A.P.M. concerned.

                                                ........................
        Date ...............                    A.P.M.    Division.
                                F.
A.P.M.,
--------
            Forwarded,
        (a) for any action possible.
        (b) will you please arrange and acquaint me with result in
    due course.

                                                        Major,
        Date ...............                    A.P.M., IX Corps.
                                G.
A.P.M., IX Corps.
-----------------
            Returned.
            Identification was (not) successful.
            Medical examination (bacteriological ) gave positive
    (negative) results.

                                        ........................
        Date ...............            A.P.M., ..............
```

Soldiers reporting with, or discovered on examination to have VD contracted from an unregistered prostitute, were made to complete a questionnaire by one diligent APM so that the source of infection could be identified and the woman removed to a lock hospital. (TNA WO 154/8)

staffed it with some winsome daughters of Rahab, and ran it as a select house of the kind. It had turned out a profitable investment.

Would Haig have had it shut down had he realised? Probably not, as he as much as every other member of the command structure knew the importance of such places to continued troop morale whatever their own personal moral stance.[37]

Another disguised outlet for venal sex was the 'pretext shop'. These were shops that sold one or other form of goods as a pretext for selling sex in the backroom: glove shops, collar and tie shop, shops selling engravings and photographs, wine merchants, perfume shops, bookshops and above all, novelty shops which had either a backroom or basement when the girls prostituted themselves. An extra-parliamentary committee noted in 1904 that there had been a considerable increase in this kind of procuring.[38] Importantly, this phenomenon also existed in the provinces. Their *modus operandi* was simple: when the client went to the counter to settle his purchases, he was made to understand that he could, for an additional sum, purchase another kind of merchandise.

It is now impossible to know how many of these pretext shops existed in the back area towns where soldiers took their leave, but it certainly provokes a reassessment of why a variety of memoirs make particular reference to pretty girls in 'glove shops' and others.[39] Gibbs felt most shop girls were innocent leaving 'the traffic of passion to women who walked the streets' but Hope went into detail describing an experience that, while no mention of a monetary transaction is made, may have been an innocent case of fraternisation, certainly closely resembles the classic description of a pretext shop transaction.[40]

A final form of indoor prostitution was that of the temporary prostitute, or amateur, who worked from home or some temporary shelter or room.[41] Gibbs found them almost in the front line in the ruined cellars of bombed out houses. Read found a 'lady' living in a cottage on our way back to camp who was available for a consideration'. This home-based prostitution was found both in the countryside and the towns. It appears to have been especially prevalent in the coal-mining towns of the Artois where, as Henry Russell tastefully reported, 'Some houses specialised in supplying the inner man which the army rations failed to satisfy, and they made many francs by doing so'.[42]

If an opportunity presented itself, it was not missed by soldiers so inclined: 'In a certain village where a mother and her two daughters offered hospitality to all comers, the soldiers waited in a long queue', found one. That 'some of them had a snack while

---

37 Dunn, *War the Infantry Knew*, p. 462; see also Crozier, *Brass Hat*, pp. 106, 143.
38 Corbin, *Woman*, p. 143.
39 Vaughan, *Desperate Glory*, p. 36, and Gibbs, *Realities*, I, p. 142.
40 Hope, *Winding Road*, pp. 196-7, 202-3.
41 Gibbs, *Realities* I, p. 229, I. L. Read, *Of Those We Loved*, p. 118.
42 Henry Russell, *Slaves*, p. 79.

waiting', suggests it may actually have been functioning as a temporary estaminet.[43] In another private home we learn from Alfred West, a NCO in the Monmouthshire Regiment, of demand appearing to exceeded supply once again with 20 men crammed into a front room awaiting their turn.[44] When any woman did 'open shop', it did not take long for the word to get around although perhaps these queues represented peaks when a single battalion was temporarily out of the line and perhaps just paid.

In all probability, these mother-and-daughter teams would only have lasted as long as their sexual health did not warrant their removal. Stagg, the RAMC nurse, on temporary secondment with the Military Police, tells of visiting a house to follow up on a woman identified as having infected a soldier. He does not describe the size of the place, but the fact that it only had a small waiting area suggests it was just a one- or two-woman operation within a private house:

> Another case was when two military police came with two gendarmes. I had to take this man with these four to a house where he had caught VD. We got to the house and he opened the door and there was a kind of bench there and there are two kilties [Scotsmen] sat on it … the MP said 'What are you chaps waiting for?'. 'Coffee, sergeant'. 'Be a funny place to wait for coffee, you'd better skip off while you are well off'.[45]

Such repartee illustrates the relaxed atmosphere surrounding the use of such places. Although confronted by MPs, the jocular response of these potential clients and their dismissal without any formal warning suggests a knowing connivance. Indeed, it would only have been illegal if the soldiers were AWOL or out-of-bounds.

Physical codes were devised to communicate to the soldier what services were on offer, like this, noted by Alfred West: 'Out of the line, the boys were all wanting women. And the women, knowing this, used to put a sign in the window saying "Washing done here for soldiers"'.[46] It seems that elaborate and well-understood codes evolved signalling a female's availability. These ranged from how washing was hung on lines, the number and arrangement of flower-pots, china ornaments and even childrens' toys placed in not too conspicuous positions on the window sill.[47] West again reporting on a colleague: 'We found out that he had a little agreement with a lady – and that when she started to hang clothes on the line, that meant her old man had gone out. When the signal came … he was up the field'. There are claims that girls working singly from cottages and houses were occasionally refugees from *maisons de tolérance* relocating from those made out-of-bounds, or shut down as 'unhealthy'.[48]

43 Dr Huot, *Psychologie du Soldat*, quoted in Fischer and Dubois, *Sexual Life*, p. 269.
44 IWM Sound Archive, No. 12236, reel 6, West.
45 IWM Sound Archive, No. 8764, reel 4, Stagg.
46 IWM Sound Archive, No. 12236, reel 6, West.
47 Ibid.
48 Tozer, *Terrible Story*, pp. 68-71.

Subterfuge was not always required. One example of the ubiquity and lack of ambiguity of the so-called 'clandestine', and the freedom in which they sometimes operated, was illustrated by a place situated in the base town of Doullens. Charles Gee, and officer in the 9th Bn Durham LI, remembered: 'that HQ had, in fact, a red light hanging out of it every night ... some girl upstairs, some casual person came each night'.[49]

While the majority of prostitutes appear to have worked from some kind of premises, they were supplemented by the streetwalker. These are perhaps the hardest category of all clandestine prostitutes to analyse. They were either the real 'amateurs', or prostitutes soliciting openly from doorways, alleyways or the corners of streets. Sometimes the girls had rooms to go to, other times it was a sordid open-air affair.[50] These girls represented a clear and ever present danger as Fred Dixson of the Surrey Yeomanry was aware; 'VD was common in the army ... you could get it from the pubs ... maybe from a civilian who you'd follow into the toilets'.[51]

In some places these were urban girls who braved the real dangers of war by staying in long-abandoned towns, living in the ruins, utilising whatever 'cover' they could and plying their trade whenever possible. In Arras, in 1917, at the height of the battle of the Artois, Cuddeford found that 'some of the less obvious kind [of resident] remained throughout, especially those who had – or conveniently adopted – aged parents to take care of. The old folks didn't seem to mind too much'.[52]

Gibbs, with his skills as a professional writer, evoked the world of the demi-monde street walker:

> There were no lights allowed at night in Amiens ... all of the streets were black tunnels and one fumbled one's way timidly, if one had no flash lamp, between the old houses ... But up to midnight there were little lights flashing for a second, and then going out, along the Street of the Three Pebbles, and in the dark corners of side streets. They were carried by girls seeking to entice English officers on their way to their billets, and they clustered like glow-worms about the side door of the *Hotel du Rhin*, after nine o'clock and outside the railings of the public gardens. As one passed the bright bull's-eye from a pocket torch flashed in one's eyes ... 'How dark it is tonight, little captain! Are you not afraid of darkness? I am full of fear. It is so sad this war, so dismal! It is comradeship that helps one now! ... A little love ... A little laughter, and then – who knows? ... *Un peu d'amour* ?'[53]

---

49 IWM Sound Archive, No.13717, Gee.
50 IWM Con Shelf, L. Gameson, 'Papers': Gameson RAMC was approached in the street.
51 IWM Sound Archive, No. 11047, reel 4, Dixon.
52 Cuddeford, *And All For What?*, p. 117.
53 Gibbs, *Realities* II, p. 278. See also similar descriptive prose of clandestines at work in Paris in Ewart, Wilfred, *Scots Guard* (London: Rich & Cowan, 1934, Strong Oak repr., 2001), p. 167.

Similar scenes would have been observable in towns and cities throughout the Western Front where soldiers congregated on leave. Linguistic ability by one party or the other came in handy when dealing with 'free-lancers' as it did in general fraternisation. 'My French came in immediately, though it being the Hotel Britannique English was also spoken. The housemaid especially spoke it quite well and did us many services, including looking after our surplus cash, a needed precaution as one man found out to his cost being taken by a pimp for seven pounds odd the first night'.[54] However, while speaking in tongues was an obvious advantage it was not an absolute prerequisite. Love, or the universal language of gesture were often adequate substitutes. Old regular army man, Bob Mariner VC, advised a comrade that he should lead 'his old Uncle Bill to her and I'll show you how a real swaddy will do a proper job of it' without a knowledge of the local 'lingo': 'Look here my young gamecock, I have had my dealings with Indian girls, half-chats, niggers, Africaners and what-not, and I'll bet you what you like, there's no woman, least of all a Froggy, who wouldn't catch on to my meaning!'.[55]

The war diary kept by the efficient APM, Captain Watson Colpitts, of the 3rd Australian Division, for six months between March and September 1917, provides an almost unique picture of the spread of contacts between soldiers and local women, illustrating their ubiquity.[56] In his monthly reports, Colpitts provided venereal disease returns and, where possible, recorded where the infection was caught. When an individual woman was identified as the source of infection, she was 'removed' by local French officials who accompanied the soldier making the accusation. Over this period alone, a total of 33 individual locations are identified. Nine are the base and leave towns of Paris, Harve, Amiens, Armentières, St Omer, Abbeville, Rouen, Calais and Boulogne, where both regulated and unregulated red lamps are known to have existed. The remaining 24 locations are villages and hamlets within just a few miles of the line (see Appendix for a list of villages and towns, with map, identifying these) and all patently in reach of a soldier with some free-time available. Four more villages are identified in this way in incomplete returns from the Royal Naval 63rd Division over the same period and more in those for the British XI Corps. The APM of the 63rd Division was perhaps overwhelmed by the problem as the file contains a report complaining that, at the end of 1918, 'there were 72 women sent to Mons who were reputed to be infected with VD and only 21 were found to be infected. There are still 3000 awaiting [sic] to be medically evacuated. I am only allowed to evacuate 12 women a month and consequently the arrangements are absolutely inadequate'.[57] In addition to these figures for France, the APM of the 3rd Division also reports cases in the much smaller Belgian occupied zone.

54   Johnson cited Boyack, *Behind*, p. 138.
55   Eyre, *Somme Harvest* p. 29/31.
56   TNA: WO 154/77.
57   TNA: WO 154/73.

What cannot be ascertained is the sort of women who were sexually active in these village cases. In all probability they were all working alone, but whether they should be classified as 'clandestine professionals', 'bully beef amateurs' or cases of innocent fraternisation can never be determined. The last is the least probable. What is important to note, however, is the widespread nature of these contacts. It is to be greatly regretted that, for whatever reason, other APM reports which might have provided even more evidence have not survived.

The general truth of the matter was noted by the young Hope, 'Wherever there are soldiers, there are women'. Wherever, in fact, a passing soldier might be. The clandestine prostitute was ubiquitous as the boys in khaki found.[58]

The 'opportunities for running up against a bit of skirt' were many, even if true fraternisation was not an option as long as the soldier was prepared to pay for his pleasure. Even 'the local farm girls always seemed willing to do their best to solve the men's problems', found Private P. G. Heath. The range of reminiscences, covering as they do airmen, officers and men of all ages, of many regiments from the 'PBI', signallers and artillery to the 'long tail' of RAMC and ASC, confirms that many men were indeed very willing to pay.

Whereas the brothel might not have been an option for those with limited money or access to rest camps and back areas, the clandestine prostitute filled the supply gap for those of limited means. She was not only readily available but offered herself at a price matching the market's ability to pay, accepting even 'bartered' goods in return for her sexual availability. She operated from a large number of locations, from the estaminet and bombed-out cellars to her own home as the circumstances demanded, sometimes surreptitiously, sometimes quite openly. The general ubiquity and number of women appearing by the wayside is an indication of the insatiable demand. Crozier summarised it in his inimitable way early in the conflict:

> It is a fact that prostitutes and loose women always followed the big drum. The more big drums there are the more prostitutes abound. There were a lot of big drums in England and France in 1915.[59]

And the noise of those big drums only increased as the war rolled on.

---

58 IWM, Heath, P. G., '*Memoirs*' (unpubl. transcript), pp. 258-59.
59 Crozier, *Brass Hat,* p. 64.

224   They Didn't Want to Die Virgins

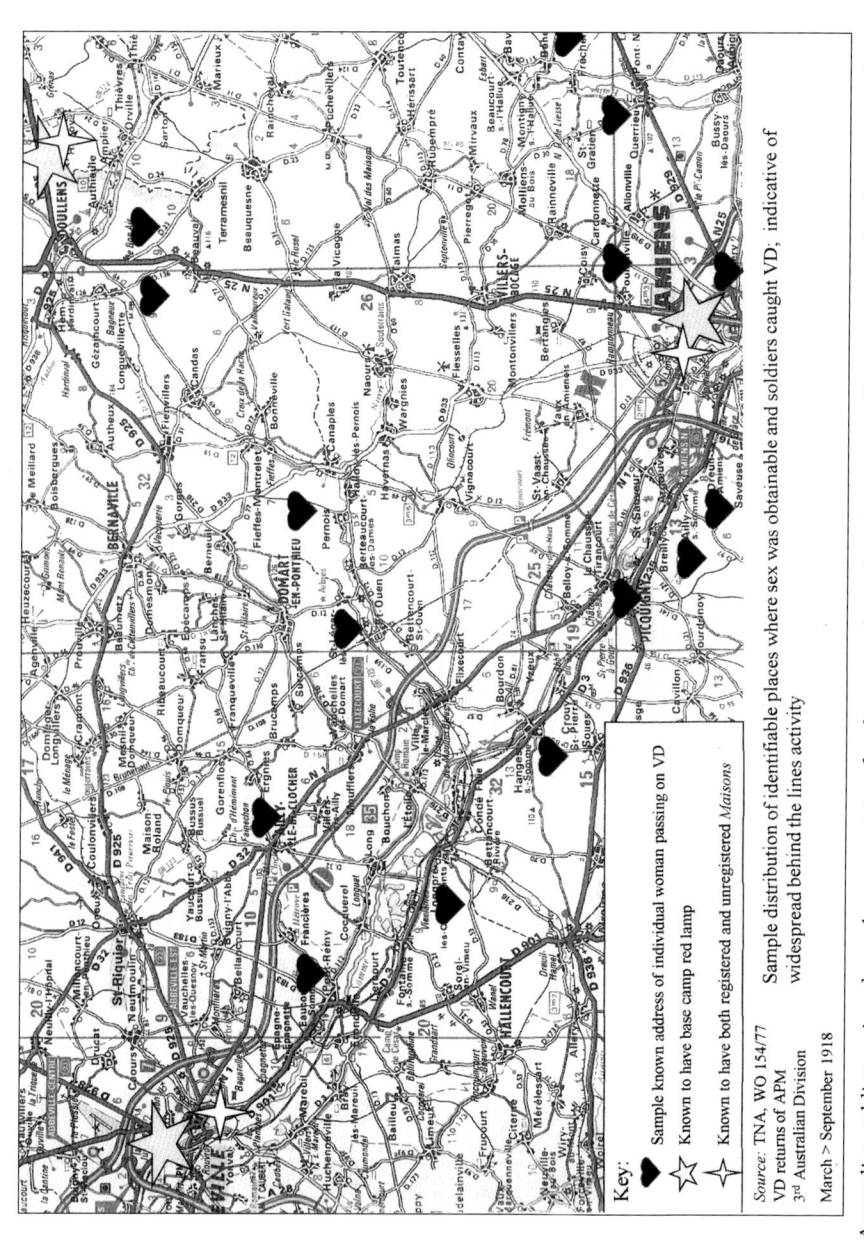

Australian soldiers enjoyed a perhaps surprising freedom to seek out female company. The map shows the distribution of army sanctioned 'red lamps', known non-regulated brothels, and – through analysis of mid-1918, 3rd Division APM returns, where VD had been reported as contracted – locations where soldiers had found sex in back area villages. (Source: TNA WO/154/77)

10

Je Ne Regrette Rien: Prostitution and the impact on morale

The easy sex enjoyed by the soldiers could for many be compartmentalised; as Dixon noted, 'it was, as it were, shut off from normal human relationships, and belonged to this lunatic world of war and to nowhere else'. If bought love was no substitute for the real thing, 'it at any rate seemed better than nothing. And in any case it worked off steam!'.[1] It bought more than just a physical release, however, and it is of interest now to enlarge on the discussion of the impact of venal sex on morale. In what way was the relatively easy access to prostitutes, either regulated or unregulated, a factor in upholding a man's morale?

We must first recognise that there would be those for whom it had no impact at all because they did not resort to their use, or did not have the opportunity presented to them. Percy Clare, was a soldier who looked, and observed, but did not buy; when asked by his billet landlady 'why he does not accompany fellow soldiers to the estaminate', replied *'Je suis marie', 'J'ai madame en Angleteter'*. In fact, for those with moral scruples, or determination to stay 'true' to a loved one at home,[2] or with a fear of catching a disease, the very existence of the brothel might have been an affront, the constant pestering of wayside prostitutes and their 'pimps' wearing,[3] and their comrades' reminiscences depressing.[4] Having to partake of 'short-arm' inspections, knowing themselves to be disease free would be an indignity; one more to add to a perceived catalogue the army imposed on the civilian-soldier.

Some men might have felt considerable post-coital remorse, their dalliance having been driven by alcohol and a loss of self-control. A quick visit might leave a man feeling dissatisfied, poorer in sprit and in pocket. Andrews summed up this particular feeling:

---

1   Dixon, *'Wheels of Darkness'*.
2   IWM 06/48/1, Percy Clare, *'Reminiscences'*, unnumbered page.
3   Hope, *Winding Road Unfolds*, p. 88; Chapman, *Passionate Prodigality*, pp. 16-17; Graves, *Goodbye*, p. 79; J. F. Tucker, *Johnny Get Your Gun*, p. 25.
4   As noted by H. Siepmann, *Echo of the Guns* (1987), p. 58. Mark VII (pseud. Max Plowman), *Subaltern*, p. 17.

> Occasionally it was possible for our men to go to a house of the red lamp, and a few would go, but they did not repeat the visit. They regretted the waste of money on a wholly unattractive experience.[5]

There may have been nagging feelings of guilt, a moral hangover as indicated by the general silence over their use. This probably had little impact on overall morale with some evidence, particularly amongst Catholic soldiers, that contrition could overcome such feelings. According to Plater's 'survey', good practising Catholics were able to overcome any moral hangover, even if a fall, *contra sextum*, was frequent and with suitable contrition, they were 'not permanently affected by ... impurity with women'.[6]

It may also have been a morale dampener simply not to be able to afford sexual services, or to believe that others were more able to take advantage of opportunities.[7] It is not unreasonable to assume that jealousies might undermine relationships or even contribute to regimental or inter-service rivalries. One thinks here, for example, of the complaints made by British troops that the Dominion contingents were forcing prices up to unaffordable levels.[8] Morale might take a tumble if the consequences of an encounter resulted in catching venereal disease, depending on the army's response, though we also read of men trying to contract the disease as a temporary way out of the war as did one of Harry Bretton RFA comrades, 'If he knew he was going into a hotspot he'd get sick with venereal'.[9] In these later cases, rather bizarrely, VD might actually boost morale.

It is also beyond conjecture that placing controls on men's activities, banning brothel visits, or closing them, exiling 'free-spirited' girls or punishing soldiers for any involvement with locals, could have detrimental effects on morale. It would have been particularly hard on those who were kept well away from a 'promised land' that was so tantalisingly close. 'Brother', wrote Dhunjibhoy Chinoy to H R Mistry (Bombay), from Kitchener's Army Hospital, Brighton in July 1915:

> it is a land of fairies... but the supervision over us is very strict, and we are not allowed to go anywhere, and we are hard-pressed, and we do not like it. At first the salas (sic) allowed us more freedom and we acted according to our pleasure – sometimes all night. We were even placed outside in billets; but some men abused the privilege, and it was entirely stopped..... Some became diseased and some were flogged... I feel afraid to write openly as perhaps the censor may open this letter.

---

5   W. L. Andrews, *Haunting Years*, p. 217.
6   Plater (ed.), *Catholic Soldiers*, pp. 73-4.
7   Regret of lost opportunity: IWM Sound Archive No. 9418, Ashby; No. 9431, Grunwell; No. 24539, Hall.
8   IWM Sound Archive No. 11111, Ferns.
9   IWM Sound Archive, No. 11029. And see also Alexander Watson, *Enduring the Great War*. p. 39.

The situation, possibly substituting Field Punishment for the flogging, could as easily have been expressed by a lad from Wigan writing to a pal in Leigh around the time of the Cayaux brothel closures.

It may have had an impact on a soldier's view of his officer had the latter's activities come under closer scrutiny or if man and officer have held divergent moral views. Clare's officer lost his respect when offering to pay for a prostitute on his behalf.[10] This could have damaged the officer/man relations that Sheffield thought so important to underpinning morale.[11] Differentiating the blue from red lamp was not simply reinforcing civilian social class differences but protecting the officer class.

On the other hand, as we have seen, the existence of paid-for sex did what the army believed it would do; eagerly anticipated,[12] it provided a release from tensions and frustrations. 'The only thing they lived for now was (1) a Blighty one; (2) the hours spent in the estaminets; (3) sometimes a bit of dick', wrote Williamson of his Patriot's Progress. It was a distraction. If a man was predisposed to seeking sexual activity, the prospect of finding women out of the line literally gave them 'hope for the future' and something to live for. Bourne contends that the British working class soldier was prepared to put up with a great deal as long as he had the occasional diversion or 'festive intermission'.[13] The army regulated brothel, for all its real and perceived drawbacks, and the general hunt for sex, would appear to have at least provided such a diversion and certain descriptions of events surrounding a brothel visit, often referred to a 'havens of joy', and Coppard's description would surely be categorised as festive;

> There were well over 150 men waiting for opening time, singing 'Mademoiselle from Armenteers' and other lusty songs. Right on the dot of 6 pm a red lamp on the doorway of the brothel was switched on. A roar went up from the troops as they lunged forwards towards the entrance ... A bloke told me a chap had his leg broken in the rush a week before, and I could well believe it.[14]

For some, surely few, it was even better than taking home leave. Harold Siepmann though so; 'At home ... the out-of-touch atmosphere of "patriotism" jarred so badly with the grim realities of the front that to spend one's time amongst the brothels of France was often the preferred option'.[15] This option was probably taken more by officers than the ranks (excluding colonial troops), as they had more regular leave.

---

10 IWM 06/48/1, Percy Clare, '*Reminiscences*', unnumbered page.
11 G. D. Sheffield, *Leadership in the Trenches.*
12 Williamson, *Patriot's Progress*, pp. 134-35.
13 Bourne, 'The British Working Man in Arms', in H. Cecil and P. H. Liddle (eds), *Facing Armageddon.* p. 349.
14 Coppard, *Machine Gun*, p. 57. Also IWM 06/48/1, Percy Clare, '*Reminiscences*', unnumbered page.
15 Siepmann, *Echo,* p. 49.

Another measure of the contribution lies in the fact that men visited prostitutes of their own free will, often seemingly on more than one occasion,[16] over an extended time period and without remorse; 'We went down to Rouen' recalled Read, fondly, 'and sampled the flesh-pots as thoroughly as we could, until funds ran low again. No doubt we were very foolish at times, but in retrospect I have no regrets whatsoever'. [17] There was no force. Where there was, as Gibbons recounted, men rebelled:

> Once in France I saw about three hundred men virtually officially shepherded to a Red Light establishment ...It was after a pretty bad smash in the Line ... and the command of the men that were left devolved temporarily upon a quite junior officer ... I suppose he thought he was doing the proper and rather sporting thing; but he got hold of a lot of lorries and had us driven as a kind of treat to the nearest town. And the lorries drew up just outside the leading Gay house, and in fact we were all to go inside and enjoy ourselves. And to the very best of my belief, not a single man that day did go inside.[18]

The army, however, if guilty of anything, was guilty of underestimating demand.

It is important to note that consummation of the sexual act that was not necessarily the key. As with sex itself, foreplay was important. A man's morale might be bolstered through the action of going to a brothel with his mates and doing little more than 'gawping'; 'I always remember it ... It was a comical affair that was', remembered Rowarth.[19] The visit itself could be a source of fun, to be remembered and recounted over and over later while in the trench.[20] Consummating the act was often secondary to the simple experience of going somewhere 'they oughtn't' and enjoying the thrill vicariously like Coppard who 'tagged on behind, irresistibly drawn'. [21] In many of the accounts there is almost a feeling of young boys having a lark, and it is not hard to imagine adventures being told and retold in trench conversations, to much laughter, and as such it indirectly led to male bonding (arguably thereby contributing to the effectiveness of the primary group). For others still it was an experience felt as a necessary rite of passage; 'It was', admitted Worcestershire Private, Edwin Bigwood, 'my first experience of life'.[22] It was, too, an affirmation of life.[23]

---

16 Chapman, *Passionate Prodigality*, p. 115, records one of many examples with 'our youngest lorry-hoping ... (with) great frequency'.
17 Read, *Of Those We Loved*, p. 337. See also Ex-Private X (Burrage), *War is War*, p. 27.
18 John Gibbons, *Roll on Next War* (1935), p. 55. Ex-Private X (Burrage), *War is War*, p. 20.
19 Lewis, *Colonel's Runner*. See also IWM 80/40/1, Rowarth, '*Misfit Soldier*' p. 29, for his account of his first visit.
20 Hope, *Winding Road*, p. 91.
21 Coppard, *Machine Gun*, pp. 56-7.
22 IWM Sound Archive, No. 10115, Bigwood.
23 Reed, *Of Those We've Loved*, p. 417.

"She Aint Arf Trey Bon'!"

Whether sex was dreamed of or a reality, whether it was paid for or freely given, the thought of a local women brightened up the soldier's life. (Author's collection)

For others, in their fight against the army, where Ashworth contends minor victories contributed to the upkeep of morale,[24] going to an unregulated brothel, or having a liaison with an amateur, sneaking out of camp to meet someone[25], represented one such victory for the individual over the system. One can see in officer's comments that, unsupervised, the men would bunk duties in preference to finding women.[26] It was not

---

24 T. Ashworth, *Trench Warfare 1914–1918. The Live and Let Live System* (1980, 2000).
25 Laffin, *'On the Western Front'* p. 124.
26 Letter to Brittain, *'Chronical of Youth'*, p. 202.

only old soldier Richards who was dismissive of Kitchener's plea to avoid wine and women.[27] In anecdotes the soldiers recalled with relish the times they had 'put one over' on their officers. Burrage told of a prostitute in the Rue de Gallennes (Havre) who reputedly wore a uniform of a British captain and was 'much in demand amongst the Tommies'. As Burrage himself concluded, 'If this were true it was a brain-wave on the part of the lady, and I expect she made enough to retire on'.[28] As unlikely as this tale is, along with the marching songs and jokes, it is illustrative of the role sex might play in the undermining of authority or pricking of military pomposity.

While noting the concern and impact of catching a sexually transmitted disease, we can see from the direct accounts of soldiers that access to prostitutes, even when actual use of their services was not taken, directly boosted morale by providing a diversion and often humorous interlude to trench life, and by providing the men with reminders of an existence not dominated by death and destruction. But in many ways morale is intangible. It is sometimes better measured by looking at things that have not happened and which are indicators of positive morale.

In releasing frustrations, it would arguably also have led to less AWOL and a stronger self-managed discipline, and as we shall see, probably contributed to lowering the level of sex crime against the civilian population. We cannot discount that such releases also helped prevent more men from getting nervous disorders, or assisted in early recovery from such.

While there were women available in significant numbers throughout the zones of occupation, there were times and places where they could not ply their trade, most notably at the front itself and where military policing had cleared the location of civilians. When there was no red lamp to light the way to Venus a mechanism of release had to be found elsewhere; the obscene and pornographic as substitutes for women and this source, too, contributed to the upholding of morale.

---

27 In addition to Frank Richards, *Old Soldiers*, see Ex-Private X (Burrage), *War is War*, p. 27.
28 Ibid., p. 18. See also Dowling, *Last Ridge*, pp. 150-4.

11

'Satisfies 'is lust, I s'pose':
The obscene, pornography and masturbation

Unfortunately for many front line soldiers there were times when the opportunities for female contact were non-existent. It was in these empty hours that erotic substitutes played their part, when the soldier sought and found stimulation and release from sexual tensions, or a boost to morale, with a range of erotic material enjoyed either in solitude or sometimes in company. A great deal of such material was specially printed or manufactured for the purpose, but other items which might have been innocent when set in the context for which they were intended (such as personal letters, or the female impersonator of the concert troupe), nevertheless could be used by the individual to feed erotic fantasies.

On the prosaic level of printed erotica, reminders of women were all-pervading: written, drawn and photographic images of the missing sex, featured in many aspects of the soldier's everyday life.[1] These materials helped to satisfy sexual desires that ranged from the simple want of a physical reminder of loved ones at home, to the satiation of immediate lust and basic physiological need. This latter need raises the question of the part masturbation played in the life of the soldier. However, as noted by Sigel and others, writing about the history of pornography, any comment on usage has to be based on reasoned speculation:

> Access ... is not the same as consumption. To say that people bought pornography does not say how they consumed the materials ... to determine how people consumed pornography, historians would need personal accounts of reading, even though these too are influenced by self-censorship and literary stylisation.

---

1 See Plater, *Catholic soldiers*, p. 75 for a rare direct reference to the existence of both 'literature, pictures'.

> Unfortunately, the letters, journals, and diaries are not available in the necessary numbers. People rarely write of illegal and 'immoral' acts, even to themselves.[2]

While the historian of the Great War is fortunate in having available some extremely frank personal memoirs, they could never be claimed as being a representative sample.

Before we investigate how soldiers related to such materials, it is helpful to look at the context of the erotic in the late Victorian and Edwardian era and at pre-war attitudes and usage patterns. During the mid-Victorian period, the amount of erotic material available had expanded and could potentially be found in a wide variety of formats, from the humble postcard to the expensive, skilfully-produced, exclusively printed book. In between there were quality prints and mass-produced photographs, moving pictures, *tableaux vivants* with partially dressed ladies, 'what the butler saw' style peep shows called mutascopes, and stereoscopes in which photographs could be viewed in three-dimensional glory. The erotic might be found in music halls and the lyrics of popular balladry, and was represented in many physical forms, from carvings on smoker's pipes to sculpture. The subject matter traversed a range from reproductions of famed artistic nude studies by the old masters, through coy pseudo-anthropological studies of nubile denizens of the Empire, to explicit sex scenes featuring fantasy group sex and even bestiality. Flagellation, cross-class seduction, the deflowering of young maidens, the nude, the action pose, the grotesque, the exotic and the humorous, all featured. Homosexuality was the only subject that a Victorian browser might not have found as readily as his modern-day equivalent. As Stephen Marcus noted, although some of the media have changed, all the elements of contemporary pornography were in place by the mid-Victorian era, 'we find then in this area of culture … the Victorian period is essentially continuous with our own'.[3]

Although there can be little doubt that producers and purveyors of the erotic were active in trying to market their wares throughout the late Victorian and Edwardian period, after the moral watershed of the mid-1880s it became increasingly hard for them to do so successfully, even to the relatively small numbers of people interested. Concerned authorities, worried that the market for pornography was filtering downward to the working classes, increased their vigilance and policing. By the Edwardian years, pornography and all manner of general erotica were driven 'underground' as prostitution and brothels had been. Crackdowns forced production of the most explicit materials overseas and any re-importation and subsequent distribution of materials was repressed with the full might of the law. It became harder to search out pornography, even for those having the resources and tenacity, as pornographers lost their freedom to display, advertise and distribute.[4]

2　Sigel, Lisa Z. *Governing Pleasures: Pornography and Social Change in England, 1815-1914* (New Jersey: Rutgers University Press, 2002), p. 98.
3　Stephen Marcus, *The Other Victorians* (London: Corgi, 1971), p. 62.
4　Sigel, *Governing Pleasures*, p. 89; Bristow, *Vice and Vigilance*, p. 202.

The strictest enforcement of the law against the sale of indecent wares so hampered the trade, boasted the authorities, 'that it is most difficult in London to obtain either pictures or books'. And this was not simply a London phenomenon: 'municipal governments vied with one another to declare their cities pure' with Manchester's chief constable claiming in 1905 that under his jurisdiction the city was known as the 'holy city'.[5] Evidence was confidently presented to the 1908 Joint Select Committee on Lotteries and Indecent Advertisements that the police crackdown on obscene materials had removed much from the streets and shop windows in cities from Liverpool to Hull.[6]

If he looked hard enough, or had been chosen as a suitable target by the pornographers, then the determined buyer might find what he sought. In 1912, the then Home Secretary, McKenna, could observe to a deputation from the powerful National Council for Public Morals that:

> Probably every man in this room and I speak for myself and I believe I shall speak for most of the others – hardly ever, if ever, sees any literature of this kind, and the ordinary public are naturally disposed to think that it does not exist ... we can spy no evidence of this kind of literature ... [However] the records of Scotland Yard show ... [it] unfortunately circulated in the most improper quarter possible amongst schools, amongst young boys and young girls.[7]

In all probability, however, the kind of literature circulated at this level was fairly innocuous, with subjects more at the titillating end of the scale than the sexually explicit. The police were inclined to follow the National Vigilance Society lead of classifying more materials as obscene and worthy of seizure (and prosecution) than the courts, and thus possibly the public, were prepared to do.

While the efforts of the local authorities, police and purity movement volunteers against local outlets usually paid off, according to Bristow the 'supplies from abroad were still largely free to pour in'.[8] The joint committee heard some interesting evidence of how the import market functioned: Dolly Ashton mailed offers of 'real hot photos at 21*s*. a dozen' from Paris to addresses in Britain.[9] Reviewing such evidence as is now available, what can be seen is that the police were not dealing with huge amounts of either the traditional type of obscene publications, or the newer postcards. The country was not 'awash' with erotica despite the scaremongering that suggested it

---

5 *Vigilance Record*, Sept. 1890, quoted in Bristow, *Vice and Vigilance*, p. 203 and p. 218.
6 Report of the Joint Select Committee on Lotteries and Indecent Advertisements (1908), paras 25, 641.
7 TNA: HO 45/10930/149778, in evidence being presented for an amendment to the 1908 Act.
8 Bristow, *Vice and Vigilance*, p. 203.
9 Report of the Joint Select Committee on Lotteries and Indecent Advertisements, paras 424, 429.

was, and supplies from abroad were probably not as great as Bristow's description of 'pouring in' implies. Those who had set up shop overseas were finding trade difficult. The British government sought official co-operation in stamping out their operations from often more-than-willing overseas governments.[10] Further, a vigilant Post Office intercepted 'sackfulls of the stuff'[11] when it legally and practically could, and the police prosecuted those agents and distributors that they identified.

The pornography industry itself contributed to the turn-of-the-century crackdown. The Newsagents Federation and Postcard Traders Association exercised a pre-publication veto of its members' designs, for example.[12] The circulating libraries, a popular way of obtaining one's reading materials during the period, applied the same self-censorship approach, and effectively 'weeded out' anything that might promote complaint or NVA action.[13]

Nearly three decades of repression – the result of the social purity campaign – had certainly put the erotic, in terms of amount and accessibility, out of arm's reach of the interested buyer. With regard to the subject matter, the social purity campaigners, using both legislation and outright social and political pressure, had so successfully managed to define what might be termed erotic as to have removed from general view even the most innocent subject matter. Much of the remaining material that could be described as 'obscene and indecent' was not erotic in the true sense of the word, unless someone found adverts for birth control or venereal disease cures erotic. Care has to be taken to discriminate the truly erotic from the socially unacceptable face of sex that 'one simply didn't talk about in public', such as prophylactics and 'abortificants'.

A challenging problem of definition is posed when trying to distinguish pornography from harmless titillation. To someone living in the twenty-first century much of the material of the Victorian and Edwardian eras seems naive and innocent, though there were undoubtedly some materials that would be comparable to today's extremes.[14] What is important is what was considered indecent and obscene in the eyes of contemporaries. Naturally this differed between individuals: moreover it was class-defined.

The actual word 'pornography' did not feature much in the vocabulary of the Edwardian civilian, or in the reminiscences of soldiers unless written a considerable time after the war, when the word had gained more common and all-encompassing currency. They preferred to use words like 'obscene', 'racy', 'risqué', 'indecent', 'lewd', 'scandalous', 'bawdy', 'dirty', 'filthy' or 'smutty' as descriptive terms, with the choice

---

10 Ibid., para. 343; see also para. 188. TNA: HO 45/10510/124433: Paris-based pornographer, Carrington, complaining of business being made impossible.
11 Report of the Joint Select Committee on Lotteries and Indecent Advertisements, para. 334.
12 Bristow, *Vice and Vigilance*, p. 223.
13 Lesley Hall, *Sex, Gender and Social Change in Britain since 1880* (2000), p. 79.
14 The Milford Haven collection of postcards at the Victoria and Albert Museum has examples.

seemingly depending on the individual's moral stance, education, social status, vocabulary and even geographic origin. The range of words used to describe sexually-related material is indicative of the difficulties the Victorians and Edwardians themselves had in defining 'obscenity'.

The broad legal definition that determined obscenity prosecutions in Britain for over 100 years, building on Lord Campbell's 1857 Obscene Publications Act, was provided by the so-called 'Hicklin test' of obscenity. It was not what it was *per se*, but who might see it that delineated its legality, though not being legally 'obscene or indecent' did not necessarily imply its social acceptability. An equally fundamental piece of legislation for controlling obscenity where it allegedly appeared, but also doing little to clarify the legal definition, was the Indecent Advertisements Act of 1889 which said, in effect, that all mention of sex in public was indecent. This effectively opened the door to anyone who wanted to categorise anything as pornographic or obscene and to prosecute or threaten to do so on that basis. The targets could range from obvious and blatant indecency to wider controversial social issues such as abortion-inducing drugs and contraception.

But what content or subject matter could be considered by the majority to be obscene or beyond the moral pale? Views ranged from those of libertines and entrepreneurial 'pornographers', on the one hand, to those of the independent busybody on the other.[15] One such 'busybody' was Alfred Dyer, an obsessed fanatic, was to prove a thorn in the army's side with his tireless campaigning in both Britain and India against regulated prostitution as well as the 'obscene' in general. The latter could hold views even more extreme than those espoused by the ever-watchful, agenda-setting National Vigilance Association. And, as Hynes has shown, somewhere in between was an intellectual elite, the early stirrings of an opinion-forming group, who implicitly and explicitly questioned the social and individual mores of the time through both their actions and art, and who were ultimately to contribute to a change in post-war social perceptions.[16]

The evidence to the Joint Select Committee on Lotteries and Indecent Advertisements (1908) gives some sense of what content could invoke accusations of obscenity: nude women showing pubic hair, nude women with men in the picture, nude paintings, women in underclothes and undressing, women sitting in certain positions. Interestingly, there was no mention of 'sexual acts' which may either imply their rarity or they were simply accepted as so obviously obscene as to not need mentioning. Abortion remedies, 'Malthusian devices' such as French letters, also described as 'rubber goods and surgical instruments', were on the list. 'Innuendo' that was likely to discomfort the magazine or newspaper reader was also a sensitive area.

Thus, by the turn of the century it was not only that which was successfully prosecuted that defined the obscene. Such was the power of the 'moral guardians' that the implicit threat of prosecution, the blocking of distribution, or the organisation

---

15 Bristow, *Vice and Vigilance*, p. 87.
16 Hynes, *Turn of Mind*, pp. 149-71.

of public boycott was sufficient to force self-censorship onto the various branches of publishing. The problems of definition were rarely tackled formally.

Was what the soldier came across in the trenches deserving of the label 'pornography'? Sigel solves the definitional question by including in her analysis all that was defined and recognised as pornography by collectors of the material; in other words, the subjective view of those who used it gave the word meaning:

> I use the word pornography as an umbrella term to cover a wide variety of variations including literature, drawings, and photographs. A focus on sexuality ties these diverse mediums together ... and has a wide range of foci and uses; it does more than just titillate. I consider pornography works that people wrote published, printed ... and collected as pornography.[17]

It is an interesting approach, though only replaces one ambiguous term, 'pornography', with another, 'sexuality'. But it does allow the inclusion of any and all media, and it was the expansion across multiple new platforms that drove the growth of the obscene. But the soldier was not a collector as such, though some may have been: it was the memories of women evoked by images and representations that aroused him, rather than the illicit or morally questionable subjects themselves. Typically, a soldier would not have derived sexual satisfaction from pornography *per se* and perhaps would not even have defined what he had as pornographic. In other words, the arousal was internalised through the image, as opposed to being directed at what was on the page itself. An advert for ladies' underwear would not normally have been considered pornographic, obscene or even indecent, for example, but, when removed from the original context of a women's magazine and pasted to a dugout wall, it became erotic material. To some, its purpose could be said to be that of any other recognised obscene image and, as such, it did more than just titillate.

Allowing the user, however, to define whether the material should be considered obscene is a useful approach. The majority of soldiers, certainly those of the middle and upper working classes, were very influenced in their attitudes, as was demonstrated earlier, by the social purity movement. They set the goalposts, prescribed what should be seen, and described what was indecent. Widespread support for the NVA tends to suggest that there was a social consensus on indecency. Look through the NVA's eyes and it can be argued that we look through the eyes of the Edwardian majority. If the Edwardian terms 'obscenity' and 'indecency' equate with the modern usage of the word 'pornography', then, by his own definition, much of the material the soldier enjoyed might be considered pornographic, however innocuous the images appear today. During the late Victorian and Edwardian period, what was 'obscene' became a moving target, with the chosen target depending largely on the whims of

---

17 Sigel, *Governing Pleasures*, p. 4.

the NVA and other busybodies. The NVA controlled the debate. The NVA defined the terms employed. The NVA broadly exercised the ultimate power of control.

These pressure groups, and the NVA in particular, could really get under the skin, so to speak. Such was their influence that the banned and harassed D. H. Lawrence complained that 'the grey ones left over from the nineteenth century ... dominate in society, in the press, in literature, everywhere, and naturally they lead the vast mob of the general public along with them'.[18]

The bulk of the army, especially the volunteer rank and file of Kitchener's Army, that 'decent middle order' of society, would have initially held a strong antipathy towards the obscene. With the majority of working- and middle-class soldiers, particularly those under 35 years of age – having lived the majority of their lives through the NVA years – marching off to war with the New Armies without having been greatly exposed to real pornography, nor to anything more indecent than an advert for family planning, a bawdy song, an 'anthropological' postcard, or perhaps a *tableau vivant*. In his relationship with sexually explicit materials, the rank-and-file soldier was, as in other aspects of his sexual life, probably a relative innocent when he crossed the Channel. Not only would he have seen little, if any, pornography, his implicit if not explicit support of social purity causes would have predisposed him initially to disdain acquiring it. Debatably, the same may not be said perhaps for the wealthier classes, those that were initially to become the officers, and for the 'old soldier' who may have been exposed to obscenity in overseas garrisons.

In a rare reference to indecent materials, Dixon, a soldier in the Royal Fusiliers, imparts a view that would have initially been felt by many:

> I don't know whether I should say this but somehow or other these elderly chaps got hold of some beastly postcards which were distributed amongst the troops of sexual habits of themselves or [I] don't know who ... which disgusted us younger chaps very much indeed.[19]

What is also pertinent here is his reticence to mention the subject, and this typical Edwardian reticence helps explain why there is so little mention in the memoirs of the common soldier.

Widespread evidence of unhindered dugout decoration shows that use of the milder pin-up and other erotica was implicitly sanctioned which explains its wider mention. With regard to the more obscene or indecent, it can be assumed that prevailing laws and attitudes governing usage and distribution in civilian life would, in theory, have applied, although other than a mention at the Inter-Allied Conference of 1917, there is no record of the authorities showing concern.

---

18   Cited in Bristow, *Vice and Vigilance,* p. 222.
19   IWM Sound Archive, No. 9343, reel 2, Davis.

If ownership and use of erotic materials became the norm rather than the exception during the war, it was because of the erosion of the soldiers' original moral positions, in a way similar to the attitude change that took place with regard to 'wild love' and paying for sex. The general range of influences that brought this about was mooted earlier, but perhaps one more may be added here: consumption itself contributed to the change. Rather than explicitly forbid photographic representations of women, the army condoned their use, and society generally helped provide them. Kirchner's provocative drawings for the *Sketch* might, for example, be accused of paving the way for more explicit materials.

Whatever level of exposure the soldier had had beforehand, temptation presented itself virtually from the moment of enlistment. He had access to the erotic and pornographic as soon as his boots hit French soil, sometimes even before. John Lucy talked of it being sold outside camp gates in England: 'The usual shoal of hawkers and bagmen descended on us in our new quarters ... lewd picture postcards ... were produced for our temptation'.[20] To the pornographers, both British and Continental, the war would have seemed a God-sent market opportunity. In France itself, the production of pornographic books boomed – some even being translated into English – as did the printing of dirty postcards and cigarette cards and the manufacturing of sex toys. As far as the soldier himself was concerned, while initially predisposed to disdain the indecent and obscene, there must have been an element of the 'forbidden fruit' about it. Given France's reputation, he would not have been human had he not been curious about what he might find there.

So what was available to the soldier on the Western Front and what can be included in the term erotica? Robb makes the point that: 'Given the sexual reticence of Edwardian society, and the sexual isolation of the soldier, it took very little to awaken desire'.[21] The most intimate erotic 'literature' was not commercially produced at all. It was the letter from home. These arrived uncensored, and full and free rein could be given to sexual reminiscence and fantasy.

Cuddeford, an officer serving in the 12th Battalion Highland Light Infantry, on the Western Front from August 1916 to July 1917, found that censoring such letters gave:

> a fine insight into the mentality of the men under our command. The sentiments expressed in some of them were crude to the extreme ... The writers believed in calling a spade a spade, without any attempt at delicacy of language.[22]

In a similar vein, men could also write letters to friends exploring or describing the sexual landscape and demanding news of the recipient's home adventures. Second

---

20 Lucy, *Devil in the Drum*, p. 62,
21 George Robb, *British Culture and the First World War* (2002), p. 54.
22 Cuddeford, *And All For What?*, p. 128.

Lieutenant Butlin's letters implored his friend for salacious news in return for his own descriptions of sexual adventures in France. Indian soldiers swapped accounts of their sexual adventures with French women.[23]

The replies from wives and sweethearts were no less open, and must have done the same job of cheering the recipient up, if only temporarily. Hiscock, the under-aged Royal Fusilier, remembers:

> Jackson's ever-loving girl in Croydon kept him supplied with adoring missives, which he read over and over again, reminding himself of sexual glories that her own particular brand of civvie street had supplied in happier days and nights. He was never averse to letting us know their contents and by candlelight he would read her halting phrases filled with love. 'Listen to this bit', he would say, 'I can't forget the last time you were home on leave … do you remember how we … [followed by a graphic description of sexual act]'.[24]

Jackson's girlfriend was undoubtedly not alone in the openness of her prose. Although the inclusion of anything quite as graphic would have been beyond the socially conscious, middle-class Vera Brittain, she confides to her diary that 'I have never thought I should be able to say to anyone such things as I write to Roland. I suppose the nearness of death breaks down the reserves and conventions, which are seen to matter so little in the light of elemental things'.[25] Many letters from wives and girlfriends would have at times contained something intimate, and not always dealing with the prosaic problems of running family and household.

Men would also confide in each other, even intimate details of home life, and some vicarious pleasure might be gained from what was essentially one person telling another, or an audience, a sex 'story'. Tilsley, who fought as a ranker and used his own experiences to create a semi-autobiographical novel, introduces a scene where the men of Lancashire are in billets, they have been singing 'Riley's Daughters' and 'Inkey-pinkey-parley-voo (sic)' and several other old favourites and one soldier implores another to recount a particularly spicy tale about a local liaison, '"..tell 'em about Georges Carponter…" The atmosphere was heavy with men's talk. Nothing loath, the black moustache (of the story-teller) wagged in the candlelight, and became the centre of a score of round eyes. *War was forgotten!*'.[26] In fact, conversations about sex dominated Tommy's conversation when not talking about the iniquities of the army or the war itself.

---

23 IMW. 67/52/1, J. H. Butlin, 'Letters'; D. Omissi, *Indian Voices of the First World War* (1999), p. 81/83/164.
24 Eric Hiscock, *The Bells of Hell*, p. 75.
25 Vera Brittain, *Chronicle of Youth*, p. 178.
26 Tilsley, *Other Ranks*, p. 29.

In addition to the letters from loved ones, the soldier also received letters from girls and women at home, who were encouraged to write out of patriotism (i.e. to show support by 'adopting' a 'Tommy'), or girlish romance. While there was no cultural equivalent to that of the *marraines de guerre*, of France – those women who 'adopted' a soldier and sometimes becoming more than simply pen-pals[27] – these letters could be important for some, and their use and content was not always completely innocent. Hirschfeld contends that not only these shared letters but gifts from home, from wives and girlfriends, and even knitted socks and scarves from anonymous sources, could take on erotic overtones: 'since these gifts were frequently destined for unknown recipients they created an erotic contact between the front and the hinterland, a contact which was considerably strengthened by the widely disseminated love correspondence'.[28] Soldiers enjoyed receiving these letters and some even carried on multiple correspondences hoping to profit by their contacts and intimacy when at home on leave.[29] Andrews mentions a variation; 'Some of our fellows would pose as 'lonely Tommy', and have a bevy of girls send them letters and parcels'.[30]

Reading matter was important in the trenches, especially for officers often living in more comfort than the other ranks, in dugouts, and perhaps, being better educated, more interested in this style of diversion. Inevitably, the material read depended on class and education. In addition to the classics, the arcadian and pastoral, poetry and the penny novel, pornographic books and periodicals were part of the staple diet, and easily obtained (especially when on leave in Paris). 'My very good Colonel bought some immodest French books which he tried to hide from me', wrote subaltern Talbot Kelly.[31] Local French pornography was sometimes translated into English.[32]

Another piece of personal erotica carried was the photograph or print. Naturally, many fell into the category of 'loved ones' rather than eroticism, as shown by Vera Brittain writing, with only a hint of sexuality, to her boyfriend, Roland: 'I have just been kissing your photograph goodnight'.[33] Cloete 'thought of women; of girls, flappers, young women. Raphael Kirchner painted pictures of them. I carried one that reminded me of Eileen'.[34] They were not always of a wife or girlfriend, however, or totally innocent – if Aldington's fictional character is to be taken as indicative of wartime reality: 'But how these men love life ... Oh, they have their "tarts", they've all got girls' photos in their pay books – and what girls! Tarts for Tommies. Cream

27 For description of the role of *marraine de guerre*, see Susan Grayzel, 'Mothers, Marraines, and Prostitutes: Morale and Morality in the First World War in France', *International History Review* 19 (1997), pp. 70-5.
28 Hirschfeld, *Sexual History*, pp. 73-4.
29 W. L. Andrews, *Haunting Year*, p. 111.
30 Andrews, Haunting Years, p 111
31 R. B. Talbot Kelly, *A Subaltern's Odyssey*, p. 77.
32 Levenstein, *Seductive Journey*, p. 339, n. 12.
33 Vera Brittain, *Chronicle of Youth*, p. 178.
34 Cloete, *Victorian Son*, p. 92.

tarts for Tommies'.[35] Huntly Gordon, Second Lieutenant, Royal Field Artillery, alluded to carrying one following a period at home on leave. In his case, it appears to have almost been a charm against other possible sexual temptations: 'The walk back through the shadows of Leicester Square past a long line of clucking old hens, whose furtive endearments only caused me to quicken my step. There was by now a girl's photograph in my breast pocket'.[36]

Without doubt, the most ubiquitous and popular reminder of feminine charms were the prints and drawings that adorned billets, dugouts, company HQs and canteens. Effectively, these were the equivalent of today's pin-up or the 'Page Three Girl' that adorns a thousand male-dominated domain of garage or workshop.

There was no distinction – unlike the red or blue lamp demarcation – between officer and other ranks when it came to an appreciation of painted beauties as Philip Gibbs noted in his 1920 *Realities of War*: 'They brought Kirchner prints of little ladies too lightly clad for the climate of Flanders, and pinned them up as a reminder of the dainty feminine side of life which here was banished'.[37] Nor were there any sites considered inappropriate for their display. Douie discovered them in billets used by subalterns of the Entrenching Battalion at the local presbytery in Henencourt: 'Unoccupied owing to the absence of the priest on military duties … the walls were adorned with the cheap sacred lithographs beloved of Catholic peasantry, interspersed with the latest photographs of famous beauties torn from the illustrated papers'.[38]

Kirchner was undoubtedly the favourite artist of all and drew for *La Vie Parisienne*, and for the *Daily Sketch*. While other artists – Sager, Herouard, Fontan, Harrison Fisher – also drew girls, Kirchner was the favourite and his were the cards predominantly pinned up in the trenches. They were the original 'pin-ups'.[39] The Tommy called Kirchner 'Kirsonner' and young officers had competitions to see who could collect the most cards.[40] The column, 'Things we'd Like to Know', in the soldiers' trench paper, *Kemmel Times* (incorporating the famed *Wipers Times* and the *New Church Times*), rhetorically asks, 'Who leads in Kirchner collections?'. That these were morale-boosting and literally brightened up the environment is beyond question. Artillery officer and brother of journalist Philip, A. H. Gibbs was not alone in making decorating a priority wherever he was posted: in moving into a new billet near S Quentin, 'We rigged up shelves and hung new fighting maps and Kirchners and got the stove to burn and declared ourselves ready for war again', and later in Bailleul, in 1918:

35 Richard Aldington, *Death of a Hero* (1929), p. 251.
36 Gordon Huntly, *The Unreturning Army: a field gunner in Flanders, 1917-1918* (London: J. M. Dent & Sons, 1967), p. 103.
37 Philip Gibbs, *Realities of War* I, p. 77.
38 Douie, *The Weary Road*, p. 48.
39 See Tonie and Valmai Holt, *Till the Boys Come Home: the Picture Postcards of the First World War* (1977).
40 *Kemmel Times* (incorporating the *Wipers Times* and the *New Church Times*), Vol 1. No. 1.

we ... sank a lot of francs in a series of highly artistic picture postcards which, pinned all round the hut at eye level, were a constant source of admiration and delight to the servants and furnished us with a splash of colour which at least broke the monotony of khaki canvas'.[41]

Vaughan appears to have believed pin-ups to be the *sine qua non* of a good billet and certainly conducive to his own good morale.[42] Mellersh, who referred to the drawings in a Freudian slip as 'provocative', also appreciated the decoration: 'He plastered our room walls with drawings of girls – there was an artist I think called Dana Gibson, nearly as effective as those in *La Vie*'.[43]

These prints, and publications like those of *La Vie Parisienne,* provided the average soldier with his staple reminder of the women he was so longing to hold. Though stylised and not at all realistic – (similar in that respect to the air-brushed beauty of today's 'mens' magazines – they were a distraction and designed to excite him and no doubt made a welcome change from the reality of local peasant girls and the often hard-bitten inhabitants of the brothels. The girls of *La Vie Parisienne* were wonderfully described by Emlyn Williams as 'plump *poules de luxe* bursting in saucy colour out of their corsages – no concession to fashion here – legs in the air, tiny aphrodisiac heels a metre apart but dimpled knees maddeningly together'.[44]

H.M. Tomlinson's appreciation of those magazine prints is illuminating in that it demonstrates that although the soldier's peacetime attitude to such things changed, it was not without some residue of guilty feelings:

> Of all the periodicals that reach the British front, the two for which there is the most competition in any officers' mess are *La Vie Parisienne* and *New York Life*. The impudent periodical from Paris is universal on our front. The work of its artists decorates every dugout. I should say almost every mess subscribes to it. It is usual to account for this as being naughty chance. Youth has been separated from the sober influence of its English home, is away from the mild and tranquil light of Oxford Street femininity, is given to death and therefore snatches in abandon in amusements which otherwise would not amuse ... *La Vie Parisienne*, it is true, is certainly not a paper for the English family. I should be embarrassed if my respectable aunts found it on my table, pointed to its drawings, and asked me what I saw in them.[45]

---

41 A. Hamilton Gibbs, *Gun Fodder*, pp. 232, 209; see also H. E. L. Mellersh, *Schoolboy into War*, p. 66; Coppard, *Machine Gun*, p. 69; Graham H Greenwell, *An Infant in Arms* (1935, 1972), p. 82; Gibbs, *Realities*, I, p. 78; Vaughan, *Some Desperate Glory*, pp. 89, 53.
42 Vaughan, *Desperate Glory*, pp. 100, 110, 138.
43 Mellersh, *Schoolboy Into War*, p. 106.
44 Emlyn Williams, *George: an early autobiography* (1961), p. 203.
45 H. M. Tomlinson, *Waiting for Daylight* (1922), p. 47.

The obscene, pornography and masturbation 243

Prints taken from magazines were pinned to dug-out and billet walls as glamour pin-ups now adorn a thousand garages and workshops. Many included a military motif. (Author's collection)

That the men sometimes were slightly ashamed of the *La Vie Parisienne* is further evidenced in a story in the *Dud*, the 11th Battalion King's Shropshire Light Infantry trench magazine. In this, the author dreams of his mother visiting his dugout:

> 'Disgracefully dear', assented mother, 'I could hardly find my way in, but, she added plaintively, 'I didn't dare to complain. I thought it one of the hardships out here, perhaps'. 'We'll soon cure that', I replied stoutly, and lit a couple of extra candles. 'There that's better'. It wasn't. Candles are hard to get, and in any case the cuttings from *La Vie Parisienne* became much too obvious. There was a gloomy silence whilst she regarded the walls of the dugout.[46]

Kirchner's girls and their like were an escape for the moment from the filth, squalor and immediate dangers of the war zone, and inevitably they were fantasised over and dreamt of. What always has to be remembered is that, for a great number of young soldiers, bereft for real-life sexual experience, these painted girls were the real thing. They had nothing to compare them with. Gilbert Franau's Wipers Times poem is perhaps unintentionally more honest about the soldier's night-time relationship with the prints.

> I dreamed of bloody spurs and bloodier sabr
> Of mention – not to modest – in despatches:
> I threw my foes, as Scotchmen toss the caber,
> And sent my prisoners home in wholesale batches;
> Led my platoons to storm the Prussian trenches,
> Galloped my guns to enfilade his flank;
> Was it HM's own royal hand, Or French's,
> That pinned the VC on my tunic ?
> SWANK!
> Those dreams are dead: now in my Wiper's dug-out,
> *I only dream of Kirchner's naughtiest chromo*:
> The brasier smokes; no window lets the fug out;
> And the Bosche shells; *and Q still issues bromo!*
> (italics in original)

It is an interesting aside here to note this trench newspaper poet's suspicion that bromide is being used to dampen ardours![47]

More socially up-market magazines, like *Tatler*, were another source of pictures. Those that were sent to the trenches by loved ones at home were devoured by officer

---

46 Cited in A. D. Harvey, *A Muse of Fire: Literature, Art and War* (1988), p. 124.
47 Gilbert Frankau, published in the *Wipers Times*. No. 3 Vol. 1 March 1916 (facsimile 1973).

The obscene, pornography and masturbation 245

'I only dream of Kirchner's naughtiest chromo'. (*La Vie Parisienne* prints from author's collection)

recipients (the *Tatler* was not a ranker's read) not only for any society news but more importantly for their pictures of models and scantily clad models.

Chapman tells of being 'guided ... to a clean and pleasant summer house with boarded walls, decorated with Kirchner drawings and portraits of English beauties from *Tatler*.'[48] And this anonymous poem, again from The Wipers Times is like all satires, close to the truth in dealing with the subject matter of a subaltern's obsession with underwear adverts. He would not have been alone in finding pleasure in gazing at these.

The Sub
He loves the Merry *Tatler*, he adores the saucy Sketch,
'The 'Bystanders' also fills him with delight;
But the pages that he revels in, the evil-minded wretch,
Are the adverts of those things in pink and white,

They are advertised in crepe-de-chine,
And trimmed with silk and lace;
The pictures fairly make him long for leave;
And while he gloats upon the frills, he cannot find the grace
To read the pars of Phrynette, Blanch and Eve.

Before the war, he'd hardly heard of lace and lingerie;
He didn't know the meaning of chemise.
But thanks to weekly papers, this astounding mystery
Has been solved by dainty Vern and dear Larise.

Before the war he only knew of corsets and of hats,
All other vogues invoked a ribald 'what-ho,'
But the last decree of fashion is a dinky nightie,
That's embroidered with his regimental motto.

It's this war, that is responsible for teaching simple youth
All sorts of naughty Continental tricks.
And already he's decided, when it's over, that, in truth,
He'll buy mamma a pairs of cami-knicks.[49]

It is also interesting that the author recognises that it is the experience of the army, and particularly of the war, that has taught him 'all sorts of naughty Continental tricks'.

---

48 Chapman, *A Passionate Prodigality*, p. 27.
49 *Wipers Times* reprinted facsimile, (London: Papermac, 1973).

The obscene, pornography and masturbation 247

EXPOSITION DE BLANC.

In the same way that simple magazine adverts could excite some, so to perhaps could the occasional reminders of women that might be chanced upon in the ruined and deserted villages and towns. Tommy could not have been too different from 'Fritz' his counterpart in sharing this sentiment of Erich Remarque:

> Some time ago there was an army theatre in these parts. Coloured posters are still sticking on a hoarding. With wide eyes Kropp and I stand in front of it. We can hardly credit that such things still exist… She is a lovely girl with a delicate nose, red lips and slender legs, wonderfully clean and well cared for, she certainly baths twice a day and never has any dirt under her nails…..The girl on the poster is a wonder to us.[50]

La Vie Parisienne was also probably read for its 'small ads', too. Using sometimes obscure code – who now knows what *'soins hygieniques'* might have implied – women advertised their varied services, but patently, with most service providers based in Paris, these would only have been able to have been enjoyed by officers and perhaps some colonial troops.

Of such stuff were dreams dreamed, conversations sparked, and moral-boosting thoughts of the future thought. It wasn't always going to be like this. There would at least be leave… sometime… and then women.

It was not only the published prints that decorated the dugouts and billets; when they had time, the men drew images themselves. Sometimes these were idealised, and sometimes they were crude. In 1915, I. L. Read, moving into new billets at Berles-au-Bois, 'marvelled at the many clever crayon and pencil sketches on the walls – of girls either nude or in various ravishing states of dishabille … This alone put everyone in high good humour'.[51]

However, there was also what was recognised to be obscenity at the depots and in the regions of the Front, where the walls were everywhere covered with obscene drawings in which the most fantastical representations of the sexual organs naturally played a prominent part. Drawings of nude women, enormous buttocks and the genital organs well in view reflected the sexual obsession that held sway in the areas denuded of women. Not all would agree that such works were morale-boosting, but even if some betrayed a deep misogyny they do show sex as top of mind when free of the distractions of war.

Halfway between the almost naive prints of Fisher, Kirchner *et al.*, and the personally executed drawings and more explicit photographs, there was the brothel advertising pamphlet and the dirty postcard. The young infantryman, Hope, describes a typical brothel calling card handed to him in the street while on leave in Calais, with an address on the front of the card and a photo of 'Yvonne, posed in her birthday suit,

---

50 Remarque, *All Quiet on the Western Front*, p. 121.
51 I. L. Read, *Of Those We Loved*, p. 36, and A. Rifleman (Aubrey Smith), *Four Years*, p. 376.

plus silk stockings and garters' on the back.[52] Hope admitted, probably like many other young men handed similar 'dangerously' smutty literature, that he tucked the advert away in his pocket rather than throw it away as litter. A snippet in an issue of the Trench newspaper, the *Somme Times*, suggests others collected such cards; 'our most recent encardine [sic – probably referring to the person being 'pink-faced'] acquisition … has a pretty taste in visiting cards and where did he go to get them?' asks the regular column 'Things We Want to Know'.[53]

Another variant, often slightly more explicit, was the cigarette card. These were photographs produced in both France and Spain that were enclosed free in packets of cigarettes. Tommy didn't often get the cigarettes, having his own brand but the cards were kept when found or had been exchanged for food or other souvenirs with the local populace.

By far and away the most pervasive format for explicit sexual imagery was the postcard. Postcards were at the vanguard of the erotic revolution. Their simple imagery, low cost, and ease of storage and concealment gave them a versatility that, to a greater extent than any other medium, put pornography in the pocket of the common soldier.[54] The subject matter ranged from the suggestive to the explicit.

The possession of what would have been considered as 'hardcore' (explicit pictures and postcards) was widespread, though it is impossible to quantify statistically. There are, however, sufficient references in memoirs of both officers and other ranks, especially in unpublished sources written in less censorious times after the war, to demonstrate that usage was not isolated, nor indeed generally shocking, to the average combatant. Chaplain Studdert-Kennedy included references to their use and ownership in his sermons to the troops.[55] Private Tilsley confirmed their ubiquity, 'Many Tommies carried a selection [of photographs] about with them – coarse or pathetic-looking naked prostitutes'.[56] Crozier found two of his officers returning from Paris with 'an envelope full of astonishing postcards'.[57] Dubois and Fischer contended that 'collections of such photographs that have been kept by ex-soldiers constitute eloquent evidence of the erotic obsession of the heroes at the Fronts'.[58] Perhaps the best evidence, however, is provided in several of the fictionalised accounts of the war that strove for realism, each of which mention the possession of obscene material. The point here is

---

52 Hope, *Winding Road*, p. 91.
53 The *Somme Times*, Vol. 1 No. 1 (31 July 1916); aka The *Wipers Times* (facs. edn, 1973).
54 A useful summary of the history of the pornographic picture postcard can be found in Lisa von Sigel, 'Filth in the Wrong People's Hands: Postcards and the Expansion of Pornography in Britain and the Atlantic World, 1880-1914', *Journal of Social History* 33 (2000), pp. 859-85.
55 Studdert-Kennedy, *Rough Talks*, p. 105.
56 Tilsley, *Other Ranks*, p. 125.
57 Crozier, *Brass Hat in No Man's Land* (1930), p. 135.
58 Fischer and Dubois, *Sexual Life*, p. 275.

that these references would not have been credible to the audiences, with presumably a fair proportion of veterans amongst them, had they exaggerated the facts.[59]

Even so, there was a certain ambivalence towards ownership and usage. Although there are the almost generic, public confessions of Graves, Sherriff *et al.*, attitudes of the time probably meant it was simply something one did not mention. While moral and religious shackles might have been loosening on the front, there was still a shame attached to the acquisition and possession of such materials, especially if they were knowingly acquired, and then later used for masturbation.

Concealment from the folks back home meant getting rid of potentially embarrassing personal effects before a battle (though this also applied to ensuring helpful materials did not fall into enemy hands). Russell, 10th Worcesters, was not alone in 'going back to the hut and burn[ing] all the letters that I was carrying in my pockets. It was a ritual that all men adopted before proceeding to the line'.[60] 'That morning we turned out our pockets, dumping postcards of naked French girls to ensure they weren't sent home with any effects should we be killed', recalled Private Clarrie Henman of the 7th Queens (Royal West Surrey Regiment).[61]

Occasionally material was concealed from fellow officers and men or, more likely, authority figures as Vaughan admitted : 'The papers [of the dead men] showed one man was an HQ man [a man probably normally stationed behind the lines], the other a sergeant in the Trench Mortars. His papers were chiefly indecent postcards and we [had] just burnt them when the padre came in'.[62] Conversely, erotic materials might be shared with fellow soldiers.[63] Inevitably, as war coarsened manners and morals, it perhaps became less of an issue to conceal the existence of this literature and photography. The padre, K.S. Shaw sadly reflected that 'the officers' messes and billets adorned with what can only be described as distinctly questionable pictures and postcards does not help to place on a high level the standard of purity generally'.[64]

If moral, social or legal ambiguities led to sketchy evidence of use and ownership, there is compensating evidence on the supply side and in the comments of the authorities and moral guardians at home. Tantalisingly, the Inter-Allied Conference on Venereal Disease of 1917 agenda lists for discussion, under item VI, 'measures against the publication and distribution of indecent literature and pictures'. Unfortunately, any record of the ensuing discussion has either been lost or re-filed, but this at least

---

59 R. C. Sherriff, *Journey's End* (1929), Act III, Scene II; Robert Graves, *Goodbye*, p. 170; Stuart Cloete, *How Young*, p. 105. F. Manning, *Her Privates We*, p. 17.
60 Henry Russell, *Slaves of the War Lords* ([1928]), p. 274.
61 Richard van Emden, *Britain's Last Tommies: Final memories … in their Own Words* (2005); Cloete, *How Young They Died*, p. 171; Richard Blaker, *Medal Without Bar* (1930), p. 463.
62 Vaughan, *Desperate Glory*, p. 192.
63 Hiscock, *Bells of Hell*, p. 75.
64 K. E. Shaw, *Jottings from the Front* (1918), p. 36.

points to the army's awareness of the prevalence of materials and sufficient concern to introduce it as an agenda topic.[65]

In terms of distribution, obscene materials were widely available commercially in the back areas of the Western Front and, apparently, easily procured: 'If you want any French women', wrote an Indian soldier to a friend in India, 'there are plenty here, and they are very good-looking. If you really want any I can send one to you in a parcel'.[66] In France and what remained of Belgium, shopkeepers regarded the postcard and picture as just another stock item for the soldiers' consumption. Hope wrote of shops in Peronne being full of '*of course*, the usual indecent items' [author's italics].[67] Cuddeford implied the same of many shops in Arras where those few civilians still resident 'seemed to do a roaring trade in picture postcards'.[68] If any explicit legal constraints on sale existed it did not appear to exercise the shopkeeper. Tilsley wrote, of a shopping trip in Poperinghe, that 'He went to one place for a coloured silk postcard, and was offered obscene ones. You could see packets in the windows bearing a note, 'These postcards must not be displayed'.[69]

The availability of such materials obviously concerned some locals. A church-sponsored newspaper, *De Poperinge Kiekop*, sold to citizens and given free to troops in Poperinghe, warned 'Soldaten, koopt niets in de winkels waar zedensschende printer en postkacrien uitgestold of te koop zijn' ('Soldiers, don't buy anything in the shops where – "violating morals" – impure printed materials and postcards are on display or for sale'). The Tommy's lack of Flemish probably precluded his taking advantage of this well-meant warning![70]

It was not only from shops that these photographs were available. Predictably, estaminets, brothels and bars were places where explicit publications could be obtained. Cloete writes that at one brothel he was 'shown dirty postcards and filthy books printed in Portugal and Spain'.[71] Tozer claims that other sources included secret houses where the colour of a window pane indicted 'that obscene or pornographic literature can be obtained there' and also 'that "certain" pictures and photographs … were disposed of through the medium of streetwalkers, who acted as agents, also they were sold secretly by some hairdressers, and by hotel and club hall-porters'. Officers acquired materials while on leave, especially while in Paris.[72]

65 TNA: WO 32/11404, Inter-Allied Conference on Venereal Disease, Agenda, Thursday 11 July 1918.
66 Omissi, *Indian Voices*, pp. 192-207.
67 Hope, *Winding Road Unfolds*, p. 197.
68 Cuddeford, *All For What?*, p. 118.
69 Tilsley, *Other Ranks*, p. 125.
70 Poperinghe town archive: *De Poperinge Kiekop, Bladje de Poperinge in't Leger*, 1-15 June 1918.
71 Cloete, *Victorian Son*, p. 207.
72 Tozer, *Terrible Life*, pp. 68-79.

Soldiers also traded them, or 'won' (as in thieving) them from each other.[73] Another highly productive source was the enemy, whether prisoner or dead. Nettleton, a subaltern in the Rifle Brigade stated that 'almost every one of the prisoners that I examined was carrying one or more pornographic postcards. I had quite an education looking at them'.[74] For some the 'education' was unwanted: 'One prisoner got a stern talking to from C Company sergeant-major, a Birmingham man, shocked at a packet of indecent photographs found in the man's haversack', recounted Graves.[75]

There was also a demand for the written word to supplement the graphical and pictorial erotica. Fischer and Dubois reported that:

> Pornographic literature was very popular. By this we do not mean the ordinary erotic novel, which does not usually arouse unnatural thoughts and does not excite the reader unduly. The trash that was sent out to the troops at the Front, and was read by them with unusual avidity, generally had a perverted tendency.[76]

Typically, their assertion is not referenced, or titles supplied and although they contend that 'hardcore' was popular, in reality it was generally not the most widely read. Much more so were cheap, throw-away paperbacks that could be purchased in Paris. Those who could read French were at an advantage and this usually meant the public-school educated officer classes. Fischer and Dubois are in no doubt that 'there was no lack of businessmen during the war who hastened to exploit the soldier's predilection for everything that was lascivious'.

New media of the time, 'moving pictures', also provided a source of erotic excitement. Films shown in working 'picture palaces' in larger towns at the rear, as well as in barns and other larger buildings nearer the front, were a great favourite with the troops. If Tommy Keele, NCO 11th Bn Middelsex, one grateful member of the audience, is to be believed, the excitement did not only lie in an opportunity to see a favourite actress:

> They used to show films in Arras to make use of the theatre in the afternoon … the projectionist used to stop the films in the bits with the girls being slightly naked but not quite … the cinema operator, he used to know the spicy bits so when a spicy bit would come and the girl had her leg in the air he would stop the machine so we could have a look at their legs.[77]

---

73 Cloete, *How Young They Died*, p. 171.
74 John Nettleton, *Anger of the Guns* (London: Kimber, 1979), p. 190.
75 Graves, *Goodbye*, p. 170.
76 Fischer and Dubois, *Sexual Life*, p. 283.
77 IWM Sound Archive, No. 9428, reel 9, Tommy Keele, NCO 11th Bn Middelsex attached to Ace of Spades concert party, 12th Division.

Another item of erotic interest were erotic toys sold at the same shops that sold postcards and the plethora of other more acceptable souvenirs. More often than not, these were lewd pictures embedded in a viewing mechanism made from a shell case. One made such a significant impression on Cloete that he mentioned it in both his 'fiction' and his autobiography: 'I was shown an aluminium ring by a corporal in the RAMC which, when you held it to the light, had a picture of a naked lady set in a hole in its face. Later I got one for myself. They were supposed to be made out of German shell fuses'.[78] The small town museum as Messines, just north of Armentières, has an interesting and rare item of trench art – a brass shell case with an amply proportioned woman etched thereon. It is interesting to speculate on who the artist might have been and whether this was etched for his own pleasure or as an item for possible sale.

In addition to the unambiguous erotic reminders of women in print and photograph, there was another that was less obvious: female impersonators at concert parties. These were performances, not unlike variety shows at home, where the 'turns' were by army personnel. In the absence of women, female parts were taken by men, usually those who, sufficiently made-up, could pass for one of the opposite sex. 'There were no women in the troupe', Huntly Gordon found attending one show, 'but two men made up so well that you would hardly know the difference'.[79]

Although the attire was in no way meant to excite, and the theatre had a long tradition of men playing female roles, in the context of an all-male society, with men starved of female company, the impersonators could provoke unintended lusts and feelings in the audience. Russell told of 'a show on one occasion that only served our appetite for some civilisation. Shorty wanted to see some real "wimmen" again'.[80] Sometimes the artistes did more than provide a simple reminder and became the objects of lust themselves: 'to sex-starved, entertainment-starved heroes of the 26th Battalion, Royal Fusiliers, he was a sight for sore eyes', remembered Hiscock:

> What astonishes me now, looking back on those rough and ready programmes, is the way ... 'females' engendered excitement among their rude and rough male audiences ... Judging by the way they sat and goggled at the drag on the stage it was obvious that they were indulging in delightful fantasies that brought to them substantial memories of the girls they had left behind ... As the Quartermaster captain lisped after performing before a particularly rapt audience: 'I bet there were more standing pricks than snotty noses tonight'. Astonishingly, I suspect he was right.[81]

---

78 Cloete, *Victorian Son*, p. 122; id., *How Young They Died*, p. 105.
79 Huntly, *Unreturning Army*, p. 104.
80 Russell, *Slaves*, p. 179.
81 Hiscock, *Bells of Hell*, pp. 41-2; for similar observations, see Tilsley, *Other Ranks*, p. 124; Groom, *Poor Bloody Infantry*, p. 63; Greenwell, *Infant in Arms*, p. 189; Charles Carrington, *Soldier*, p. 185.

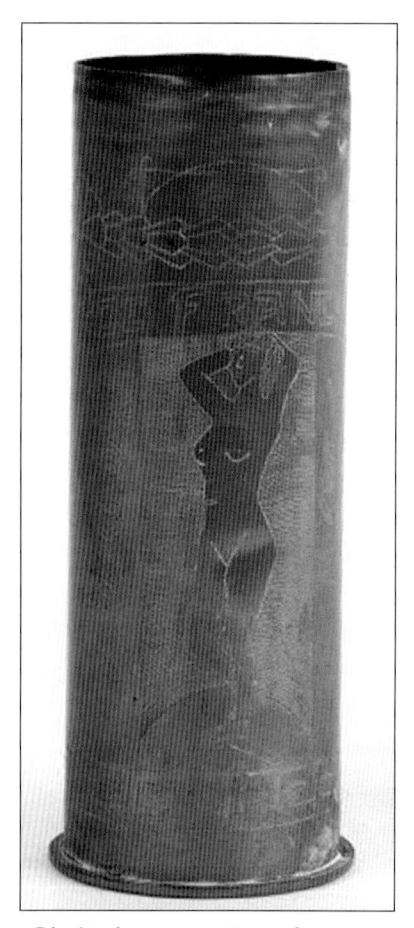

254   They Didn't Want to Die Virgins

Representations of women found themselves onto all manner of souvenirs that could be bought by the soldiers from shops in back areas. Sometimes it was trench art made by the men themselves. (From collection 'In Flanders Fields', Ieper)

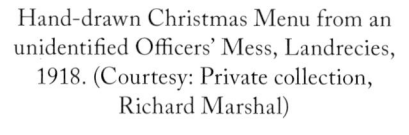

Idealised representations of women, drawn by the soldiers themselves, found their way onto many different objects such as shell cases. (Courtesy: Mesen Museum)

Hand-drawn Christmas Menu from an unidentified Officers' Mess, Landrecies, 1918. (Courtesy: Private collection, Richard Marshal)

Fisher and Dubois intimate that some of the impersonators in German concert parties crossed the sexual line, becoming – or perhaps always having been – homosexual. There is some evidence to suggest that it may well also have been the case occasionally in the British Army, as the 'insider' Keele, of the Ace of Spades, 12th Division Concert Party recalled: 'Nearly all these girl parts in the concert parties were … nearly all "nancies"'.[82]

The interest in and ownership of pornographic material of all types was thus prevalent amongst the troops. Key questions, however, are 'why?' and 'what underpinned this interest?' In part, erotic materials functioned as souvenirs of conquest or sexual adventure.[83] In addition to being another category of item from which war profiteers could make money, they had value as items traded amongst the soldiers themselves. Indisputably, the object and effect of the erotic is to arouse sexual desire. That desire has to be satisfied. Desire is not a substitute for sexual pleasure but one constituent. Fictional accounts of the soldiers' lives during the war perhaps capture the motives most accurately and prosaically. Trotter, a central character in Sherriff's *Journey's End*, comments, when sorting through a dead fellow-officer's effects, "Ere's Hibbert's postcards. Funny a bloke carrying pictures like this about. Satisfies 'is lust, I s'pose – poor fellow'.[84]

It is beyond the scope of this study, which deals with the historical rather than psychological, to delve into the drives that underlie usage. The existence of so much erotic material – which must have been an aid to masturbation – is evidence that sexual needs were not sublimated. Absolute proof is almost impossible to discover, and thus the historian is left with inference.[85]

It might be argued that the general moral climate, and the historically strong antipathy towards masturbation, would have suppressed its practice. One soldier, otherwise sexually active, claims that general tiredness limited his desire and opportunity.[86] There can be little doubt that, whatever the individual's natural urges, any fulfilment would have invoked anxiety, if not shame and possibly the disapproval of peers.[87] As Hall has argued, 'the amount of literature produced in this connection and its wide dissemination would perhaps suggest that the era of greatest masturbation anxiety

---

82 IWM Sound Archive, No. 9428, reel 7, Keele.
83 Crozier, *Brass Hat,* p. 135.
84 Sherriff, *Journey's End,* Act III, scene II; also Manning, *Her Privates We,* p. 17.
85 Porter and Hall, *The Facts of Life,* p. 105, and S. Audoin-Rouzeau and A. Becker, *1914-1918: Understanding the Great War,* p. 43.
86 IWM 80/40/1, Rowarth, *'Misfit Soldier'* (unpubl. memoir), p. 10.
87 The antipathy, and indeed fear, exhibited towards masturbation, especially in the middle and upper classes, is discussed in Lesley Hall, 'Forbidden by God, Despised by Men: Masturbation, Medical Warnings, Moral Panic, and Manhood in Great Britain, 1850-1950', *Journal of the History of Sexuality* 2 (1993), pp. 365-87.

was not (as is usually thought) the mid-Victorian period but the late Victorian to Edwardian era, indeed up to the outbreak of World War I'.[88]

There were, however, counter arguments challenging the status quo, largely beginning with Havelock Ellis's *AutoEroticism*, first published in 1899.[89] In this and subsequent writings, Ellis challenged and began to undermine the traditional view that autoerotic practice was inevitably physically, mentally, or morally debilitating. However, Ellis's extremely limited circulation blunted any initial effect and Hall argues that, even throughout the late 1920s, when general writings and advice on the subject had ceased to amplify the physical dangers of masturbation, 'an often almost unconscious repugnance to the idea of masturbation was still prevalent'.[90]

What is apparent is the widespread and long-lasting impact that the anti-masturbation teaching had: 'While the influence of social purity on sexual behaviour in general is difficult to determine, its instructional efforts certainly kept the campaign against masturbation going for another two generations and increased the burden of anxiety on the young'.[91] Writing in 1937, the sexologists Fischer and Dubois could still refer to masturbation as an 'unnatural practice' which soldiers:

> often resorted to … [and] leads to very serious consequences. The military hospitals contained many a soldier with an emaciated face, sunken eyes, and a jumpy nervousness that was not attributable to war experiences.[92]

Perhaps wisely, they do not venture to explain how they arrive at their diagnosis from the symptoms observed.

No doubt, purity leaflets and quack pamphlets had an effect on young men, and individuals could not altogether ignore a climate of opinion that blamed masturbation for a variety of ailments as well as the corruption of his posterity. The large number of printed and photographic materials in the soldiers' possession, however, suggests that the incidence of masturbation must have been high. It is possible that soldiers preferred to masturbate rather than visit prostitutes, with the attendant risk of venereal disease. And, as with many other aspects of soldiers' sexuality, that the working class did not share the taboo against masturbation must be taken into account.

Hirschfeld was in no doubt as to the prevalence of masturbation and its cause, though interestingly at the time of publication of *Sexual History of the War* in 1931, he was still hostile to masturbation:

---

88   Hall, 'Forbidden by God', pp. 365-87.
89   Havelock Ellis, *Studies in the Psychology of Sex*, I, *AutoEroticism* (1899).
90   Hall, *Hidden Anxieties*, p. 24.
91   Bristow, *Vice and Vigilance*, p. 127.
92   Fischer and Dubois, *Sexual Life*, pp. 278-9.

> The evil of self-abuse (or self-satisfaction) was widespread in every army ... On this point I have interviewed hundreds of men of all nationalities, and in general have received the answer that was expected under the circumstances ... Indeed not a few older men, who at home were accustomed to regular sex[ual] intercourse, confessed that they had chosen this way of escape from the torture of the senses, to avoid the scruples of conscience, and the dangers consequent upon illegitimate sexual intercourse.[93]

It is perhaps unsurprising that memorialists' references to masturbation were generally those of men remembering and recording their experiences from the safety of the more liberal 1960s. Hiscock, for example, remembered, 'Obviously, we masturbated (but not each other)'. It is instructive to note that not only does he admit to personal masturbation, but talks of 'we' and goes so far as to publicly identify another by name. 'Also from Rochdale, was Martin, a sex-starved bachelor of forty ... he was a poor soldier in the line, masturbated most nights, and only came to life out on rest when he could get to grips with the local whore'.[94] For Martin at least, sex, or the promise of it, was important in sustaining morale.

The subject was also introduced through fiction, as in the case of Stuart Cloete's *'How Young They Died'*:

> There were flashy looking girls in the estaminets who offered themselves for cash on the line ... Riddled with VD most of them ... These public women were not his cup of tea so he satisfied himself by masturbating.[95]

Cloete's comment is important. His fiction closely mirrors his own autobiographical work and his characters are often saying and doing things that he might not find it possible or permissible to admit in a personal memoir, though he does say 'My father told me not to touch myself and I didn't. Not till the war'.[96] While neither author mentions the use of pornography for the process of stimulation, its use cannot be discounted. And, as Manning had one character say, "Tis all in human nature'.

One unanswerable question is where the men indulged in this normally solitary activity, although it is not at all certain that we should assume that shame enforced solitude.[97] By its very nature the army forced men together; life, even for officers, was lived cheek-by-jowl with one's comrades. One German soldier commented that 'masturbation was virtually impossible for my regiment while it was in position. Whoever has been in the field with front line divisions knows the dense concentration

---

93 Hirschfeld, *Sexual History,* pp. 75-6.
94 Hiscock, *Bells of Hell,* pp. 36, 44.
95 Cloete, *How Young They Died,* p. 104.
96 Id., *Victorian Son,* p. 163.
97 Both Hirschfeld, *Sexual History,* p. 77, and Erich Maria Remarque, *All Quiet on the Western Front* (1969), p. 165, refer to communal masturbation.

of men in wooded positions which never permits men, and especially young officers, to be alone'.[98] However, discreet and quick fumbles under a great coat or in the relative privacy of a billet were almost certainly prevalent.

The extent of the soldier's solitary (or even public) sexual practices will never be known, but what can be argued with some certainty is that he would have suffered substantial emotional and moral torment over the issue, with his upbringing and the overriding social code of the time militating against 'self-abuse'. Yet when overcome with natural urges, absent from a wife or sweetheart and unable or unwilling to seek temporary relief from either a compliant or paid-for local, his moral scruples would have been sorely tested, with desire inflamed by the often explicit sexual imagery that surrounded him.

Despite little acknowledgement of the fact, what is today described as 'pornography', and at the time as 'obscene', was an essential and important part of the Western Front sexual experience. A wide range of material, from the mildly erotic, fantasy drawings contained in popular magazines, to titillating postcards and the more graphic photographs was readily available at an affordable price and from a range of sources. Such material was often a substitute for absent women. It was ubiquitous, decorating billet and trench and, at times, carried in the wallet or pocket. It allowed the release of sexual tensions, substituted for 'the real thing' and helped keep morale high. In an all-male society it was inevitable and its absence would have been inexplicable. One soldier summed up very simply the benefits of being exposed to some sexual titillation; it was, he wrote, 'amazingly good for the morale of the war weary troops'.[99]

---

98 Hirschfeld, *Sexual History*, p. 76.
99 Sergeant J. M. Russell, cited in N. Boyack, *Behind the Lines: The lives of the New Zealand Soldiers in the First World War* (1989), p. 139.

12

Not Guilty! Sex crimes: Assault, rape and sodomy

Across the Western Front, or while at home on leave, soldiers channelled their sexual urges into the sometime successful chase for a 'bit of willing skirt' or, more regularly, by circumventing the chase and paying for sex. Access to pornography provided a further release for sexual frustration. These responses, though frowned on by peacetime society, were implicitly sanctioned by the army partly for the maintenance of morale, and because they were seen as a way of deflecting what the army saw as the potentially worse problem of venereal disease. There was also an implicit hope that by taking such an 'understanding' view those sexual activities which were unambiguously illegal, those proscribed in both civilian and military law, would also be minimised. How successful was the policy?

Regulations in the Army Act that covered sexual offences were:

AA sec. 36: Indecent Assault on Female
AA sec. 37: Rape
AA sec. 39: Procuration (woman or girl under 21 to have unlawful carnal connection)
AA sec. 43: Indecency/Gross Indecency (with another male person)
AA sec. 38: Carnal Knowledge (various, but mostly with young women under 16)
AA sec. 79: Bigamy
AA sec. 42: Sodomy

When in doubt, the army resorted to AA sec. 40, a catch-all that involved 'Any act, conduct, disorder, or neglect, to the prejudice of good order and military discipline' (and which could be construed to include adultery), or (for officers only) AA sec. 16, 'Disgraceful Conduct': 'behaves in a scandalous manner, unbecoming the character of an officer and a gentleman'.[1]

---

1   For further reading, see Hugh Godley (ed.), *Manual of Military Law* (sixth edn, 1914).

It will be noted that homosexuality was listed as a crime under AA sec. 42. For that reason, and no other, it is included here as part of the soldier's sex life.

On the evidence of disciplinary records, the soldier of the Western Front could largely be judged innocent of involvement in the crimes of a sexual nature normally associated with armies in war and specifically covered by the Army Act. A total of 304,262 men (5,952 officers and 298,310 other ranks) appeared before courts martial in the period between August 1914 and 31 March 1920 (the end date for the official statistics on the war effort). It is not clear from the official figures whether Empire and Dominion soldiers were included in the court-martial statistics as the statistics only record the soldiers' nationality where the death penalty was given. No precise figure exists for the number of men serving abroad, but from a total of some 5,700,000 British men who enlisted in the army during the war (an estimated total of 8,400,000 men enlisted including 980,000 from the Empire and a further 1,500,000 with the Indian army), approximately 4,000,000 served overseas in all theatres (5,400,000 including the troops of the Dominions and the coloured labour corps). Of all courts marshal, 163,174 were overseas. Approximately 89 per cent ended with a conviction. Assuming the statistics are only including soldiers of the British army, the percentage of British men facing a court martial on all fronts was no more than 4 per cent and the majority of these crimes were unrelated to sex.[2] Of the court-martial convictions 30 per cent were for absence without leave; drunkenness contributed 17.5 per cent; insubordination just under 10 per cent; and desertion 12.7 per cent. To this one has to add cowardice, mutiny, striking an officer, sleeping on guard duty, casting away arms in the face of the enemy, and wilful disobedience. Included in the balance would be sundry offences relating to sex.[3]

That 'innocent' must be the general verdict on the Great War soldier's behaviour is perhaps unsurprising, given the nature of the conflict and composition of Kitchener's armies. Sex crime, even with the caveats of under-reporting and military obfuscation, was apparently low, especially given the huge number of soldiers stationed along the Western Front. Perhaps it was the outcome of the largely stationary nature of the line. Lily has shown in reference to World War Two that most rapes, for example, take place noticeably at times of 'break-out' and forward movement.[4] It might be argued that the low incidence was, in part, a result of the army's policy of allowing access to women, and sustaining morale by such.

It is interesting that in other wars, statistics tend to confirm that sex crime of this nature drops when some form of provision is made to satisfy a soldier's lust. The British soldier was, however, not a saint despite the low level of reported crime.

2   *Statistics of the military effort of the British Empire during the Great War, 1914-1920* (1922), pp. 364-365 for recruitment and pp. 663-70 for courts marshal statistics.
3   Ibid, pp. 30, 363, 669.
4   Lilly, J. Robert, *Taken By Force: Rape and American GIs in Europe during World War II* (Basingstoke: Palgrave Macmillan, 2007), p.12.

Tommy cannot get off totally 'scot free' and with reputation totally unsullied. He was not always the 'veray parfit gentil knight'. There were rapes and assaults; they did have sex with under-age girls; there was bigamy and sodomy, and even one reported case of bestiality. In addition, crimes, such as robbery were committed against prostitutes (who were counted by some as fair game) to pay for sexual pleasure. Soldiers were also guilty of behaviour that, while not strictly a crime, was certainly of a reprehensible or questionable nature, such as taking advantage of those unable to look after themselves.

Sexual violence is synonymous with warfare. It occurs on a number of levels. At its most extreme it is a strategic weapon of war, utilised where a specific, if unstated, war aim is the physical destruction of a race or culture; the Japanese in Nanking in 1938; the Pakistan army in Bangladesh in 1971; and Bosnia in the late 1980s and early 1990s; Rwanda, 1993; the continuing Congo civil wars; and most recent examples of the Boko Haram and ISIS movements. It can, and has, been threatened or used as an instrument of terror, or as torture during the interrogation process. Sexual violence, specifically rape and murder, can also be a weapon designed to humiliate the opposing male opponent, demonstrating the latter's inability to protect their women. Sexual violence can be seen, and condoned, as a legitimate means of revenge on an enemy for actions it has itself perpetrated: the mass raping of German women by Russian troops in 1945 is often cited as an example, as is American behaviour in post-war Japan and in Vietnam. The literal rape of civilians during the figurative rape of 'poor little Belgium', in August 1914 might also fall into this category.[5] It can be both implicitly and explicitly condoned as a facet of military culture, reinforcing masculinity norms and group bonding; it has been implied by Bourke that the US Marine Corps is an example of such. The Serbian 'White Eagles', of the most recent Balkan Wars, being another example.[6] Sex is sometimes part of the reward structure; implicitly or explicitly a 'spoil of war' to be taken where found. Sexual violence, notably rape, is finally a random act of individual gratuitous violence meted out by one person on another and motivated by one or more psychological or perhaps biological impulses. Unlike the preceding list, where there is a measure of formal organisational support, gratuitous violence is prohibited by military law with punishment levied on those who transgress. Where individual gratuitous violence occurs it represents the breakdown of army discipline; an army may have one philosophical and cultural outlook but this breaks down at the operational level through the undirected actions of the soldiers themselves.

The sexual violence in the Great War, specifically that involving British army soldiers, generally falls into this final category. That is not to say that other examples of sexual violence, such as sadism, did not perhaps occur but, despite Fischer and Dubois's somewhat hysterical belief that 'the war was one huge brothel in which sexual maniacs could indulge their mania to their heart's content, and were very

5   See Beevor, *Berlin: the downfall, 1945*.
6   Bourke, *Rape: A History from 1860 to the Present* (London: Virago, 2007), pp. 364-366.

often decorated and promoted for their bestiality', there is insufficient hard evidence to warrant wide discussion. There is one highly controversial, and banned, novella, Hanley's *The German Prisoner* (1930), which has torture and sexual depravity as its theme and might be cited as evidence, however limited. However, despite Hanley briefly serving on the Western Front in the Canadian Army, this is one work of fiction by a veteran that is unlikely to have had any truth at its core. Inevitably, it is unsupported 'finger-pointing' directed against the enemy that survives, not admissions of personal guilt or accusations levied at a soldier's own comrades. Arthur Harris, of the Royal Naval Division, falls into the category of accusing the enemy of unspeakable crimes, recounting the incident of finding a woman strapped to a bed in a cellar near Arras who had been kidnapped by Germans and raped to death.[7] The obvious question is, what credence can we give to this and other similar accounts given the general vilification of the enemy?

Irrespective of the wider crime, exploring the incidence of individual rape is complicated by three factors; firstly, debate over what constitutes 'consent' in term of acceptance or willingness to perform a sexual activity; secondly, because the official records are inaccurate, and either knowingly, or perhaps unwittingly, they disguise or hide the crime; finally, the level of prosecutions does not reflect the actual level of crime due to its being under-reported by the victims, or the failure of the military authorities to bring charges or successful prosecutions.

The difficulty of delineating prostitution from fraternisation was discussed earlier in this book. Was a woman who exchanged use of her body for food necessary for her or her family's survival a prostitute? Was a woman who knowingly exchanged use of her body in return for a night out or a gift a prostitute? How far can such 'survival sex' be truly described as consensual? The same semantic issues occur when attempting to determine whether sexual congress is enjoyed by mutual consent, or a woman permits or submits to performing a sexual act because refusal is not an option – for whatever reason.

The description 'taken by force' can be widely interpreted. It might be argued that the women who populated the regulated brothels in France were being subjected to continual rape since the conditions of their 'employment' were dictated to them and they had little choice as to whom they had sex with. In this way, perhaps they were akin to the 'comfort women' forcibly recruited from conquered and subjugated nations to service the Japanese soldiers throughout the Pacific theatre in World War II. Or indeed the Japanese women who themselves became prostitutes in post-war Japan, servicing the American and Australian occupying forces within the framework of the 'Recreation and Amusement Association'. Joanna Bourke argues that some women in this latter example effectively sacrificed themselves by becoming prostitutes as a way of helping control and limit the rape of other women.[8] Their consent to selling their

---

7 IWM Sound Archive, No. 24871. Harris, Arthur, Royal Naval Division.
8 Bourke, *Rape*, p. 358.

bodies was made under duress. There can be little doubt that the women who became prostitutes for German soldiers, or inmate 'trustees' in German prisons and concentration camps during the Second World War, did so under duress, even though they received a payment for such. The payment in these cases was often simply a promise of continued life.

Interestingly, army chaplain Studdert-Kennedy – famously better known as 'Woodbine Willie' – could, in one of his *'Rough Talks by a Padre'*, equated the use of a red lamp prostitute to being a crime, albeit couched in the rhetoric for which he became famed;

> Prostitution, as a traffic, is just slow murder, and not so slow at that. The beauty of the harlot perishes, her body becomes diseased, and she dies quickly, not only of direct venereal disease, but of all sorts of intercurrent [sic] diseases to which the constant nervous strain has made her liable … The woman that you use in turn with other men is the potential mother of children, and you kill them for the pleasure by your act.
> Are Our Hands Clean of Woman's Blood?[9]

This consideration did apparently not prick the conscience of too many Tommies given their unbridled usage of the lamps. Neither, it seems, did it occur to them that in the context of the Western Front, perhaps a woman gave herself out of fear. Soldiers could be insistent in their demands, getting annoyed when refused. It has been claimed that the soldiers expected to be provided with sex 'at a reasonable price and complained and became hostile and sometimes violent if the women they approached were not interested'.[10] Though there is little evidence to support the accusations of hostility and violence, there was certainly coercion involved on occasion with, for example, a Lieutenant Jamieson, court martialled for scandalous conduct 'annoying a woman by soliciting her to immorality'.[11] Dressed in uniform and carrying guns one can perhaps understand they would have presented an intimidating presence. However, in an area routinely populated with unregulated, wayside prostitutes, and even perhaps an element of more promiscuous women, is it also easy to understand how a soldier would assume any individual woman willing and an initial rejection on her part as ritualistic, an opening negotiating ploy or indeed, flirtatious foreplay. Bourke contends that at times in World War Two 'Women would 'consent' to sexual intercourse, fearful that any sign of resistance would lead to something worse'. 'Courtship', she notes, 'is conceived as "different" in wartime'.[12]

---

9   Studdert-Kennedy, G.A., *Rough Talks By A Padre* (London: Hodder and Stoughton 1916), p. 109.
10   Margaret H. Darrow, *French Women and the First World War: War Stories of the Home Front* (Oxford: Berg 2000), p. 45.
11   TNA: WO 90/6, 22 Apr. 1917.
12   Bourke, *Rape*, p. 373.

Consent, too, might be given on the assumption that there would be no recourse to justice should the woman make a complaint, or a feeling that the official process was unfairly weighted against them and to submit was a better option. Even language difficulties could have raised a barrier. Here we enter the realms of under-reporting and the possible failings of the military justice system on behalf of the civilian population.

There can be little doubt that the military statistics under-report the incidence of sex crime. Many minor, and perhaps even major crimes would have been unreported because the victim chose not to report an alleged offence out of shame. Schrijvers in his *'Taken by Force'*, a study of sexual violence in World War Two, makes the point that he did not find, as he expected, references to rape or sexual violence within the more general complaints about GI behaviour during and after the Bulge campaign in the Belgian Ardennes, and this leads him to wonder 'how many women (and their families) in this traditional and Catholic area have remained silent out of shame'.[13] Given the little difference in time or space between the two wars, it is a comment that can equally be made about the Great War.

Even in the event of reporting an act of violence, there would have been doubt in a victim's mind as to the army's sincerity in pursuing an investigation. Peers makes the interesting observation of crime in the Indian army that 'As the army could only be expected to punish what it acknowledged, the less diligently it searched out particular acts, at particular times, and in particular places, the more it was left undisturbed'.[14] The same underlying philosophy may have been implicit during the Great War as witnessed by the comments of one General to two chaplains, the Reverends T. M. Pym and Rev. G. Gordon, owning up to 'seeing my men commit atrocities, and should expect to see it again' but not doing anything about it.[15] There may even have been intimidation of both complainants and potential witnesses. This was the situation in the case of Australian Major Carl Speckman accused of attempted rape where the woman refused to testify having allegedly been intimidated by fellow soldiers of battalion.[16]

Many complaints were dealt with unofficially at a lower level of command and went unrecorded; others never came to court because of the death of the accused. Even where there are official data to be mined, across the range of army records much of the official language is discreet, if not evasive, in matters of sex. The material is suspect and somewhat statistically unreliable. Rape, for example, might be obscured or hidden by the less provocative and less punishable description of 'Offence against inhabitant'. Potential charges of sodomy at courts martial became 'Indecency' or 'Disgraceful Conduct', and there were cover-ups to protect individual reputations, or

---

13 Schrijvers in Lilly, Foreword to *'Taken by Force'*, p. xxx.
14 Peers, 'Privates off Parade', pp. 823–55.
15 Rev. T. M. Pym and Rev. G. Gordon, *Papers from Picardy by Two Chaplains*, London (Constable, 1917).
16 AWM 17/1/85.

where regimental honour was at stake as both Peers and Balhatchet claim happened in India and Burma where fearful of publicity, the army was more concerned with protecting its own reputation, than in obtaining justice for civilians. John Lucy was certain there was a desire to maintain the reputation of his Irish regiment when in France. Probably there were cases of direct or indirect suicide by the accused before a case could be brought to court martial; Vera Brittain's brother, Edward, effectively took his own life by throwing himself into enemy fire rather than be publically exposed as a homosexual.[17]

Perhaps the greatest challenge in ascertaining the true level of sex crime is the level of under-reporting at the lowest level of the disciplinary process. All army crimes went through several levels of investigation, first of all being considered by the company commander or equivalent. If a case merited punishment beyond his powers (which were limited to confining men to barracks or advising pay stoppage), the case would be referred to the commanding officer who could mete out wider punishments, including Field Punishment, fines and up to 28 days in the guardroom. If a charge was considered by a CO as too serious for his jurisdiction, then the procedure was referral for possible court martial to brigade level. A soldier had the right to elect for a court martial where the CO proposed discipline exceeding the minimum punishment. There were three levels of courts martial: District Court Martial, General Court Martial for serious crimes (at this level the death sentence could be passed), and Field General Court Martial employed at the front.

As with any civilian prosecution, firm evidence was required before a case was referred for court martial. Evidence was often difficult to secure in the fog of war. It would have been difficult to find witnesses. The APM of 5th Division, for example, records for 3 September 1914, 'Several cases of looting and robbery reported and one case of attempted rape'. With no subsequent record of how this accusation was treated it can perhaps be assumed that, given the rapid advance, with the division quickly moving on, this was one example of a case being lost.[18] Equally, there would probably have been cases where those in authority would not have been confident in their understanding of the law and were thus reticent to follow up on accusations. A request by the Poperinghe Town Major asking the Belgian liaison officer for clarification of local laws relating to statutory rape hints at such.[19]

On the incidence of rape along the Western Front, we are left with Bourke's conclusion that;

---

17 Peers, 'Privates off Parade', p. 834. Lucy, *Devil in the Drum*, pp. 295-6. For a discussion of the example of Vera Brittain's brother, see A. Bishop and M. Bostridge (eds), *Letters from a Lost Generation: the First World War letters of Vera Brittain and four friends* (London: Gollancz, 1981, Phoenix, 2000), p. 6.
18 TNA: WO 154/33; APM Report, 5th Division 1914-15, entry for 3 Sept. 1914.
19 TNA: WO 95/4042, Town Marshal, Poperinghe, 22 June 1916.

An historical portrait of the prevalence of rape in any war lies somewhere among the recorded voices of its victims and their supporters, and the willingness of a victorious military to permit or control it. Within these limitations it is reasonable to conclude that until mechanisms are in place to address each of these factors, the prevalence or wartime rape will be impossible to determine.

However, what we do have are the comments of the men themselves, though few and we must pay heed to the contention of Bourke and others that with rape being such a heinous crime with 'sexual transgressions ... even more taboo than state-legitimised killing in combat situations', it has been written out of history.[20] Hirschfeld contends that 'the war saw numerous cases of rape perpetrated on all fronts by soldiers of all armies'. It is 'a sexual crime, always connected with war ... [due to] continuous stimulation of the sexual sphere through the bloody work of war and the sight of violent acts'.[21] More recent studies would contend that rape has more to do with power than sex but, leaving aside the psychological explanations for individual behaviour, rape, at least that reported and leading to a successful court martial, was rare in the allied armies. G. S. Hutchison, a soldier himself involved in a sexual misconduct case, implies that cases of rape might have occurred but in such small numbers that, though 'many men who served could recollect a case of rape', it would not be a truthful overall picture capturing the real spirit of the times. Any recollection would merely be with the aim of 'making a book of character and importance equal to many which have been published'.[22] It is possible that Charles Gain of the 2/5th Manchesters was more truthful admitting that: 'the men I was with were rough with women, boasted of their conquests, many of whom were actually raped', but as he added, 'there were no prosecutions to my knowledge'.

Sexual atrocities are normally associated with open warfare, as soldiers move through towns and villages, and are less likely to be perpetrated by static armies of occupation. The British Army found itself immobile from the winter of 1914-15, but it was not an occupying force: the soldiers found themselves amongst allies and a generally welcoming population. Brownmiller, author of an influential work on rape, concedes that:

> it seems ... rational to conclude that the opportunity for rape was effectively cut down by the new system of trench warfare, the frequency curtailed by military stalemate, and the horror of it superseded by the staggering loss of life as the war went on.[23]

---

20 Bourke, *Rape*, p. 379.
21 Hirschfeld, *Sexual History*, p. 315.
22 Hutchison, *'Footsloggers'* (London: Hutchinson, 1933), p. 179.
23 Susan Brownmiller, *Against Our Will* (New York: Simon & Schuster, 1975. Bantam, 1976), p. 37.

One further possible explanation may be that there is little need of forced sex when soldiers find themselves to be living amongst 'war nymphomania', complemented by the general availability of clandestine prostitution. Indeed, perhaps the incidence of rape was perhaps not widespread, and that women made up the allegations to cover their own 'guilt' and, as Ruth Harris recognised, sometimes confused reality with imagination which would in turn lead to false erotic charges'.[24] Richards was witness to one event where infidelity during the absence of a husband at the front needed to be covered on his unexpected return by false accusations against British soldiers.[25] Lucy certainly felt that it was probably the case that soldiers sometimes 'got blamed for things which they were innocent of'.[26] But it would sometimes be difficult for a woman to prove her case to a disbelieving or prejudiced authority as is evidenced in several APM diaries where accusations were not followed up due the unreliability of the woman involved.[27]

On balance, it seems likely that the British soldier of the Western Front was unusually restrained, perhaps because his character was so different to that of the traditional soldier. He had a moral predisposition not to commit such crimes, and felt horror and repulsion when he learnt of any infringement to his moral code. He was obviously also aware of the consequences of his action should guilt be proven – 'that would have been the shortest step to a firing party and a wall' recalled Burrage.[28] The same cannot be said of the ANZAC contingent, whose general disciplinary record was notorious and who had shown, or learnt, disrespect towards both prostitutes and local civilian populations in Egypt which resurfaced at times on the Western Front, including an alleged gang rape incident in Bouzincourt in 1917 and the sacking of brothels in Boulogne in 1918.[29] Equally, there is evidence of similar problems in other colonial troops.[30]

An unavoidable conclusion, however, must be that release from otherwise dangerous sexual tensions was in large part the outcome of having the army brothels. The low incidence of sexual offences against the person is perhaps a better vindication of the army's policy toward the formal provision of sex than its hoped-for efficacy in holding down VD rates.[31]

It is obvious, from the records of the APMs, town marshals and local police, that there was remarkably little coercion involved, unless perhaps of an economic

---

24 Hirschfeld, *Sexual History*, p. 317. See also R. Harris, 'Child of the Barbarian', *Past & Present* 141 (1993), pp. 170-206.
25 Frank Richards, *Old Soldiers never die*, p. 151.
26 Lucy, *Devil in the Drum*, p. 296.
27 TNA: WO 154/8, App. LVII, 16 Sept. 1917.
28 Ex-Private X (pseud. A. M. Burrage), *War is War* (1930), p. 47,
29 TNA: WO 154/112, and Sir Wyndham Childs, *Episodes and Reflections* (1930), p. 144. Wilfred Galway, '*The Silver King*' quoted Stanley, *Bad Characters* (Australia: PS 2010), p. 125.
30 David Omissi, *Indian Voices*, p. 115.
31 Fischer and Dubois, *Sexual Life*, p. 462.

kind. Even taking into consideration the caveats explored above regarding reporting and prosecution levels, both rape and assault cases were relatively few. While Lucy thought that 'one or two were shot for rape', and Dolden claimed that entering the town of Moule just after a member of a previously-billeted, kilted regiment 'had rather ungraciously strangled one of the village maidens' led to 'excessive politeness' from the inhabitants,[32] on the whole, however, British soldiers were reasonably courteous towards French and Belgian women. Surfleet claimed that he 'never saw any girl molested in any way: they were invariably treated with the utmost respect by most of the troops'.[33]

Although there was little reported rape there is evidence of a range of other misdemeanours. In what appears to be an extremely rare case, a charge was brought against a Major Sandwich, a regular in the 8th Hussars, in the first weeks of the war, in St Omer, 'of having carnal knowledge of a girl under 16 years of age' and unspecified scandalous conduct. In this case the first charge was unproven though the second earned him a cashiering. There is no evidence of the charge of having sex with an under-age girl ever being brought again.[34]

Sex was important enough for a soldier to commit fraud for, or to pass fraudulent cheques to prostitutes and effectively to cheat and lie for. Two Canadian officers, for example, faced a court marshal for passing dud cheques to pay for prostitutes while on London leave.[35] Robbing prostitutes to pay for their pleasure was not unknown. Sergeant Dixon of the Army Service Corps related how 'two jocks', in a red lamp in Béthune, robbed a prostitute after visiting her.[36] This was evidently not reported and the two Scottish soldiers got away with their crime. Similarly, 'doing a runner' and not paying for services rendered was not unheard of. Brugger discovered this amongst ANZAC troop in Cairo who would enter brothels and sometimes refuse to be parted from their money for services rendered'.[37]

Thomas Dinesen VC, paints a picture of troops whose moral code, or at least apparently that part of it relating to the treatment of women, had certainly taken a battering: 'utterly abandon[ing] the gentlemanly idea of fair play. With girls you may use any trick, however mean and shabby – the only thing is to get what you want from them and then beat it ... "Oh hell, she was only a whore, anyway!"'. Interestingly, Burrage, a soldier with an ear and an eye for matters sexual, claimed 'I never heard of a case of rape...' but hints at poor behaviour: 'war has a way of bringing out the wild

32 Lucy, *Devil in the Drum*, p. 296. Dolden, *Cannon Fodder*, p. 124.
33 IWM P126, A. Surfleet, *Blue Chevrons*, p. 126.
34 TNA: WO 90/6, Court Martial record.
35 Canadian Court Martial records. B 07/01/1918, Lt R. J. Beck and B 28/11/1918, Lt E. S. Fowles, from microfilm in the possession of Julian Putkowski.
36 IWM Sound Archive, No.11047, reel 4, Dixon.
37 .Susan Brugger, *Australians and Egypt*, p. 146.

beast in man, and boys with gentle mothers and sisters, and clean sweethearts waiting for them at home, said and did things which I can only hope they lived to regret'.[38]

Perhaps the troops made a conscious differentiation between prostitutes and 'girl-friends', treating the latter better, though general evidence gives support to the conclusion that for many 'all's fair in love and war' was more of a guiding principal. This lack of fair play is illustrated in an incident reported by Williams, an NCO in the King's Liverpool Regiment. He recalled being billeted in an unfriendly village, the unfriendliness being the result of some previously billeted troops 'misbehaving', and leaving behind a pregnant 16-year old sufferer of *le petit mal* (epilepsy).[39] This is not the only example of unfair advantage being taken as F.A.J. 'Tanky' Taylor of the Worcesters found at Bapaume in 1918 where a mentally retarded but sexually compliant young woman was generally abused by some of his fellow battalion.[40]

Reported assaults were more common, though the fact that it was often difficult to identify the alleged assailant meant that charges could not be brought, and we cannot now know whether the alleged assault was of a sexual nature or related to theft in some way. It is also possible that sometimes soldiers may have carried out revenge attacks on girls suspected of giving them venereal disease. The APM returns for the 63rd Division, May 1916 to December 1918, record several incidences of civilians alleging unspecified assault where the assailant could not be identified.[41]

Dissatisfaction with a particular brothel or an individual prostitute in it could spark off trouble, and prostitutes were sometimes considered 'fair game for blaguardism' as one Canadian APM recorded in his monthly war diary.[42] Lance-Sergeant Wickins, 9th Rifle Brigade, was executed for the apparently motiveless murder of a prostitute in Le Havre.[43] A prostitute betrayed another deserter with whom he was hiding. She might have betrayed him because of his conduct toward her, or because his money had run out. Private Hall, of the 47th Battalion Machine Gun Corps, recorded an incident in a Calais brothel where the brothel owners called the Military Police to eject a soldier who was causing problems.[44] Occasionally incidents could be serious, such as those in Cairo's Wassa and, later, in Boulogne where brothels were burnt down, and prostitutes and their pimps assaulted.[45] Interestingly, Tozer claims that brothels were the first place the MPs looked for AWOL officers.[46]

38 Thomas Dinesen, *Merry Hell!*, pp. 185-7. Ex-Private X (Burrage), *War is War*, p. 47,
39 IWM Sound Archive, No.10604, reel 7, Williams.
40 Taylor, *Bottom of the Barrel*, p. 138.
41 TNA: WO 154/73, entries for 17 Apr. 1918, 11 July 1918 and 25 July 1918.
42 TNA: WO 154/112, entries for 8 July, 9 July and 12 July 1918.
43 J. Putowski and J. Sykes, *Shot At Dawn* (Barnsley: Wharncliffe Publishing, 1989, Leo Cooper, 1999), pp. 237-8; also A. Babington, *For the Sake of Example: capital courts-martial, 1914-1920* (London: Leo Cooper, 1983).
44 IWM Sound Archive, No. 14599, reel 4, Hall.
45 Brugger, *Australians and Egypt*, pp. 145-7. Gammage, *The Broken Years*, pp. 39-40.
46 Tozer, *Terrible Life* (1929), p. 85. Other ranks too might 'hide out', see TNA: WO 93/49.

General assaults, perhaps in the nature of horseplay, would also have occurred. Some incidents may have been more serious than others but patently many would have gone officially unreported. RFA Driver Lawson, told of an incident when they were going up the line in a cattle truck: 'We stopped at a station and [there were] some French girls there and some of the chaps started to maul the girls'.[47] It does seem probable, given the number of girls reported to be offering sex as clandestine prostitutes or amateurs that innocent girls and women might be unintentionally accosted by a soldier looking for sex, especially if drunk. Claims of assault on innocent civilians, if received, were, it appears, taken seriously by at least some APMs.[48]

Other sex-related crimes which the army identified were adultery (AA sec. 40) and bigamy (AA sec. 79). The former is curious, given the army's attitude to both marriage generally and towards regulated brothels specifically, but perhaps venal sex did not count as adultery. Adultery in the strictest sense of having sex outside of marriage was, as we have seen, rife including multitudinous affairs conducted by the highest ranking officers. Sir John French reputedly even had an affair with a young guardsman's widow whom he had initially met when offering condolences.

Ironically, bigamy became a greater problem for the army with the introduction of Kitchener's New Armies, comprising a larger number of married men than the army had ever had to accommodate previously. Bigamy occurred both with men marrying local French and Belgian women, and with colonials 'taking up' with British women. The latter problem was of a sufficient size to exercise the popular press and for warnings to be issued in the News of the World during March of 1918. The Times of 31 October 1919, reported a soldier who was married eight times during the war in France. He had married a new girl virtually everywhere his unit was stationed taking the concept of fraternisation to an entirely new level![49] While there were war brides especially towards the end of the war who followed their men home, the option was not open to all. Bird tells of one of his platoon who 'became confidential with us and owned he was married to a girl in the next village. He went there at every opportunity and lived well. When his leave came through, I was surprised that he went to Scotland – until he confided he was married to another girl in Edinburgh….and he said he had a wife and three children in Quebec'.[50]

One sexual crime for which the Army Act had no category was bestiality. It was not unknown in the old British Army, and the court-martial records list one case involving intercourse with a dog during the South African War. Unnatural sexual activities had also cropped up in the Gibraltar and Malta stations.[51] It was perhaps inevitable, given the army's broad demographic composition, that a 'country crime'

---

47 IWM Sound Archive, No. 24882 reel 2, Lawson.
48 TNA: WO 154/112, July 1915 entries, for example.
49 *News of the World*, 13 Jan. and 24 Mar. 1918; see also *The Times*, 31 Oct. 1919, p. 11 also Dinesen, *Merry Hell!*, p. 178.
50 Bird, *Ghosts*, p. 85.
51 TNA: WO 90/6.

be occasionally committed. Proof of its existence on the Western Front occurs in at least one APM's diary with a local farmer's complaint about soldiers sodomising a pig, and similarly later, a calf,[52] though other such offences were probably never recorded officially, given their upsetting and embarrassing nature.

The final sex crime to be considered is sodomy. The army's toleration of regulated prostitution was, as earlier noted, partly driven by fear of homosexuality and its potential impact on troop efficiency and ultimately morale. Not surprisingly, for the 'love that dare not speak its name', neither memoirs nor army statistics throw much light on its prevalence.[53] Vickers has demonstrated that homosexuality was tolerated in the Second World War if the man concerned was considered to be a good soldier. This may have applied equally in the Great War, especially among the traditional officer class. Toleration would patently have led to a lower level of reported 'crime' and interestingly, some authors have held that 'there was a clear understanding that soldiers in monogamous relationships ought not to be penalised'.[54] Further, because only officer courts martial have left any detailed records, it is difficult to discover any details of the circumstances under which NCOs and other ranks were prosecuted. To understand the general reticence of the old soldiers to commit themselves to paper, and to try to draw some conclusions from such evidence as there is, a brief overview of the context of how homosexuality was viewed by society is useful.[55]

There were two distinct strands to society's views on homosexuality during the period, reflecting attitudes to sex generally. On the one hand there was the strongly felt general abhorrence of the newly discovered 'homosexual' (the term is relatively modern), as well as the long-recognised sodomite, which was orchestrated by the forces of social purity and the popular 'penny press', aided by the police.[56] On the other hand, there was the much smaller but increasingly influential 'defence' being mounted by sexologists, artists and other interested parties such as Edward Carpenter

---

52 TNA: WO 154/112, August 1915.
53 Emma Vickers, '"The Good Fellow": Negotiation, Remembrance and Recollection: Homosexuality in the British Armed Forces, 1939-1945', in Herzog (ed.), *Brutality and Desire;* also Richard S. Fogarty. 'Race, Sex, Fear and Loathing in France during the War' in the same volume.
54 Holmes, *Tommy,* p. 599.
55 This section owes much to J. Weeks, *Sex, Politics and Society* (London: Longman, 1990); R. Davenport-Hines, *Sex, Death and Punishment, Attitudes to Sex and Sexuality in Britain since the Renaissance* (London: Fontana, 1991); H. Montgomery Hyde, *The Other Love: an Historical and Contemporary Survey of Homosexuality in Britain* (London: Heinemann, 1970); K. Plummer (ed.), *The Makings of the Modern Homosexual* (London: Hutchinson, 1981).
56 Davenport-Hines, *Sex, Death,* pp. 138-46. The author illustrates the social and legal 'attempt to suppress all public mention of homosexuality, and compromise artistic individualism for a generation'. See also Robb, *British Culture,* p. 57, 'The public embraced the addition and the "general negative attitude toward homosexuality" continued to grow with the law on its biased side as well'.

and Havelock Ellis (though publication in Britain of the latter's work was banned) who formed the beginnings of a homosexual 'counter-culture'.[57]

With the start of World War I, cultural anxiety and prejudice escalated, as it did over other aspects of what was perceived as promiscuous sexual activity. According to George Robb 'no aspect of human sexuality aroused greater anxiety during the war than homosexuality'.[58] Increasingly, there was not only legal but also social opprobrium attached to practitioners, which partly stemmed from the belief that, before the war, England's elite class had been corrupted and compromised from within by homosexual decadence (in the figure of Oscar Wilde and others), resulting in wartime military and political degeneration.

A reflection of how wider society back in Blighty saw homosexuality is illustrated by the accusations – in Captain Harold Spencer's *Imperialist* magazine and by Pemberton Billing MP – that a 'black book' existed, compiled by German agents and containing the names of 47,000 British men and women including 'Privy Counsellors, youths of the chorus, wives of cabinet ministers, dancing girls and even cabinet ministers themselves … diplomats, poets, bankers, editors, newspaper proprietors, and members of the King's household' who had 'engaged in the propagation of evils all decent men had thought had perished in Sodom and Lesbia'. Homosexuality was seen as a vice purposely being employed by the Germans to corrupt British youth.[59]

Indeed, as Britain's war against Germany went increasingly badly, the association of male homosexuality with Germany increased on the British home front. In 'Efficiency and Vice', which appeared in the conservative *English Review*, Arnold White claimed that the 'efficiency' of Germans led them to a sustained effort to 'undermine the stamina of British youth' through a 'moral invasion of England'. This moral invasion consisted of 'the systematic seduction of young British soldiers by the German urnings [male homosexuals] and their agents … The tendency in Germany is to abolish civilising as we know it, to substitute Sodom and Gomorrah for the New Jerusalem, and to infect clean nations with Hunnish erotomania'. Here White alleges German use of male homosexuality as a tool against its enemy. 'This rhetoric served to mitigate any lingering pre-war sympathies for Germany and to incite patriotic fervour for the war both at home and abroad with notions of cleansing Britain of its foreign contaminants, protecting both the nation and its allies from further infection'.[60]

---

57 Weeks, *Sex, Politics*, p. 113, 'a small-scale homosexual reform movement which began to develop in the early years of the twentieth century who saw themselves very much as fighting for "the Cause" against legal and moral repression'.
58 Robb, *British Culture*, p. 57.
59 Pat Barker, *The Eye in the Door* (1993), pp. 154-5, cited in DeGroot, *Blighty*, p. 193; and for a full account of the Billings–Alan episode, see Philip Hoare, *Oscar Wilde's last Stand* (1997).
60 Deborah Cohler, 'Sapphism and sedition: producing female homosexuality in Great War Britain', *Journal of the History of Sexuality* (2007).

This was the attitude, however, of the educated elite, and was probably above the heads of most people. In 1986, John Boon, who had been an air mechanic at HQ Fienvillers Chateau, would tell his Imperial War Museum interviewer, 'the word homosexual means something to me now but I didn't know what it meant then'.[61] This is not perhaps a surprising statement, given his age some 70 years prior to the interview, but it cannot be taken purely as a sign of a young man's innocence or naivety. It is probable that a large number of young soldiers would not have know what a 'homosexual' was: not only was the concept of a person defining himself in terms of his sexual orientation new, but the very word itself had only been in use for three or so decades. What Boon and his peers would undoubtedly have known of was sodomy, and the possibility of other 'indecent' same-sex acts, though the notoriety of the Oscar Wilde trials had certainly had a general impact on public perceptions of the 'homosexual'. Weeks holds that the trials were in effect 'labelling processes of a most explicit kind drawing a clear border between acceptable and unacceptable behaviour'. Boon and his generation grew up during a period where attitudes to same-sex relationships were undergoing change and when, as a number of historians of sexuality have demonstrated, there was 'the emergence of new conceptualisations of homosexuality'.[62] 'The sodomite' as Foucault has put it, was a temporary aberration. The 'homosexual, on the other hand, belonged to a species' and a recognisable 'modern' male homosexuality was beginning to emerge, even if the man in the street could not yet recognise him as such, or distinguish him from the 'dirty' and corrupt sodomite.[63]

Social and legal antipathy to sodomy had a long history in Britain, although by the mid-Victorian period society no longer executed the sodomite, the act itself was still looked on as a 'sin against nature'. However, following what is known as the Labouchere Amendment to the 1885 Criminal Law Amendment Act, there was a marked change in atmosphere, with the act widening the scope of what was considered irregular or depraved behaviour. From that point any 'male person who, in public or private, commits, or is a party to the commission of, or who procures, or attempts to procure the commission by any male person of any act of gross indecency with another male person, shall be guilty of a misdemeanour, and being convicted thereof shall be liable at the discretion of the court to be imprisoned for a period of not exceeding two years, with or without hard labour'. It was no longer simple sodomy that evoked a prosecution but any form of same-sex contact.

Though it is felt that this amendment was conceived as something of an ironic joust by its sponsor,[64] it did actually fit the mood of the moment, a mood that had hardened against the sodomite and a mood yet again dominated by the forces of social purity. This particular attack on the sodomite has to be seen within the context of the general

61 IWM Sound Archive No. 9476, John Henry Boon, air mechanic HQ Fienvillers Chateau.
62 Weeks, *Sex, Politics*, p, 108.
63 Ibid., pp. 101-3.
64 Ibid., pp. 102-3.

attack being mounted on male promiscuity by the social purity brigade. It was not the immorality of the action itself that raised concern but that it was perceived along with other sexual vices as corrupting youth and deviant from the true aim of sex, the healthy reproduction of the race. 'As usual,' comments Bristow, 'the homosexuals had been getting the worst of the moral storm'.[65]

Ironically, despite the army's pronounced fear of homosexuality, cases had been recorded in the military. The court-martial register WO 90/6 records several cases of 'sodomy' and attempted sodomy, with six cases in South Africa between 1900 and 1905. Historically, 'the predominant form of male prostitution was military. This was casual and traditional'.[66] Certain regiments, notably the Brigade of Guards, were notorious for being sexually available to other men – and of 'learning of how to be "goosed" before they'd learnt the goosestep'. 'Oh! The gallant Blues! Oh, my Beautiful Boy! My Brave Screw! What recollections!' was how one middle-aged homosexual eulogised a young guardsman on his death in 1850. An obsession with utilising their services was referred to as having 'Scarlet Fever'. And, in the 1880s, a guardsman described how 'When a young man joins, someone of us breaks him in and teaches him the trick; but there is little need of that as it seems to come naturally to almost every young man, so few have escaped the demoralisation of schools or crowded homes. We then have no difficulty in passing him on to some gentleman ... Although of course we do it for money, we also do it because we really like it'.[67] J. A. Symonds was accosted in 1865 by a young grenadier off Leicester Square, and in 1877 was taken to a male brothel near the military barracks in Regent's Park: 'it was a far more decent place than I expected'. The 'nice' young soldier he encountered there seemed to find 'nothing unusual, nothing shameful' in it at all. Symonds was also told by a corporal in the Lifeguards that some men enlisted on purpose to indulge their propensities.[68] Fred Jones, who had been a soldier in the Foot Guards relates his experiences as Jack Saul in the *The Sins of the Cities of the Plain*: 'There are lots of houses in London,' he says, 'where only soldiers are received, and where a gentleman may sleep with them. The best known is now closed. It was the tobacconist's shop next to Albany Street barracks in Regent's Park, and was kept by a Mrs Turman. The old lady would receive gentlemen and let us know ... there are still six houses in London that I know of'. This was written in 1881 but also a position defended verbally as late as 1890.[69]

Were these practices still current in 1914? Victor Purcel thought it worth recording in 1914 that every trooper in the Household Cavalry has his schoolboy catamite,[70] and even though the Guards reputation was not as publicly vicious as of old at least

65 Bristow, *Vice and Vigilence*, pp. 171, 193.
66 Hyam, *Empire*, p. 63.
67 Davenport-Hines, *Sex, Death*, p. 146, Weeks, *Sex, Politics*, p. 109.
68 Letters of John Addington Symonds, H. M. Sueller and R. L. Peters (1969); P. Grosskurth, *John Addington Symonds: A Biography* (1964), quoted in Hyam, *Empire*, p. 63.
69 Montgomery Hyde, *History of Pornography*, p. 148.
70 Victor Purcel, *Memoirs of a Malaysian Official* (1965), quoted in Hyam, *Empire*.

one notable self-confessed homosexual of the war years, J. R. Ackerley, claimed to be availing himself of their paid-for charms.[71] However much such activities and proclivities existed, these soldiers were old army regulars from the lower rungs of society. There was a 'widespread belief that the working class was relatively indifferent to homosexual behaviour, partly because they were "closer to nature"', and 'the two great swathes of male prostitution with working class youths in their teens, and with Guardsmen ... seemed to justify this belief.'[72] Yet it would be wrong to cast the entire BEF of 1914 as having homosexual leanings. In fact, the number of courts martial for indecency or scandalous conduct, which predictably went up during the war with the increased size of the army, led Major-General Childs (of the Home Office) to attribute the increase in crimes such as sodomy and murder, which had been relatively unknown in the pre-war army, directly to the influx of wartime recruits and officers.[73]

The accuracy of this accusation is debatable[74] but the 'decent' soldier-citizens of the new armies, with the possible exception of some of their officers who might have developed a tendency, or least had an experience while at public school, were certainly not cut of the same cloth as the earlier regulars. By the time of the war, despite there being the stirrings of a pro-homosexuality faction, the popular feeling was against not just the act but against the character. As with other sexual activities, such as casual sex, obscene literature and self-abuse then 'recognised' as deviant, the soldier lined up against them with the social purity concerns. To many homosexuality was an unknown. Basil Farrer, a Private in the 3rd Bn Green Howards would be typical in his admission that, 'If I tell this story it will show you how young and naïve I was ... I was in Trafalgar Square ... and a man walked beside me, offering me a cigarette ... he followed me into a cinema ... I thought he was after my money ... I was scared of the man and I ran off. I realise now he was a homosexual'.[75] Unlike the soldiers' change of heart towards other deviations, they do not appear to have come out in favour of same-sex activities, at least not in public and not in any great number. If there was one area of activity where sublimation can be said to have taken place it was this.

The statistics record that between the outbreak of the war and 31 March 1920, 23 officers and 293 other ranks appeared before a court martial for indecency. An incorrect figure of 292 courts martial for 'indecency' has been recorded elsewhere but

---

71 Ackerley, *My Father and Myself* (1968), p. 135.
72 Weeks, *Sex, Politics*, p. 113.
73 Beckett and Simpson, *Nation*, p. 23.
74 Though the peak in the number of courts martial for indecency did indeed correspond with the influx of Kitchener's recruits, the records indicate that old regular army and territorial officers were amongst those convicted of offences. Harvey identifies three (Llewellyn, Rudderborg and Boyd) from the register of general courts martial who had seen action in the Boer War, see WO 92/3 and A. D. Harvey, 'Homosexuality and the British Army During the First World War', *Journal of the Society of Army Historical Research* 79 (2001), pp. 313-9.
75 IWM Sound Archive No. 9552 Reel 2, Farrer, Basil, Pte 3rd Bn Green Howards 1916-1918.

the exact figure is unimportant given the overall scale. These figures do not include the 206 hearings for 'scandalous conduct' over the same period, which would have included some relevant cases. Other soldiers were tried in civilian courts. The majority of alleged offences appear to have taken place in Britain though this may not reflect activity, just those caught and tried. Prosecutions peaked during the 12 months ending 30 September 1916, when almost one fifth of the officers prosecuted were charged with either indecency or scandalous conduct.[76] Statistically, given the four million or more who served on the Western Front alone, the incidence of homosexuality would appear to be statistically negligible and certainly well below the accepted norm for peacetime society as a whole.

Should these figures be taken at face value as evidence of a low incidence of homosexuality in the army, or perhaps lack of opportunity? Perhaps men simply chose not to reveal their sexuality. Or were these just the tip of the iceberg, prosecutions that took place when no cover-up could be made? Or are they an indication of changing attitudes towards the crime? Peers proposes that the historical difficulty of bringing a successful prosecution explains why few were brought; their number cannot, therefore, be used as a measure of homosexual activity.[77] Baynes contended that homosexuals were extremely rare, particularly amongst the rank and file, and a man with a reputation for being a homosexual would be totally ostracised – as well as being likely 'to get a "hiding" whenever a couple of drunks were looking for someone to beat up'.[78] Private Holbrook, of the 4th Battalion Royal Fusiliers, makes a revealing statement: '[They were] very strict against homosexuality ... I didn't see much'.[79] If we can take him at his word, it is a comment revealing in its brevity: 'I didn't see much'. We do not know what might constitute 'much' but what is interesting is that he should have seen any evidence at all. The statistical probability of his seeing any at battalion level, with a full-strength complement of just 1000 men in an army of over 4 million, when just 293 cases in total were officially recorded, is too small to compute. That he, by his own admission, should have seen some activity, along with a number of other independent qualitative references, implies that there was probably a great deal more homosexuality than the bald official statistics show. Cassel believes that the Canadian official history perhaps inadvertently admits to homosexual activity in its claim that 'men deliberately infected themselves with the milder form of the disease (i.e. VD) from a favoured comrade'.[80]

---

76 *Statistics of the military effort*, p. 669. Samuel Hynes, *A War Imagined: The First World War and English Culture* (New York: Atheneum, 1991), p. 225, gives an incorrect total of 292 courts martial for 'indecency'. This figure is repeated both by Niall Ferguson, '*The Pity of War*' p. 349. Richard Holmes, *Tommy* (2004), p. 598,
77 Peers, 'Privates off Parade', p. 884, quoting William Hough, *Precedents in Military Law* (1855), p. 467.
78 John Baynes, *Morale*, p. 151.
79 IWM Sound Archive, No. 9339, reel 6, Holbrook.
80 Cassel, *The Secret Plague*, pp. 130-1.

Apart from the usual problem of unravelling army statistics and having to read between the lines, we also have to differentiate between deep homoerotic friendship, and the true homosexual relationship. This area is admirably covered in Paul Fussell, *The Great War and Modern Memory*, so will not be dwelt on here other than to quote the ardently heterosexual Hiscock who cogently captures the enigma: 'Trench warfare bred a monasticism not unlike which was lived at Eton (or any other Public School) … Many a soldier dies and was mourned by his fellow man with even more intensity than by some bereft wife at home in England'.[81] In a culture that demonised homosexuality, male wartime relationships were honourably exempt though writers, like Aldington, were quick to ensure there was no suspicion: 'Let me at once disabuse the eager-eyed sodomites among my readers by stating emphatically once and for all that here was nothing sodomitical [sic] in these friendships'.[82]

This male bonding, this love, was not confined to the British soldier but was a common trench experience touching all combatants. Remarque illustrates the point: 'Kat and I … have a more complete communion with one another than even lovers have' and 'we are nearer than lovers, in a simpler, a harder way'.[83] The non-sexual love that could legitimately exist between trench companions has to be seen in the context of the masculine friendships that existed before the war in civilian society. Men could be close and still heterosexual and manly. Weeks contends that it was widely accepted in Victorian society that strong and indeed often emotional relationships were normal.[84] Even the redoubtable morality campaigner, W. T. Stead, could write to Edward Carpenter that 'A few more cases like the Wilde case and we could find the freedom of comradeship now possible to men seriously impaired to the permanent detriment of the race'.[85] Hiscock provides a rather tender 'confession' of his love for his friend Brook, which illustrates the point:

> We were in love with each other and such a feeling left us immune from the need or urge for sex … doing things together might have included masturbation but somehow we steered clear of it. Ours was a pure love … difficult to write about, impossible to forget, and in that hospital [on hearing of Brook's death] … I wept like a child.[86]

Sometimes the intimacy of the trenches, however, can seem to suggest that men played out deeper fantasies, or were unaware of their own leanings. In a remarkable letter to his girlfriend in England, one soldier recounted an incident that illustrates this well. He tells how he and a fellow subaltern were exchanging a ritual of kisses:

---

81 Fussell, *The Great War*, Hiscock, *Bells of Hell*, p. 76.
82 Aldington, *Death of a Hero*, p. 26.
83 Remarque, *All Quiet,*, pp. 85, 182.
84 Weeks, *Sex, Politics and Society*, p. 109.
85 Ibid, p. 110.
86 Eric Hiscock, *The Bells of Hell Go Ting-a-ling-a-ling*, p. 98.

> As we arrived at the barn door he said, 'just a moment Frank, before we go in I've got something else to give you – put that light out'. I put the lamp out and into my pocket, wondering what was coming. Then I felt an arm around my neck, and the dear lad kissed me once – 'that's from Evelyn' he said; then he kissed me again and said 'that's from your mother'. I returned his tender salute and said 'that's from me'. There we were like a couple of girls but there was no one about, and the matter was a secret between us – and you.[87]

Interestingly, the writer asks for secrecy, perhaps demonstrating his own feeling that he has crossed a line.

But what of those who sublimated or repressed their desires, or who experienced short-term or temporary homosexual desires, or who only 'came out' later? Hiscock, again in confessional mood, admits to his own feelings and draws a useful distinction between the homoerotic and the predatory homosexual:

> There is a strain of homosexuality in most men. Some want to keep it under control, others let it rip and behave like Oscar Wilde ... Brook had a feminine streak in him, but not enough to allow him to yield to such pursuers as Lieutenant Clarke.... Brook, Jackson and myself all had some homosexual tendencies (despite Jacko's infatuation with his Croydon belle) and in the days and nights of stress we masturbated, but kisses on unshaven faces were rare, and only in moments of acute danger ... [88]

The predatory were very different, however, with 'Lieutenant Clarke's [tendencies] ... a wholly different cup of tea. They were destroyers, devoid of feelings'.

In the years succeeding the war, many of those who had served would, like Graves, admit to their temporary homosexuality:

> In English preparatory and public schools romance is necessarily homosexual. The opposite sex is despised and treated as something obscene. Many boys never recover from this perversion. For every one born homosexual, at least ten pseudo-homosexuals are made by the public school system; nine of these ten as honourably chaste and sentimental as I was.[89]

Hiscock met a product of this system. Talking of a fellow member of the Public Schools Battalion of Royal Fusiliers he remembered: 'I never saw him with women

---

87 Santanu Das, 'Kiss me, Hardy: *Modernism/Modernity* 9 (2002), pp. 51–74.
88 Hiscock, *Bells of Hell*, p. 76.
89 Robert Graves, *Goodbye to All That*, p. 23.

and although there was no evidence that he was homosexual I realise now that he was certainly queer, however latently'.[90]

With others, suppressed homosexuality became a more permanent aspect of their sexual lives. Siegfried Sassoon, J.C. Ackerley, Herbert Read, Ivor Gurney, Tom Driberg, T. E. Lawrence, Wilfred Owen, Christopher Isherwood, and Ivor Novello were just a few of those who 'came out', at least to an extent that law and society allowed them to. While these famed literary homosexuals are well-known, many others likewise discovered their sexuality but kept their virginity, perhaps then spending a lifetime suppressing their real sexual desires. Ackerley is particularly intriguing in that he admits to visiting a brothel, but finds he cannot consummate the heterosexual act.[91] Would this have been a common occurrence? Did men go to the brothels for reasons of 'face' or because it was a manly joke and a 'step in the right direction' albeit disguising a different and developing sexual orientation?

Most men, given the attitudes surrounding the question, would naturally have maintained a low profile. Hall contends that 'several leading pacifists were homosexual, and though there were probably even more homosexuals among the serving troops, these were relatively invisible, except in the infrequent cases when matters reached a court martial'.[92] As the courts-martial statistics show, however, not all men could hide their predilections. Men openly displayed their sexuality and in doing so incurred military sanction for what was considered a serious crime even though the statistics belie the army's concern.

Sometimes the crime was exposed by the censor intercepting a letter written by a man to a willing partner. Subaltern Graham Seton Hutchison, of the 3rd Argylls, had a relationship with his batman, and with one of the sergeants in his battalion, arranging an assignation at a house in Armentières. The letter fell into the hands of the authorities, but, even with insufficient evidence to justify a court martial, Sir John French wrote that in his opinion 'he was not the class of officer whose services it is desirable to retain'.[93] Another unguarded letter was also the undoing of Second Lieutenant Wilfred Marsden of the RFC and led to his being cashiered for behaving in a scandalous manner unbecoming the character of an officer and gentleman.[94] Another whose fate was decided by a wayward letter was Vera Brittain's brother, though his indiscretions took place on the Italian front.[95]

90 Hiscock, *Bells of Hell,* p. 13.
91 Parker, *Ackerley*, p. 21.
92 Hall, Lesley, *Sex, Gender and Social Change in Britain Since 1880* (Palgrave Macmillan 2000), p. 96.
93 Hutchison, *Footslogger (*London: Hutchinson, 1933), pp. 142-53; for the military's view of this affair see TNA: WO 374/36057.
94 TNA: WO 339/24241.
95 Miles Hudson, *Soldier, Poet, Rebel. The Extraordinary Life of Charles Hudson VC* (Stroud: Sutton 2008). See also Paul Berry and Mark Bostridge, *Vera Brittain – a Life* (1995).

More often it appears that the court martial was a result of a complaint made by another, less willing participant. Occasionally, the men might be caught *in flagrante delicto*: Captain A. C. Boyd of the 3rd Battalion 1st Herts (a Territorial) and Lieutenant Fally of the 10th Battalion Seaforths, were caught at a male brothel in London's West End during a combined police and army raid.[96] Lieutenant Pope Hennessy of the 49th Battalion CEF was court-martialled under Section 40, for behaviour 'prejudic[ial] to good order and military discipline'. The army clerk compiling the register noted that it was for 'Scandalous Conduct, Indecency', having 'got into bed with a private soldier'.[97] Unfortunately, other clerks were not as descriptive and we will never know how many of the other men charged under Section 40 had their behaviour concealed. Pope Hennessey was, however, acquitted, as were several others who appeared before Field General Courts Martial on Section 41 indecency charges. For example, 2nd Lieutenant Trustam of the Lincolnshires in December 1917, Temporary Major Courau of the RFC at Cassell in September 1917, Temporary Lieutenant Abell of the Royal Field Artillery at Reningelst in 1916, Temporary Captain Goodwin, Lieutenant Russell of the Army Services Corps in 1915, and Lieutenant Rudolph of the RAMC at Arras in 1917.[98] No surviving court records explain why these men were initially charged or what defence procured them 'not guilty' verdicts. Other ranks escaped censure too.[99] One might assume that there was no smoke without fire, but perhaps their actions were considered temporary aberrations caused by drink (as some Section 41 cases also list drunkenness along with the indecency charge).

Not all men, however, escaped censure. Temporary Captain G. N. Ganet of the Remount Services was convicted for attempting to procure a private and a gunner to commit an act of gross indecency with him at Le Havre in 1917. Section 40 was invoked to successfully prosecute 2nd Lieutenant McBean of an infantry battalion of 'being unduly familiar with a private soldier'; 2nd Lieutenant Chaplin of the Essex Yeomanry, 2nd Lieutenant Odlum of the ASC, and 2nd Lieutenant Newman of the RFA were all separately cashiered in 1916 and 1917 for proven indecency. All were junior subalterns, all from Kitchener's New Armies and – it might be assumed from their being officers at this stage of the war – from a public-school background.[100]

When the military authorities successfully prosecuted a man, he faced a number of possible official sentences, the toughest being prison with hard labour, as well as being cashiered. Private H. Taylor, of the 47th London Division, was found guilty on 15 July 1918 on two charges of 'disgraceful conduct of an indecent kind' and sentenced to two

---

96 See also TNA: WO 38/24, XC21082.
97 TNA: WO 90/6; Mar. 1917.
98 TNA: WO 90/6, a register of Field General Courts Martial, has provided the sample of indecency cases.
99 See TNA: WO 154/52, APM Diary 3 Nov., 'Cpl Logan of 2nd Manchesters tried for indecency'.
100 TNA: WO 90/6.

years with hard labour.[101] The same fate, but for a single year's hard labour, befell 2nd Lieutenant Spence of the Royal Engineers for an offence in the field at Abbeville in the same year. Not all were tried at military court. Lieutenant Marsden of the RFC was convicted at the Old Bailey and given two years hard labour.[102]

Few men went to prison: more commonly, officers were 'discharged with ignominy' and cashiered. Captain (acting major) Dakin of the ASC, Lieutenant Rodeck of the Army Service Corps, and Captain Warburton of the Leinsters all lost their pips. Captain G. M. Goodall, attached to the Gurkha Rifles, also forfeited his Military Cross. The Reverend Rogers of the Church Army Workers was discharged with ignominy, as was another chaplain, Harwood, who in December 1917 also got six months.[103] Occasionally, where the case was difficult to prove, the man might get off with a reprimand. Second Lieutenant Faulkes, RFA, received one at a General Court Martial in October 1918, as did Major Alford of the 3rd Cameron Highlanders, but his career was blighted.[104] Sometimes those sentenced to imprisonment re-enlisted as private soldiers on their release, but then not all who applied to be despatched to a theatre of war were sent.

Discharged, cashiered, reprimanded, sent home to Britain, refused the right of re-enlistment: these were probably the easiest of sentences to take. Although there was no official death sentence for this crime, there is evidence that many men effectively received just that. In the case of Lieutenant Reginald Fuller 42nd CEF Battalion, 1st Army, his sentence stated that 'The court wish to recommend that the services of this man should be utilised, if possible, in a fighting unit'.[105] In other words, he was given a death sentence. Perhaps more chilling is the kangaroo court justice apparently meted out by men in the field. Private Howell Phillips, Machine Gun Corps, 1916-18, illustrated the extreme attitude that could be taken by the men and told of what was effectively summary justice:

> We didn't know this old business of homosexual, they call it. We didn't know such a thing was in the country then. Terrible thing that; if we had one of those he wouldn't come back alive from the front I can tell you … No nonsense like that … if we came across a homo at the front he'd never come back, we'd finish him off … oh, the buggers, what a terrible thing.[106]

---

101 TNA: WO 154/69.
102 TNA: WO 339/24241.
103 The register of General Courts Martial, which briefly records name, rank, offence and sentence is TNA: WO 92/3, WO 92/4 and WO 90. Unfortunately, the actual court transcripts were not always kept but some records of courts martial, with the court finding and sentence, can be found at TNA: WO 71 and WO 213.
104 TNA: WO 339/77793 and TNA: WO 374/887.
105 Julian Putkowski, private collection of Canadian records.
106 IWM Sound Archive, No. 9498, reel 6, Phillips.

General Sir Wyndham Childs, writing in his biography, confirmed that summary justice might well have been delivered in the field. While not specifically referring to cases of indecency, he reflects that, should the death penalty be lifted as the ultimate deterrent:

> I am perfectly convinced that the fighting troops would take matters into their own hands and offenders caught red handed would be shot by their comrades. I would not go so far, even, as to say that this did not happen during the war.[107]

The general antipathy to homosexuals is reflected in Tommy Keele's memories of the female impersonators at the concert parties. 'They used to come to our film shows in the afternoon and we could sit there and hear them talking to each other … pansy noises all the time and we hated them', but he could also reflect, more tolerantly, following an unwanted homosexual approach that, 'Everybody was sex starved … there was no such things as girls around … he was probably in that mood and anything was good enough.[108]

The low incidence of homosexuality supposedly evidenced by the official court-martial statistics must be considered a fiction. Many cases never made it to court. F.A.J. ('Tanky') Taylor, an infantryman with the Worcesters, told of an 18-year old comrade who was sexually harassed while acting as batman for his officer. He got away, talked to another batman but was advised not to say anything as it would only be his word against the officer's.[109] If justice was to be done, it was often executed by the men themselves, as Tommy Keele testified:

> Our bandmaster … nice bloke … offered to share double bed … first couple of nights we slept quite comfortably, but on the third night I woke up with a funny little movement around my bottom … I push a hand away quickly and said 'don't you dare … you so and so'. This time he'd gone much further and he was practically raping me … so I really battered his head and face for trying to bugger me![110]

The young officer training recruit, Cloete, had similarly to resort to his own protection measures: 'He [a senior officer] was a homosexual and he made a pass at me. I opened my new jack-knife, put it under my pillow and said, 'if you try to get into my bed again I'll stick it into you'.[111]

107 Childs, *Episodes and Reflections*, p. 144.
108 IWM Sound Archive, No. 9428, reel 7, Keele.
109 Taylor, *Bottom of the Barrel*, p. 106.
110 IWM Sound Archive, No. 9428, reel 7, Keele.
111 Cloete, *A Victorian Son*, p. 200.

The unfortunately named Hiscock, who seemed to attract homosexual attention, found that public humiliation of the 'bugger' was the most effective policy, at least for getting rid of unwanted attention:

> I awoke from an uneasy sleep to find him pressed up close to me and that his hand was undoing my fly-buttons … and murmuring in my ear something that went like this: 'Don't say a word … I'm sorry but I must … I won't hurt you … don't say anything'. I groaned inwardly. Another bugger. Was I ever to be free of them … I raised my voice and said something about telling the whole carriage what was going on. The hand that was attempting to undo my fly-buttons went to its owner's pocket. It came out again clutching a ten-shilling note. 'Don't say anything … I'm sorry … Be a good boy … Don't say anything … I'm sorry'.[112]

Hiscock also tells of another occasion of unwanted attention from an officer who had to be 'warned off' with threats of going public. Other memorialists relate stories of being importuned, the common strand being their own innocence leading them into compromising situations. It is also often someone in a position of relative power who is the one making the advances. 'Tanky' Taylor, another whose looks apparently made him a target of homosexuals, told of an unwanted incident while sharing a room with a colonial officer at a training camp: 'I was quite aware of my youthful, not to say, girlish, appearance with my blue eyes, that I was an object of attraction to the sex-starved older men'. The unfortunate Taylor was even to 'enjoy' the unwelcome attentions of men in the Chinese Labour Corps![113]

With Private Bigwood, another Worcester, it was a corporal who tried to exploit the power relationship:

> At night, he came and lay down beside me when I was going to sleep and all of a sudden I felt something kind of poke my backside … I had no idea what he was trying to do … 'what the devil's going on', I said. I had no idea of anything like that in those days … but he did … but he got away then … It was long after war that I realised that sort of thing went on; queers, we called them.[114]

That Bigwood did not immediately appreciate that something was 'going on' is not surprising, as, in the trenches, the norms of tactile contact between men changed profoundly, and the concepts of personal space and privacy were different from those of civilian life, at least for the upper working and middle classes who were not used to the overcrowding of the slums. This in itself would have both allowed and prompted

---

112 Hiscock, *Bells of Hell*, p. 25; at p. 36.
113 Taylor, *Bottom of the Barrel*, pp. 118–119
114 IWM Sound Archive, No. 22733, reel 2, Bigwood.

a certain degree of intimacy, of which any sexual dimension might not have been immediately appreciated or even apparent.

Power suborning innocence was seemingly not uncommon but the problem was probably very quickly solved without apparent recourse to any official channels. John Henry Boon, an air mechanic, recounted that:

> We had a ... French interpreter and he used to make himself very friendly with the boys, young boys, and he used to try and interfere with them and they just didn't know what was happening, they'd never met anybody like that before ... our corporal was a worldly-wise man, he'd been in the navy, and we told him what was going on ... he went round all the boys to find what was going on and then he went and saw our staff captain and told him what was going on; within an hour he was out, back to his unit.[115]

Boon makes no mention of subsequent investigations or trial. It seems that most of these incidents went unrecorded either because those involved did not think them serious enough to report or, if they did, the event was quietly hushed up. As has been shown in relation to other crimes, perceived or actual, no regiment wished to blacken its name if it could be avoided.

Perhaps the most interesting claim concerning acts of indecency was its use as a cynical ploy to get away from the front, virtually a reworking of a 'self-inflicted wound' ruse. According to Osburn of the RAMC, one man officially accused another of indecency. It usually led to a court martial and if it worked:

> one or both of you implicated in the alleged offence would rely on getting two years imprisonment for 'indecency' to be spent in Wormwood Scrubs or some other English prison.[116]

The true incidence of homosexual love, or basic same-sex encounters, will never be uncovered. What also clouds the issue is the existence of what Weeks has referred to as 'situational' homosexuality, 'activities which were often regarded as legitimate, or at least acceptable, in certain circumstances, without effecting [sic] self-concepts'.[117] This would doubtless include the many *ad hoc* occasions when the frustrations of the soldier's life, or the special circumstances of incarceration as prisoners of war simply became too much to bear. Perhaps in these conditions, the much vaunted trench comradeship made individuals more understanding of each other's sexuality. The needs and a 'temporary' aberration in an individual's sexual behaviour might be tolerated and even accepted.

---

115 IWM Sound Archive, No. 9476, reel 4, Boon.
116 Osburn, *Unwilling Passenger*, p. 87.
117 Weeks, *Sex, Politics & Society*, p. 109.

The range of sex crimes considered here are those recognised in the Army Act of the time. It is highly likely that at the fringes there were a number of other, wider sex crimes including 'white slaving', sexual murder and sadism, some of which might now fall into the modern definition of 'war crime'. In a war that saw personal brutality taken to extreme levels it is now impossible even to attempt to classify the acts that were the work of sexual maniacs from those that were carried out by "normal" combatants'.

On balance, considering the complete gamut of possible sex crimes, it is astounding that the British Army behaved with the restraint it apparently did. In addition to the safety valve of recognised prostitution, and the abundant availability of clandestine prostitutes, this is a further indication of the moral stance of the Edwardian middle classes. While they might change their attitudes towards certain sexual matters, they also had moral boundaries that could not be transgressed even in a period of unprecedented social rupture.

Sex crime, like any other military crime, represents a breakdown in discipline. A breakdown in discipline leads to a bad morale. Thus although there is no direct link, its incidence can be said to be an indicator of discipline and morale. Sex crimes committed by an individual also reflect on the standing of a regiment. The importance of regimental pride in sustaining morale has been well demonstrated by David French;[118] consequently, loss of 'face' or regimental disgrace could have had an impact on morale and on battlefield performance. The low level of sex crime is thus arguably more than simply a reflection of Edwardian morals; it can also be taken as a measurement of the success of the army's policy on how it handled the issue of sex, and ultimately of the overall morale of the men.

---

118 French, *Military Identities*, p. 256 and pp. 282-3.

13

'Inkey Pinkey, Parlez-vous': Conclusion

The book set out to reappraise the sex life of the soldier serving on the Western Front and challenge the long-accepted view that sexual activities played little part in the life of the combatant. By illustrating the range and scope of activities, it is possible to argue that, far from being of little significance in their lives, sex played a role in sustaining morale, if not in all men, and at all times, then in a sizeable number and on many occasions. Morale has many underpinnings, and 'not all of these factors will operate with constant or equal force'.[1] There is, however, a growing case for including sexual relief as one of those underpinnings.

By looking behind the official figures for venereal disease it has been shown that there was under-recording of the incidence of the disease. Reliance on the statistics as a measure of sexual activity has perhaps created a 'blind-spot' in terms of investigating the importance of sex in the daily life of the soldier and its contribution to his morale. It was hoped that the soldier's own voice, muted but not silent on the issue, would tell the story more accurately than the questionable statistics. In listening to his story, the historian can find another view of the soldier's life outside the constraining prism of 'the trench'. The cultural sensitivity of the subject, and recognition that 'people rarely write of illegal and 'immoral' acts, even to themselves'[2], are reminders that this story is to be treated with caution. It cannot be claimed to have been a universal story, experienced by all; indeed over a war of nearly four years and involving nearly four million men on the northern European front alone, it would be hard to find any thesis that could be universally applied.

However we read the statistics for venereal disease derived from medical records, they are not a guide to total sexual activity, nor, of course, do they give any indication of wider sexually-related experiences. A number of factors contributed to an

---

1   Michael Snape, *God and the British Soldier. Religion and the British Army in the First and Second World Wars* (2005), p. 91.
2   Lisa Z. Sigel, *Governing Pleasure: Pornography and Social Change in England, 1815-1914* (2002), p. 98.

understating of the real number of infections, including medical and individual ignorance, basic non-reporting, and possibly official fudging for political reasons. It is clear that for many individuals there was no sublimation or suppression of desire and, despite an assumption that sexual activity might be limited to certain social classes, it knew no such boundaries:

> There were fastidious soldiers, and straight laced soldiers; there were faithful as well as unfaithful husbands; there were middle-aged men who regulated their conduct; but the popular line the army followed at every grade, was the pursuit of sex, on the rare days when opportunity offered.[3]

Was the soldier's behaviour predictable, an inevitable consequence of Hynes's 'Turn of Mind'? 'If we examine the relations of the sexes before the war', claimed Hirschfeld:

> we see a revolutionary shift, for the whole realm of sexuality is different from the past. Whereas, formerly, sexuality had, in accordance with bourgeois concepts of chastity, been enveloped in mystical darkness, there arose at the turn of the century a tremendous current of thought, an erotic enlightenment movement. This was a reaction against the earlier repression of sexuality from society.[4]

Although attitudes towards sex were clearly changing as the Victorian period gave way to the Edwardian and, as Hirschfeld noted, 'the outbreak of war fell at a time pregnant with sultry anticipations which had partly destroyed the ancient values and pronounced the death verdict on them', this change was still in its infancy at the start of the war. New attitudes and behaviours had yet to filter down from the innovators and opinion formers. The men who comprised the new citizen army mostly held 'Victorian' morals on enlistment, morals which should perhaps have put a brake on casual and venal sexual activity, if not on libido. For many, the moral position changed in the conditions of war. The British soldier fraternised with compliant locals in billet and bar, was often a regular visitor to the official red and blue lamps, and to regulated brothels when finance and time permitted, and availed himself of the services of myriad clandestine and 'amateur' prostitutes when opportunity knocked.

Perhaps because opportunity was comparatively rare and effectively rationed to times and places not of the individual's own choice, lust appears to have been heightened. The pioneer sexologists Fischer and Dubois noted the conclusions of Dr Maestan, a French 'scientist':

> No one thinks so much of sexual pleasure as the person in whom the sexual instinct is repressed. Just as starving people think more of food than those who

---

3   Carrington, *Soldier*, p. 184.
4   Hirschfeld, *Sexual History*, p. 12.

are normally nourished, so the unsatisfied sexual need leads to a constant preoccupation with the subject, which is reflected in the choice of reading matter, strange perversions and more or less obscene talk.[5]

This would certainly appear true of the British soldier, whose daily conversations centred on women, when they were not pre-occupied by war. Further, when he found himself 'skint', beaten to the prize by others, or simply in an area bereft of women, he relied on pornography and other obscene or erotic material as substitutes for the real thing.

The soldier was implicitly encouraged in his pursuits by an army which acknowledged that sex was important for its men, realised the impossibility of controlling natural urges, and worried about the potentially worse barrack-room problems of homosexuality and sex crime. While it worried mainly about the impact of unrestrained sexual activity on health (and thus on available manpower), it also implicitly understood that morale was dependent at least in part on men satisfying their sexual urges. The army, realising that reliance on individual self-control, and/or providing leisure entertainments and religious support as a diversion, would not be sufficient, and not initially being able to even contemplate sanctioning the use of prophylactics, it turned to a traditional solution – sanctioning regulated prostitution. It further exercised a light touch with regards to fraternisation with local women and the use of pornography. While perhaps the primary reason for the tolerance of regulated brothels lay in controlling health, it had the fortuitous result of also helping bolster the morale of men missing the company of women. It ran counter, however, to contemporary moral standards. The policy could not be made explicit and explains the absence of formal sources directly linking morale with the provision of sex; it effectively left the army in a moral 'no man's land' of its own making.

Despite the inherent contradiction in the army's position, and the various controversies this led to throughout the war, its policy of 'looking the other way' while the soldier entertained himself outside of the infrastructure the army provided, to some extent achieved its objectives. Venereal disease rates were held down, thereby maximising the number of men kept healthy and combat ready, and, perhaps while never as readily available as some men might have wished, sexual activities contributed with other variables to the upholding of morale.

Sex, or the anticipation of it, was an undoubted morale-booster for many men. It brought distraction and contributed to relief and recovery.[6] 'Flirtation with French girls' wrote Russell, 'made the chief mental relief of the men'.[7] I.L. Read called his

---

5 Fischer and Dubois, *Sexual Life*, p. 271.
6 See Allinson, *The Bantams*, p. 215 for a vivid picture of the role of sex in the post-battle recovery process.
7 H. Russell, *Slaves of the War Lords* (1928), p. 141:

sexual adventure a 'legitimate youthful longing rudely interrupted and stifled by more than two years of war'.[8]

It was important both to those who were missing the company of wives and girl-friends (and having a sexual encounter was not always seen as being unfaithful to, or incompatible with an existing relationship), as well as to those who had no home ties or were experiencing the first awakening of manhood. It did not have to be consummated sex to achieve this; vicarious experiences such as simply visiting a brothel, chatting up a local, hearing of a mate's adventures or dipping into pornographic materials all had their place. The lines of this end-of-war song summed up the attitudes of many soldiers and how they felt about their war time experiences:

> We came on business only – not expecting any fun;
> But when we got to 'la belle France' we found you M'amoiselle,
> Intending, if we did this work, we'd have some fun as well.
> You flirted, danced and sang with us – taught us 'parley-vous';
> Life would have been so rotten if it had not been for you.[9]

Independent, contemporary observers such as Nurse La Motte, were also aware of how the army connived at allowing women, though not wives, access to the forward areas for the sake of morale:

> always there are plenty of women. Never wives, who mean responsibility, but just women, who only mean distraction and amusement, just as food and wine. So wives are forbidden, because lowering to the morale, but women are winked at, because they cheer and refresh the troops.[10]

Why the relative silence surrounding the issue, if sexual activity was as prevalent and as important variable in upholding morale as it now appears to have been? A number of theories can be advanced, including scholarly myopia, with a concentration on sex on the home front, gender issues, the problems arising from venereal disease and, for others, an obsession with the actual trench experience on the war front – to the exclusion of other aspects of the soldier's life. A good case can also be made, however, for there being an historical and yet subliminal cover-up: 'In wartime discussions of controversial sexual topics like VD, the soldiers, as the nation's heroes, were beyond reproach'.[11] Let sleeping dogs lie: why besmirch the good name of the ranks of decent

---

8   Read, 'Of Those we Loved', p.p. 234 – 237.
9   'Homeward', 1919, quoted by D. Kent, *From Trench and Troopship: the Experience of the Australian Imperial Force, 1914-1919* (Sydney: Hale & Iremonger, 1999). p. 197.
10 Ellen Newbold La Motte, *The Backwash of War: the Human Wreckage of the Battlefield as Witnessed By an American Hospital Nurse* (G P Putnam's Sons, New York, 1916, reprint 2008), p. 65.
11 Robb, *British Culture*, p. 55.

The Soldier's Dream.
A "Bitter" disappointment on waking.

The fantasy of the girl in the estaminet helped a soldier dream of better times, even if he had eventually to wake to harsh reality. (Courtesy Mark Warby. ©2015 Estate of Barbara Bruce Littlejohn.)

men who gave their lives so cheaply? Ian Hay, one of the very first writers to describe the experience of war, noted this:

> We proceeded to idolise our War. We saw ourselves as a nation of Crusaders … we ascribed to our soldiers and sailors a nobility of character which they – and they were probably the most normal and rational members of the community at that time – would have been first to disclaim.[12]

Gibbs equally saw the truth;

> These men were heroic soldiers, yet our hero worship should not blind us to the truth of things. There is nothing more utterly false than to imagine that war purges human nature of all its frailties and vices, and that under the shadow of death a great body of men gathered … from any class and cities, became suddenly white knights, *sans peur et sans reproche*, inspired by the highest ideals of faith and chivalry.[13]

Hay's caveat, implicitly advising us to listen to the soldier's own story, was largely forgotten as the myth of the 'Crusader' grew.

This book did not set out to question how the soldiers' wartime sexual experiences, if proven, might have affected their post-war attitudes and behaviour. But it can perhaps make a contribution to the debate.

Historians such as Bristow have contended that: 'It is generally accepted that the war speeded the decline of Victorian attitudes to sex'.[14] For Eric Leed, the war represented a complete break, a discontinuity, rather than being part of a speeding-up of general trends.[15] Not all agree, however. Thompson argues that, although post-war illegitimacy rates were down, divorce rates up, fashions more overtly sexual, and birth control more widely practised, all these were trends that were already in evidence before the war.[16] Marwick argued that the long-term effect of the war on social attitudes and social structure was profound but 'reacted within the broader trend'.[17] Fuller goes even further: 'The war acted … to reinforce certain values and to foster a cultural conservatism which made the troops in many ways the last of the Edwardians rather than the first of the moderns, as they are so often depicted'.[18] Bourke advances the

---

12 R. T. Rees, *A Schoolmaster at War* (London: Haycock, 1931). Quoted from the forward written by Ian Hay.
13 Gibbs, *Soul of War*, P. 310.
14 Bristow, *Vice and Vigilance*, p. 146.
15 Leed, *No Man's Land: Combat and Identity in World War One* (1979).
16 Thompson, *The Edwardians*, pp. 269-71.
17 Marwick, *The Deluge*, p. 290.
18 Fuller, *Troop Morale*, p. 141.

theory that returning soldiers yearned for domesticity and the security that it offered.[19] Hall believes that post-war letters to Marie Stopes (in response to the publication of *Married Love* in 1918) indicate, however, a 'stunning level of sexual ignorance and timidity in both sexes. Women often married in complete ignorance of the physical facts, but men also found their knowledge very inadequate'.[20] In other words, wartime experiences were either forgotten, discounted or perhaps their incidence over-exaggerated. 'In terms of the history of formal sex education, 1914-1918 was no turning point in the emancipation of the public'.[21]

Perhaps the findings in this study will add to a wider debate over the extent and speed of changes in post-war sexual attitudes, and their cause. What cannot be doubted is that a generation must have been enormously altered by the experience of war both at home and abroad in ways that are hard to pin down, precisely because they were not widely discussed. The banter of large bodies of men thrown together in close proximity in a volunteer – later a conscripted – army, the sharing of sexual anecdote to fill the tedium of trench warfare, even the army's oft-repeated lectures about personal sexual hygiene, must all have been an education for many soldiers. Those who had seen France now had some acquaintance with a culture in which sexual activity outside the marriage bed was accepted, venal sex was tolerated, and in which there was much readier access to a literature which in England would be condemned as obscene. They might have found themselves in close proximity to homosexual men – of whom they were largely unaware before the war – and even, perhaps to their own surprise, have formed homoerotic bonds with other men out of friendship and a shared desire to survive. They might have seen – and taken advantage of – women forced into prostitution by desperate circumstances or who had discovered for themselves a sexuality made vulnerable by the absence – or loss – of husbands. These were not, for Edwardian men, ordinary experiences. Moreover, our soldier discovered that 'authority' – not least in the shape of the military hierarchy and the army's chaplains – was not only aware of this 'illicit' behaviour, but sometimes actively condoned it, some individuals even drinking deeply from the same well.

How that experience was digested lies outside the remit of this book. It has been noted that, other than in a small number of examples, there was a hiatus of around a decade between the end of the war and the first serious autobiographical and fictional attempts to record and assimilate the sexual experience of war, but the fact remains that a genie had been let out of its bottle and could never be forced back in. It was not only on the Western front that the stock of sexual knowledge and experience was enlarged but on the Home Front too, where women had access to a whole range of novel experiences and freedoms outside the marital bed. Perhaps the point about Mrs Stopes's post-war correspondents is not their ignorance, but the fact that for the

---

19   Bourke, *Dismembering the Male*, p. 162.
20   Hall, *Hidden Anxieties*, p. 108.
21   Bristow, *Vice and Vigilance*, p. 147.

first time married people had an awareness of what they were missing through their inadequacy or inexperience, and sense of the way in which their experience within marriage fell short of the potential pleasure that could be achieved. It was an awareness that sex was normal, and sexual experiences could be shared.

One concluding observation can be made. In filling a lacuna in the history of the Western Front, the sex life of the Tommy himself, one particular, if clichéd, aphorism rings true: *plus ça change, plus c'est la même chose.*

Leave; the ultimate morale booster but it was not always taken at home, and not always with what might have been a recognised 'girlfriend'. (Courtesy Mark Warby. ©2015 Estate of Barbara Bruce Littlejohn)

Appendix

Imperial War Museum oral records cited

The sound archive of the Imperial War Museum contains approximately 1250 interviews with soldiers who had direct experience of the Western Front. Archived digitally, they comprise interviews which usually took place in the respondent's home, each conducted by an IWM researcher, either male or female, although some were conducted by independent interviewers and recorded as part of documentary making by the BBC or a similar broadcaster. The earliest interview is in 1975 with the bulk being made in the late 1980s and early 1990. Generally, the more recent the interview, the older the respondent, and many were in their ninth decade. Respondents were not selected with reference to any sampling frame and, with the relatively low number, statistical analysis cannot be justified.

Notes:
- The file number indicates the date of the recording with the large numbers being the more recent. Where no year is noted for the interview, the record is blank.
- All oral records with some allusion to sex, brothels, venereal disease, homosexuality and pornography or obscenity are included
- 12% are Officers; 8%, NCOs; the remaining 80%, rank and file
- 65% are Infantry; 15%, Artillery; the remaining 20%, support troops
- All those recorded from 1989 are numbered 11000 and up, with the earliest recording (300s) recorded from 1974
- Those interviewed from 11000 were all more than 84 years of age, with age then increasing as the file numbers get higher.

Name	Record No.	Rank	Regiment	Date of Interview	Age
Alban	6678	Private Fitter	Royal Ordnance Corps	1982	93
Amatt, Sidney	9168	Private	Infantry		
Armstrong, Thomas	9758	Officer	RFC		
Ashby, John	9418	Private	2nd and 5th Bn Infantry	1986	
Ashurst, George	9875	Private	2nd Bn Lancs	1987	
Baxter, Arthur	9346	Private	51st Machine Gun Corps	1986	
Bigwood, Edwin	10115	Private	7th Bn Worcestershire Regt	1996	
Bigwood, Eddie	22733	Private	4th Bn Worcestershire Regt	1996	
Bird, Robert Cecil	10656	Driver	147 Bde, RFA	1989	
Blunt, Harry	645	Private	Machine Gun Corps	1980	
Boon, John Henry	9476	Private/air mechanic	HQ Fienvillers Chateau	1986	
Booth, Eustace R.	9263	Private	Army Service Corps (MT) motorcycle dispatch	1986	
Bretton, Harry	11029	Private	Royal Field Artillery	1989	
Bromley, Tom	9544	NCO	Army Service Corps	1986	
Brown, T. H.	24546	Private	18th King's Liverpool Regt		
Calvert, Horace	9955	Private	1/6th Bn West Yorks and Hussars	1987	
Cole, James	24876	Private signaller	1st Devonshire and 2nd Bn Middlesex		
Collins, Norman W.	12043	Officer	Seaforth Highlanders	1991	94
Craske, Clifford W.	4066	Ranker	Infantry	1963 BBC	
Davis, Gordon	9343	Private	22nd Bn Royal Fusiliers 1915-17 and RFC 1917-18	1986	
Davis, Jim	9750	NCO	12th Bn Royal Fusilliers/ officer 8th/9th Royal	1987	
Day, Albert	24854	Private	1/4th Bn Gloucesters	1975	
Dennys, Cyril G.	9876	Officer	RGA 212 Siege Bty 1917-1919	1987	
Dixon, Fred	737	Private trooper	Surrey Yeomanry	1974	
Dixon, James	11047	NCO	Army Service Corps No. 2	1989	97
Edwards, Norman	14932	NCO	1/6th Bn Gloucestershire Regt	1991	97
Esler, Maberly S.	378	Officer	RAMC	1974	
Farrer, Basil	9552	Private	3rd Bn Green Howards	1986	
Ferns	11111	Private			

Name	Record No.	Rank	Regiment	Date of Interview	Age
Field, Laurie	1137	Private	Oxs and Bucks LI	1990	
Gee, Charles	13717	Officer Lft Cornel	9th Bn Durham LI		
German, Matthew	25204	Private	RAMC		
Gillman, Arthur	9420	Private	2/2nd London Regt (Royal Fusiliers) 1918	1986	
Goodman, Frederick C.	9398	Private	RAMC 2/1st London Field Ambulance	1986	
Greener, Martin	8945	Officer	9th Bn Durham Light Infantry 1915		
Grunwell, George	9431	Private	West Yorks	1986	
Hall, Lawrence	14599	Private	47th Bn Machine Gun	1994	96
Harding, John T.	380	Private trooper	Montgomery Yeomanry	1974	
Harris, Arthur	24871	Private	Royal Naval Division	1976	
Higgins, Charles F.	9884	Private	Infantry, no regt	1986	
Hill, W.	24539	Private	8th Bn Rifle Brigade	1989	94
Holbrook, William	9339	Private	4th Bn Royal Fusiliers	1986	
Holdstock, Henry T.	20	Driver	Kite balloon section Royal Naval Air Service	1973	
Holmes, William	8868	Private	12 Bn London Regt	1985	
Hopthrow, Harry	11581	NCO	Signals	1990	
Jarman, Clarence W.	12925	Private	7th Royal West Surrey	1992	96
Keele, Tommy	9428	NCO	11th Bn Middelsex attached Ace of Spades concert party 12th Division	1991	
Lane, Clifford James	7257	NCO	1st Bn Hertfordshire Regt 7th Bn Bedfords	1983	
Lawson, R. H.	24882	Driver	Royal Field Artillery	1975	
Lovegrove, James Leslie	8231	Private	RFA and Officer Loyal North Lancs Regt	1984	
Lyons, Michael	11216	Private	250th Bde RFA	1990	
Maberly, Squire					
McCormack, Leo	22739	Driver ?	RFA	1996	99
McIndoe, Thomas W.	568	Private	12th Middlesex	1975	
Miller, Ralph	11961	Private	1/8th Bn Warwickshire Regt		
Mundy, Hawtin L.	5868	NCO	1st Ox and Bucks	1996	
Payne, Fitz	7256	NCO	Royal Engineers Signals Service	1983	

Name	Record No.	Rank	Regiment	Date of Interview	Age
Phillips, Thomas Howell	9498	Private	Machine Gun Corps 1916-1918	1986	
Pickard, Joseph	8946	Private	1/7th Northumberland Fusiliers	1986	
Powell, Frederick J.	87 Reel 6	Officer	RFC 1915-17 Chief Flying Instructor	1973	
Price, Donald	10168	Private	20th and 30th Royal Fusiliers	1988	97
Raine, Frank	9751	NCO	18th Bn Durham Light Infantry	1987	
Rhodes, Ernie		Ranker	8th Reserve Bn MR and 16th Bn MR		
Rimmer, Ted	22745	Private	South Lancs Regt	1996	
Rogers, Henry	19072	Private	2/7th Sherwood Foresters	1999	95
Shuttleworth	4228	Private	Served as pensions and allowances clerk		
Smathers, William	10769	Private	2nd Bn Kings Liverpool Regt	1989	
Smithers, Herman	22732	Private Sapper	Royal Engineers Signals	1996	
Stagg, Leonard John	8764	Private – nursing orderly	RAMC 2/3rd South Midland Field Ambulance	1985	
Stammers, Alfred Charles	12575	Driver	Army Service Corps	1992	99
Taylor, Raynor	11113	Private	Glamorgan Yeomanry	1990	
Taylor, Sidney	10615	Private	RFA 250 Coy	1989	
Taylor, William George	9430	Officer	2nd Hon. Artillery Company	1986	
Taylor, Harry	6617	NCO	1/6th South Staffs	1983	
Trafford, Richard,	24540	Ranker	1/9th Bn Kings Liverpool Regt		
Wallworth, Wilf	22748	NCO	7th Bn South Lancs	1996	
Wedderburn-Maxwell, John	9146	Officer	RFA 45th 1st and 36th Batteries	1985	
Wells, Harry	22740	Private	17th and 23rd Bn Royal Fusiliers 1918	1996	96
West, Alfred	12236	NCO	Monmouth Regt	1991	
Williams, Edmund	10604	NCO	19th Bn King's Liverpool Regt	1986	
Williamson, J.				1948	

Bibliography

MANUSCRIPTS AND UNPUBLISHED SOURCES

Manuscripts held at The National Archives

CAB 23/5/WC366	Lord Derby Memorandum.
CAB 24/45/g.t.3932	Letter / Cabinet sanction of use of French regulated brothels for army.
CAB 24/162	Royal Commission on Venereal Disease, 1916, Final Report.
HO 45/10510/124433	Paris-based pornographer, Carrington, complaining of business being made impossible.
HO 45/10724/251861/29A	Submission of London Borough of Lambeth for the Criminal Law Amendment Bill 1917.
HO 45/10837/331148/38	Ernley Blackwell, Internal memo, 6 Mar. 1917 Expressing fear that lack of sex leads to homosexuality in army.
HO 45/10930/149778	File relating to evidence for Joint Committee on Indecent advertising.
FO 141/466/2	Cairo Purification Committee report part one, Cairo, 1916.
WO 213	Courts Martial transcripts.
WO 90	General Courts Martial register: name/rank/offence/sentence.
WO 92/3	General Courts Martial register: name/rank/offence/sentence.
WO 92/4	General Courts Martial register: name/rank/offence/sentence.
WO 154/101	Assistant Provost Marshal.
WO 154/112	Assistant Provost Marshal Reports Canadian 2nd Division.

WO 154/114	Assistant Provost Marshal, HQ IGI August 1914-November 1916
WO 154/13	Assistant Provost Marshal Reports, 1st Anzac Corps, Nov. 1917–Oct. 18.
WO 154/33	Assistant Provost Marshal Reports 5th Division, Aug. 1914 – Apr. 1915.
WO 154/6	Assistant Provost Marshal Reports V Corps.
WO 154/72	Assistant Provost Marshal Reports 62nd Division, Jan. 1917–Mar. 1919.
WO 154/73	Assistant Provost Marshal Reports 63rd Division, May 1916–Dec. 1918.
WO 154/77	Assistant Provost Marshal 3rd Australian Division.
WO 154/78	Assistant Provost Marshal.
WO 154/8	Assistant Provost Marshal Reports IX Corps.
WO 162/3	Statistics of the Military Effort of the British Empire 1914–1920.
WO 32/11404	Proceedings of the Imperial War Conference / 1918/ temptations of overseas troops.
WO 32/5115	Annual Report on Infectious Diseases in the British Army in France 1916.
WO 32/5597	File on controversy over Harve brothels, 1918.
WO 339/77793	Courts Martial C Faulkes 2nd Lieutenant, RFA Special Reserve of Officers.
WO 374/ 887	Courts Martial Major H. Alford 3rd Res Btn Cameron Highlanders.
WO 71/659	Courts Martial Pte B. O'Connell, 1SR Btn Irish Guards.
WO 90/6	Courts Martial log.
WO 93/49	Courts Martial Pte J. Graham, 2nd Munster Fusiliers.
WO 95/4042	Town Marshal, Poperinghe, 22 June 1916.
WO 95/4047/4047	Senior medical Officer reports.

Unpublished memoirs held at the Imperial War Museum

IWM 76/153/1	McGregor, P., 'Letters'
IWM P185	Runcie, A 'Territorial Mob', unpubl. Account
IWM P126	Surfleet, A., 'Blue Chevrons', unpubl. Account
IWM P246	Jones, P.H., 'Diary', 1919, unpubl. Account
IWM 06/48/1	Clare, Percy, 'Reminiscences 1914-18'
IWM 77/47/1	Chaney, Bert, 'Journal'

IWM 86/30/1	Cordy, John, My Memories
IWM 04/19/1	Wood, J.W.
IWM 82/3/1	Mudd, 'Letters to wife'
IWM 03/15/1	Proctor, M. Papers
IWM 06/30/1	Holmes, T. H.
IWM 01/51/1	Eachus, S. T., 'Memoirs'
IWM 67/52/1	Butlin, J. H. 'Letters collection'
IWM 74/102/1	Esler, T. 'Memoirs'
IWM 80/40/1	Rowarth, John William, 'Misfit Soldier'
IWM 84/52/1	Stanley, C. S., 'Letters'
IWM 87/51/1	Bowyer, W. H., 'Letters' to girlfriend Dorothy
IWM 87/8/1	Pond, P, 'Old Soldiers Never Die'
IWM 92/36/1	Dixon, R. Graham, 'The Wheels of Darkness'
IWM Con Shelf	Gameson, L., 'Papers'
IWM Con Shelf	MacGregor, A. E., 'Memoirs'
IWM 88/27/1	McKechnie 'Reminiscences'
IWM PP/MCR/48	Cain, C.A.,'The Footsloggers'

Manuscripts held at West Flanders Archive / Provincaale Achief West-Vlaanderen

Richsarchief Brugge Archif de Panne	Un-indexed files contained in main *Eerste Wereldoolog* file; subfiles numbering 1613-1614, 1617, 1620, 1625-1626, 1661, 1666, 1681-1682, 1698.
Poperinghe Town Archives	Un-indexed files.

Unpublished Manuscripts, Belgium

In Flanders Fields Museum, document section	Diary of Achiel Van Walleghem, under Priest of Dikkebus

Unfiled and un-indexed manuscripts held at Centre de Documentation, Musee Royal de l'Armee et D'Histoire Militaire, Brussels

Boxes   2789; 5616; 3679.

Government of South Australia State Library transcripts
http://www.slsa.sa.gov.au/saatwar/collection/transcripts.

Australian War Museum (Internet collection)
AWM L/12/11/2122, Adcock G. I., 'Letters from the Front'.

Manuscripts held at Archives de l'armee de terre, Chateau de Vincennes (ATT)
Series ATT 16; Rapports de la commission de controlle de la correspondence au bureau frontiere W et zone Britannique.

Canadian Expeditionary Force Courts Martial records
B 07/01/1918, Lt R. J. Beck and B 28/11/1918, Lt E. S. Fowles.
Source: microfilm in private possession of Julian Putkowski.

The Women's Library, formerly the Fawcett Library
National Vigilance Association Collection.
Ladies National Association Records (from 1915, the Association for Moral and Social Hygiene. Especially the *Journal of the Association for Moral and Social Hygiene*, 'British Troops in France: provision of Tolerated Brothels', The *Shield*, 3rd series, 1916-1917.

Trench Journals in Cambridge University Library
The Whizz Bang, Territorial 1916, WRC 404
The Gasper, New Army (Universities and Public Schools Brigade) 1917, WRA487
Minden Magazine, Regulars 1915, WRC 489
Trench Echo, Canadian 1915, WRB 494
Dead Horse Corner Gazette, Canadian, WRB 422
The Dump, New Army 1915, WRB 515
The Cinque Ports Gazette, Territorial 1916, WRA 574
The Dagger, Territorial 1918, WRC 415
The Salient, VI Corps 1915, T537

Imperial War Museum: oral archive
See Appendix I for listing of respondents.

PUBLISHED PRIMARY SOURCES

Government publications

Macpherson, Sir W.G., *History of the Great War based on official documents by direction of the Historical Section of the Committee of Imperial Defence. Medical Services: General History* Vol. 2 (Macmillan, 1923).
——, *History of the Great War based on official documents by direction of the Historical Section of the Committee of Imperial Defence. Medical Services: General History* Vol. 3: *Medical Services during the operations on the Western Front in 1916, 1917 and 1918; in Italy; and in Egypt and Palestine* (HMSO, 1924).
Michell, T. J. and Smith, G. M., *History of the Great War based on official documents* (HMSO, 1923).

Report from the Joint Select Committee on Lotteries and Indecent Advertisements (HMSO, 1908).
Statistics of the military effort of the British Empire during the Great War, 1914-1920 (War Office: 1922, repr. Naval & Military, undated).

Newspapers and Periodicals

Journal of the Western Front Association, *Stand to!*
*The Wipers Time*s, including the *New Church Times*, etc., 1914–17.

Official Diaries and Unit Histories

Riddell, Brigadier General E. and Clayton, Colonel M. C., *The Cambridgeshires 1914 to 1919* (Cambridge: Bowes and Bowes, 1934).

Published Memoirs, Diaries, Letters and Reminiscences

Aldington, Richard, *Life for Life's Sake: a book of reminiscences* (London: Cassell, 1941, Penguin repr., 1968).
Adams, Bernard, *Nothing of Importance: a record of eight months at the Front with a Welsh battalion October 1915 to June 1916* (London: Methuen, 1917).
Andrews, William Linton, *Haunting Years: the commentaries of a war territorial* (London: Hutchinson, 1930, Naval & Military repr., 2001).
Arthur, Max, *Forgotten Voices of the Great War: a New History of WWI in the Words of the Men and Women Who Were There* (London: IWM/Ebury, 2002).
Barnes, D. *It made You Think of Home: the haunting journal of Deward Barnes, Canadian Expeditionary Force, 1916-1919,* ed., B. Cane (Toronto: Dundurn Group, 2004).
Becker, J. H., *Silhouettes of the Great War: the memoir of John Harold Becker* (Ontario: CEF Books, 2001).
Behrend, Arthur, *As From Kemmel Hill* (London: Eyre & Sottiswood, 1963).
Bird, Will R., *Ghosts Have Warm Hands: a memoir of the Great War, 1916-1919* (Toronto: Clarke, Irwin, 1968, CEF Books edn, 2000).
Blunden, Edmund, *Undertones of War* (London: R. Cobden-Sanderson, 1928, Penguin edn, 2000).
Bourne, J., 'The British Working Man in Arms', in H. Cecil and P.H. Liddle (eds.), *Facing Armageddon. The First World War Experienced* (London: Leo Cooper, 1996).
Bowman, T., *The Irish Regiments in the First World War. Discipline and Morale* (Manchester: Manchester University Press, 2003).
Brenan Gerald, *A Life of One's Own: childhood and youth* (London: Hamish Hamilton, 1962).
Brittain, Vera, *Chronicle of Youth: Great War Diary 1913-1917*, ed. Alan Bishop with Terry Smart (London: Gollancz, 1981, Phoenix, 2000).

——, *Testament of Youth: an autobiographical study of the years 1900-1925* (London: Gollancz, 1933, Virago, 1982).

Burrage A.M. [writing as Ex-Private X], *War is War* (London: Victor Gollancz, 1930, 2010).

Carrington, Charles, *Soldier from the Wars Returning* (London: Hutchinson, 1965, Arrow Books repr., 1970).

Carstairs, Carroll, *A Generation Missing* (London: W. Heinemann, 1930, Stevenage: Strong Oak repr., 1989).

Casson, Stanley, *Steady Drummer* (London: G. Bell & Sons, 1935).

Cecil, Hugh, *The Flower of Battle: How Britain Wrote the Great War* (Vermont: Steerforth Press, 1996).

Chapman, Guy, *A Passionate Prodigality: fragments of autobiography* (London: I. Nicholson & Watson, 1933, Buchan & Enright repr., 1985).

Childs, Wyndham, Sir, *Episodes and Reflections* (London: Cassell, 1930).

Christie, N. M. (ed.), *Letters of Agar Adamson, 1914 to 1919, Lieutenant Colonel, Princess Patricia's Canadian Light Infantry* (Ontario: CEF Books, 1997).

Clapham, H. S., *Mud and Khaki: the memories of an incomplete soldier* (London: Hutchinson, 1930, Naval & Military repr., 2004).

Cloete, Stuart, *A Victorian Son: an autobiography* (London: Collins, 1972).

Coppard, George, *With a Machine Gun to Cambrai: a story of the First World War* (London: HMSO, 1969, IWM rev. edn, 1999).

Corday, Michel. *The Paris Front: An Unpublished Diary: 1914-1918*, (New York: E.P. Dutton & Co., 1934).

Croney, Percy, *Soldier's luck : memoirs of a soldier of the Great War* (London: Stockwell, 1965).

Crozier, F. P., *A Brass Hat in No Man's Land* (London: Jonathan Cape, 1930, Gliddon Books repr., 1989).

Crutchley, C. E., *Machine Gunner* (Northampton. Published by the Editor on behalf of the Machine Gun Corps Old Comrades' Association. Printed by Mercury Press; Barnsley: Pen & Sword Military Classics rev. edn, 2005).

Cuddeford, D. W. J., *And All For What? Some war time experiences* (London: Heath Cranton, 1933, Naval & Military repr., 2004).

Dinesen, Thomas, *Merry Hell! A Dane with the Canadians* (London: Jarrolds, 1930, Naval & Military repr., undated).

Dolden, A. Stuart, *Cannon Fodder* (Poole: Blandford Press, 1980).

Douie, Charles, *The Weary Road* (London: John Murray, 1929, Naval & Military repr., 2001).

Dowling, W. H., *To the Last Ridge* (London: Grub Street, 2002).

Dunn, Captain J. C., *The War the Infantry Knew 1914-1919* (London: P. S. King, 1938, Abacus repr., 1994).

Eddy, Sherwood, *With Our Soldiers in France* (New York: Association Press, 1917).

Edmonds, Charles, *A Subaltern's War* (London: Peter Davies 1922, Anthony Mott repr., 1986).

Emden, Richard van, *Britain's Last Tommies: Final memories… in their Own Words* (London: Abacus, 2006).
Ewart, Wilfred, *Scots Guard* (London: Rich & Cowan, 1934, Strong Oak repr., 2001).
Eyre, Giles E. M., *Somme Harvest* (London: Jarrolds, 1938, Stamp Exchange repr., 1991).
Fraser, Donald, *The Journal of Private Fraser, 1914-1918*, ed. R. H. Roy (Victoria, B.C: Sono Nis, 1985, CEF Books repr., 1998)
French, Anthony, *Gone for a Soldier* (Kineton: Roundwood Press, 1972).
Gibbons, John, *Roll on Next War* (London: Frederick Muller, 1935).
Gibbs, Hamilton A., *Gun Fodder* (Boston: Little, Brown, *c*.1919. Naval & Military repr.).
Gibbs, Philip, *Now It Can Be Told* (New York: Harper, *c*.1920).
——, *Realities of War* (2 vols, London: W. Heinemann, 1920, repr., 1938).
——, *Soul of War* (London: W. Heinemann, 1915, repr., 1938).
Gladden, N.E., *Ypres 1917* (London: Kimber, 1967).
Gladden, N.E., *Across the Piave* (London: H.M. Stationery Office, 1971).
Graham, Stephen, *A Private in the Guards* (London: Macmillan, 1919, Heinemann edn, 1928).
Graves, Robert, *Goodbye to All That* (London: Jonathan Cape, 1929, Penguin edn, 1960).
Greenwell, Graham H., *An Infant in Arms* (London: Lovat Dickson & Thompson, 1935, Allen Lane, 1972).
Griffith, Wyn, *Up To Mametz* (London: Faber & Faber, 1931, Seven House edn, 1981).
Groom, W. H. A., *Poor Bloody Infantry* (London: Kimber, 1976, Picardy edn, 1976).
Hankey, Donald, *A Student in Arms* (London: Andrew Melrose, 1917).
——, *A Student in Arms (Second Series)* (London: Andrew Melrose, 1917).
Hynes, Samuel, *Flights of Passage: Reflections of a World War II Aviator* (Annapolis MD: Frederick C. Biel Naval Institute Press, 1988).
Hilton, Richard, *Nine Lives* (London: Hollis & Crater, 1955).
Hiscock, Eric, *The Bells of Hell Go Ting-a-ling-a-ling: an autobiographical fragment without maps* (London: Arlington Books, 1976).
Hope, T. S., *The Winding Road Unfolds* (London: Tandem Books, 1965).
Huntly, Gordon, *The Unreturning Army* (London: J. M. Dent & Sons, 1967).
Hutchison, Graham Seton, *Footslogger* (London: Hutchinson, 1933).
Jackson, John, *Private 12768* (Stroud: Tempus, 2004).
Kelly Talbot, R. B., *A Subaltern's Odyssey* (London: Kimber, 1980).
Kipling, Rudyard, *The New Armies in Training* (London: Macmillan, 1915).
Laffin, John, *On The Western Front* (Stroud: Sutton, 1997).
La Grange, Clementine de. *Open House in Flanders 1914-1981*, trans. Melanie Lind. (London: John Murray, 1929).

La Motte, Ellen Newbold, *The Backwash of War: the Human Wreckage of the Battlefield as Witnessed By an American Hospital Nurse* (G P Putnam's Sons, New York, 1916, reprint 2008).
Levine, Joshua, *Forgotten Voices of the Somme* (London: IWM/Ebury, 2008).
Lewis, C.S. *Sagitarius Rising* (London: Peter Davies, 1936)
Lewis, F., *The Colonel's Runner. The Account of 1713 Pte F. Lewis (Royal Warwickshire Regt)*, ed. T. Oates, at http://www.hellfire-corner.demon.co.uk/runner.htm (accessed 19 June 2010).
Lucy, John F. *There's a Devil in the Drum* (London: Faber & Faber, 1938, Naval & Military, 1993).
Marks, T. Penrose, *The Laughter Goes from Life: in the trenches of the First World War* (London: Kimber, 1977).
Masters, John, *Bugles and a Tiger* (London: Michael Joseph 1956).
Mellersh, H. E. L., *Schoolboy into War* (London: Kimber, 1978).
Milne, John, *Footprints of the 14th Leicester Regiment, August 1914 to November 1918* (Leicester: Edgar Backus, 1935).
Montague, C. E., *Disenchantment* (London: Chatto & Windus, 1924).
Moran, Lord (Wilson C.), *The Anatomy of Courage* (London: Constable, 1945).
Nettleton, John, *The Anger of the Guns* (London: Kimber, 1979).
Noakes, F. E. *The Distant Drum, A Memoir of a Guardsman in the Great War* (private printing, 1952. Barnsley: Frontline Books facsimile 2010).
Omissi, D., *Indian Voices of the Great War* (London: Macmillan, 1999).
Orpen, Sir William, *An Onlooker in France 1917-1919* (London: Williams & Norgate, 1921, Dodo repr.).
Osburn, Arthur Carr, *Unwilling Passenger* (London: Faber & Faber, 1932, Second edition 1936).
Penrose Marks, Thomas, *The Laughter goes From Life: in the trenches of the First World War* (London: Kimber, 1977).
Plater, Charles, (ed.) Catholic soldiers by sixty chaplains and many others (London : Longmans & Co., 1919).
Plowman, Max [writing as Mark VII], *A Subaltern on the Somme* (London: J. M. Dent & Sons, 1927, Naval & Military repr., undated).
Priestley, J. B., *Margin Released* (London: Heinemann 1962. repr.,1962).
Read, Herbert, *The Contrary Experience* (London: Secker & Warburg, 1973).
Read, I. L., *Of Those We Loved* (Bishop Auckland: Pentland, 1994).
Rees, R. T., *A Schoolmaster Goes to War* (London: Haycock, 1931).
Richards, Frank, *Old Soldiers Never Die* (London: Faber & Faber, 1933, Berkeley Publishing Corporation, 1966).
Smith, Aubrey [writing as A. Rifleman], *Four Years on the Western Front: Being the Experiences of a Ranker in the London Rifle Brigade* (Oldhams, 1922, Naval & Military repr., undated).
Rule, E. J., *Jacka's Mob* (Sydney: Angus & Robertson, 1933).

Russell, Henry, *Slaves of the War Lords* (London, [1928], Naval & Military repr., undated).
Sassoon, Siegfried, *Memoirs of an Infantry Officer* (London: Faber & Faber 1933, 1965 edition).
——, *Memoirs of a Fox Hunting Man* (London: Faber & Faber 1931, 1999 edition).
——, *Diaries 1920 1922*, Ed. Rupert Hart Davis (London: Faber, 1981).
Shaw, K E., *Jottings from the Front* (London: Allen & Unwin, 1918).
Siepmann, Harry, *Echo of the Guns* (London: Robert Hale, 1987).
Snook, J. F., *Gun Fodder* (London: Allen & Unwin, 1930).
Studdert-Kennedy, G.A., *Rough Talks by A Padre* (London: Hodder & Stoughton).
Taylor, F. A. J., *The Bottom of the Barrel* (London: Regency, 1978).
Tilsley, W. V. *Other Ranks* (London: Cobden Saunderson, undated).
Tiplady, Thomas, *The Cross at the Front: Fragments from the Trenches* (1917), chs. VIII-XIII, http://www.gwpda.org/memoir/cross/crossTC.htm#TC (accessed 19 June 2010).
Tomlinson, H. M., *Waiting for Daylight* (Private Printing, 1922).
Tozer, Bazil. *The Story of a Terrible Life* (London: T Werner Laurie Ltd, 1929).
Tucker, John F., *Johnny Get Your Gun* (London: Kimber, 1978).
Vaughan, Edwin Campion, *Some Desperate Glory* (London: Warne, 1981, New York: Henry Holt, 1988).
Voigt, F. A., *Combed Out* (London: Jonathan Cape, 1929).
Watson, W. H. L., *Adventures of a Motorcycle Despatch Rider* (London: Diggory, 2006).
Wheatley, Dennis, *Officer and Temporary Gentleman* (London: Hutchinson, 1978).
Wheeler, Victor W., *The 50th Battalion in No Man's Land* (Ontario: CEF Books, 2000).

Monographs

Adam-Smith, Patsy, *The Anzacs* (Ringwood Victoria: Penguin, 1978).
Allinson, Sidney, *The Bantams* (London: Howard Baker, 1981).
Arthur, Max, *When this War is Over: Soldiers Songs of the First World War* (London: Piatkus, 2001).
Arthur, George Life of Lord Kitchener (New York: Cosimo, 2000, reprint of 1920).
Ashworth, T., *Trench Warfare 1914-1918. The Live and Let Live System* (London: Macmillan, 1980, 2000).
Audoin-Rouzeau, S., *Men at War 1914-1918: National Sentiment and Trench Journalism in France* (Oxford: Oxford University Press, 1992).
Audoin-Rouzeau, S. and Becker, A., *1914-1918: Understanding the Great War* (London: Profile Books, 2002).
Balhatchet, Kenneth, *Race, Sex and Class under the Raj* (London: Weidenfeld & Nicolson, 1980).
Barret-Ducrocq, Francoise, *Love in the Time of Victoria* (Harmondsworth: Penguin, 1991).

Bartley, Paula, *Prostitution: Prevention and Reform in England, 1860-1914* (London: Routledge, 1999).
Baynes, John, *Morale – A Study of Men and Courage 2nd Scottish Rifles at Neuve Chapelle* (London: Cassell, 1967).
Bean, C., *Official History of the AIF* (Sydney: Angus & Robertson, 1929).
Becket, I. F. W. and Simpson, K. (eds), *A Nation in Arms: a social study of the British army in the First World War* (Manchester: Manchester University Press, 1985).
Beevor, A., *Berlin: the downfall, 1945* (Harmondsworth: Penguin Viking, 2002).
——, *D-Day, The Battle for Normandy* (Harmondsworth: Penguin Viking, 2009).
Bell, P. M. H., *France and Britain: entente and estrangement* (Harlow: Longman, 1996).
Bergen van, Leo, *Before My Helpless Sight Suffering, Dying and Military Medicine on the Western Front, 1914-1918* (trans. Liz Waters from Zach en Eervol, Antwerp/The Hague 1999. English publication Farnham: Ashgate Publishing, 2009).
Berry, Paul and Bostridge Mark, *Vera Brittain 'A life'* (London: Chatto & Windus, 1995).
Bland, Lucy, *Banishing the Beast: Sexuality and the Early Feminists* (Hammond IL.: New Press, 1995).
Blizzard, Dr Leon, *Les Maisons de prositution de Paris pedant la guerre.* (Poitiers: Societé Française d'Imprimerie, 1922).
Bond, B.(ed.), *The First World War and British Military History* (Oxford: Clarendon Press, 1991)
Bourke, Joanna, *Dismembering the Male – Men's Bodies, Britain and the Great War* (Chicago: University of Chicago, 1996, Reaktion Books edn, 1999).
Bourke, Joanna, *Rape: A History from 1860 to the Present* (London: Virago, 2007).
Bourke, Joanna, *An Intimate History of Killing. Face to Face Killing in the Twentieth Century* (Granta, 1999).
Bourne, J. 'The British Working Man in Arms', in H. Cecil and P.H. Liddle (eds.) *Facing Armageddon. The First World War Experienced* (London: Leo Cooper, 1996), pp. 336-52.
Boyack, N., *Behind the Lines: The lives of the New Zealand Soldiers in the First World War* (Wellington, NZ: Allen & Unwin/Port Nicholson, 1989).
Bowman, Timothy, Irish Regiments in the Great War, Discipline and Morale (Manchester: Manchester University Press, 2003).
Bristow, Edward, *Vice and Vigilance: purity movements in Britain since 1700* (Dublin: Gill & Macmillan, 1977).
Brophy, J. and Partridge, E., *Songs and slang of the British soldier: 1914-1918* (London: Eric Partridge at the Scholartis Press, 1930).
Brown, C. G. *The Death of Christian Britain. Understanding Secularisation 1800-2000* (London: Routledge, 2001).
Brown, Malcolm, *Tommy Goes to War* (Stroud: Tempus, 2001 paperback).
Brownmiller, Susan, *Against Our Will* (New York: Simon & Schuster, 1975. Bantam, 1976).

Cains, D. S. The *Army and Religion; an Enquiry into the Religious Life of the nation* (London: Macmillan & Co. 1919).
Cassel, Jay, *The secret plague. Veneral disease in Canada, 1838-1939* (Toronto: University of Toronto, 1987).
Cecil, Hugh & Liddle, Peter, eds, *Facing Amageddon* (London: Leo Cooper, 1996).
Chapman, Guy, *Vain Glory* (London: Cassell, 1968).
Chapman, Paul, *A Haven in Hell* (London: Leo Cooper, 2000, Pen & Sword).
——, *In the Shadow of Hell* (London: Leo Cooper, 2001, Pen & Sword).
Clausewitz, von, Carl, *On War* (Ware: Wordsworth Edition, 1997).
Compton, Piers, *The Colonel's Lady and Camp Follower* (London: Robert Hale, 1970).
Corbin, Alain, *Women for Hire: Prostitution and Sexuality in France after 1850* (Harvard: Harvard University Press, 1990).
Costello, John, *Virtue under Fire: how WW2 changed our sexual attitudes* (Boston: Little, Brown, 1985).
Darrow, Margaret H. *French Women and the First World War: War Stories of the Home Front* (Oxford: Berg 2000).
Das, Santanu (ed.), Race, Empire and First World War Writing (Cambridge: Cambridge University Press, 2011)
Davenport-Hines, Richard, *Sex, Death and Punishment* (London: Fontana,1991).
De Groot, Gerard, *Blighty. British Society in the Era of the Great War* (Harlow: Longman, 1996).
Devon, James, *The Criminal and the Community* (London: John Lane, 1912).
Eksteins, Modris, *Rites of Spring, The Great War and Birth of the Modern Age* (London: Doubleday, 1989).
Ellis, John, *Eye-Deep in Hell* (London: Croom Helm, 1976).
Falls, Cyril, *War Books* (London: Peter Davies, 1930).
Farwell, Byron, *Mr Kipling's Army: all the Queen's Men* (London: W.W. Norton 1991, repr., 1987).
Fellows, Carol, *Love and War: stories of the War Brides from the Great War to Vietnam* (Sydney: Bantam, 2002).
Ferguson, Niall, *The Pity of War* (London: Basic Books, 1999).
Ferris, Paul, *Sex and the British: a Twentieth Century History* (London: Michael Joseph, 1993, Mandarin,1994 edition).
Fischer, H. C. and Dubois Dr. E. X., *Sexual Life During the World War* (London: F. Aldor, 1937, Private printing edition).
Fishbein, M. and Ajzen, I., *Belief, attitude, intention, and behavior: an introduction to theory and research* (London: Addison-Wesley, 1975).
Fisher, Kate, *Birth Control, Sex, and marriage in Britain 1918-1960* (Oxford: Oxford University Press, 2006).
Flexner, Abraham, *Prostitution in Europe*: *The regulation of prostitution in Europe* (New York: American Social Hygiene Association, 1915).
French, David, *Military Identities. The Regimental System, the British Army, and the British people 1870-2000* (Oxford: Oxford University Press, 2005).

Friedenson, Patrick. ed. *The French Home Front, 1914-1918*, trans. Bruce Little (Providence, RI: Berg, 1992).
Foucault, Michel, *The History of Sexuality*, I, *The will to knowledge* (Paris: Gallimard 1976, trans., Vintage Books, 1990).
Fuller, J. G., *Troop Morale and Popular Culture in the British and Dominion Armies 1914-1918* (Oxford: Clarendon Press, 1990).
Fussell, Paul, *The Great War and Modern Memory* (Oxford: Oxford University Press, 1975).
Gammage, Bill, *The Broken Years, Australian Soldiers in the Great War* (Canberra: ANUP, 1974).
Godley, Hugh (ed.), *Manual of Military Law* (London: War Office, sixth edn, 1914).
Grayzel, Susan, *Women's Identities at War: Gender, Motherhood and Politics in Britain and France During the First World War* (Chapel Hill NC: University of North Carolina Press, 1999).
——, *Women and the First World War* (Harlow: Longman, 2002).
Gregory, Adrian, *The Last Great War* (Cambridge: Cambridge University Press, 2008).
Hall, Lesley, *Sex, Gender and Social Change in Britain Since 1880* (Basingstoke: Macmillan, 2000).
——, *Hidden Anxieties: Male Sexuality 1900-1950* (London: Polity Press, 1991).
Harries-Jenkins, Gwyn, *The Army in Victorian Society* (London: Routledge & Kegan Paul, 1977).
Harsin, Jill, *Policing Prostitution in nineteenth-century Paris* (Princeton NJ: {Princeton University Press, 1985).
Harvey, A. D., *A Muse of Fire: Literature, Art and War* (London: Hambledon, 1998).
Herzog, Dagmar (ed.), *Brutality and Desire, War and Sexuality in Europe's Twentieth Century* (Basingstoke: Palgrave, 2009).
Hicks, George, *The Comfort Women. Japan's Brutal Regime of Enforced Prostitution in the Second World War* (New York: W.W. Norton, 1997).
Hirschfeld, Magnus, *Sexual History of the World War* (New York: Panurge, 1934, Falstaff edn, 1937).
Holmes, Richard, *Tommy* (London: HarperCollins, 2004).
Holt, Tonie and Valmai, *My Boy Jack? The search for Kipling's only Son* (London: Leo Cooper, 1998).
Holt, Tonie and Valmai, *Till the Boys Come Home: the Picture Postcards of the First World War* (London: Macdonald & Janes, 1977).
Hubert, M. (ed.), *La Population de la France pedant la Guerre* (Paris and New Haven: Les Presses Universaitaires de France and Yale Press, 1932).
Hudson, Miles, *Soldier, Poet, Rebel. The Extraordinary Life of Charles Hudson VC* (Stroud: Sutton 2008).
Humphries, Steve, *A Secret World of Sex* (London: Sidgwick & Jackson,1988).
Hyam, Ronald, *Empire and Sexuality* (Manchester: Manchester University Press, 1990).

Hyde, H. Montgomery, *The Other Love: an Historical and Contemporary Survey of Homosexuality in Britain* (London: Heinemann, 1972).
Hynes, Samuel, *The Edwardian Turn of Mind* (Princeton: Princeton University Press, 1975).
——, *A War Imagined: The First World War and English Culture* (New York: Atheneum, 1991).
Ivelaw-Chapman, John, *The Riddles of Wipers* (London: Leo Cooper, 1997).
Jackson, Jack, Private 12768: memoir of a Tommy (Stroud: Tempus, 2004)
Keegan, John, *The First World War* (London: Vintage Books, 2000).
Keller, Nora Okja, *Comfort Woman* (Harmondsworth: Penguin, 1998).
Kendrick, Walter, *The Secret Museum: Pornography in Modern Culture* (Harmondsworth: Penguin, 1987).
Kent, David, *From Trench and Troopship: the Experience of the Australian Imperial Force, 1914-1919* (Sydney: Hale & Iremonger, 1999).
Keshen, Jeffrey A., *Saints, Sinners, and Soldiers: Canada's Second World War* (Vancouver: University of British Columbia, 2004).
Kinsey, A., Pomeroy M. and Martin C., *Sexual Behaviour in the Human Male* (Philadelphia: Saunders 1948).
Leed, Eric, *No Man's Land: Combat Identity in WW1* (Cambridge: Cambridge University Press, 1979).
Lengel, Edward G. *World War I Memories: an Annotated Bibliography of Personal Accounts Published in English Since 1919* (London: Scarecrow, 2004).
Levinstein, H., *Seductive Journey* (Chicago: Chicago University Press, 2000).
Liddle, Peter H., *The Soldier's War 1914 – 1918* (Poole: Blandford Press, 1988).
Lilly, J. Robert, *Taken By Force: Rape and American GIs in Europe during World War II* (Basingstoke: Palgrave Macmillan, 2007).
Longden, Sean, *To the Victor, the Spoils: reality behind the heroism* (Gloucester: Arris, 2004).
Lowry, Thomas P., *The Stories the Soldiers Wouldn't Tell* (Mechanicsburg PA: Stackpole Books, 1994).
Macdonald, Lyn, *Somme* (London: Michael Joseph, 1983, repr., 1993).
MacKenzie, S. P., *Politics and Military Morale. Current Affairs and Citizenship Education in the British Army 1914-1950* (Oxford: Oxford Historical Monographs 1992).
Macintyre, Ben, *A Foreign Field* (London: HarperCollins, 2002).
Marcus, Stephen, *The Other Victorians* (London: Corgi, 1971).
Marshall, S.L. *Men Under Fire: The Problem of Battle Command* (Norman OK: University of Oklahoma Press, 2000)
Marwick, Arthur, *The Deluge: British Society and the First World War* (London: The Bodley Head, 1965).
Mason, M, *The Making of Victorian Sexuality* (Oxford: Oxford University Press, 1994).
McCartney, Helen B., *Citizen Soldiers. The Liverpool Territorials in the First World War* (Cambridge: Cambridge University Press, 2005).

McMillan, James F., *Housewife or Harlot: the place of Women in French Society 1870-1940* (New York: St. Martin's Press, 1981).
McMillan, James F., France and Women, 1789-1914 (London: Routledge 2000).
McPhail, Helen, *The Long Silence, Civilian Life Under German Occupation, 1914-1918* (London: I. B. Tauris, 2001).
Messenger, Charles, *Call to Arms: the British Army*, 1914-1918 (London: Cassell, 2005).
Montgomery, Hyde, H., *A History of Pornography* (London: New English Library, 1966).
Moore, William, *See How They Ran* (London: Sphere, 1970).
Moynihan, M. (ed.), *People at War 1914-18* (Newton Abbot: David & Charles, 1973).
Nasson, Bill, *Springboks on the Somme: South Africa and the Great War 1914-1916* (South Africa: Penguin, 2007).
Nicolson, Juliet, *The Perfect Summer* (London: John Murray, 2000).
——, *The Great Silence 1918-1920: Living in the Shadow of the Great War* (London: John Murray, 2009).
Paritt, George, *Fiction of the First World War* (London: Faber & Faber. 1988).
Parker, Peter, *Ackerley. The Life of J. R. Ackerley* (New York: Farrar, Straus, Giroux, 1989).
——, *The Old Lie: The Great War and the Public School Ethos* (London: Constable, 1987).
Pearsall, Ronald, *The Worm in the Bud* (London: Pelican, 1971).
Perry, F.W. *The Commonwealth Armies, Manpower, and Organisation in two World Wars* (Manchester : Manchester University Press 1988).
Plummer K. (ed.), *The Makings of the Modern Homosexual* (London: Hutchinson, 1981).
Porter, Roy and Hall, Leslie, *The Facts of Life: the creation of sexual knowledge in Britain 1650-1950* (London: Yale University Press, 1995).
Putkowski, Julian and Sykes, Julian, *Shot at Dawn* (Barnsley: Wharncliffe Publishing, 1989, Leo Cooper, 1999).
Reader, W. J., *At Duty's Call: a study in obsolete patriotism* (Manchester: Manchester University Press, 1988).
Rearick, Charles, *The French in Love and War: Popular Culture in the Era of the Two World Wars* (London: Yale University Press, 1997).
Robb, George, *British Culture and the First World War* (New York: Palgrave, 2002).
Rosenman, Ellen Bayuk, *Unauthorised Pleasures Accounts of Victorian Erotic experience* (Cornell: Cornell University Press, 2003).
Rousseau, F., *La Guerre Censurée: une Histoire des combatants Européens de 14-18* (Paris: Editions du Seuil, 1999).
Sheffield, G.D., *Leadership in the Trenches – Officer-Man Relations, Morale and Discipline in the British Army in the Era of the Great War* (Basingstoke: Macmillan 2000).
Sigel, Lisa Z von, *Governing Pleasures Pornography and Social Change in England 1815-1914* (New Jersey: Rutgers University Press, 2002).
Simkins, Peter, *Kitchener's Army: the Raising of the New Armies, 1914-1918* (Manchester: Manchester University Press, 1988, Pen & Sword repr., 2007).

Snape, M, *God and the British Soldier. Religion and the British Army in the First and Second World Wars* (London: Routledge, 2005).
Snyder, David R., *Sex crimes under the Wehrmacht* (Lincoln NE: University of Nebraska Press 2007).
Spiers, E.M., *The Army and Society*, 1815-1914 (London: Longman, 1980).
Stanley, Peter, *Bad Characters: Sex, Crime, Mutiny and Murder in the Great War* (Sydney: Pier 9, 2010).
Theabald, Francoise. *La Femmme au temps de la Guerre de 1914* (Paris: Editions Stock, 1986).
Thompson, Paul, *The Edwardians: The Remaking of British Society* (London: Paladin Press, 1979).
Tolerton, Jane, *The Life of Ettie Rout* (Auckland, NZ: Penguin, 1992).
Tombs, Robert and Isabelle, *That Sweet Enemy: the History of a Love-Hate Relationship* (London: Random House, 2009).
Toynbee, A. J., *The German Terror in Belgium* (London: Hodder & Stoughton, 1917).
Trustram, Myrna, *Women of the Regiment* (Cambridge: Cambridge University Press, 1984).
Turner, E.S., *Dear Old Blighty* (London: Michael Joseph, 1980).
Venning, Annabel, *Following the Drum: The Lives of Army Wives and Daughters* (London: Headline, 2005).
Walkowitz, Judith R., *Prostitution and Victorian Society* (Cambridge: Cambridge University Press, 1983).
——, *City of Dreadful Delight* (London: Virago, 1994).
Watson, Alexander. *Enduring the Great War. Combat, Morale and Collapse in the German and British Armies, 1914-1918* (Cambridge: Cambridge University Press: 2008).
Watson, Janet, *Fighting Different Wars: Experience, Memory, and the First World War in Britain* (Cambridge: Cambridge University Press, 2007).
Weeks, Jeffrey, *Sex, Politics, and Society: The Regulation of Sexuality Since 1800* (London: Longman, 1990).
——, *Coming Out: homosexual politics in Britain, from the nineteenth century to present* (London: Quartet 1977).
Weerdt, Denise De, *De vrouwen van de Eerste Wereldoorlog* (Gent, 1993).
Westlake, Ray, *Kitchener's Army* (Staplehurst: Spellmount, 1989).
Wilson, J. M., *Siegfried Sassoon. The Making of a War Poet. A Biography 1886-1918* (London: Duckworth, 1998).
Winter, Denis, *Death's Men: soldiers of the Great War* (London: Allen Lane 1978, Penguin, 1979).
Winter, J. M., *The Great War and the British People* (Harvard: Harvard University Press, 1986).
Young, R. J., *Under Siege: Portraits of Civilian Life in France during WW1* (New York: Berghahn Books, 2000).
Zeigler, Philip, *King Edward VIII: the official biography* (London: Collins, 1990).

Zeldin, T., *France 1848-1945: Ambition, Love and Politics* (Oxford: Clarendon Press, 1973).
Yoshimi, Yoshiaki, *'Comfort Women. Sexual Slavery in the Japanese Military During World War II'*, Asia Perspectives (New York: Columbia University Press, 2000).

Articles and book chapters

Beardsley, Edward, 'Allied Against Sin: American and British Responses to Venereal Disease in World War I', *Medical History* 20 (1976), pp. 189-202.
Buckley, Suzanne, 'The failure to resolve VD amongst Troops in Britain during WW1', in Bond, Brian and Roy, Ian (eds), *War and Society Year Book of Military History* 2 (Croom Helm, 1977).
Cecil, Hugh, 'British War Novelists' in Cecil, H and Liddle, Peter (eds), *Facing Armageddon. The Forts World War Experienced* (London: Leo Cooper 1996).
Cohler, Deborah, 'Sapphism and sedition: producing female homosexuality in Great War Britain', *Journal of the History of Sexuality* 16(1):69-94 (2007).
Das, Santanu, 'Intimacy, Gender and gesture in First World War Trench literature'. *Modernism/Modernity* 9 (2002), pp. 51-74.
Dean, Carolyn J., 'The Great War, Pornography the Transformation of Modern Male Subjectivity', *Modernism/Modernity* 3 (1996) pp. 59-72.
Denhooven, D., 'Living Apart together; Belgium civilians and non-white troops and workers in war time Flanders', in Das, Santanu (ed.*)*, *Race, Empire and First World War Writing* (Cambridge: Cambridge University Press, 2011).
Englander, David, 'The French Soldier, 1914-1918', *French History* 1 (1987), pp. 49-67.
Englander, David, 'Discipline and Morale in the British Army, 1917-1918' in Horne, J. (ed.) *State, Society and Mobilisation in Europe during the First World War*, Cambridge, Cambridge University Press 1997.
Fogarty, Richard S. 'Race, Sex, Fear and Loathing in France during the War' in in Herzog (ed.), *Brutality and Desire, War and Sexuality in Europe's Twentieth Century* (Basingstoke: Palgrave, 2009), pp. 75-78.
Gibson, C., 'My Chief Source of Worry: an Assistant Provost Marshal's View of Relations between 2nd Canadian Division and Local Inhabitants on the Western Front, 1915-1917', *War in History* 7 (2000), pp. 413-41.
——, 'The British Army, French Farmers and the war on the Western Front, 1914-1918', *Past & Present* 180 (2003), pp. 175-239.
——, 'Through French Eyes: the BEF and the records of the French postal censor', *History Workshop Journal* 55 Spring 2003, pp. 177-88.
——, 'Sex and Soldiering in France and Flanders: The British Expeditionary Force along the Western Front, 1914-1919', *International History Review* 23 (2001), pp. 535-79.
Gilbert, A. N., 'Buggery in the British Navy 1700-1861', *Journal of Social History* 10 (1976), pp. 72-98.

Gilfoyle, Thomas, 'Prostitutes in History: From Parables to Metaphors of Modernity', *American Historical Review* 104 (1999), pp. 117-41.
Grayzel, Susan, 'The Mothers of our Soldiers' Children: Motherhood, Immorality and the Baby Scandal 1914 – 1918', in Nelson and Holmes (eds), *Maternal Instincts, Motherhood and Sexuality in Britain* (New York MacMillan, 1997).
Grayzel, Susan, 'Mothers, Marraines, and Prostitutes: Morale and Morality in the First World War in France', *International History Review* 19 (1997), pp. 66-82.
Greenhut, Jeffery, 'Race, Sex and War: The impact of Race and Sex on Morale and health Services for the Indian Corps on the Western Front 1916', *Military Affairs* 45, 2 (1981), pp. 71-4.
Hall, Lesley, 'Forbidden by God, Despised by Men: Masturbation, Medical Warnings, Moral Panic, and Manhood in Great Britain, 1850–1950', *Journal of the History of Sexuality* 2 (1992), pp. 365-87.
Harris, Ruth, 'Child of the Barbarian', *Past & Present* 141 (1993), pp. 170-206.
Harrison, M., 'The British Army and the problems of Venereal Disease in France and Egypt during the First World War', *Medical History* 39 (1995), pp. 133-158.
Harvey, A. D., 'Homosexuality and the British Army During the First World War'. *Journal of the Society of Army Historical Research* 79 (2001), pp. 313-19.
Horn, M., 'More than Cigarettes, Sex and Chocolate: the Canadian Army in the Netherlands 1944-45', *Journal of Canadian Studies* 16 (1981), pp. 156-73.
Horne, J. and Kramer J., 'German "atrocities" and Franco-German Opinion, 1914: the Evidence of German Soldiers' Diaries', *Journal of Modern History* 66 (1994), pp. 1-33.
Howe, D. Glenford, 'Military Civilian Intercourse, Prostitution and Venereal Disease amongst Black Soldiers in the Great War', *Journal of Caribbean History* 31 (1997), pp. 88-102.
Land, Inoye P. and Hogan D., 'Venereal Disease and the CEF of the First World War', *Annals Royal College of Physicians and Surgeons of Canada* 31 (1998), pp. 401-5.
Levine, Philippa, 'Walking the Streets in a Way No Decent Woman should: Women Police in World War One', *Journal of Modern History* 66 (1994), pp. 34-78.
——, 'Battle Colors: Race, Sex and Colonial Soldiery in World War I', *Journal of Women's History* 8 (1998), pp. 104-30.
Makepeace, C, 'Punters and Their Prostitutes: British Soldiers, Masculinity and Maisons Tolerees in the First World War' in John H. Arnold and Sean Brady (eds) What is Mascuilinity? *Historical Dynamics from Antiquity to the Contemporary World* (Palgrave Macmillan, 2011), pp.413-30.
McKenzie, S.P., Morale and the Cause: The Campaign to Shape the Outlook of Soldiers of the British Expeditionary Force, 1914-1918', *Canadian Journal of History* XXV (1990), pp. 215-32.
O'Connor, P. S., 'Venus and the Lonely Kiwi: the War Effort of Miss Ettie A. Rout', *New Zealand Journal of History* I (1967), pp. 1-32.

Peers, Douglas, 'Privates off Parade: Regimenting Sexuality in the Nineteenth-Century Indian Empire', *International History Review* 20 (1998), pp. 823–55.

Pryke, Sam, 'The popularity of nationalism in the early British Boy Scout movement', *Social History*, 23 (1998) pp. 309-24.

Payne, E., 'The Weather, the Seasons, and the Loss of Sexual Innocence in the Great War', *Stand To!* 72 (2005), pp. 32-4.

Razzell, P. E., 'Social Origins of Officers in the Indian and British Home Army, 1758-1962', *British Journal of Sociology* 14 (1963), pp. 248-60

Rhoades, Michelle K., '"There Are No Safe Women": Prostitution in France during the Great War', *Proceedings of the Western Society for French History* 27 (1999), pp. 45-50.

———, 'Renegotiating French Masculinity: Medicine and Venereal Disease in the Great War'. *French Historical Studies* 29 (2006), pp. 293-327.

Roy, Kaushik, 'Discipline and Morale of thr African, British and Indian Army units in Burma and India during World War II: July 1943 to August 1945', *Modern Asian Studies* 44 (2010) pp.1255-1282

Sheffield, G.D, 'Officer-Man Relations, Discipline and Morale in the British Army of the Great War' in Cecile H. and Liddle (eds.), *Facing Armageddon: the First World War Experienced* London Leo Cooper 1996

Sigel, Lisa von Z., 'Filth in the Wrong People's Hands: Postcards and the Expansion of Pornography in Britain and the Atlantic World, 1880-1914', *Journal of Social History* 33 (2000), pp. 859-85.

Simpson, D., Morale and sexual morality amongst the British Troops in the First World War, in Douglas Mackaman & Michael Mays (ed.), *World War One and the Cultures of Modernity* (Jackson: University of Mississippi 2000).

Silberbauer, H. L., 'Reminiscences of the First World War', *South African Military History Journal*, 10 (1997), pp. 167-74.

Snyder, Cindy S., Gabbard, May and Zulcic 'On the Battleground of Women's Bodies: Mass Rape in Bosnia-Herzegovina', *Affilia (*2006); 21; 184.

Springhall, J. O., 'The Boy Scouts, Class and Militarism in relation to British youth movements, 1908-1930', *International Review of Social History*, 16 (1971), pp. 125-58.

Strachan, Hew., 'Training, Morale, and Modern War', *Journal of Contemporary History*, 41 (April 2006),

Swanson, Chris and Smith, James, *Soldiers in East Grinstead*, at http://www.spartacus.schoolnet.co.uk/FWWcamps.EG.htm (accessed 18 June 2010).

Tosh, John, 'What Should Historians do with Masculinity? Reflections on Nineteenth-century Britain' *History Workshop Journal* (1994) 38(1): pp. 179-202.

Towers, Bridget A., 'Health Education Policy, 1916-1926: Venereal Disease and the Prophylaxis Dilemma', *Medical History* 24 (1980), pp. 70-87.

Vickers, Emma, 'The Good Fellow: Negotiation, Rememberance and Recollection – Homosexuality in the British Armed Forces, 1939-1945, in Herzog, Dagmar,

Brutality and Desire, War and Sexuality in Europe's Twentieth Century (Basingstoke: Palgrave McMillan, 2009).

Watson, Alexander and Porter, Patrick, 'Bereaved and aggrieved: combat motivation and the ideology of sacrifice in the First World War', *Historical Research*, 83 (February 2010), pp. 146–64.

Watson, Janet S. K., 'Khaki Girls, VADs, and Tommy's Sisters: Gender and Class in First World War Britain', *International History Review* 19 (1997), pp. 32-51.

Weeks, Jeffrey, 'Inverts, Perverts, and Mary-Annes: Male Prostitution and the Regulation of Homosexuality in England in the Nineteenth and Early Twentieth Centuries', *Journal of Homosexuality* 6 (1980), pp. 113-34.

Wessely, Simon, 'Twentieth-century theories on combat motivation and breakdown', *Journal of Contemporary History*, 41 (April 2006).

White, R., 'The Soldier as Tourist: the Australian experience of the Great War', *War and Society* 5 (1987), pp. 63-78.

Woollacott, Angela, 'Khaki Fever and its control: Gender, Class, Age and Sexual Morality on the British Home Front in the First World War', *Journal of Contemporary History* 29 (1994), pp. 325-47.

Novels and Plays from Experience

Ackerley, J. R., *Prisoners of War* (London: Chatto & Windus,1925).
Aldington, Richard, *Death of a Hero* (London: Chatto & Windus,1929).
Baker, Richard, *Medal Without Bar* (London: Hodder & Stoughton,1930).
Barbussse, Henri, *Under Fire* (Harmondsworth: Penguin, 2003).
Bennett, Arnold, *The Pretty Lady* (London: Cassell and Co. 1918).
Cloete, Stuart, *How Young they Died* (London: Collins, 1969, The Book Society edition, 1969).
Cloete, Stuart, *Rags of Glory* (Garden City, N. Y. : Doubleday,1963).
Ewart, Wilfred, *Way of Revelation* (New York: G. P. Putnam's, 1922).
Forester, C. S., *The General* (London: Michael Joseph, 1936, repr., 1965).
Graves, Robert *Goodbye To All That* (London: Jonathan Cape, 1929. Penguin Books, 1960).
Hanley, James, *The German Prisoner* (NYC: Exile Books, repr., 1923).
Harrison, Charles Yale, *Generals Die in Bed* (London: William Morrow, 1930, repr. Annick 2002).
Henel, Otto, *Eros im Stacheldraht* [Love on Barbed Wire] (Leipzig: Freidenker Verlag, 1926).
Hodson, James Lansdale, *Grey Dawn–Red Night* (London: Victor Gollancz, 1929).
Jones, David, *In Parenthesis* (London: Faber & Faber, 1963).
Junger, Ernst, *Storm of Steel* (New York: Zimmerman & Zimmerman, 1985).
Keable, Robert, *Simon Called Peter* (London: Constable 1924).
Manning, Frederick, *Her Privates We*: *the Middle Parts of Fortune* (Piazza, issued to subscribers by Peter Davies, 1929, Penguin edn, 2005).

Mottram, R. H., *The Spanish Farm Trilogy* (London: Chatto & Windus 1928, repr., 1930).
Mottram, R. H. *Through the Menin Gate* (London: Chatto & Windus, 1932).
Rathbone, Iris, *We That Were Young* (London: Chatto & Windus, 1930, Virago,1988).
Remarque, Erich Maria, *All Quiet on the Western Front* (London: Mayflower, 1969).
Saint-Mandé, Wilfred (John Henry Parkyn Lamont), *War, Wine and Women* (London: Cassell, 1931, repr., 2003).
Sherriff, R. C., *Journey's End* (London: Victor Gollancz, 1929).
Smith, Helena Zena (Edvane Price), *Not So Quiet: Stepdaughters of War* (London: Albert E. Marriott, 1930, NY: Feminist Press edn.).
Tozer, Basil, *The Story of a Terrible Life* (London: T. Werner Laurie, 1928).
Williamson, Henry, *The Patriot's Progress* (London: Geoffrey Bles, 1930, Sphere reprint).

Theses

Gibson, K. C., Relations between the British Army and the Civilian population on the Western Front 1914-1918 (Leeds University PhD Thesis, 1999).

Index

INDEX OF GENERAL & MISCELLANEOUS ENTRIES

Alliance of Honour Society 89
Army Act 45, 259-260, 270, 285
Autoeroticism 256
AWOL xv, 63, 220, 230, 269

Bigamy 89, 259, 261, 270
Blue Lamps vii-viii, 45, 179, 188-192, 241
Boer War 52, 81, 275
Brothels viii, 17-18, 24-25, 31, 37, 41, 46-47, 52-59, 61-62, 66, 70, 75, 77, 79, 84, 88-89, 93, 96, 102, 104, 106, 116-117, 120, 133, 137, 142, 156, 179, 181, 183-187, 189-190, 192-195, 197-202, 206, 209, 212-214, 216, 224, 227, 232, 242, 251, 262, 267-270, 279, 287-288, 295, 299-300, 302, *see also* Estaminets

Catholicism 92, 100, 104, 106, 135, 144, 204, 226, 231, 241, 264, 306
Commonwealth War Grave Commission, The 160
Conseil National des Femmes Françaises 158
Contagious Diseases Act 39, 54-55
Criminal Law Amendment Act 273

Defence of the Realm Act xv, 40, 51, 206
District Court Martial 265

Estaminets 26, 109, 116, 137, 140, 154, 162, 166, 169, 174, 197, 212-216, 227, 251, 257, *see also* Brothels

Executive Committee of the National Relief Fund 95

Field Punishment 227, 265
Flagellation 193, 232

General Court Martial 265, 281

Haldane reforms 93
Home Front 24, 27-28, 51, 54-55, 74, 90, 95-96, 110, 206, 263, 272, 289, 292, 309-310, 317
Home Office 46, 275
Homosexuality 24, 27, 31, 46, 93, 232, 260, 271-279, 282, 284, 288, 295, 299, 311, 314-317

Indecency 236, 264, 275, 284
Indecent Advertisements Act 235
Inter-Allied Conference 39, 44-45, 56, 69, 75, 237, 250-251

Joint Select Committee 233-235, 303

Labouchere Amendment 273
Ladies' Association against the Contagious Diseases Act 55

Maison des Aliénés 61
Maisons de Tolérance 56, 178-179, 181, 185, 189, 197, 200, 220
Masturbation v, 24, 31, 89, 93, 109, 231, 250, 255-257, 277, 315

319

Mutascopes 89, 232

National Council for Public Morals 233
National Vigilance Association xv, 235, 302
National Vigilance Society 93, 233
Newspapers and journals:
  Daily Mail 68
  Daily Sketch 241
  Dead Horse Corner Gazette 139, 302
  English Review 272
  Kemmel Times 241
  La Vie Parisienne vi-vii, 98, 129, 241-242, 244
  New Church Times 139, 241, 303
  News of the World 270
  The Shield (Journal of the Association for Moral and Social Hygiene) 53, 189, 197, 302
  The Times xiii, 31, 72, 230, 266, 270
  Times Literary Supplement 31
  Wipers Times 139, 241, 244, 246, 249, 303
Newsagents Federation 234

Obscene Publications Act 30, 235

Pornography v, 21, 25, 31, 36-37, 88-89, 93, 95, 97, 117, 231-232, 234, 236-237, 240, 249, 257-259, 274, 286, 288, 295, 311-312, 314, 316
Postcard Traders Association 234
Prostitution v, vii, 17, 21, 24-25, 40-41, 43-47, 50-55, 59-63, 66, 69, 77-79, 82, 88-89, 93, 95-97, 102, 104, 108, 110, 116-117, 124, 126-128, 135-136, 138, 142, 150, 154, 158, 164-166, 169, 174, 177-181, 188-189, 193, 199-200, 202, 204-207, 209-212, 215-216, 219, 221, 223, 225, 228, 230, 232, 235, 240, 249, 256, 261-263, 267-271, 274-275, 285, 287-288, 292, 308-310, 313, 315-317

Public women 61, 62, 133, 204
Purity League 102

Red lamp areas viii, 25, 40, 224
Royal Committee on Venereal Disease 40

Salvation Army 88, 101
Samaritans 75
Secretary of State for War 57-58
Sodomy v, 45, 259, 261, 264, 271, 273-275
Stage and television plays/programmes:
  Blackadder 28
  Journey's End 28, 103, 250, 255, 318
  Oh, What a Lovely War 26, 240, 268, 274, 281
  The Monocled Mutineer 27
Stereoscopes 232

Tableaux Vivants 232

Trinity College 91

University College Dublin 91

Venereal Disease vi, viii, xvi, 17, 21, 23-25, 28-30, 39-40, 42-43, 46-47, 51-52, 54-56, 58-63, 67-70, 72-80, 83, 92, 96, 101, 107-109, 120-121, 123, 150, 178-179, 184, 187, 192, 197-199, 206-207, 210, 212, 215-216, 218, 220-222, 224, 226, 234, 250-251, 256-257, 259, 263, 267, 269, 276, 286, 288-289, 295, 299, 314-316

War Cabinet 40, 57
War Office 46, 49, 54, 56, 69, 72-73, 303, 310
White Cross Society 89

YMCA xvi, 52, 100-102, 114-116, 121

INDEX OF PEOPLE

Ackerley, J.R. 275, 279
Adcock, Major-General I. G. 160
Alban, Private 53, 187, 296
Anderson, Andrew 160
Andrews, W.L. 132, 138, 146, 225, 240
Armstrong, Sir Thomas 92, 296
Ashton, Dolly 233
Ashurst, Sergeant George 101, 164, 186, 195, 201, 296

Baert, Albert 150
Barnes, Deward 29, 36
Baxter, Arthur 108, 296
Behrend, Subaltern Arthur 139, 168
Bigwood, Private Edwin 228, 283
Bird, Robert Cecil 84, 143,
Bird, Will R. 155, 165, 171, 195, 270
Blackwell, Sir Ernley 46
Blizzard, Dr Leon 199, 212
Blunt, Private Harry 95, 296
Boon, John Henry 120, 273, 284, 296
Boyd, Captain A.C. 280
Bretton, Private Harry 226, 296
Brittain, Vera 138, 240, 265, 279
Bromley, Tom 121, 187, 195, 201, 296
Brown, Private T.H. 120, 296
Burrage, A.M. 31, 113, 145, 148, 152, 155, 177, 185, 188, 230, 267-268, 304
Butler, Josephine 39, 55
Butlin, Lieutenant J.H. 29, 72, 127, 239

Campbell, Lord 235
Carpenter, Edward 271, 277
Carrington, Charles 31-32, 40, 50, 53, 82, 88, 90, 104, 113, 115, 132, 135, 137, 181
Casey, Edward 29
Chaney, Bob (Bert) 184, 188, 200
Childs, Major-General Sir Wyndham 69, 275, 282
Chinoy, Dhunjibhoy 226
Clare, Private Percy 32, 126, 136, 138, 147, 149, 155, 158, 166, 189, 193, 207, 209, 214, 225, 227

von Clausewitz, Carl 34
Cole, Private James 136, 296
Colpitts, Captain Watson 222
Coppard, George 72, 113, 186, 189, 227-228
Cordy, John 117
Crozier, F.P. 23, 32, 43, 73-74, 85, 99, 109, 140, 142-143, 161-162, 168, 172, 223, 249

Davis, Private Gordon 121, 296
Davis, Private Jim 190, 296
Derby, Lord 53, 57-58, 78
Dinesen, Thomas 20, 107, 112, 268
Dixon, R. Graham 21, 106, 149-150, 165, 192, 225
Downing, W.H. 128
Dufferin, Lord 41
Dulom, François 116
Dyer, Alfred 235

Edwards, Norman 165, 296
Elgin, Viceroy 46
Ellis, Havelock 256, 272

Farrer, Private Basil 275, 296
Ferens MP, T.R. 57
Flexner, Abraham 51, 82
Foch, Field Marshal 34
Forbes, Lady Angela 140
French, Sir John 270, 279

Gain, Charles 266
Gee, Charles 221
Gibbons, John 41, 54, 66, 72-73, 75, 111, 135, 145, 155, 158, 228, 305
Gibbs, A. H. 241
Gibbs, Philip 85, 108, 114, 124, 126, 135-136, 152, 154, 172-173, 183, 193, 219, 221, 241, 291
Goodman, Private 92, 297
Gordon, Rev. G. 264
Graham, Guardsman Stephen 42, 45, 104, 111-112, 123

Graves, Robert 18, 23, 104, 149, 152, 155, 172, 190, 192, 200-202, 250, 252, 278
Greenwell, Lieutenant 49
Groom, W.A. 137
Gurney, Ivor 279

Haig, Sir Douglas 47, 57-58, 112, 151, 206, 219
Hankey, Donald 102, 120-121
Heath, Private P. G. 223
Henman, Private Clarrie 250
Henry, Sir Edward 69
Herschfeld, Magnus 27, 80, 177
Hill, Private P. 65, 121
Hill, Private W. 32, 184, 201, 297
Hilton, R. 29
Holbrook, Private William 276, 297
Holmes, Private William 151, 214
Hope, T.S. 25, 105, 145, 165, 183-184, 188, 209, 214, 219, 223, 248-249, 251
Hughes, Thomas 89
Hutchison, Graham Seton 266, 279

Isherwood, Christopher 279

Jackson, John 146
Jarman, Private Clarence Walter 210
Jarvis, Lieutenant-Colonel 213, 215
Jones, P.H. 165

Kahn, Rissaldar Farz Ali 160
Keele, Tommy 252, 255, 282, 297
Kelly, Talbot 23, 240
Kipling, Rudyard 34, 39, 108
Kirchner, Raphael 190, 238, 240-241, 244-246, 248
Kitchener, Herbert Lord 63, 72, 81-82, 86, 90-91, 93-94, 97, 108, 111, 131, 168, 173, 226, 230, 237, 260, 270, 280

La Motte, Ellen 21, 289
Laffey, John 184
Lane, Clifford 25, 120, 297
Lawrence, D.H. 237
Lawrence, T. E. 279

Lawson, Driver R.H. 115, 164, 169, 185-186, 188, 201-202, 207, 270, 297
Lewis, Private F. 26, 183, 215
Lovegrove, Private James 65, 297
Lucy, John 150, 238, 265, 267-268

MacPherson, Sir W.G. 77
Maestan, Dr 287
Manning, Frederick 21, 112, 159, 257
Mariner VC, Bob 19, 133, 162, 222
Marsden, Ronald 132
Marsden, Lieutenant Wilfred, 279, 281
Massey, W.F. 50
McCormack, Gunner Leo 31, 202, 297
McGregor, Private Peter 65
McIndoe, Thomas Walter 72, 287
McKendrick Hughes, John 151
McKenna, Home Secretary 233
McKenzie, Sir Thomas 50
McMillan, James 141, 143
Mistry, H R 226
Money, R.C. 83
Moore, Dr W. J. 44, 51
Moran, Lord 35, 90, 115
Morgan, Lieutenant William, xiv, 139, 188-191
Mottram, R. H. 161, 166

Novello, Ivor 279

Orpen, Sir William 105, 134, 136, 166
Osburn, Arthur 19, 284, 306
Owen, Wilfred 279

Plowman, Max 213
Priestley, J. B. 90
Purcel, Victor 274
Pym, Reverend T.M. 264

Rawlinson, General 51
Read, Herbert, 279
Read, I.L. 37, 110, 115, 122, 155, 163, 219, 228, 248, 288
Remarque, Erich Maria 248, 277
Reynolds, Captain Jack 160
Richards, Frank 18-19, 36-37, 81, 85, 127-128, 152, 159, 230, 267

Riddell, Sir George 78
Rogers, Private Henry 107, 298
Rout, Ettie 23
Rowarth, John William 29, 174, 184-186, 199, 228, 301
Russell, Henry 138, 219, 250, 253, 288

Sandwich, Major 268
Sassoon, Siegfried 30, 279
Saul, Jack 274
Scott, Sir George 82
Shaw, Chaplin K.E. 78, 111, 142, 147, 250
Sherriff, R.C. 103, 250, 255
Shuttleworth, Private 114, 298
Siepmann, Harry 112, 148, 151, 227
Silberbauer, H.L. 66, 316
Smathers, Private William 96, 298
Smith, Aubrey ('A Rifleman'), 37, 135, 139, 148
Smith, Helen Zena 162
Speckman, Major Carl 264
Spencer, Captain Harold 272
Stagg, Leonard 21, 77, 120, 211, 220, 298
Staniforth, J. 91
Stanley, Colin C. 108
Stead, W.T. 277
Studdert-Kennedy, G. 249, 263
Sydenham, Lord 40

Symonds, J. A. 274

Taylor, F.A.J. 'Tanky' 120, 269, 282-283
Taylor, Harry 54, 73, 298
Taylor, Raynor 95, 298,
Taylor, Sidney 99, 114, 121, 298
Tilsley, Private W.V. 112-113, 239, 249, 251
Tiplady, Chaplain Thomas 26-27
Tomlinson, H.M. 242
Tucker, Private John 110, 149-150, 158

Van Walleghem, Father Achiel 144, 151, 216
Vaughan, Edwin 140, 165, 242, 250

Waite, Major H. 53
Wallworth, Wilf 187
Ward, Joseph 50, 75
Wedderburn-Maxwell, J. 207, 298
Wells, Private Harry 45, 96, 298
West, Alfred 21, 220, 298
Wheatley, Denis 72, 102, 109, 192-193
Wheeler, Victor W. 104, 141, 170
White, Arnold 272
Wickins, Lance-Sergeant 269
Wilde, Oscar 46, 88, 272-273, 277-278
Williams, Edmund 77, 242, 269, 298
Williamson, H. 27, 137, 227,
Williamson, J. 108, 298

INDEX OF PLACES

Abbeville 140, 162, 165, 195, 222, 281
Aldershot 108
Amiens viii, 31, 53, 63, 73, 107, 128, 132-133, 140, 152, 172, 192-193, 195-196, 200, 216, 221-222
Armentières 112, 135, 161, 195, 222, 253, 279
Arras 136, 146, 153, 169, 193, 221, 251-252, 262, 280
Artois 219, 221
Australia 23, 109, 117, 160, 267, 301

Bailleul 137, 204, 241
Bapaume 269

Béthune 29, 31, 117, 137, 143, 153, 165, 186, 195, 268
Bombay 44, 226
Boulogne viii, 132, 140, 153-154, 159, 162-164, 193, 195-196, 210, 222, 267, 269
Bouzincourt 267
Bromley 120, 122, 156, 187, 195, 201, 296
Brussels 37, 301
Busseboom 170

Caestre 213
Cairo 37, 99, 109-110, 268-269, 299

Calais vii-viii, 155, 180, 188, 193, 195-196, 222, 248, 269
Canada 24, 28, 89, 109, 117, 309, 311, 315
Cayeux sur Mer viii, 40, 46, 53, 56, 102, 195, 197-199, 201
Chicago 24, 31, 56, 308, 311

Dickebusch 216
Doullens 195, 221
Dranoutré 213
Dunkerque 152, 192, 195

Egypt 23, 52, 55, 75, 85, 102, 109, 111, 267-269, 302, 315
Étaples 140, 151, 186, 195
Eton 277

Festubert 138
Fienvillers Chateau 121, 273, 296
Flanders ix, xiv, 27-28, 59-62, 68-69, 91, 138-139, 141, 143-145, 151-152, 154, 168, 204, 206-207, 211, 216, 241, 254, 301, 305, 314

Gallipoli 23, 84, 110
Glasgow 91
Granville Ste Honorine 53, 79

Harfleur 195
Harronville 173
Hedsin 195

India 40, 44, 49, 52, 59, 81-82, 84-85, 112, 117, 179, 235, 251, 265, 316, 321
Ireland 86, 109
Italy 37, 302, 321

La Gorgue 139
Lambeth 46, 299
Laventie 213
Le Havre viii, 101, 140, 181, 195-197, 269, 280, 300
Lens 115, 133, 169, 171
Lille 135
Locre 213

London 31, 49-50, 55, 69-70, 88-89, 106, 233, 268, 274, 280

Malakoff Farm 107
Manchester 21, 27, 33, 38, 67, 81, 96, 233, 303, 308, 310, 312
Marseilles 37

Neuve Chappelle 136

Paris viii, 50, 63, 71, 79, 97, 126, 131, 138, 140, 142-143, 151, 153-154, 158, 161, 177, 179, 181, 195-197, 199, 205, 212-213, 221-222, 233-234, 240, 242, 248-249, 251-252, 299, 304, 308, 310, 312-313
Petit Paris 205, 213
Picardy 28, 137-138, 264, 305
Ploegsteert 213
Plymouth 108
Pont St Neep 165
Poperinghe viii, 61-62, 132, 137, 144-145, 150-151, 160, 174, 195-196, 205, 213, 251, 265, 300-301
Portsmouth 108

Rouen 29, 73, 77, 122, 127, 140, 160, 192, 195, 199, 204, 222, 228

Saffron Walden 110
St Omer viii, 65, 137, 195-196, 222, 268
St Quentin 136
Steenvoord 137

Vermelles 115
Villaret 141
Vimy 169

Warploy 195
Watten 149
Westoutré 169, 213
Wimereux 163

Ypres xiv, 19, 60-61, 133, 135, 213, 305, 321

INDEX OF MILITARY UNITS & FORMATIONS

Canadian Expeditionary Force xv, 160, 302-303
Australian and New Zealand Army Corps (Anzac) vii, xv, 23, 50, 68, 140, 157, 195, 267-268, 300
Chinese Labour Corps 41, 283
Indian Army 21, 44, 46, 51, 74, 83-84, 109, 154, 260, 264, 316
Kitchener's New Armies 86, 270, 280
Machine Gun Corps 95, 108, 269, 281, 296, 298, 304
New Zealand Expeditionary Force (NZEF) xv, 30, 50, 68, 75, 160, 258, 308
Officer Training Corps xv, 85, 93
Royal Army Medical Corps (RAMC) xv, 21, 28, 77, 106-107, 211, 220-221, 223, 253, 280, 284, 296-298
Royal Army Service Corps 28
Royal Field Artillery 65, 202, 241, 280, 296-297
Royal Garrison Artillery 29
Royal Ordnance Corps 53, 187, 296
Territorials 60-61, 85-86, 108, 111, 133, 149, 165, 185, 188, 275, 280, 300, 302-303
Yeomanry xv, 85, 95, 106, 221, 280, 296-298
XI Corps 222

Guards Division 62
2nd Canadian Division 69, 213, 215, 299, 314
3rd Division viii, 70, 224
3rd Australian Division 215, 222, 300
35th Division 214
42nd Division 86
47th London Division 280
56th Division 26
63rd Royal Naval Division 222, 262, 269, 297, 300

8th Hussars 268
9th Hussars 28
Cameron Highlanders 83, 281
Cheshire Regiment 41
City of London Regiment 120
Devonshire Regiment 136, 296
Dorset Regiment 127
Durham Light Infantry 221, 297
East Surrey Regiment 126
Glamorgan Yeomanry 95, 298
Gloucestershire Regiment 139, 165, 296
Green Howards 275, 296
Highland Light Infantry 28, 238
King's Liverpool Regiment 74, 96, 269
Lancashire Fusiliers 17, 71, 74, 101, 132
Leicestershire Regiment 66
London Regiment 214, 297
Manchester Regiment 266
Middlesex Regiment 72, 120, 297
Monmouthshire Regiment 21, 220
Oxfordshire and Buckinghamshire Light Infantry 184, 297
Queen's Westminster Rifles 171
Rifle Brigade 32, 37, 65, 122, 184, 252, 269, 297, 306
Royal Berkshire Regiment 94
Royal Dublin Fusiliers 91
Royal Fusiliers 45, 91, 95-97, 111, 121, 153, 185, 201, 237, 253, 276, 278, 296-298
Royal Sussex Regiment 28
Royal Warwickshire Regiment 26, 306
Royal Welch Fusiliers 17, 162
Royal West Surrey Regiment 210, 250
Scottish Rifles 24, 81, 308
King's Shropshire Light Infantry 244
South Lancashire Regiment 187, 298
South Staffordshire Regiment 54, 73, 298
Worcestershire Regiment 120

Wolverhampton Military Studies
www.helion.co.uk/wolverhamptonmilitarystudies

Editorial board

Professor Stephen Badsey
Wolverhampton University

Professor Michael Bechthold
Wilfred Laurier University

Professor John Buckley
Wolverhampton University

Major General (Retired) John Drewienkiewicz

Ashley Ekins
Australian War Memorial

Dr Howard Fuller
Wolverhampton University

Dr Spencer Jones
Wolverhampton University

Nigel de Lee
Norwegian War Academy

Major General (Retired) Mungo Melvin President of the British Commission for Military History

Dr Michael Neiberg
US Army War College

Dr Eamonn O'Kane
Wolverhampton University

Professor Fransjohan Pretorius
University of Pretoria

Dr Simon Robbins
Imperial War Museum

Professor Gary Sheffield
Wolverhampton University

Commander Steve Tatham PhD
Royal Navy The Influence Advisory Panel

Professor Malcolm Wanklyn
Wolverhampton University

Professor Andrew Wiest
University of Southern Mississippi

Submissions
The publishers would be pleased to receive submissions for this series. Please contact us via email (info@helion.co.uk), or in writing to Helion & Company Limited, 26 Willow Road, Solihull, West Midlands, B91 1UE.

Titles

No.1 *Stemming the Tide. Officers and Leadership in the British Expeditionary Force 1914* Edited by Spencer Jones (ISBN 978-1-909384-45-3)

No.2 *'Theirs Not To Reason Why'. Horsing the British Army 1875-1925* Graham Winton (ISBN 978-1-909384-48-4)

No.3 *A Military Transformed? Adaptation and Innovation in the British Military, 1792-1945* Edited by Michael LoCicero, Ross Mahoney and Stuart Mitchell (ISBN 978-1-909384-46-0)

No.4 *Get Tough Stay Tough. Shaping the Canadian Corps, 1914-1918* Kenneth Radley (ISBN 978-1-909982-86-4)

No.5 *A Moonlight Massacre: The Night Operation on the Passchendaele Ridge, 2 December 1917. The Forgotten Last Act of the Third Battle of Ypres* Michael LoCicero (ISBN 978-1-909982-92-5)

No.6 *Shellshocked Prophets. Former Anglican Army Chaplains in Interwar Britain* Linda Parker (ISBN 978-1-909982-25-3)

No.7 *Flight Plan Africa: Portuguese Airpower in Counterinsurgency, 1961-1974* John P. Cann (ISBN 978-1-909982-06-2)

No.8 *Mud, Blood and Determination. The History of the 46th (North Midland) Division in the Great War* Simon Peaple (ISBN 978 1 910294 66 6)

No.9 *Commanding Far Eastern Skies. A Critical Analysis of the Royal Air Force Superiority Campaign in India, Burma and Malaya 1941-1945* Peter Preston-Hough (ISBN 978 1 910294 44 4)

No.10 *Courage Without Glory. The British Army on the Western Front 1915* Edited by Spencer Jones (ISBN 978 1 910777 18 3)

No.11 *The Airborne Forces Experimental Establishment: The Development of British Airborne Technology 1940-1950* Tim Jenkins (ISBN 978-1-910777-06-0)

No.12 *'Allies are a Tiresome Lot' – The British Army in Italy in the First World War* John Dillon (ISBN 978 1 910777 32 9)

No.13 *Monty's Functional Doctrine: Combined Arms Doctrine in British 21st Army Group in Northwest Europe, 1944–45* Charles Forrester (ISBN 978-1-910777-26-8)

No.14 *Early Modern Systems of Command: Queen Anne's Generals, Staff Officers and the Direction of Allied Warfare in the Low Countries and Germany, 1702-11* Stewart Stansfield (ISBN 978 1 910294 47 5)

No.15 *They Didn't Want To Die Virgins: Sex and Morale in the British Army on the Western Front 1914-1918* Bruce Cherry (ISBN 978-1-910777-70-1)